Beki.

GW00360084

A HISTORY OF THE MODERN WORLD

Richard Poulton

HAPPY CHRISTMAS BEK.I

Oxford University Press

Oxford University Press
Walton Street, Oxford OX2 6DP

London Glasgow New York Toronto
Delhi Bombay Calcutta Madras Karachi
Nairobi Dar es Salaam Cape Town Salisbury
Kuala Lumpur Singapore Hong Kong Tokyo
Melbourne Auckland

and associate companies in
Beirut Berlin Ibadan Mexico City Nicosia

For my Parents, Christopher and Aileen Poulton.

The publishers would like to thank the following for permission to reproduce photographs:
BBC Hulton Picture Library, pp. 11, 33, 93, 122, 124, 227; Camera Press, pp.189, 220, 244, 255, 271, 277, 283, 284, 286, 305, 338, 350; Central Press Photos, p. 251; Mary Evans Picture Library, pp. 22, 24 (left), 52, 75, 152; Stanley Gibbons Magazines Ltd., p. 8; Robert Hunt Library, pp. 20, 96; Imperial War Museum, pp. 23, 24 (right), 146, 168, 80, 186, 193, 194, 342; Keystone Press Agency, pp. 69, 70, 88, 90 (left and right), 143, 164, 199, 203, 209, 218, 232, 238, 243, 253, 267, 273, 290, 299 (left), 300, 304, 307, 312, 313, 321, 328, 329,330, 345; Labour Party Library, p. 262; Library of Congress, p. 38; Billie Love Collection, p. 116; Mansell Collection, pp. 13, 17, 51, 54, 73, 81, 82, 113, 117, 118, 127, 135, 137, 141, 156, 166; Mirror Group Newspapers, p. 334; Novosti Press Agency, pp. 211, 213, 234, 269; Popperfoto, pp. 43, 172; Private Eye – Edward McLachlan, p. 299 (right); Franklin D. Roosevelt Library, p. 225; S.C.R. London, p. 61; J.Sennep S.P.A.D.E.M. Paris 1980, p. 103; Wiener Library, p. 157.

Although every effort has been made to trace copyright holders, this has proved impossible in some cases. If any copyright holders incorrectly acknowledged will contact the publisher, corrections will be made in future editions.

Printed in Great Britain by Cambridge University Press, Cambridge.

Contents

List of Maps

Preface

In writing this book, I have tried to balance the provision of essential factual information, arranged in clearly defined sections, with a number of themes, patterns and parallels. It has always worried me that the O-Level student is liable to be presented with unrelated islands of material. For this reason, I have often taken a starting date which predates the requirements of the various examination syllabuses. I have also made frequent cross-references to other countries, so that the pupil is encouraged to develop a sense of perspective.

The majority of chapters are self-standing, and clearly focussed on specific countries or geographical areas. But Chapters 1, 3, 11, 13, 19 and 23 are intended to reach across national frontiers, and to present themes which are either more abstract, or lend themselves to wider discussion. Within the 'national' chapters, I have attempted to highlight the universality of certain features: the pressures of accelerated economic growth; the fine distinction between efficiency and dictatorship; the conflict between national security and national selfishness; the growth of representative government, and the corresponding problem of where responsibility lies.

I hope that this blend of material will enable O-Level students to form something more than a fragmented impression of the evolution of the modern world.

Of all the deep debts of gratitude incurred in writing this book, none is greater than that to the Headmaster (the Reverend David Jones) and Governors of Bryanston School, who gave me not only a generous allocation of time but also a generosity of encouragement and support, without which the project would have been impossible. Subsequently I depended heavily on the unstinting goodwill of my colleagues on the Bryanston staff and the tolerance of the pupils; I would like to acknowledge individually the other members of the History Department, Neil Boulton, Robert Allan, Peter Brewin and John Watson, each of whom offered constructive and sympathetic criticism while carrying an extra work-load on my behalf, and Julia Lawson, who cheerfully took on an extra pastoral load.

Every author seems to acknowledge his wife's support. It is a tribute for which every formula has been tried and every superlative used, but it is not merely a convention nor a piece of essential domestic diplomacy. I simply know that, as a bachelor, I could not have written this book. From Sally I have received every assistance that one person can give.

Richard Poulton, Head of History, Bryanston School 1980

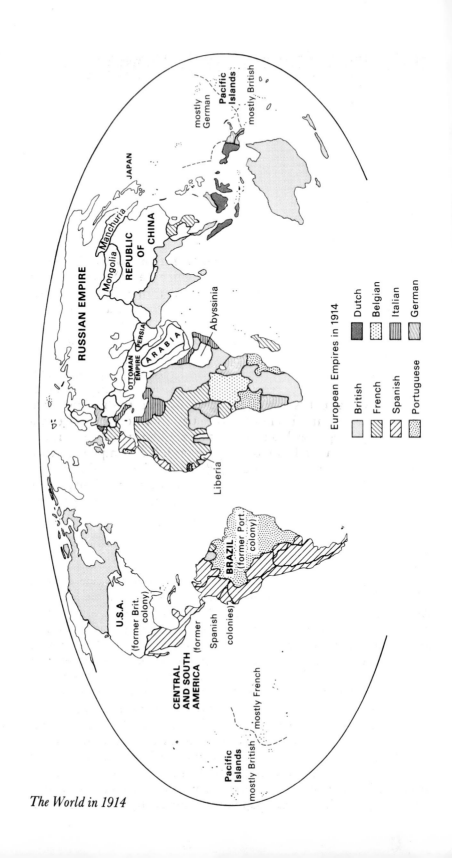

The World in 1914

European Empires in 1914

British
French
Spanish
Portuguese
Dutch
Belgian
Italian
German

RUSSIAN EMPIRE

Mongolia

Manchuria

JAPAN

REPUBLIC OF CHINA

OTTOMAN EMPIRE

PERSIA

ARABIA

Abyssinia

Liberia

Pacific Islands

mostly German

mostly British

BRAZIL (former Port. colony)

U.S.A. (former Brit. colony)

CENTRAL AND SOUTH AMERICA (former Spanish colonies)

Pacific Islands

mostly British

mostly French

Into the Twentieth Century 1

The Turn of the Century

In its first issue of the year 1900, the magazine *Punch* published a list of 'Principal Questions', the first of which was 'Did January 1st commence the twentieth century?'. It was a question which was puzzling many people, for at stake were all the extra celebrations that only the turn of a century could justify. The sad truth was that the would-be revellers had to wait another 12 months before they came to the right date.

Man was not made for fitting dates. There are no perfect time-boundaries in History, least of all when one century succeeds another. We cannot 'stop the world' at the end of the nineteenth century and start it afresh in the twentieth, for nothing came to a halt and nothing absolutely new started. The twentieth-century world inherited a restless moving pattern, full of competing ideas, ever-growing technology and a rapidly increasing population. For the first time, *world* history was coming to mean something, as the ease of communication destroyed the narrowness of people's knowledge and understanding.

European Dominance

Nothing could disguise the fact that as the new century started, Western Europe and its once-colonial offshoot, the United States of America, dominated the economic developments that were taking place. The Europeans also treated most of the rest of the world as areas which they could use to their own advantage in a complicated game of power politics. Britain claimed some kind of power over nearly one third of the land area of the world. France, Germany, Belgium, Holland, Spain, Portugal and Italy also enjoyed colonial empires which between them swallowed up most of the rest of Africa. Non-European empires existed in Russia, Ottoman Turkey, China and Japan, but if these are excluded, European powers controlled the rest of the Middle East and Far East, except for Siam and Tibet. The subcontinent of South America was technically a group of independent countries, but in practice their roots were European, as they were populated largely by descendants of

Spanish and Portuguese emigrants, and their economic strength was largely based on European capital.

It was, then, a white man's world. Western Europe had developed its own political pattern with the 'nation state', and the competing nation states had in turn developed forms of economic efficiency which became known as 'the agricultural revolution' and 'the industrial revolution'. More advanced and more confident than any other human group in the world, the Europeans proclaimed their power and their influence across the globe. When, in Jules Verne's book, Phineas Fogg went *Around the World in Eighty Days*, it was entirely natural for the author to presume that his hero would find civilization wherever the European influence was strong, and savagery where it was not. Such arrogance was not uncommon, and superficially at least, the facts supported it, though not for long. For underneath European progress in the nineteenth century were five fundamental, and often competing, ideas. As they too spread across the world, they helped to fashion the twentieth century pattern. These ideas – imperialism, nationalism, capitalism, socialism and democracy – must therefore be defined more closely.

Imperialism

Imperialism became highly developed in the nineteenth century, though its origins went back many hundreds of years. In modern usage, it can be a disapproving word, but in the nineteenth century it implied honour, vigour and power. 'We hold a vaster Empire than has been' proclaimed a Canadian stamp in 1898, with pride on behalf of Great Britain.

Imperialism involved a country conquering, administering and then developing another more backward area or country, usually with a mixture of motives. Trade was the most obvious one, as it had been ever since Vasco da Gama, the first European to reach

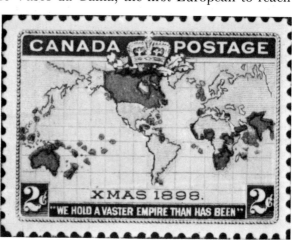

The British Empire depicted on the Canadian Christmas stamp, 1898.

India by sea, admitted in 1498 that he had come looking for
'Christians ... and spices.' Mechanization and mass production in
Western Europe meant that new sources of raw materials were
required, and new markets for finished goods. Imperialism was
bound to be stimulated by capitalist success, though often the
capitalist trader trod along the track that a missionary had
previously marked out. David Livingstone (1813–73), in exploring
Africa and spreading the Christian Gospel, unknowingly opened
the way for later economic exploitation which he would have
deplored. So did others who believed in the duty to pass on the
benefits of Western standards:

> Take up the White man's burden –
> Send forth the best ye breed –
> Go bind your sons to exile
> To serve your captives' need;
> To wait in heavy harness,
> On fluttered folk and wild –
> Your new-caught, sullen peoples,
> Half-devil and half-child.
> (Rudyard Kipling, 1865–1936)

Thus, for gain or glory, for strategic security in this life or for
salvation in the next, the strong powers of Western Europe took
their grip upon the world, while the decaying empires of Austria,
Russia, Turkey and China wrestled with the problems of their
collapsing influence. Not the least of their problems was
nationalism.

Nationalism

Nationalism grew strongly in the nineteenth century. Whereas
eighteenth-century peacemakers (right up to the Treaty of Vienna
in 1815) had distributed chunks of land and their occupants as if
they were properties on a giant 'Monopoly' board, nineteenth-
century populations were not prepared to be treated thus, and
demanded the right to be able to settle their own fate. Sometimes
'nationalism' demanded the uniting of what had previously been
'mere geographical expressions' like Germany and Italy; sometimes it involved breaking up old empires like those of the Austrian
Hapsburgs and the Ottoman Turks into small units. It is difficult
to define, because many 'nations' incorporate different races,
different colours, different creeds, different cultures and different
languages, and still have something special which makes them
distinctive. It has been suggested that the vital ingredient is no
more than the will of those people to be 'a nation', and their belief
that this grouping is the best guarantee of human security and
progress.

Capitalism

Western Europe was the cradle of capitalism, the economic system where individuals work for their own gain in the form of money, that money being paid to them as wages or salaries, profit, interest or rent. In a slave system, a man works because he has no choice; under feudalism, he works in exchange for protection by his lord; in a capitalist society, he wants a reward in cash or in something that has a clear cash value. Most men work for others. They sell their labour to a firm that produces goods for sale to the community or that provides a service for members of the public. The system is based on the fact that in order to set up the firms and buy the machines and produce the goods, businessmen borrow other people's savings and 'invest' them, turn them into 'capital' in the form of buildings and machines. Without the belief that they can make a profit, men would neither lend nor borrow money; without the borrowing of money, no-one could collect together much 'capital'. There would be no investment, no employment, no wealth in society. Capitalists can therefore be very powerful, because they control the financial resources of a community. They accumulate wealth, and their decisions can be matters of life and death for their employees, if there are no controls on them.

One of the most powerful capitalists was Andrew Carnegie (1835–1919), who emigrated to America from Scotland because of his parents' poverty. He rose from being a bobbin-boy to be the creator and controller of a vast steelworks empire, including the necessary iron- and coal-mines, railways and ships. His annual income was more than $12,500,000; in 1901, he sold his share in United States Steel for $350,000,000, a figure larger than the estimated value of all businesses in the United States a century earlier. But in 1892, his employees in Pennsylvania had their wages cut to less than $10 a week because Carnegie felt that they were demanding too much through their trade union.

Socialism

Trade unions were one outcome of socialism, which was a philosophy which grew strongly in the nineteenth century, stimulated by the growth of capitalism. Socialists believe that 'society' – in other words, everyone – should have some control over the production of goods and services in a community, and over how the wealth is distributed. Reacting against the unfairness that capitalism brings, socialism stresses equality, classlessness and the dignity of the worker. It took many forms in the nineteenth century. Robert Owen (1771–1858), a reforming millowner, set up a model industrial community at New Lanark in Scotland (where incidentally he increased his profits as a result of spending much more than usual on the welfare and conditions of his workers). He also

The iron gaze of the 'steel king of America': Andrew Carnegie.

endeavoured to promote trade unionism, especially among the unskilled workers, who were the most exploited. His was a gentle form of socialism compared with that of a German refugee, Karl Marx, whose outspoken views caused him to flee via France to England, where he settled in 1850 for the rest of his life.

Marx did not accept that members of the capitalist classes (the 'bourgeoisie') would ever share their wealth and power with the workers (the 'proletariat'). For him, all History was 'the History of class struggles', because the workers, especially the industrial workers, always produce more value by their labours than they use up in their lifetime. This surplus value becomes the profit of the employers, who thus become unfairly rich and powerful. In his best-known works *The Communist Manifesto* (1848) and *Das Kapital* (1867), Marx prophesied that the proletariat would become the ruling class by means of a revolution, and that the state would take over total control of the economy on behalf of the whole community. 'Let the ruling classes tremble at a Communistic revolution. The proletarians have nothing to lose but their chains. They have a world to win. Working men of all countries, unite!'

Wherever industrialization had taken place, and especially in England, Germany and France, the followers of Marx were watching for The Revolution. Each new outburst of strikes called by the trade unions and the Syndicalists (groups demanding workers' control of industry) seemed to herald the dawn of the new era. It was only after the success of the Bolshevik Revolution in Russia in 1917 that they realized that they had been looking in the wrong direction.

Democracy

The *idea* of democracy, rule by the people, was strongly voiced in
the eighteenth century, especially in the American and French
Revolutions, but the *practice* of democracy was introduced only very
slowly in the nineteenth century. In 1867, Walter Bagehot, a liberal
political commentator, complained that if England were to accept
the idea of 'one man, one vote', 'upon this theory, the rich and wise
are not to have ... more votes than the poor and stupid'. The
possibility of 'one *woman*, one vote' was so outrageous as to be
unmentionable. In fact Britain, with Parliamentary Reform Bills
passed in 1832, 1867 and 1884, was more stable and more confident
of the people's opinion than, for example France. Elsewhere in
Europe, monarchy prevailed in a more or less comfortable partnership with some form of elected assembly, while in Russia and
Turkey the central governments remained totally autocratic. Only
the U.S.A., with the advantage of being a new nation which had
deliberately created its own political system as a contrast to the old
regimes of Europe, could claim to be democratic, and even that
claim meant turning a blind eye to the condition of the blacks.

Europe and the World

These five features of European life – imperialism, nationalism,
capitalism, socialism and democracy – helped to fashion not only
European politics but also world developments around the turn of
the century. Though the United States of America and Japan were
also making rapid advances in technology, their political attitudes
kept them in relative isolation, and it was the Europeans who
prospered around the globe. Imperialism and capitalism are both
expansionist; they seek power and profit, and so they can often
expand together. In Africa, the Middle East, India and Indo-
China, Europeans competed for land and for political influence,
while the areas which today dominate world affairs (the U.S.A.,
Russia and China) seemed relatively unimportant.

   In Africa, the last 30 years of the nineteenth century witnessed
a massive 'scramble' for territory. Whereas in the 1870s (when
Livingstone was still exploring) only a few coastal regions had been
officially colonized by Europeans, by 1914 only Liberia and
Abyssinia were free of European control, the former because it was
a wretchedly poor state made over to emancipated slaves and the
latter because it had bloodily fought off the Italians at the battle of
Adowa in 1896. Elsewhere on the 'Dark Continent', seven European powers – eight if we count the nominal presence of Turkey –
had annexed a total of 11,500,000 square miles of territory. The
British, French and Portuguese were long established; the Spanish
took a chunk of coastal desert in 1860, but the real scramble started
in the 1880s, when King Leopold of Belgium claimed the Congo

'It was, then, a white man's world'. The Englishman's essential cup of tea is brought on a carefully laid tray to a waiting train in an Indian station.

after commissioning an American, Stanley, to explore it. At the same time, the German Chancellor, Bismarck, in spite of his avowal 'I am no man for colonies', not only laid claim to the Cameroons and German South West Africa, but also encouraged the Italians into Eritrea and Somaliland. In the Middle East, Britain, with its hold on the Suez Canal and India, reckoned to exercise the dominant European opinion as the Ottoman Empire slowly broke up, though Germany and Russia each had hopes of gains there. India was firmly in the British grip, while beyond that subcontinent the French claimed dominion over Indo-China, while the Dutch still clung to the East Indian islands that they had won in the seventeenth century.

In all these areas, the European imperialists and capitalists would eventually meet with resistance in the form of nationalists, socialists and those who wanted democracy. But there were few signs of them at the turn of the century, except the Boers in South Africa, and the Boxer Rebels in China. Japan and Russia were two autocracies relatively safe from colonization by the Europeans, yet China had nearly succumbed to European control by the end of the nineteenth century. The ruling Manchu Dynasty was a hollow shell, beneath which European traders and missionaries vied for real control.

The only remaining continent, America, was largely disinterested in the political aspirations of the Europeans, and had been ever since the enunciation of the Monroe Doctrine of 'isolationism' in 1823. For the Europeans there was neither threat nor promise on the far side of the Atlantic, only the prospect of a gradual increase in trade.

Europe's Internal Structure

With so much European energy being directed outwards in the nineteenth century, the continent itself enjoyed a period of unprecedented peace. After the end of the Napoleonic Wars and the Treaty of Vienna (1815), there was no lengthy war in Europe in the nineteenth century. The Crimean War saw little more than a year of fighting despite its dates of 1854–56; the Austro-Prussian War of 1866 was the 'Seven Weeks War', while the Franco-Prussian War of 1870 lasted for less than six months. Although there was little fighting, there was keen rivalry, especially after about 1860. Two Empires, those of Austria-Hungary and Turkey, were falling into decay, and as their power ebbed, new nations emerged to claim at least the right to exist and sometimes the right to expand. The most significant of these was Germany.

Germany as a unified country dates only from January 1871; in less than ten years, the kingdom of Prussia under William I and his minister Bismarck absorbed 38 other states by conquest and by treaty, defeating Austria and France on the way and enabling Italy also to complete its unification as a nation. Under the 1871 Constitution of the German 'Reich' (Empire), the King of Prussia became the Kaiser (the same word as Caesar or Czar), and he appointed his own Chancellor. For the next 19 years, Bismarck served three Kaisers in this role (one of them ruled for only three months) and dominated European politics. Sitting squatly in the centre of Europe, Bismarck's Germany built up all the economic, political and military strength required to control continental diplomacy. Even in 1870, it had mobilized 1,830,000 soldiers in 18 days, and its peacetime army never fell below 400,000 troops, whose efficiency became a byword. Between 1871 and 1913, its coal production increased by 700 per cent, and its iron production by 1,150 per cent, to a tonnage nearly twice as large as Britain's.

To the west of Germany was France, smarting under its defeat by the Germans in 1870 and resentful of the loss of Alsace and Lorraine. The constitution of the Third Republic, accepted in 1875, provided a loose form of government with little executive control at the top. It was Bismarck's policy to isolate France diplomatically, creating several 'War Scares' to indicate to his own Reichstag (Parliament), and to the rest of Europe, how untrustworthy and unstable the French were.

To the east of Germany were two fading empires. One of these, the Austro-Hungarian Empire, was the area at whose expense Germany had grown as a nation. For centuries, the Hapsburgs had dominated the centre of Europe through the Holy Roman Empire and then the Austro-Hungarian Empire, but a wave of revolutions in 1848 marked the beginning of the final phase of their decline. The Emperor Francis Joseph, who came to the throne in 1848 and died in 1916 (thus achieving the longest reign in European history) could not stem the collapse of a country whose institutions were out of date and whose economy was hopelessly overburdened. Further east, the Ottoman Turks similarly could not maintain their old supremacy over the Balkans and the Danube provinces. Their former subjects, sharing neither their race nor their religion and often encouraged by the self-seeking 'sympathy' of the Russians or the British or the French or the Austrians, rebelled against the Turks with ever-growing success. First Greeks, then Serbs and Slavs challenged the Turks, forming as they did so new 'nations' like Serbia, Bosnia, Montenegro and Bulgaria. Meanwhile to the north hovered the Russians, seeking expansion around the Black Sea, access to the Danube, and most of all, the chance to control the Straits of the Bosphorus and the Dardanelles.

The Split into Two Armed Camps

Bismarck's strategy in the period 1871–90 was to consolidate his new Germany, not to expand it any further. In his view, the major threat to peace would come from France, and he summed up his own method of preventing trouble thus: 'In a world governed by five powers, try to be in a group of three.' In 1872 (and again in 1881) he created the Dreikaiserbund, the 'League of Three Emperors' (Germany, Austria-Hungary and Russia) for defence against France. In 1879, he made a closer Dual Alliance with Austria, expanding it to a Triple Alliance in 1882 by the inclusion of Italy, while still keeping on good terms with Russia by signing a Reinsurance Treaty in 1887. However, the flavour of German diplomacy was soon to change. In 1888, William II came to the Imperial throne, and in 1890 he sacked Bismarck. Cautious consolidation now gave way to ambitious arrogance. 'I will not rest until I have brought my navy to the same height at which my army stands.' 'Germany, like the spirit of Imperial Rome, must expand and impose itself.' In 1897, he sent his fleet to the Far East and wrote 'Hundreds of thousands of Chinese will quiver when they feel the iron fist of Germany heavy on their necks; and the whole German nation will be delighted that its Government has done a manly act.'

By that time, the French had already clawed their way out of isolation by finding unexpected friendship in Russia. Eastern in attitude and backward in business, the Russians had come to suspect the real value of the Reinsurance Treaty, guessing correctly that if Germany had to choose between Russia and Austria in the event of a Balkan crisis, William would give all his support to Austria. So the eastern empire shared its worries with the western republic. In 1888, Russia borrowed 500,000,000 francs on the Paris Exchange, and thereafter about 25 per cent of all French exported capital went to Russia, where it supported the highest growth rate in the world. In 1891, a French naval squadron came to Kronstadt on a ceremonial visit, and within 12 months military negotiations had begun. They led to the alliance of France and Russia in 1894 specifically against attacks by Germany, Austria or Italy. The continental powers were thus split into two clear 'sides', and there was a general assumption that Britain, if she had to opt for either, would support the Triple Alliance of Germany, Austria-Hungary and Italy.

The End of Britain's 'Splendid Isolation'

In 1848, Palmerston had declared 'We have no perpetual allies, we have no eternal friends. Our interests are eternal, and these interests it is our duty to follow.' In the final quarter of the nineteenth century, Britain tried to remain aloof from European entanglement, for British interests now lay in her Empire, on which 'the sun never set'. For every square mile of its own islands, Britain ruled one hundred square miles overseas. She preferred 'informal empire', where the profits of trade and the benefits of firm government were enough to keep an area under control. But when it proved necessary, as in the Boer War in 1899, she could mobilize 500,000 troops.

The vital requirement of the British Empire was an invincible navy, which would protect the trade-routes, carry troops and link the nations. For this reason, the Admiralty believed that security depended upon having a fleet bigger than the next two fleets in Europe put together, namely those of the French and the Russians. Therefore, their alliance in 1894 was unwelcome and slightly threatening news, and the French became even more suspect in 1898, when a small army force marched across Africa and established itself at Fashoda, claiming the Upper Nile for France. Though the claim was soon withdrawn, Britain was jolted by this and by the Boer War into considering the end of her isolation. In 1899, a formal treaty of alliance was offered to Germany, who from 1887 to 1889 had tried unsuccessfully to get Britain to accept direct alliance. Now in 1899 it was William who rejected the diplomatic overtures.

Suddenly the German Navy Laws of 1898, authorizing a massive ship-building programme, plus the Kaiser's encouragement of the Boer leaders, plus the build-up of international tension following the Boxer Rebellion in China in 1900, made it questionable whether Germany was Britain's natural ally. In 1902, Britain and Japan signed a defensive alliance that would operate if either were attacked by *two* other powers, and in 1904 Britain pledged herself to friendship (but not to firm alliance) with France, in the 'Entente Cordiale'. This resolved the nagging uncertainties about French control in Morocco and British influence over Egypt and the Sudan, and reassured both governments. The Anglo-Russian Entente of 1907 was a similar agreement, whereby those two countries clarified the extent of their interests in Persia, China and Afghanistan.

Uncle and nephew: King Edward VII and Kaiser William II pose at Windsor in 1907, in the days when all the royal families seemed to be on the same side.

Thus Britain, though not committed to any major power, had come out of her 'Splendid Isolation' on the unexpected side. Bismarck's 'Triple Alliance' was now faced by the 'Triple Entente'.

Steps towards War

Once the two camps were established, there were plenty of incidents which illustrated their opposing attitudes. Kaiser William had already been bitterly critical of the British position in South Africa and had offered military aid to the Boers. In 1905, as if to test the strength of the Entente Cordiale, he challenged the establishment of French supremacy in Morocco. The other major powers of the world were however also colonial powers, afraid to overturn a principle by which they too were benefiting in various corners of the world. At the International Conference held at Algeciras in 1906, Germany was outvoted and rebuffed, and France retained her position.

In 1911, Germany again put up a challenge by sending a gunboat, the *Panther*, to the Moroccan port of Agadir. Again, William gained no international support, and in exchange for some small strips of the French Cameroons, he at last acknowledged the

French protectorate over Morocco. These two 'Moroccan Crises' of 1905 and 1911 represented the peak of tension in the area of *expanding* imperialism, but in the Balkans, the area of *declining* empires, nationalistic competition triggered a new series of confrontations. The weakness of Turkey and Austria-Hungary in the nineteenth century had enabled Greece, Montenegro, Serbia, Moldavia and Wallachia (jointly called Romania) and Bulgaria to establish some form of restless independence. Macedonia and Albania were still under savage Turkish rule, while Bosnia and Herzegovina were theoretically still Turkish but in practice were administered by Austria.

In 1908, revolution in Turkey encouraged the Austrians to claim Bosnia and Herzegovina, and the Bulgarians to announce total independence. In 1911, the Italians took advantage of Turkish weakness and the Second Moroccan Crisis to occupy Tripolitania in North Africa and the Dodecanese Islands, and in 1912 Greece, Serbia, Bulgaria and Montenegro thrust Turkey out of Europe except for a toe-hold around Constantinople.

This First Balkan War led directly to the Second (1913), when the former allies squabbled over their spoils, particularly the valuable coast of Albania. With the major powers mediating, peace was reached at the Treaty of Bucharest (1913), but it was a peace which left Bulgaria bitter, Serbia resentful of Austrian interference, Bosnia aggrieved at its lack of independence and Albania in newborn chaos (with six groups simultaneously claiming to govern it in 1914). Away to the north, Russia too resented the peace. Since the Austrians had grabbed Bosnia in 1908, Russia had supported Serbia in all matters, in an attempt to keep some influence in the Balkans, but had achieved nothing.

In July 1914, two pistol shots in this backwater of the Balkans focussed the attention of the world on the two armed camps of Europe, with their improved weaponry, their ambitions around the world, their economic needs, and their national pride. With the rest of the world now parcelled out among the various colonial powers, the competition returned to the mainland of Europe. The alliances that had originally been defensive turned into harnesses, dragging country after country into war.

The First World War 1914-18

Sarajevo – the Immediate Cause

It was tactless of the Archduke Francis Ferdinand, heir to the throne of Austria, to visit Sarajevo, capital of Bosnia, on 28 June 1914, for that was St. Vitus Day, a Serbian national festival, and Bosnia contained a million Serbs. Furthermore, the Archduke was coming to see great army manoeuvres, and neither Serbs nor Bosnians looked favourably on any show of Hapsburg armed strength. In the circumstances, security arrangements were pathetic: 120 policemen and a few detectives covered the four-mile route of the Archduke's drive, and they were more excited by the unprecedented sight of six motor cars at one time than by worries of who might be in the crowd.

So, for members of the 'Young Bosnia' movement, a Slav nationalist secret society, it was easy to plan the death of the Archduke. Assassins waited along the processional route, armed with bombs or pistols. One even checked with a policeman which car the Archduke was in before throwing his bomb, only to see it explode too late to harm its intended victim. Gavrilo Princip, the best marksman of the group, had better luck further along the route. He was presented with a virtually stationary target at a distance of two metres. His two shots hit the Archduke and his wife, who were both dead within 15 minutes.

It was quickly established that the conspirators had received arms from the 'Black Hand', a terrorist group led by the head of the Serbian Intelligence Service. Within four weeks, the frustration and fury of the Austrian government was vented on Serbia, with whom relations had been especially bad since the Balkan Wars. A ten-point ultimatum was presented, which the Serbs could not fully accept without sacrificing their rights to genuine self-government. Within three days of a reasoned but negative reply from Serbia, the Austrians declared war, in the hope of forcing Serbian cooperation. It was a bluff, because the Austrians were not ready to fight, only to mobilize. The Russians, self-appointed guardians of Serbian interests, did not realize this and started their long-winded mobilization to indicate that they would not stand by and watch Serbia being bullied. The Germans, alarmed to see what they had considered a

Sarajevo 1914. Wreckage marks the spot of the first attempt to assassinate Francis Ferdinand. Within hours, the Archduke had been shot by Gavrilo Princip.

private quarrel between Austria and Serbia getting out of hand, asked the Russians to stop mobilizing; the Russians made no positive reply. What the situation required, in the German view, was a decisive military demonstration, a power-display such as she had put on in 1866 and 1870. To do this meant wiping out French power quickly, even quicker than in 1870, and then turning eastwards to bring peace to the rest of Europe. German mobilization plans were much more efficient than any others, and the sheer arrogance of the idea gave it a chance of success.

Three uncalculated factors took the dangerous squabble from this point to world war. One was the inflexibility of mobilization plans that depended on railway timetables; the second was the British diplomatic response to the continental confusion; the third was the speed and efficiency with which Britain blocked the German knock-out blow against France, so turning a short, sharp scrap into a four-year nightmare.

The Schlieffen Plan, and Britain's Response

Count von Schlieffen, German Chief of Staff from 1891 to 1905, had devised a plan to outwit the Dual Alliance of France and Russia. It depended on capturing Paris within six weeks of any declaration of war, thus causing France to surrender and leaving Germany free to deal with the still unprepared Russians. Railways were the key to speed, and the Schlieffen Plan, worked out over a period of years, included a vast timetable of movement aimed at Paris. 840,000 men had to be pumped through Aachen, near the German border with Holland and Belgium: 11,000 trains would be moving simultaneously. The aim of the plan was to sweep round to the west of Paris, where there were least fortifications. Even in retirement, Schlieffen updated the timetable annually, according to the railway track open at the time. Aachen was the bottleneck; troops funnelling out of Germany could not be held there because of the shortage of marshalling space. They therefore had to be dispersed into and through neutral Belgium.

Belgium was the only European country (apart from Portugal) with which Britain had a firm alliance, since signing the Treaty of London in 1839 which guaranteed Belgian independence and neutrality. This 'scrap of paper', as the German Chancellor Bethman-Hollweg called it, had also been signed by Prussia and Austria, but neither expected Britain to honour the agreement. On 4 August 1914, just five and a half weeks after Sarajevo, Britain demanded a promise from Germany that Belgium would be safe, but the trains were already rolling, and the timetable could not be put into reverse. At midnight, having received no reply, Britain declared war.

The British Expeditionary Force, some 90,000 soldiers, was moved across the Channel between 12 and 20 August, while the French flung their main armies recklessly and disastrously into Lorraine and the Germans advanced steadily through Belgium. On 23 August, the German First Army met Sir John French's British troops at Mons, just inside the Belgian border, and for the first time, their progress was stopped. The rapid rifle fire of the B.E.F. was believed to be from machine guns, and even a three-to-one superiority in numbers could not carry the Germans forward. But the British withdrew, that night and every night for the next fortnight, despite spirited resistance to the German advance at Le Cateau and St. Quentin. Von Moltke, German Chief of Staff, was sufficiently confident of success to remove four divisions and send them off to the Eastern Front. But the pace of advance was nonetheless slower than intended, and led to a fatal decision to short-circuit the Schlieffen Plan, bringing the First and Second Armies to the east of Paris rather than encircling it. Despite the shortened line of advance, a gap developed between the German units, into which Joffre, French Commander in Chief, thrust his Fifth Army and the B.E.F. The Germans fell back from their position south of the Marne to the Aisne. The Schlieffen Plan was thus destroyed, and the war which both sides had reckoned would be 'all over by Christmas' had to be re-planned. The Battle of the Marne saved France from defeat, and condemned all the combatants to a long war.

PUNCH, OR THE LONDON CHARIVARI.—November 4, 1914.

THE EXCURSIONIST.

Scene: Ticket Office at —— *(censored).*

Tripper Wilhelm. "FIRST CLASS TO PARIS."   Clerk. "LINE BLOCKED."
Wilhelm. "THEN MAKE IT WARSAW."   Clerk. "LINE BLOCKED."
Wilhelm. "WELL, WHAT ABOUT CALAIS?"   Clerk. "LINE BLOCKED."
Wilhelm. "HANG IT! I *MUST* GO *SOMEWHERE!* I PROMISED MY PEOPLE I WOULD."

Punch *picks on the failure of the Schlieffen Plan, and the frustration of the Kaiser as the French, Russian and British forces bar his way.*

The Character of the War

It has been said that the First World War had causes but no objectives. The soldiers of each side felt that they were *defending* something against the aggression of the other side, though what they were defending was not clear. 'Civilization' was a common answer, but the fact that both sides believed that Right – and the Christian God – was on their side, was confusing. So too was the fact that the generals in charge of the defence of civilization could do nothing but attack. 'To make war means always attacking' wrote Foch, later to be Supreme Commander of the Allied forces on the Western Front.

Worse still was the fact that the attack philosophy had to be put into practice with, and against, the weapons of defence. Rifles with magazines and machine-guns destroyed the chance of a courageous cavalry or infantry attack. The only means of obliterating a well-situated machine-gun nest, namely bombardment with heavy artillery, also made the ground unsuitable for the rapid charge that the machine-gun had previously prevented. Barbed wire and trenches added to the immobility of the fighting, and the development of gas warfare and ever heavier artillery made little difference. Railway lines and motor lorries and 'buses could hasten troops to the front line, but until the development of the tank, they had to fight forward on foot, and then rely on supplies which had to be brought over the same devastated ground. It is interesting to note that the decisive battles of the war – those which brought a sudden reversal of what seemed likely, such as the Marne, Tannenberg and Caporetto – were battles of the 'old' kind, where courage and good generalship deflected an enemy thrust and produced a counter-attack. Most other battles, and all the weary weeks of warfare which filled the gaps between those climaxes which are called battles (the Somme, Verdun, Ypres), were static triumphs of defence over attack, of courageous obstinacy over courageous stupidity. Only the tank broke the deadlock, and even that was not always taken seriously by either side: Kitchener, the British Secretary for War whose death in 1916 meant that he only saw early development of the tank, referred to it as a 'pretty mechanical toy'.

One of the early tanks, which Kitchener referred to as 'pretty mechanical toys'.

The defensive nature of the weaponry took a horrific toll of the victims who were served up by the optimistic aggression of the generals. More than 8,000,000 fighting men and women were killed, and three times as many were injured, taken prisoner or declared missing. German military losses were estimated to be about 2,000,000 dead; Russia lost 1,700,000 in three years of fighting; France, Austria-Hungary and Britain with its Empire each lost over a million. It is impossible to assess accurately civilian deaths that can be attributed to the war. But there is no doubt that man-made blockades and overstrained supply lines contributed heavily to deaths from famine and disease, on a scale similar to the military casualties. Then, as a postscript, a world-wide 'flu epidemic killed many millions more in 1919.

The Western Front

The German response to the failure of the Schlieffen Plan was to

A Call
from
the Trenches.

(Extract from a letter from the Trenches.)

"I SAW a recruiting advertisement in a paper the other day. I wonder if the men are responding properly —they would if they could see what the Germans have done in Belgium. And, after all, it's not so bad out here—cold sometimes, and the waiting gets on our nerves a bit, but we are happy and as fit as fiddles. I wonder if————has joined, he certainly ought to."

Does "————" refer to you?

If so

ENLIST TO-DAY.

God Save the King.

'What the eye does not see. . . .' Appeals to patriotism kept Britain's army fully manned by volunteers until 1916. But life in the trenches was more testing than recruiting propaganda could admit.

appoint the War Minister, von Falkenhayn, as Chief of the General Staff, in place of von Moltke, who had tampered with the Plan. Falkenhayn's strategy was to capture the Channel ports through which the B.E.F. had entered France, and to strike again towards the unprotected western flank of the French. October 1914 thus saw a 'race to the sea' as each side tried to outflank the other. The bloodiest fighting occurred at Ypres and the nearby ridges of Messines and Passchendaele, where a quarter of a million casualties were sacrificed in establishing a savage stalemate. The B.E.F. was transferred to this sector from the Aisne, and this first Battle of Ypres ('Wipers' to the troops) virtually destroyed it. For the next two years, Kitchener's volunteers filled the gaps in what the Kaiser had apparently called 'that contemptible little mercenary army'. (In fact, this phrase was invented by the *Daily Mail*. Its insulting tone was carefully calculated to increase British patriotic resentment.)

By the end of 1914, trenches ran from the English Channel to Switzerland, snaking across the clay plain of Flanders, swinging south where the Germans had pushed towards Paris and turning north-east again to drape around the vital French fortress of Verdun, which symbolized national resistance more than anywhere else. From Verdun to Switzerland was the line of the common border between France and Germany, which the French had fortified heavily. It was here that they most expected German attacks, and from here that they hoped to recapture the disputed territories of Alsace and Lorraine. Trench warfare was a new phenomenon, though it had occurred briefly in the American Civil War half a century earlier. It led to new diseases (e.g. trench foot, trench fever) because many trenches became rat-infested open drains, and the tensions of continuous bombardment and possible attack caused a special form of nervous breakdown known as 'shell-shock'. It also encouraged new forms of weapon designed to break the deadlock, most notably gas and the tank.

1915 showed the incompetence of the generals on both sides. The British made a conventional attack and break-through at Neuve-Chapelle – and withdrew in confusion. The Germans used gas for the first time a month later (the Second Battle of Ypres, April 1915), and followed up too slowly to exploit their position. At Loos and at Aubers Ridge in the same Ypres salient, costly attacks gained no strategic ground for the Western allies, nor did an offensive in the Champagne region.

1916 saw a vast increase in the size of offensives and in the resultant losses of men, but no increase in the gains of land. Falkenhayn once again concentrated on defeating France, so that he could then send his German forces eastwards against Russia. By focussing on Verdun, he believed that he would destroy either the manpower or the morale of the French. From February until December 1916, the weight of the German attack surpassed anything in the previous history of warfare. The artillery, some of it firing at a distance of twenty miles, beyond the horizon, could be heard a hundred miles away. Some shells weighed more than a ton each, but many men also died on the end of bayonets, or from gas, or from snipers' bullets. General Pétain voiced French determination in the phrase 'Ils ne passeront pas' ('They shall not pass'), and by April, French counter-attacks were exacting huge losses from the Germans. Reinforced by men and materials brought to the front by 3,000 lorries a day, the French showed such gallantry that Falkenhayn was caught in his own trap: he could not withdraw the Germans without admitting a humiliating set-back. In August 1916 he was sacked, but his policy at Verdun ran on for another four months; eventually the casualties numbered more than 800,000, and nearly half of them were German.

To relieve pressure on Verdun, Haig (who had taken over from Sir John French in 1915) brought forward the planned Franco-British offensive on the Somme, which had been intended for August. After five days of intensive bombardment, 100,000 men went 'over the top' on 1 July. The Germans, alerted by the intensity of the bombardment and then its cessation, emerged from the deep shelters which they had dug in the previous 18 months and manned their machine guns. By nightfall, the British had lost 57,770 men, almost as many in a day as the French were losing in a month at Verdun. In four months, nearly a million men were killed or wounded, fairly equally divided between attackers and defen-

The Schlieffen Plan and the Western Front

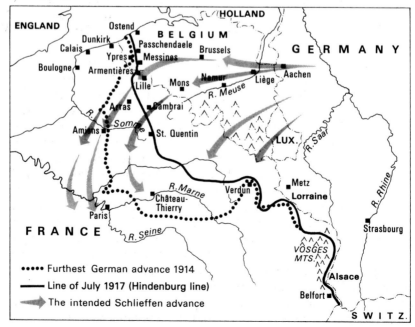

ders. The relentless pressure by the Western allies astounded the new German commanders on the Western Front, Hindenburg and Ludendorff, who made a slight withdrawal; by November, the Battle of the Somme had petered out, but not before tanks had gone into battle at Flers in September 1916. Their effect on the outcome of the Somme was negligible – hardly any of the first 50 tanks survived their first day in action – but those who had argued for the development of this secret weapon were encouraged to press for more money and more resources. The British and French recognized the tank's potential more quickly than the German High Command did, and there was a plan for a new Franco-British offensive in the spring of 1917. However, in late 1916 Joffre, the French Commander in Chief was sacked, and replaced by Nivelle, foolhardy and overconfident to the point where he proclaimed that he had 'a formula' which in 48 hours would turn the tide of the war.

Thus, 1917 opened with a strategic withdrawal by the Germans to new, well-prepared defences (the 'Hindenburg Line'), and with a lunging, short-sighted attack by the French under Nivelle (the Second Battle of the Aisne), the calamitous clumsiness of which led to mutiny in the French army and the rapid replacement of Nivelle by Pétain, the hero of Verdun. The fact that the U.S.A. declared war on Germany in April 1917 (see below) increased the German desire to win victory on the Western Front as soon as possible, and British and Canadian troops in Flanders held the key to the outcome of the war. Successes at Vimy in March and Messines in June led to the bitter Third Battle of Ypres, or Passchendaele, four months of muddy murder for little gain and nearly a quarter of a million casualties. Further south, at Cambrai, a massive tank attack on 20 November 1917 broke through the German lines significantly, but the lack of reserves destroyed the advantage.

1918 was expected to be decisive, but a race against time. The collapse of the Russian army released German forces to fight in France, but fresh American troops were arriving across the Atlantic. Ludendorff pressed for victory with an offensive (March to July) which saw more movement than at any time since September 1914; his troops crossed the Somme, the Aisne and the Marne and were closer to Paris than they had ever been, before they were held up by a mixture of exhaustion, lack of reserves, bad supply lines, and a new coordinated resistance from French, British, Empire and American troops under the unified command of Marshal Foch. Counter-attacking on the Marne in July and at Amiens with 800 aircraft and 540 tanks in August, the Allies fought their way north and east, and by November had moved for the most part onto Belgian soil. When the Kaiser abdicated on 9 November 1918 because of the internal collapse of his Empire, no enemy troops were in any part of Germany: the end of the war was decided by civilians and not by soldiers (see Chapter 10).

The Eastern Front

The Eastern Front ran from the Baltic to the Black Sea: for the Germans it was a Second Front; for the Russians, it was two fronts because they were fighting against both Germany and Austria-Hungary. When the Germans invaded Belgium in 1914, the French implored their only direct allies, the Russians, to attack East Prussia in order to suck some German troops away from the Western Front. In this they were successful, but the Russian advance was ill-prepared, a fact which an early victory by Rennenkampf's First Army disguised. The Russian Second Army, led by Samsonov, pressed rapidly westwards, moving too fast for its own lines of communication and supply, and eventually getting confused and uncoordinated in the forests around Tannenberg. The Germans, led by Hindenburg and Ludendorff (who were transferred to the Western Front in 1916), surrounded Samsonov and closed in. 30,000 Russians were killed, and 92,000 captured, along with armaments which the Russians desperately lacked thereafter. Samsonov committed suicide, and so did not see his rival Rennenkampf also defeated by the Germans at the Battle of the Masurian Lakes ten days later (September 1914).

Simultaneously, the Russians were being more successful against Austria. Early in September 1914 they captured Lemberg, capital of the Austrian province of Galicia, and for a while they planned further attacks on Austria. The Germans therefore decided to mark time in the west, while preparing a massive attack with the Austrians on the Russian province of Poland, and a counter-attack on Galicia. By the end of 1915 the Russians had lost a million casualties and a million prisoners, and the Tsar himself had assumed command of the army in an effort to boost its morale. In 1916, the Germans changed the emphasis back to Verdun on the Western Front, and in despair the French asked the Russians to draw the enemy's fire once more.

The 'Brusilov offensive' of June 1916 was Russia's most brilliant achievement of the war. This new surge into Galicia captured 400,000 prisoners and seemed to mark the beginning of the end of the Austro-Hungarian Empire. Romania, after two cautious years as a neutral power, now signed a military alliance with Britain and France, and thus divided the Central Powers into two distinct blocs, Germany with Austria, and Turkey with Bulgaria. But before the year was out, Romania had capitulated to the Central Powers, and the Russians were reeling back again as internal tensions and a hopeless supply system ruined their effectiveness.

In March 1917, the Tsar realized that he could no longer count on the total loyalty of the troops in his capital or at the front, and abdicated. He left a self-styled Provisional Government to cope with the problems of the war and of several revolutionary groups (see Chapter 5). The Germans hesitated: should they attack Russia

CHICHESTER CATHEDRAL

Yuuki Bouterey-Ishido, cello
&
Tianyang Han, piano

Frank Bridge (1879–1941)
Four pieces for cello and piano
    I. Berceuse
    II. Serenade
    III. Élégie
    IV. Cradle Song

Johannes Brahms (1833–1897)
Sonata for cello and piano no. 1 in E minor, op.38
    I. Allegro non troppo
    II. Allegretto quasi Menuetto
    III. Allegro

Tuesday 20th February 2024

Welcome to Chichester Cathedral

We hope that you enjoy this concert.

This series is entirely self-supporting and we gladly welcome your donations. The continued generosity of you, our audience, allows us to bring high-quality live music to Chichester on Tuesday lunchtimes.

Please remember to switch off your mobile phone. We would ask you to refrain from taking photographs and from making recordings. Feel free to eat your sandwiches in the nave. At the end, we would be grateful if you would take away this programme and recycle it.

Donations can be made:

- via the cash plates at the end of the concert
- using the contactless card readers, dotted around the cathedral
- by scanning this QR code
- on the lunchtime concerts web page

Yuuki Bouterey-Ishido is a professional cellist performing around the UK and Europe. Yuuki has been invited to perform at major festivals around the world, including the Schnittke Festival in London and the Semaine Internationale de Piano et musique de chambre in Switzerland. Other significant performances include solo recitals in Japan, Italy and New Zealand. He has also toured Europe extensively as a member of the Menuhin Academy Soloists under the direction of Maxim Vengerov.
Yuuki is currently on trial with the Royal Scottish National Orchestra. Yuuki is also a passionate chamber musician and has been awarded various chamber music prizes, as well as being invited to perform in various chamber festivals in Europe. He currently performs as a member of the Trio Kagura.

Masterclasses include those with, amongst others, Julian Lloyd Weber, Christoph and Miklós Perényi. Major prizes and awards include a Diploma of the Royal Academy of Music, the String Player Award at the Gisborne International Music Competition 2017, First Prize in the Barbirolli Cello Prize 2018, and 2nd Prize in the National Concerto Competition in New Zealand, among others.

A graduate of the Royal Northern College of Music, **Tianyang Han** is a pianist currently performing and teaching in the UK. Tianyang Han was inspired to pursue music as a profession after hearing the famous Chinese pianist Yundi Li perform. In 2009 she left middle school and started to study professionally with the esteemed teacher Danwen Wei at the Shenyang Conservatory of Music.

In 2014, Tianyang moved to England to study at the Royal Northern College of Music (RNCM) with Professor Graham Scott, having received the prestigious Lord Rhodes Scholarship. She graduated with a Master of Music. Tianyang currently holds the Resident Accompanist post at Brighton College. Other than solo performance, Tianyang also regularly plays chamber music, performing alongside Yuuki Bouterey-Ishido and in her trio, the Valette trio, in various venues in England. The Valette piano trio has won various awards including the Hirsch Prize, Nossek Prize and Weil Prize. She has participated in masterclasses with, amongst others, Daumantas Kirilauskas, Pavlina Dokovska and Solomon Mikovwky.

In 2010 and 2012, she attended the Italian Music Fest, Perugia, where she performed the Mendelssohn Piano Concerto No.1 with Sergei Babayan conducting. In 2018, she received a scholarship to join the 29th Semaine International de Piano & Musique de Chambre festival in Switzerland. Other awards include winning prizes in both the Youth Class and the Chopin Ballade/Scherzo Class at the 16th Hong Kong-Asia Piano Open Competition, Third Prize in the Shenyang Conservatory of Music Competition in 2011 and 2013, and finalist at the 2017 Concerto Competition (RNCM).

Spring 2024

Lunchtime Concerts
Tuesdays at 1.10pm

9 January	Andrew Garrido, piano
16 January	Meera Maharaj, flute, & Dominic Degavino, piano
23 January	Kassia Trio (two saxophones and piano)
30 January	Tim Ravalde, organ
6 February	Caroline Tyler, piano
13 February	Clarinet Quintet (string quartet with clarinet)
20 February	Yuuki Bouterey-Ishido, cello & Tianyang Han, piano
27 February	Charles Harrison, organ
5 March	Nataly Ganina, piano
12 March	Larisa Trio (violin, cello and piano)
19 March	Mikeleiz-Zucchi Duo (saxophone and accordion)

in her moment of chaos, or would such an attack bring all the Russian factions together to face the external enemy? Would German interests be served better by encouraging the chaos – for instance, by allowing troublemakers like Lenin to travel across Germany into their homeland from which they had been exiled for years? The Provisional Government finally forced the decision on the Germans by taking the offensive in June. The Germans fought back, and began to press up the Baltic coast towards Petrograd, the Russian capital. Lenin and his followers, promising 'Bread, Peace and Freedom', gained control of Petrograd early in November, and proclaimed peace with Germany. It was not easy to achieve in practice but the Treaty of Brest-Litovsk (March 1918) finally took Russia out of the war, conceding much of Poland to Germany and acknowledging the Ukraine as an independent state. The Eastern Front thus ended in victory for the Central Powers, but at a heavy cost to Germany. Fighting for Austrian interests was like 'fighting fettered to a corpse', which divided German aims and forces.

Italy

The Italians were never entirely happy about their place in the Triple Alliance of 1882 with Germany and Austria-Hungary, because the latter still occupied several Italian-speaking areas near the Adriatic coast ('Italia Irredenta', or 'Unredeemed Italy'). Political indecision in 1914 led to a rapid declaration of neutrality when the European war broke out, but in May 1915, hopes of expansion into the disputed territory persuaded the government to declare war on Austria-Hungary, with the full backing of Britain, France and Russia as promised in the Treaty of London (April

The Italian Front, 1917–18

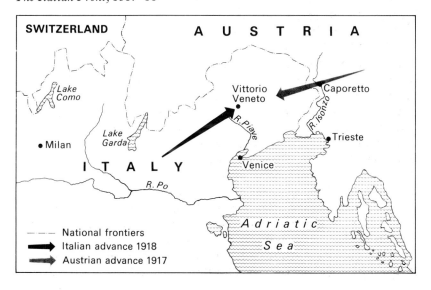

1915). Geography gave the Austrians a superb defensive position in the mountains, dominating the Italian north-east frontier. Cadorna, the Italian general, was forced to launch a series of attacks with limited objectives, so that he could inch forward and then consolidate. Each 'Battle of the Isonzo' lasted about two weeks and was very costly for the Italians. Four such battles were fought in 1915; another seven followed in 1916–17, and the Austrians were beginning to doubt whether they could withstand any more. Conrad, the Austrian commander, decided to change the pattern and attack rather than defend, and with German support, he initiated the 12th Battle of the Isonzo in October 1917. The Italians collapsed. Short of ammunition, dispirited by their own losses and lack of success, and worried by the presence of Germans against them, they fled from Caporetto where the battle began, to the Tagliamento River, and then on 30 miles to the Piave River. Although they lost 40,000 casualties and 290,000 prisoners, some Italians behaved as if they were relieved at the result; they simply wanted to get home. But a new commander, Diaz, regrouped and rediscled his men, and in October 1918 he launched a savage attack from the Piave. Within a week his forces had captured the Austrian Headquarters (optimistically called 'Venetian Victory' – Vittorio Veneto), and inflicted a crippling blow on the Central Powers, for the Austrians now sought peace.

Turkey

Turkey and Germany were friends but not allies until August 1914, when the arrival of two German warships, the *Goeben* and the *Breslau*, convinced the Turks of the security of joining the Central Powers. Thus the war grew much more complex. There was not much to be gained merely by inflicting a defeat on Turkey, but if a way could be forced through the Dardanelles and on to Constantinople and the Black Sea, the Allies would not only be putting a ring around possible German expansion, but also would be providing a new and favourable answer to the old 'Eastern Question' of 'Who will take the place of Turkey?'

However, Anglo-French attempts to storm the Dardanelles in February 1915 were laborious and ineffective; heroic action on the Gallipoli peninsula by British and ANZAC troops from April 1915 to January 1916 produced no better result. The final evacuation was the most skilfully conducted part of the whole campaign. Elsewhere, British forces in the Persian Gulf fought their way slowly up the Tigris Valley in 1914 and 1915 until they stood less than 20 miles from Baghdad. But they had gone too far, and falling back on the town of Kut did not save them. In April 1916, 10,000 officers and men surrendered to the Turks, a defeat which was avenged in the spring of 1917 when Kut was recaptured and Baghdad fell.

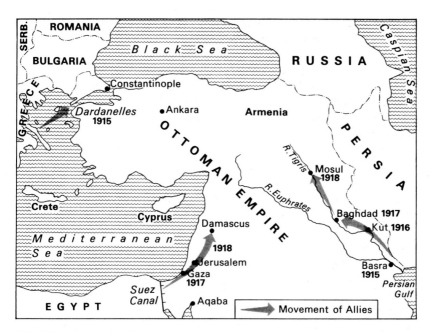

The War against the Ottomans

Potentially more important than either of these campaigns was that in Palestine, where Turkish victory would lead to their seizure of the Suez Canal and the disruption of all the British trade that flowed through it to India, Malaya, Hong Kong, Australia and New Zealand, while British victory would lead to Arabs overthrowing their Turkish masters and thus dealing the death-blow to the Ottoman Empire in the Middle East. To this end, Arab rebellion was encouraged and sometimes led by the sensitive, flitting figure of T.E. Lawrence 'of Arabia', archaeologist and volunteer Intelligence Officer. With his success and with General Allenby's more conventional cavalry advance through Palestine proceeding steadily in 1917 and 1918, Turkish influence collapsed. When Damascus fell in October 1918, the Turks sued for peace.

During the First World War, the Turks tried to eliminate one of their subject races, the Armenians, whose position as Christians on land adjoining enemy Russia made them highly suspect to the nationalist Muslim Turks. 1,500,000 men, women and children were callously slaughtered in 1915 and 1916, a cowardly and complicated reaction to the pressures of war.

The War in the Balkans

Only by the end of 1915 could the Austrians, with the aid of Germany and land-hungry Bulgaria, subdue the Serbs, whose tattered army withdrew through the snows of Albania to the coastline that they had coveted after the First Balkan War. They

returned to the mainland at Salonika, where, with a motley mixture
of British and ANZAC troops evacuated from Gallipoli, some
French conscripts and some Greek partisans, they waited until
June 1918. Then, as 'the Army of the Orient', they drove
northwards. By the end of September, Bulgaria had collapsed and
signed the 'Salonika Armistice'. The Serbs and their French allies
fought their way back to Belgrade, which they entered in triumph
on 1 November. The British troops turned eastwards against
Turkey, providing a further reason for Turkey's desertion of the
Central Powers in October 1918.

The War at Sea

In 1906, Britain had launched H.M.S. *Dreadnought*, the fastest,
heaviest, most fully armoured and most deadly warship ever
devised until then. It was a deliberate reaction to the German naval
expansion which William II had entrusted to Admiral von Tirpitz,
and the Germans retaliated by designing their own improved
version of the *Dreadnought*. When the war broke out, Britain enjoyed
an advantage of having 29 capital ships (i.e. battleships or heavy
cruisers) to Germany's 17, but the Germans were better equipped
with battle-cruiser raiders, fast and well-gunned, and had given
much more attention to the development of the submarine, of
which they had 28 in 1914 and over 100 in 1917. It was fear of these
submarines that restricted the British use of their Grand Fleet, and
early naval engagements – Britain's first of any consequence since
the Battle of Trafalgar – went Germany's way. In 1914, the *Goeben*
and *Breslau* shelled French bases in North Africa and then escaped
to Constantinople, making a big impression on the Turks. The
Emden, the *Karlsruhe* and the *Königsberg* proved to be spectacular
and costly raiders, and at Coronel off the Chilean coast, a British
squadron of four ships was destroyed by Admiral von Spee. But in
1915, this defeat was avenged at the Falkland Islands, and German
raids on the English east coast were stopped. The German
declaration of submarine warfare against neutrals as well as
belligerents did not affect the military balance. In 1916 came the
only major confrontation between the two battle fleets – 259 surface
vessels were involved – at Jutland in the North Sea.

Admiral Scheer, noting the relative failure of the 1915 submarine campaign, wanted to draw the British Grand Fleet to
destruction by committing all his surface and submarine strength
to one battle, but the scrap that developed was indecisive. The
British lost twice the tonnage and twice the casualties that the
Germans suffered, and were shown to have defective armour, shells
and signalling equipment. On the other hand the Germans were in
more danger of annihilation than the statistics suggest, and the
Kaiser lacked the confidence to use the High Seas Fleet again when
the risks were so great. The German High Command swung back

The Union Jack flies over a captured German U-boat in 1917.

to the use of unrestricted submarine warfare in 1917, leaving the High Seas Fleet resentful, and eventually mutinous.

The submarine campaign of 1917–18 nearly succeeded, though it drove the Americans firmly into the Allied camp. One ship in every four that left British ports in April 1917 failed to return. One million tons of British and neutral shipping were sunk in that month, ten times more than could be replaced by fresh launchings. Britain, the habitual blockading power, was within six weeks of starvation. Zig-zag courses, mines, depth-charges and Q-ships (merchant ships with concealed armaments) were not enough to hold off the U-boats, and only the emergency introduction of compulsory convoys brought down the rate of sinkings. Of the 88,000 ships that travelled in convoy between May 1917 and November 1918, only 456 were sunk, despite a peak figure of 140 German submarines in operation. It is an interesting comment on the dread of German submarines that when the war ended, the armistice-makers allowed the Germans to keep six battleships and six light cruisers, but not a single U-boat, for that was the weapon which had been largely responsible for the sinking of more than 12,000,000 tons of shipping during the war.

The World At War

The German colonial possessions in Africa (East Africa, South West Africa, the Cameroons and Togoland) were early targets for British, French or South African forces. All except East Africa quickly succumbed, deprived as they were of any help from their mother country.

In the Pacific and on the Chinese mainland, Japan took advantage of its alliance with Britain to increase its power as a trading and military empire. China, already torn by its own political divisions, eventually also declared war on Germany, largely in order to be represented at any peace conference which might parcel up former German spheres of influence (see Chapter 8). The Japanese and Chinese were never directly involved in the battle of the European armed camps on the Western Front, but Indians, Senegalese, Australians, Vietnamese, Algerians, and many other peoples were, for when Britain and France declared war, they did so in the name of their colonies also. Only the continent of South America escaped the upheaval and the wastage, though the naval war came close to it.

It was the war at sea that brought the United States into the conflict in April 1917. For the past hundred years, America had carefully avoided any entanglement with European politics and alliances, and had been proud of its neutrality, a necessary policy when so many American citizens had direct links with England and with Germany, with Ireland and with Italy, indeed with every nation. Proud of being the 'melting pot' of former nationalities, it was nonetheless afraid of internal tensions boiling up. So in 1914, the government of President Wilson had neither experience nor understanding of the strained relationships in Europe, but responded to popular feeling in declaring its neutrality, which in practice meant continuing trade and financial arrangements with both sides. But the German threat of submarine warfare against neutral powers tipped American sympathies towards Britain and France. The actual sinking of the *Lusitania* in May 1915, with the loss of 128 American lives, caused such fury that the Germans eventually promised safety to unarmed passenger liners. In 1916, goodwill was restored between Germany and the U.S.A., and Wilson was re-elected President on the slogan 'He kept us Out of War'. But on 31 January 1917, the Germans announced that unrestricted submarine warfare would start at midnight, and before the end of February American lives were lost in the sinking of the *Laconia*. The declaration of war in early April was as popular as neutrality had been 12 months before, and American intervention meant that the European stalemate had to end soon. It was not so much what the Americans did, but what they might do in the future, that made Germany bid for outright victory in March 1918, and gave the Allies the resilience to hold off the attack.

The Civilian Contribution to War – and to Peace

No previous war had affected so many civilians. Because of the static nature of most of the Fronts, there were relatively few refugees streaming away from their homes. But it was this very immobility which raised the cost of every mile gained in terms of men, money and materials, and which introduced the idea of 'total' war, which involved everyone, and in which governments took unprecedented measures to maintain their war efforts.

Although each country varied in the details of its arrangements, Britain provides an example of the types of changes brought about. For the first time ever, military service was made compulsory for men aged between 18 and 41; suspected spies were locked up without trial; a rationing system was introduced; ships were commandeered by the government, who also took a major say in the running and financing of railway companies and coalmines; 'Daylight Saving Time' was introduced by Act of Parliament (despite the protests of farmers who complained that it would upset their animals); taxes on excess profits went as high as 80 per cent; hemlines went significantly higher too, in order to make it easier for women to move as they took over the countless jobs vacated by men now at the Front; pubs were forced to shut in the afternoons. These and a host of further regulations brought the whole population into the war on what was called 'the Home Front'.

More important than the details, most of which ended when the war ended, was the long-term effect of the war on society. The war centralized the country; it focussed the attention of the nation on one overriding aim – to win the war – and it brushed aside old attitudes and old ways of doing things. The skilful use of advertising by the Government unlocked a flood of volunteers for the army and private savings for the Treasury. After the war, the same advertising was going to be used with great success by commercial companies. The war emancipated the women, who until 1914 had fought against the men to get political recognition: now they fought with the men against a common enemy, and within a month of the end of the war, women over 30 had been granted the vote. Furthermore, they were now accepted in many spheres of economic life which had been previously closed to them. Most of all, the war established the right of the Government to get on and govern, to use its initiative and to demand loyalty and obedience as the situation required. No nineteenth-century ministry would ever have dared, or have wanted, to be so demanding of its populace. In this respect Britain, with its positive response to Asquith and Lloyd George, differed from France, Russia and Germany.

In France and Russia, the presence of invaders imposed severe strains. Six ministries came and went in France as bitter debates raged between those who wanted victory and those who wanted a negotiated peace. In Russia, two million civilian deaths from starvation or invasion gave substance to the arguments of revolutionaries who eventually won power in 1917, partly because of their opposition to the war.

In Germany, the strain of war brought increasing political chaos. Bethmann-Hollweg was sacked in 1917, and three other men held the rank of Chancellor before the war ended. Strikes increased even in key industries: food and raw materials were desperately short, and red flags symbolizing workers' revolution flew from an increasing number of buildings. In 1918, the Germans viewed with deep pessimism the Bulgarian armistice of 30 September, the Turkish armistice of 3 October, and the Austrian surrender of 3 November. The strain, not only on soldiers and sailors but also on civilians, was so great that it became clear that the nation would not make one huge final effort. 'Collective suicide is not practical policy,' said a minister.

Ludendorff fled to Sweden, and Kaiser William to Holland, for neither of them could hold the demoralized country together. On 11 November 1918, the people of Germany forced their government to request an armistice, in order to stave off the inevitable military defeat.

Woodrow Wilson and the Ideals

One man dominated diplomacy in 1917 and 1918 because of his country's power and his own ideals: Woodrow Wilson, 28th President of the United States. A professor turned politician, he had a strong sense of responsibility for the improvement of the political and social life of all mankind, as well as a great belief in the ability of America to sort out the confusions of a world hitherto dominated by Europe. Having regretfully committed his forces to fight for peace in April 1917, he began to shape that peace in January 1918 when he submitted to the American Congress the following '14 Points', which he believed should be the basis of international negotiation:

1 Open covenants of peace, and the end of secret diplomacy;
2 Freedom of navigation in international waters, in peace and in war;
3 The removal of as many economic barriers as possible, and equality of trading conditions among the nations accepting the peace;
4 The reduction of armaments to the lowest point consistent with national safety;
5 The settlement of all colonial disputes, with equal recognition being given to the interests of the colonial population and the legitimate claims of the mother country;
6 The evacuation of all Russian territory, and the acceptance of the fact that Russia could and should develop in whatever way suited her;
7 The restoration of Belgian sovereignty;
8 France to be evacuated by the Germans, and Alsace and Lorraine returned to the French;
9 The readjustment of Italian frontiers according to clear lines of nationality;
10 The unhindered development of self-government among the peoples of the old Austro-Hungarian Empire;
11 Romania, Serbia and Montenegro to be evacuated; Serbia to be given access to the sea; new and acceptable boundaries to be drawn in the Balkans;

President Wilson (left) with members of his Cabinet.

12   Self-government to be allowed to the subject races of the old Ottoman Empire while the Turkish areas retained their own security and sovereignty. The Dardanelles to be opened permanently to the ships and commerce of all nations;

13   The creation of an independent Polish state, with free and secure access to the sea; its political and economic independence to be internationally guaranteed;

14   A general association of nations to be formed, pledged to guarantee political independence and territorial integrity to great and small nations alike.

The 14 Points were not particularly original, but Wilson put them together authoritatively. In many subsequent speeches, when he picked out the 'Four Principles' or the 'Four Ends' or the 'Five Particulars', he dwelt on those things which related to the concepts of nationalism (as opposed to imperialism), democracy and self-determination, as well as the idea that the general association of nations would provide 'collective security'. This meant that all associated states would rally to defend the interests and welfare of any country being attacked, which would render the attack not only useless but even dangerous for the attacker.

The Allies had many reservations about Wilson's theories, but in November 1918 Britain and France announced that they accepted the broad principles of the 14 Points, as did Germany and Austria. The Central Powers were perhaps more willing than the Allies, but at that stage they had less to lose.

Clemenceau, Lloyd George, and the Practical Problems

Ideals were all very well for a country like America, whose history and geography isolated her from the tensions of European development. But Clemenceau, Prime Minister of France since November 1917 and nicknamed 'the Tiger' and 'The Father of Victory', could remember the humiliation of 1870, when he had witnessed the handover of Alsace and Lorraine to the swaggering Germans. Furthermore, his country had suffered to an unprecedented extent: more than a million Frenchmen were dead, a third of a million homes had been destroyed, thousands of factories looted and hundreds of mines flooded, all at the hands of the invaders, and some even in the last hours of the war when the Germans were actually suing for peace while continuing acts of unnecessary destruction. French hatred ran deep; the desire not only to beat the Germans but to continue to punish them remained strong throughout the 1920s, as was illustrated by French stubbornness over reparations and the occupation of the Ruhr, 1923–25 (see Chapter 10). The population that Clemenceau spoke for had no intention of forgiving or trusting.

Similarly the British Prime Minister Lloyd George had fought and won a flag-waving election as soon as the war was over. Despite his personal moderation and desire to calm the international scene, he found himself bearing the load of bitter British expectations. Too many men had died or been maimed, too many ships had been sunk in icy waters. 'Hang the Kaiser' and 'Make Germany Pay' were honest expressions of popular feeling, and because of the election campaign, they became near-commitments for the politicians who were returned to Westminster.

To implement the 14 Points raised other, practical, problems. France and Britain were both colonial powers: what would the principle of self-determination do to their empires? They had attracted Italy away from the Triple Alliance in 1915 by a secret promise of Austrian and Turkish territory: were they now bound by such secret diplomacy, and could they ever find satisfactory boundaries for Italy? Must they accept as equals the revolutionary Russian government led by Lenin, which they considered as being treacherous after it had left the Triple Entente? Was it wise to return Alsace and Lorraine to France when the former contained many people of German extraction? And could there be an acceptable redrawing of the map of Central and Eastern Europe in keeping with the ideals of the 14 Points, or was it impossibly complex? These were among the major questions that had to be thrashed out at the Peace Conference that met in Paris in January 1919, and produced the Treaty of Versailles which was signed in June 1919.

The Treaty of Versailles, 1919

Strictly speaking, the name 'Treaty of Versailles' belongs solely to the agreement made with Germany, though it is sometimes used to include the treaties made with the other defeated powers (Austria and Hungary which were now treated separately, Turkey and Bulgaria).

Only the Allied and Associated Powers were represented at the Peace Conference, i.e., the victorious ones and those on whom they looked sympathetically. The Germans were allowed to make written comments on the draft treaty which was ready in May, but little notice was taken of them. This was to be a dictated peace and not a truly negotiated one, for much of it was based on the terms of the armistice which the desperate Germans had signed in November 1918. Significantly, this had included a promise to pay for damage done, which set the tone of the whole treaty.

After opening with 26 articles which formed the Covenant of the new League of Nations (see section below), the Treaty of Versailles swiftly outlined the frontiers of the 'new' Germany. Starting from the north and working clockwise (see map on p.147), Germany lost: 1,500 square miles of northern Schleswig which voted to join Denmark; most of West Prussia and Poznan, which became part of Poland and gave the Poles their promised access to the sea; the port of Danzig which became a 'free city' looked after by the League; Memel, a strip of land to the north of East Prussia which went to Lithuania (East Prussia remained a part of Germany though separated from the rest of it); parts of Upper Silesia, which although they voted to stay in Germany were clumsily split between Germany and Poland; on the western side, Alsace and Lorraine which reverted to France; the Saar, rich in coal, which was to be administered by France for the League for 15 years until it could vote on its own future; and finally, three tiny areas near Aachen which were given to Belgium. All German areas left on the west of the Rhine were to be demilitarized, as well as a strip 30 miles wide on the eastern bank.

Germany's colonies were also taken away and distributed as 'mandates' to other members of the League. A 'mandate' granted a country the administrative rights over an area, with the ultimate responsibility for bringing that area to true independence. Britain made the major gains from this, being granted East Africa, the Cameroons and Togoland, but Belgium, France, South Africa, Australia, New Zealand and Japan also benefited.

The armaments allowed to Germany were also severely restricted: the Navy was limited to 15,000 men and 36 ships, the army to 100,000 men, and the Air Force was totally banned. This emphasized again Germany's 'war guilt', which was further stressed by the sections accusing the Kaiser of 'a supreme offence against international morality', by arranging the trials of anyone whom the Allies might accuse of war crimes, and by establishing that Germany should pay 'Reparations' over the next thirty years. (The Allied Commission's 'bill', when it arrived in 1921, was initially for £6,600,000,000.)

The Germans, remembering that it was Britain who had declared war on them over a 'scrap of paper', bitterly resented the punitive attitude of the Allies, a fact which contributed strongly to the appeal of the *National* Socialist (Nazi) Party in the 1930s.

The Remaining Treaties, and the New Face of Europe

In 1919 conditions of peace were signed with Austria (Treaty of Saint-Germain) and with Bulgaria (Treaty of Neuilly). In 1920 it was the turn of Hungary, a kingdom without a king, (Treaty of Trianon) and of Turkey (Treaty of Sèvres). The Turkish treaty had to be renegotiated in 1922 and 1923 because of continued war between Turks and Greeks and the emergence of a new Turkish regime. The final settlement was made at Lausanne in 1923.

All the treaties started with the Covenant of the League of Nations (see next section) and then went on to prescribe frontiers, military limitations and reparations payments. The result of the treaties was a band of new countries running from the Arctic to the Mediterranean (see maps on pp.46–47). In 1900, a journey in a virtually straight line from the north-western tip of Russia to Athens would have taken the traveller through the Russian Empire, the German Reich, the Austro-Hungarian Empire, Serbia, the Ottoman Empire and into Greece. In 1922, the same journey would have started in Finland and passed through Estonia, Latvia, Lithuania, Poland, Czechoslovakia, Hungary, the Kingdom of the Serbs, Croats and Slovenes, and finally Greece. The four empires had gone. Whereas Austria-Hungary had had a population of 50 million in 1914, in 1920 the two separated countries could claim only eight million between them. Turkey had only half the population of the old Ottoman Empire. Bolshevik Russia had lost 40 per cent of her former imperial population.

Not only these former empires felt aggrieved about the new Europe. The principle of self-determination was inconsistently applied, and all the new nations had reasons for dissatisfaction. Poland and Czechoslovakia disputed the Teschen area of Silesia. Poland and Russia fought about their common frontier, fixed on ethnic lines by Lord Curzon in 1919 and then moved eastwards in 1921, bringing many Ukrainians under Polish rule. Three million Sudeten Germans formerly ruled by Austria now found themselves in the new country of Czechoslovakia. Out of such disputes sprang the roots of a further major war, while out of the resentment of Greeks, Turks, Serbs, Magyars, Bessarabians, and many other racial groups now settled in the 'wrong' countries, arose a series of negotiators' nightmares.

The League of Nations

Wilson's 14 Points had ended with a call for a general association of nations to guarantee the political independence of all states. The League of Nations was that association, and it was set up initially by a Covenant which was built into all the 1919 peace treaties which concluded the Great War.

The Covenant formed the constitution of the League. In its 26 articles, it laid out who could and could not join the League, and how other nations could be elected. It established the mechanisms and methods by which it would work, and it set out a number of obligations and objectives.

42 self-governing states and dominions were named as founder-members of the League; Germany, Russia, Austria and Turkey were specifically excluded. Other states could apply to join, and could become members if approved by two-thirds of the Assembly.

The *Assembly* was the main meeting-ground of the League: each nation could send three representatives to it, although each country had only one vote. The Assembly met in Geneva, usually once a year, to discuss any matters relating to the peace or welfare of the world. Also in Geneva was the permanent *Secretariat*, responsible for all the international preparation and administration. The Secretary-General in charge of this Civil Service presided over the meetings of the Assembly (Sir Eric Drummond of the British Foreign Office was the first to hold the post). There was a third branch of the League, the *Council*, consisting of representatives from Britain, France, Italy and Japan, who considered disputes and difficulties and who made recommendations to the Assembly. The four permanent member-countries of the Council were assisted by four (later six) temporary members chosen by the Assembly. Council meetings occurred three or four times a year.

By the terms of the Covenant, members of the League bound themselves not to fight against fellow-members. They were encouraged to refer all disputes, with members or non-members, to the League for settlement, and if this failed, they were required to give three months' notice of any unilateral action. Any state that committed an offence against the League could be curbed in one of two ways: either the member-states could refuse to supply it with necessary goods – this was called 'imposing economic sanctions' – or they could use 'military sanctions', though this was never clearly defined nor brought into operation. Secret diplomacy between members was strongly discouraged, and disarmament was positively encouraged, though it was conceded that a nation must always be able to defend itself.

The overriding principle behind the League was that of 'collective security', which had been the intention of the last and most emphatic of Wilson's 14 Points. Ironically, the failure of the American Senate to ratify the Treaty of Versailles and the incorporated Covenant of the League meant that America never became a member of the League (see Chapter 5 for a fuller explanation), and the strength of the League was always conditioned by which countries were or were not members. Germany eventually became a member in 1926 but left again in 1933, despite

THE GAP IN THE BRIDGE.

The European view of America's refusal to join the League of Nations.

failing to meet a requirement that withdrawal should be notified two years in advance. Russia was a member only from 1934 until 1939. Japan and Italy withdrew in 1933 and 1937 respectively, after attracting criticism from the other nations. The result was that the full force of a 'collective' decision seldom, if ever, applied among the Great Powers of the world, and so there was little sense of security either.

The Covenant also laid down other duties for the League: the Mandates Commission was to supervise the welfare of the former German and Turkish colonies, and the League was to be responsible for the International Labour Organization, which was also set up by the Versailles Treaty to improve and standardize workers' conditions. The Permanent Court of International Justice was set up at The Hague to settle judicial and legal disputes between nations (as opposed to political disputes which came before the Council or the Assembly). Certain other smaller Commissions were set up to cope with immediate problems: the Repatriation Commission, the Health Organization, the Minorities Commission, and the Disarmament Commission (see below and Chapter 11).

The League of Nations – Virtues and Weaknesses

The League embodied all the optimism which made men believe that they had just come through 'the war to end all war'. It was the most ambitious, forward-looking and wide-ranging international partnership that had ever been created. From its experiences, not only its immediate successor the United Nations Organization but also the British Commonwealth, the European Community, the Organization of African Unity, the Arab League and other voluntary associations of countries have learned much. For all the economic and technical development of the nineteenth century, little had been achieved that was cooperative rather than competitive, except the foundation of the International Red Cross Society. Henceforth famine, drug-running, the white slave trade, stateless refugees, international communication systems and all manner of social and technical problems were matters for shared attention and therefore simpler solution.

It is very easy to criticize the League for its spectacular 'failure' in not preventing the Second World War and to forget that it *did* solve disputes of a political nature, which seem small now only because they were solved. The argument between Sweden and Finland over the ownership of the Aaland Islands (1921), the status of Upper Silesia (1921), the population exchanges in the Balkans (1923), the Greek reparations to Bulgaria (1925) and the Yugoslav-Hungarian dispute (1934) brought positive decisions or actions from the League which solved the problems and captured few headlines. It must also be remembered in defence of the League that the very treaties that established it also set up the explosive issues that were to destroy it. The proclamation of German war guilt and the discrimination against Germany becoming a member were fundamental errors of statesmanship and not failings of the League.

Yet there were weaknesses. Nearly all decisions of the League had to be unanimous, which meant that any international decision could be obstructed by just one nation, and amendments to the Covenant were in practice impossible. It was by nature an indecisive body, lacking not so much the strength of its convictions, but the convictions themselves.

It had no armed force of its own, and so its ideas about military sanctions were useless from the start. Economic sanctions therefore became the main weapon available to the League, but they were so slowly and incompletely used against Italy in 1935 that they were equally useless. The fact was that the League had no way of defending its decisions or beliefs against any power, big or small, that would not voluntarily accept them. It certainly had no answer to the use of force, and it could not even make a country accept criticism: Japan withdrew from the League in 1933 because of the condemnation of the Lytton Report (see Chapter 8).

The absence of several of the Great Powers undermined the League, none being missed more than the U.S.A., whose economic power alone would have vastly increased its strength and influence. It was narrowminded to allow countries like Brazil, Honduras and Siam to join the League merely because they had nominally declared war on Germany, while Germany itself was excluded. The

League was associated too much with the victorious allies and therefore with vindictive peace treaties, and was also inconsistent in its membership policy. The British Empire was represented as one unit at the first meeting, but soon Canada, Australia, New Zealand, South Africa and India – the last not even being a self-governing Dominion – were given separate representation: a cynical Frenchman suggested instant admission of Monaco (all 370 acres of it) as a full member.

The Struggle for Peace With Security

One of the great contradictions of the League was that in encouraging disarmament, it was making nations feel threatened because they would no longer be able to defend themselves. A sure sign of this worry was the large number of private treaties made inside and outside the League. France was still afraid of Germany, and so made protective treaties with two of Germany's neighbours, Poland in 1921 and Czechoslovakia in 1924. Poland feared Russia, and so made a similar defensive treaty with a Russian neighbour, Romania, in 1921. Czechoslovakia, afraid of Hungary, brought about the Little Entente of 1920–21, a complete network of two-way treaties between Czechoslovakia, Yugoslavia and Romania, while Italy also made a treaty of 'friendship and collaboration' with Yugoslavia in 1924. Meanwhile at a Conference in Washington in 1921–22, the power structure of the Pacific and the Far East was being clarified in the Five Power Naval Treaty which fixed a ratio of capital ships for the U.S.A., Britain, France, Japan and Italy at 10:10:6:3.3:3.3.

The League tried to balance defence with disarmament in a Draft Treaty of Mutual Assistance which was produced in 1923. The British Labour government squashed it in 1924, but then combined with the French Socialist government to produce the Geneva Protocol, a plan which bound all signatories to abide by the decisions of the Court of International Justice whatever other treaties they might have signed, and never to use force until sanctions had been tried. This received unanimous approval from the League, but was wrecked in 1925, when a new Conservative government in Britain announced that it would not support such an agreement. At this point the future of the League hung in the balance, and the alternative arrangement that Britain, France and Germany now produced looked attractive, but had ominous implications. It was known as the Locarno Pact, though it was signed in London in December 1925.

Locarno guaranteed the French and Belgian borders with Germany, a German proposal gladly accepted by the Western powers; it acknowledged the continuation of the demilitarization of the Rhineland; it ensured that Germany, France, Belgium, Czechoslovakia and Poland would never go to war over their frontiers but

Europe before the First World War

would seek arbitration, a procedure which Britain, Italy and
France variously guaranteed; finally, it suggested the admission of
Germany not just to the League, but to a permanent seat on the
Council of the League. This proposal caused considerable jealousy
and bickering, but in 1926 Germany joined the League. 'Peace for
Germany and for France,' proclaimed Briand, the French Foreign
Minister. 'That means that we have done with the long series of
terrible and bloody conflicts which have stained the pages of
History.' In 1928 he was responsible, with the American Secretary
of State, for the Kellogg-Briand Pact, a renunciation of war as an
instrument of national policy which most nations signed, especially
after Kellogg had stated that he did not include wars of self-
defence.

Thus by the end of the 1920s, a new framework for international affairs had been created. Although the League had been
embarrassed by its occasional failure to handle political confrontations, for example the Polish seizure of Vilna in 1920 and the
Italian occupation of Corfu in 1923, and although even a treaty like
Locarno implied that parts of the Versailles settlement were now
open to further negotiation, the decade drew towards its close with
a sense of international achievement. Europe's boundaries seemed
at last to be largely settled; the mandates were working; France and

Europe after the First World War

Germany were at ease with each other diplomatically, and the U.S.A., while not a member of the League, was bringing a benevolent interest to bear through the Kellogg-Briand Pact. Since 1926, a Preparatory Commission had been working towards a full-scale Disarmament Conference, which it was hoped would finally remove the spectre of major war from the world.

But as the 1920s gave way to the 1930s, international optimism fell foul of stubborn realities. The Wall Street Crash of 1929 and the Depression destroyed the economic foundations of most Western countries, and drastically altered their politics. In the east, Japanese expansion in 1931 threatened the stability and the principles of the League. Furthermore, the much-heralded Disarmament Conference achieved nothing between 1932 and 1934. The 1930s witnessed a rapid slide from optimistic peace to disastrous war, details of which are considered in Chapter 11.

4 Russia 1905-41

'Bloody Sunday', 1905

In January 1905, an orderly procession of men, women and children approached the Winter Palace in St. Petersburg. Led by an Orthodox priest, Father Gapon, and bearing a plaintive petition, this group provided a touching illustration of the faith of the Russian people in the powers of the Czar, their 'Little Father', to protect them against any wrong – until an ill-judged command sent volleys of rifle fire into the heart of the crowd. Nobody knows the casualty figures, for the dead and wounded were hidden from the authorities as far as possible; estimates range from two hundred to fifteen hundred. It was a forceful example of the power of the Russian monarchy (though the Czar himself was not at the Winter Palace on that day).

'Bloody Sunday' marked the start of the 1905 Revolution in Russia. The other spectacular event of the year was the mutiny on the battleship *Potemkin* over the refusal of the crew to eat maggoty meat. But more important were the riots, demonstrations and strikes which flared up throughout the country without apparent leadership. This significant lack of a revolutionary leader shows that the causes of the trouble were widely felt and deep-running.

Having been undeveloped economically throughout the nineteenth century (serfdom was abolished only in 1861), Russia was trying to scramble into the new century. Between 1892 and 1901, the Russian growth rate was only exceeded by those of the U.S.A. and Japan, because of a policy of rapid industrialization introduced by Witte, Minister of Finance. On money borrowed largely from France, Witte enabled coal production to increase by 350 per cent in the 1890s and iron and steel by 850 per cent in the same period. Railway building doubled, mainly on the Trans-Siberian line, and the output of the cotton industry doubled. Industrial towns grew rapidly and without much planning, so that living conditions were atrocious and the distribution of food was always inefficient. A rapidly rising population meant plenty of cheap labour for the employers, who therefore still treated their workers, in town or country, as if they were serfs from an earlier era. It was this

A scene from Eisenstein's powerful film The Battleship Potemkin. *The Tsar's troops menace the helpless workers despite the pleading hands. The film was made in 1925, on the direct orders of the Russian Central Executive Committee.*

combination of new economic pressures and old social and political attitudes that encouraged the emergence of revolutionary or terrorist groups like 'Land and Liberty' in the 1860s, the 'People's Will' in the 1870s and 1880s, and the Social Revolutionaries (1901) and the Social Democrats (1898). The S.R.s were representatives of rural discontent, peasant terrorists and intellectual idealists always liable to resort to violence and assassination to achieve their ends. The S.D.s were Marxists, men and women who believed in Karl Marx's theory that all history is the history of class struggles. They looked to the 'proletariat', the new urban working classes packed into the slums of St. Petersburg, Moscow and other major towns, who would overthrow capitalism and the Czar, and produce a new world of equality.

The Soviet, and the October Manifesto

It was none of these groups that produced the most revolutionary action in 1905, despite all the tension and unrest, the strikes and the national humiliation of losing a war against Japan, which had been deliberately started in 1904 to take men's minds off internal troubles. More 'revolutionary' than the negative expressions of dissatisfaction were two attempts to produce positive change, one from the workers and one from the liberal advisers to the Czar.

The workers produced the idea of the Soviet, first in the textile town of Ivanova-Voznesensk and then in St. Petersburg. A Soviet was simply a meeting of workers (and later, soldiers as well), run by themselves for themselves. Anyone could speak, on any subject. Chairmen were chosen from the crowd for a day or a week or a month, but otherwise, organization was informal. It was totally democratic and had power in an area because the workers would do what it (i.e. *they*) said. In St. Petersburg, a Soviet started in October 1905, and by the end of November contained representatives of all the big factories. It also published its own paper, *Izvestya*.

The liberals led by Witte meanwhile persuaded the Czar to issue the October Manifesto, which guaranteed to the Russian people freedom of speech, freedom from arbitrary arrest, freedom of association, and, most revolutionary of all, an elected Assembly (the Duma) with power to make laws. Though the Duma was not responsible for appointing ministers, and though the elections had to be held in two stages through electoral colleges, the fact was that the Czar was allowing the existence of political parties. Before the Duma, parties had no place to speak and so were all considered subversive; now they were out in the open, and bound to spread.

Nicholas II himself was a nervous, chain-smoking man who loved his family, believed in the greatness of Russia and the supremacy of the Czar, and wanted to carry out the sacred trust vested in him, but lacked the personality and the imagination to lead others. His wife Alexandra, German by birth, showed much more toughness, though she was over-emotional and dangerously outspoken at times. She nagged Nicholas with endless encouragement: 'You have never lost an opportunity to show them your love and kindness; now let them feel your fist... They must learn to fear you; love alone is not enough.'

1905–17 – Stolypin and the Great War

The tide of revolution ebbed after the October Manifesto. The Soviets were put down by force in December, their leaders being arrested or forced to flee, and in the middle of May 1906 the First Duma met, elected for five years. It lasted for two months: its members tried to discuss too many fundamental issues, and the ministers (Witte had been sacked by now) did not want to work with them. In 1907, a Second Duma met, with little more success. On the trumped-up charge that it had been trying to organize a mutiny, it too was dissolved, and Stolypin, the Prime Minster from 1906 to 1911, used the old autocratic powers to manipulate the electoral system until it would return a more moderate group of representatives. The Third Duma met in 1907 and lasted its full five years. The Fourth Duma also worked fairly harmoniously with the Government from 1912 to 1917.

Stolypin was prepared to work with the Duma, but on his own terms. He believed that carefully controlled reforms would be more effective in calming Russia, and that the peasantry, the largest group in Russia, was the key to the unrest. If the peasants could be turned into owners of their land, with incentives to produce a lot of food, they would become forces of stability and wealth rather than restless and wretched tenants in an impersonal village community. So by crushing terrorists and encouraging agrarian reform, he not only restored order but also gave a new boost to the economic development of the country. More efficient farming supported more industrial workers: steel, machinery, coal, oil – all the necessities of a modern economy – increased the wealth and power of Russia. Although trouble still flared sporadically, (Stolypin himself was assassinated by an anarchist in 1911, and from 1912 to 1914 there was an unprecedented number of serious strikes), the position of the Czar was apparently fully secure again in 1914 when the First World War broke out. A succession of good harvests had relieved tension: 50,000 new primary schools were fulfilling some of the demand for education for all; local councils ('zemstva') were increasingly responsible and cooperative. Moreover, the outbreak of war was popular. The capital city immediately changed its name to Petrograd, the Russian version of the Germanically-named St. Petersburg. (German connections were universally disliked. At the same time the English Royal Family changed its surname, Saxe-Coburg-Gotha, to the utterly English 'Windsor'.)

There is no simple picture of Russia at war; only a series of contrasts. Mobilization of men went better than expected (6½

Nicholas II and Alexandra out hunting in 1901. After the abdication in 1917, the Czar and his family were held under house arrest, until in July 1918 they disappeared. Officially, they were killed by Bolshevik guards at Ekaterinburg, but many doubt this story.

million by the end of 1914 and 15½ million by 1917) but there was never more than a third of the necessary rifles, and only 12 per cent of the required machine guns in 1917. A brilliant victory against the Austrians at Lemberg in September 1914 came between the disastrous defeats of Samsonov and Rennenkampf at the hands of the Germans (see Chapter 2 for the narrative of the war). While thousands of tons of grain and butter rotted in their stores, men starved in Central Siberia because there were no railway wagons to bring the food to them. At the front, empty wagons were pushed off the tracks to get them out of the way. The military authorities did not consider it their job to send them back. The most consistent characteristic of the Russians was the loyalty which they showed to their allies in the west despite appalling losses. The Galicia campaign of 1915 cost 1,410,000 killed and wounded and 976,000 prisoners, but Brusilov launched a new campaign in 1916 in order to divert the German attack on Verdun.

The Czar took control of his forces in 1915, moving from Petrograd to staff headquarters at Moghilev. He had no military brilliance or experience, but the ruinous result of this decision was political, not military. In Petrograd, power passed to the neurotic Alexandra and the man she called 'Our Friend', Rasputin.

Rasputin

'Rasputin' is not a Russian surname. It is an adjective meaning 'foul, filthy, debauched' which became connected with a wandering

'Our friend' Rasputin, surrounded by some of his friends. Many ladies at court were spellbound by him.

'Holy Man' from Siberia who first came to the capital in 1903. In 1907, the Czar's only son fell desperately ill with haemophilia (uncontrollable bleeding), and Rasputin saved his life, probably by using hypnotism to calm the boy. The joy and gratitude of the parents was boundless. Despite his unwashed, unkempt state, his drunkenness, his sexual and social crudity, Rasputin was always welcome in the Imperial Palaces. By 1911, he had political influence: by 1916, he was powerful enough to have the Prime Minister Goremykin sacked and his own nominee Sturmer appointed. Some of his ideas were good. He wanted the Czar to make more use of the Duma, and he tried to organize the chaotic transport system, but his personality and influence over the Czarina nauseated the politicians and courtiers, especially in view of the absence of the Czar. In December 1916, he was murdered by Prince Yusupov, having done irreparable damage to the reputation of the Royal family and the authority of the Czar. But his death did not improve the situation. Petrograd and Russia were now in the hands of Alexandra, 'that German woman'.

The 'February Revolution', 1917

In February 1917, the unplanned combination of four factors in Petrograd had the unexpected result of toppling the Czar from his throne. After 300 years of power, the Romanov dynasty evaporated with a suddenness that took even the revolutionary parties by surprise. The four factors were a socialist holiday (Women's Day), a strike at the Putilov steel works, large but not abnormally large bread queues, and the obvious reluctance of the police and troops to quell the consequent disturbances. From headquarters 500 miles away, the Czar demanded suppression of the troubles, while the President of the Duma began to sense emergency and pleaded for a new form of government. He was too late. 'This fat Rodzianko has written me some nonsense to which I will not even reply,' said the Czar on the receipt of an urgent telegram. Within a few days, there were no loyal troops left in Petrograd. The Duma had been dismissed by a telegram from the Czar, and had used its own initiative to form a Provisional Government in the Tauride Palace. In another part of the Tauride Palace, a Soviet had spontaneously formed itself from representatives of factories, regiments and districts of Petrograd. Alexandra was cowering at Tsarskoye Selo a few miles away, and as Nicholas tried to reach her, his train was diverted to Pskov, 150 miles away. Here he realized at last that he had lost the support of his troops, even of some of his exasperated generals, and so abdicated to his brother Michael. Michael refused the throne, and the 'February Revolution' was over. The only things missing were real revolutionaries.

Lenin and the Bolsheviks

In 1903, the banned Russian Social Democratic Party held its
Second Congress, first in Brussels and then in London. The
participants were all Russian Marxists, refugees or exiles from
Russia because of their beliefs: Plekhanov, the 'Father of Russian
Marxism'; Trotsky, a brilliant young organizer and propagandist;
Lenin, intellectual brother of an executed S.R. terrorist, and editor
of a Marxist newspaper, *The Spark*; Martov; Axelrod; and about 50
others. Debate centred on 'What is to Be Done?' (Lenin had
written a pamphlet with that title in 1902), and the movement was
split in its opinions. The majority (or 'Bolsheviks') favoured a
tough, disciplined party organization, strongly led and pledged to
political revolution to bring about the dictatorship of the proletariat. They were led by Lenin. The minority group, the
Mensheviks, were more concerned to foster mass appeal. They
were more moderate, and prepared to wait for the inevitable
revolution which Marx had forecast (see Chapter 1). Despite their
name, the Mensheviks had many more followers in Russia at large
than did the more fanatical Bolsheviks.

Neither group was ready for the 1905 Revolution, though
Trotsky became a member of the St. Petersburg Soviet and was
arrested when it came to an end. The October Manifesto made it

*Lenin addresses the Petrograd crowds in 1917. The figure at the corner of the
rostrum is Trotsky. When he was subsequently disgraced, his image was
removed from this well-known photograph, and that of Stalin was
superimposed.*

easier for the S.D.s to exist in Russia, and some Mensheviks sat in the Dumas, but attempts to heal the split in the party failed.

In 1914 the Bolsheviks condemned the outbreak of hostilities as an 'imperialist' war, destroying the brotherhood of working men. The Mensheviks argued that patriotic support of the war might produce democratic reforms. In lonely exile, Lenin clarified his ideas. 'Capital has created all the prerequisites for the realization of Socialism,' he wrote in 1916. Less confidently, at the beginning of 1917 he forecast a huge European revolution but 'We of the older generation may not live to see the decisive battles'. Five weeks later, the Czar had abdicated, and the Bolsheviks had done nothing significant to contribute to his downfall.

In April 1917, Lenin and 18 other Bolsheviks were allowed by the Germans to travel across Germany to Russia. It was hoped that he would accelerate the internal collapse of Russia by spreading his revolutionary ideas.

February to October 1917

For eight months Russia was in the grip of uncertainty. The Provisional Government, representing the upper-class liberals and respectable radicals from the former Duma, claimed the authority to govern. Led by Prince Lvov until July, when the moderate socialist Kerensky took over, the Provisional Government tried to maintain its commitment to its Western allies and to fight the Germans while restoring order internally. It was impossible. Four deep currents, the near-invisible underlying causes of the sudden effectiveness of the February Revolution, now welled up to the surface and brought about the October Revolution.

The first was the break-up of the Russian Empire, no longer held together by the presence of the Czar, and already invaded by foreigners who could offer independence to Poland or the Ukraine. This was bound to upset the war effort. The second was the increasing mutiny of the troops, who were disheartened by the losses and failures of the war, unconvinced of the need to keep fighting, and undermined by the Soviet's 'Order Number One' which destroyed army discipline. The third was the firm intention of the urban workers to have more say in the control of the economy, especially where wages, conditions and hours were concerned. The last was the desire of the peasants to leave the village communities which had controlled most of them since the end of serfdom in 1861, and to become owners of their own land, as Stolypin had intended. The tensions created by these four trends were clearly reflected in the strained relationship between the Provisional Government and the Petrograd Soviet.

The Provisional Government may have had the authority to govern, but the Soviet had most of the power, because it was the direct mouthpiece of the workers and soldiers. Electricity supply, food distribution, railway priorities were all decided by the workers who would carry out the decision. The Provisional Government could only exist as long as the Soviet wished it to do so.

The individual with the most influence was Kerensky, the vice-chairman of the Soviet and also Minister of Justice, then of War, in the Provisional Goverment. In May and June he persuaded the troops to undertake one more major offensive against the Germans. It failed abysmally and ended in desertion and dishonour. In July he became Prime Minister and had to crush riots in Petrograd – the July Days, whose outcome included the flight of Lenin to Finland, the arrest of Trotsky and the apparent humiliation of the Bolsheviks. In August, Kerensky found himself threatened from a new direction as Kornilov, the man whom he had put in charge of the army, attempted a military takeover which was foiled only by the lack of cooperation of the railway workers and telegraph operators. As the Germans pressed in from the Baltic coast towards Petrograd, Kerensky's position became more and more hopeless. Nonetheless, it was the Bolsheviks and not the Germans who brought him down.

The October Revolution

The fortunes of the Bolsheviks varied greatly in 1917. Always a small group, they attracted enmity as well as support with the forcefulness of their slogans: 'All Power to the Soviets', 'End the War', 'Bread, Peace, Freedom' or 'Bread, Peace, Land'. In June they called and then cancelled massive street demonstrations. In the July Days, they lost control of the Petrograd crowds and found themselves branded as criminal troublemakers. The right-wing attempted coup by Kornilov in August and September retrieved all their fortunes. Overnight, Bolshevik majorities appeared in the Petrograd and Moscow Soviets. The Socialists, the Mensheviks and the S.R.s preferred to throw in their lot with the Bolsheviks rather than risk a military dictatorship. Trotsky was released from prison, and Lenin moved nearer the Finnish-Russian border. By now, he was convinced that Marx's proletarian revolution could take place even in relatively undeveloped Russia, and he communicated a new slogan to his comrades in Petrograd: 'Insurrection Now'. Kamenev and Zinoviev, long-standing Bolsheviks and friends of Lenin, violently disagreed, but Trotsky, chairman of the Soviet's new Military Revolutionary Council, laid plans for the capture of key points by 'Red Guards' (armed workers). On 22 October, the 'ten days that shook the world' began with remarkable calm, as increasing numbers of soldiers and workers accepted the authority of the Bolsheviks.

On 23 October the key fortress of Peter and Paul succumbed to

the mere words of Trotsky. On 25 October the main railway
stations were seized by Red Guards, as were the main post office,
telephone exchange and bank. At 9.00 p.m., on Lenin's order, a
blank shot from the cruiser *Aurora* signalled the attack on the
Winter Palace, now defended by less than 1,000 people, including a
women's battalion. It capitulated without a struggle. Kerensky was
not captured, but he could raise only a handful of troops to oppose
the Bolsheviks. On 1 November he fled, leaving Lenin in charge of
Petrograd, and any parts of Russia he could command.

The Beginning of Reconstruction

Both the Provisional Government and the Petrograd Soviet had
tried to plan ahead in the summer of 1917. The Provisional
Government had organized elections for a Constituent Assembly,
and set up a Pre-Parliament to fill the gap until the new Assembly
was ready. The Soviet had called the First All-Russia Congress of
Soviets in March 1917, and a Second Congress met in Petrograd on
25 October, while the Bolsheviks were seizing power throughout
the city. The Bolsheviks had a clear majority in the Second
Congress when it opened, and their position was strengthened by
the walk-out of Martov and the Mensheviks. 'Your role is played
out,' shouted Trotsky at them. 'Go where you ought to be; go to the
dustbin of history.' Now scarcely challenged, the Bolsheviks in the
Second Congress cemented themselves into power, giving approval
to a Council of People's Commissars which would run the country,
and a larger Executive Committee of the Congress of Soviets which
would add weight and support. Lenin was appointed Chairman of
the Council, Trotsky took on Foreign Affairs. Stalin became
Commissar for Nationality Affairs and Lunarcharsky became
responsible for Education.

Two Decrees were issued by the Second Congress in October
1917. The first, on Peace, withdrew Russia from the World War,
thus fulfilling a policy that only the Bolsheviks had dared to
consider. The second, on Land, also seemed to be fulfilling the
Bolsheviks slogan of 'Bread, Peace, Land', but its details were more
in keeping with S.R. philosophy than Marxist doctrine. It
abolished the power of all landlords and said that land could only
be used by the people who worked it themselves, a ruling that won
important support from the peasantry. At least temporarily secure,
the Bolsheviks allowed the elections to go ahead for the Constituent
Assembly, but when it met in January 1918, with its clear S.R.
majority, it was disbanded after one day of discussion. Thereafter
the Bolsheviks, shortly to be renamed the Communists (Reds),
held unchallenged power in Petrograd, Moscow and western
central Russia, but they had to fight to establish themselves
elsewhere.

The Civil War

The Russian Civil War lasted from 1918 to 1921, a savage and complicated series of campaigns. The Reds had one overriding aim – to maintain and extend the power that they had won – and with Lenin to inspire them and Trotsky to organize them in the field, the Red Army became an efficient, brutal force, with a sense of purpose and with interior lines of communication. Their opponents, the 'Whites', had none of these qualities or advantages: they were a mixed bunch of Czarists, landlords, liberals, S.R.s and foreigners who had no single final objective but who could agree only on their hatred of the Reds. There were also 'Greens', groups of self-interested partisans and anarchists, who fought on whichever side suited them better.

Three times the Communist regime faced defeat. The first was

Russia in Revolution

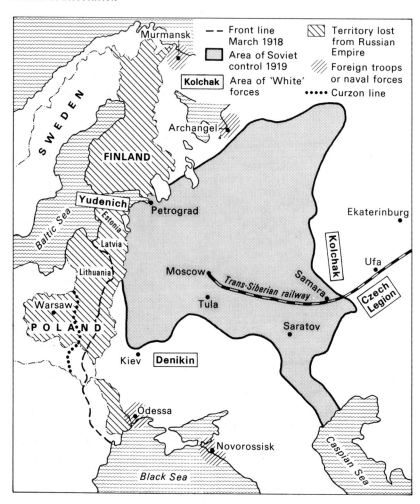

in 1918 when the Reds tried to transport to Vladivostok 30,000 Czechoslovaks who had fought against Austria-Hungary, and who wanted to carry on fighting for national self-determination even though Russia had pulled out of the war. From May to September, the Czechs took over much of the Trans-Siberian railway, hoping that the Czar's former allies would support them. British troops did land at Murmansk, Americans and Japanese at Vladivostok, and French at Odessa, but there was no coordination or common purpose, and the Reds survived. In 1919 and 1920 came a second crisis as Kolchak, Denikin and Wrangel all led strong attacks against the Communists while the Poles were trying to extend their territory, and attacking in the south-west. This threat to *Russia* increased internal support for the Reds. Again they survived, to face a third crisis in 1921, when revolt sprang bloodily out of a former Red stronghold, the naval fortress of Kronstadt near Petrograd. For 18 days, Trotsky had to turn his skill and his soldiers against his former supporters, who even now were only demanding what the Bolsheviks had asked for in 1917: free elections to the Soviets, freedom of speech and the press, liberation of political prisoners, and equal rations for all. Eventually white-robed soldiers moved unseen across the frozen river Neva to the island fortress, and suppressed the revolt. This ended the Civil War, but made the Communists look again at their policies.

War Communism and the New Economic Policy

The Russian economy had collapsed under the strains of world war, revolution and civil war. Money meant nothing – the value of the rouble in 1920 had dropped to one per cent of its 1917 figure – and production had dwindled drastically. With influenza and typhus ravaging the population, supply lines had broken down, and men struggled only for their own survival. The Communists nationalized all industry and agriculture in mid-1918, and for the next three years 'War Communism' prevailed. To call it a system would be an exaggeration. It was a bid for survival. 'Committees of the Poor' were authorized to search for food and to requisition anything they found. Compulsory labour was forced on anybody. All production, sowing and distribution came under the direction of the Supreme Economic Council or the Food Commisariat. Rationing was introduced on a sliding scale: a manual worker in Petrograd in 1919 getting the biggest possible allocation of food received 15½ pounds of bread, six pounds of fish, one pound each of salt and sugar, and small amounts of vegetable oil, butter and mustard, all to last him for a month. Payments for rent, water, electricity, postage and rail travel had to be abolished, as the irregularity or frequent non-existence of such services made their administration uneconomic.

The ruthless ordering of the population was backed up by the power of the CHEKA, the All-Russian Commission for Fighting Counter-Revolution and Sabotage, set up by Lenin in 1917 under the supervision of Dzerzhinsky. Based in Moscow, this secret police organization was more powerful than anything managed by the Czars. Extortion, imprisonment, forced labour and murder were its regular weapons. It was the CHEKA that organized the roving Committees of the Poor, compelled the censorship of the press and removed those who opposed the regime.

By the end of 1920, Lenin was ready to abandon War Communism, and the Kronstadt Rising confirmed the decision. In February 1921 he announced the end of grain requisitions and the substitution of a tax-in-kind. This New Economic Policy (N.E.P.) was a complete reversal of Communist thinking, for it encouraged the peasant to produce more food by promising him a greater personal gain. Instead of risking requisition of his whole crop, the efficient peasant could pay the required tax in kind, and sell his surplus on the open market. It looked suspiciously like capitalism, and the class of wealthy peasants who benefited, the kulaks, looked like the group on whom Stolypin had based his faith in the days of the Czar.

This conciliation of the peasantry marked the beginning of a new phase politically and economically. NEPmen, private traders stimulated by the open market in grain, turned their attention to light industry. Though 'the commanding heights of the economy' (as Lenin called mining, steel-production, power and transport) always remained in State hands, private enterprise was responsible for 80 per cent of small-scale factories in 1924 and 83 per cent of all retail trade. From 1921 to 1925, the annual industrial growth rate averaged 40 per cent, and by 1926 Russian production at last achieved the level it had reached in 1913, before the First War. The N.E.P., like War Communism and like the CHEKA, was a way to survive, a price which Lenin was prepared to pay to keep the power which the October Revolution had delivered into the hands of the Communists. It was left to Lenin's successors to reassert 'true' Communism, for Lenin himself suffered a series of strokes in 1922 and 1923, and died early in 1924.

The Triumvirate and Trotsky; the Emergence of Stalin

From January 1924 to December 1927, a power-struggle raged for control of the Communist Party, and therefore of Russia. At the time of Lenin's first stroke in 1922, Trotsky seemed destined to succeed him, but his self-confident and high-handed brilliance made him few friends in the Party. Kamenev and Zinoviev, founder-members with Lenin of the Bolsheviks when the S.D.s split in 1903, were also strong contenders. Kamenev was chairman of the Moscow Soviet, Zinoviev of the Petrograd Soviet. Both were open men, whose opinions were known and who had not feared to resign from the Party briefly in 1917 when they disagreed with Lenin. Last of the obvious candidates was Stalin, 'Man of Steel', a dour, shrewd, tough man, six times imprisoned for his Marxism by the Czar's forces but rewarded by his promotion to the posts of Commissar for Nationalities (1917–23), Commissar for State Control (1919–23) and Secretary General of the Central Committee of the Party, a post which he held from 1922 until his death. Though severely criticized in Lenin's 'Testament', a message dictated in five-minute snippets by the dying leader, Stalin was strongly in evidence at Lenin's funeral, and by using the support of Kamenev and Zinoviev, he held the loyalty of the Party and got Trotsky sacked from his post of War Minister in 1925. Alarmed by Stalin's forcefulness, Zinoviev joined up with Trotsky in 1926 to oppose the Secretary General, but after 18 months of regular debate, less than one per cent of the Party voted for the Trotsky-Zinoviev policies at the 15th Party Congress in 1927, and, within a month, both Trotsky and Zinoviev were expelled from the Party for 'factionalism', a political crime which even Lenin had condemned. Trotsky was exiled to the Chinese borders and then deported altogether in 1929, stripped of his Russian citizenship. He was murdered in Mexico in 1940. Zinoviev and Kamenev, pawns in the power game, suffered turbulent careers near the top of Party

Stalin (right) shares a joke with Marshal Voroshilov.

politics until in 1936 they were executed on a charge of conspiracy after a public 'show trial'. Stalin was supreme, and remained so.

Stalin and the Economy

The N.E.P. produced economic and political problems. As farm production increased, prices and therefore farmers' incomes went down, while simultaneously industrial prices went up. This reduced trade between town and country, and made the farmers reluctant to further increase food production. This 'scissors crisis' provoked state intervention in the price of manufactured goods, but politically such intervention was necessary anyway, if Russia were not to return to capitalism. In the winter of 1927, kulaks were refraining from selling their corn until scarcity had driven up the price: early in 1928 came the First Five Year Plan (1928–32) and the end of the N.E.P.

Planning was not new. Gosplan, a State Planning Commission, had been set up in 1921 and Goelro, a ten-year plan for electricity production, dated from 1920. However, the targets were new: coal production was to increase in five years from 35 to 75 million tons, pig iron from three to ten million tons. Heavy industry was to have priority, but production of transport, electricity, agricultural machinery and consumer goods were all to be boosted. No punches were pulled: two versions of the Plan were produced, and the tougher one was adopted, and by 1929 the slogan was 'The Five Year Plan in four years'. Stalin was completing what Witte had begun, the transformation of Russia into a modern industrial state.

This could not be achieved without a new revolution in agriculture which would produce more grain from less farmers, freeing others for work in industry. 'Collectivization' of agriculture, a process which had begun in a few places after 1917 and involved 3 per cent of the total farmed acreage in 1928, was thrust upon an unwilling peasantry in 1928 and accelerated in 1929. By March 1930 Stalin claimed that 14,250,000 peasant households, or 55 per cent of the peasant population, were members of collectives. By 1936, 90 per cent of the peasantry were in a total of 246,000 collective farms. The kulaks had been forced out of existence, some into collectives, some into concentration camps and some into their graves. Their land and machinery provided one base for the new *kolkhozy* (collectives) and *sovkhozy* (state farms with wage-earning workers). Machine Tractor Stations, where tractors were lent out along with a good deal of propaganda, were another. (There were only 1,300 tractors in the whole of Russia in 1928.) The efficiency of the collective farms is dubious (grain production was improved by 15 per cent in the 1930s, but the total number of livestock decreased) and their unpopularity amongst the wealthier peasants is certain, but they did assert socialism over semi-capitalism, and form part of Stalin's total programme for the economy.

The Second Five Year Plan (1933–37) and the Third (1938–42 but actually curtailed by the war) kept up the pressures despite massive errors in planning and wastage in production in some places. Workers were taught not to expect equal pay, but pay which rewarded the strong and stung the sluggards into more action. 'Norms' were set, and much was made of Stakhanov, a miner who so exceeded what was demanded of him that he was made a cult hero. Pressure, propaganda and purges were relentless, showing that the individual was a servant of the State. 'Why is a Russian citizen like Adam and Eve?' asked a cynical popular riddle. 'Because he lives in Paradise but has no clothes.' But the results came. By 1940, annual production of coal had risen to 463 per cent of the 1928 figure. Electricity output had increased by 940 per cent, tractors 2,300 per cent, steel 400 per cent and pig iron 440 per cent. Such economic improvement gave Russia a platform for survival against the Nazi invasion in the Second World War.

Stalin and the Party

Control of the economy was essential to Stalin's programme of 'Socialism in One Country' which he first suggested in 1924, when arguing against Trotsky's idea of 'Permanent World Revolution'. With the advanced countries of the world looking securely capitalist, Stalin's attitude was that Russia could and should create its own Socialist State without waiting for world-wide revolution. In order to do this, the power of government, the State, had to be increased, and the Communist Party had to be ready to play its essential part.

Since 1919, the State and the Party had consisted of similar structures, with overlapping personnel. Democracy in the State was served by the regular meetings of the All-Russia Congress of Soviets; the Party held regular All-Russia Party Congresses. The State had a permanent Central Executive Committee; the Party a Central Committee. At the pinnacle of the pyramids, the State consisted of the Council of People's Commissars ('Sovnarkom'); the Party had the 'Politburo' and 'Orgburo'. Lenin, Trotsky, Kamenev and Stalin were all members of Sovnarkom and the Politburo, but increasingly it was *Party* rank which carried influence. Stalin ran Russia as Secretary of the Party, and only became Prime Minister of Russia in name in 1939.

In 1917, the Party was small and select, with 23,000 members. By 1919 it had a quarter of a million members, by 1933 three and a half million. Such an organization was dangerously unwieldy, and from the time of his triumph over Trotsky, Stalin used purges to root out opposition, real or imagined. In 1928, 1929 and 1930, a tenth of all members were expelled from the Party for 'failure to carry out their duties'. From 1933 to 1935, all recruitment to the Party stopped, and a further third of the members, 'enemies and deceivers', lost or gave up their membership. But more ominously, in 1934 Kirov, a member of the Politburo, was assassinated and the purges started to spill blood. Over 100 men were executed at once. From 1936 to 1938 Moscow show trials condemned Party officials, political commissars and army officers to death with clinical efficiency. Their extent was staggering. By 1939, four of the 15 members of the original Bolshevik government had died of natural causes, ten had been purged or executed. Only Stalin remained. Half of the 1932 Politburo were dead, all but five out of the 80 members of the Supreme Military Soviet had vanished. Historians cannot agree on the final total of victims. Their estimates of between one million and ten million indicate the indiscriminate, ruthless nature of the purges which Stalin called 'unavoidable, and on the whole beneficial'. He certainly benefited: 500,000 new Party officials would never risk disloyalty to him while he lived.

Soviet Foreign Policy, 1917–39

The Bolshevik promise to end Russian participation in the First World War was quickly honoured. In December 1917 a Russian delegation began negotiations at the German Field Headquarters at Brest-Litovsk, while the fighting stopped. German terms were harsh, and the Bolsheviks were divided in their opinions. Lenin wanted peace at any price, while others argued for continued fighting because they believed that Germany was about to burst into revolution. Trotsky played for time, announcing to the astonished Germans a state of 'Neither War nor Peace'. In February 1918, the Germans began their advance again, and the Russians accepted their terms, surrendering their claims to Poland, the Ukraine, Finland, the Baltic Provinces and much of the Caucasus. Statistically they had given away 34 per cent of their population, 54 per cent of their industrial plant and nearly 90 per cent of their mines, but they had won a necessary 'breathing space' for the establishment of their government.

The German defeat in 1918 cancelled the terms of Brest-Litovsk, but Russia was enmeshed in civil war and living in a diplomatic twilight. The Communists were refused recognition at the Paris Peace Conference, and strangely it was the German Weimar Republic which first recognized them in 1922 in the Treaty of Rapallo. Britain's first Labour Government opened diplomatic relations with Russia in 1924; the U.S.A. held back until 1933. In 1934 Russia joined the League of Nations. Peace was what Russia wanted: the Polish War of 1920–21 had cost her more territory, and the only foreign policy that seemed possible in the 1920s and 1930s was the surreptitious encouragement of Communist parties around the world.

The U.S.A. 1917-41 5

Politics, Parties and the Emergence of Wilson

American Presidential elections are held every four years, and Congressional elections are held every two years for one third of the Senate and all of the House of Representatives. These elections always take place in November of an even-numbered year, but the term of office starts six or eight weeks later, in January of an odd-numbered year. Thus, for example Woodrow Wilson won the election of 1912 and took office in 1913.

The Republican Party provided every President but one from 1861 to 1913, but after 1877 most of them lacked distinction or individual ability. They were 'front-men' for business interests, usually able, usually honest, usually uncontroversial. The other major party, the Democrats, drawing most of their support from Southern whites, urban workers and ethnic minorities, had little power at the top compared with the influence of the Republicans, who had waxed strong on the reputation of Abraham Lincoln, the North's victory in the Civil War and the strength of their business interests. The Democrats won a majority in the House of Representatives eight times out of ten at the end of the century, but the Presidency and the Senate nearly always went to the Republicans.

The Republicans had little political philosophy nor did they need any, until the pressures of economic expansion and imperialism thrust up problems like slums, corruption, poverty, and the use of power at home and overseas. Huge business organizations, the 'trusts', controlled every aspect of life through their economic power, but the reaction against them was evident in what was called the 'Progressive Movement'. From 1901 to 1909, Theodore Roosevelt, a reforming Republican of wide political interest and skill, revitalized the Presidency by using the office to tackle the trusts, root out corruption, preserve lands and forests from ruthless speculators and to raise the standards of public responsibility generally. In 1909 his personal friend W.H. Taft won the Presidency for the Republicans, after Roosevelt had said that he would not stand for election again. But the Taft era lacked Roosevelt's energy and strength. Before four years were up, the Republican party had split between those who wanted Roosevelt back and those who supported Taft. In the election of 1912, it was a reforming Democrat, Woodrow Wilson, who was elected to power because of that split.

Woodrow Wilson, 1913–21

Wilson called his political programme 'The New Freedom', and it was very much in line with the Progressive Movement. His first four years in office were devoted to cutting tariffs, breaking the power of the trusts and sorting out the system of currency and banking. This was true leadership. Wilson picked his way through a political minefield knowing that he had one great source of strength. His office represented the people of the United States, *all* the people of *all* the states, and it was his role to defend them against small but powerful sections of the country. Under his guidance the Democrats in Congress could now pass reforms on behalf of the weak and the poor and the under-represented. LaFollette's Seamen's Act of 1915 and the Workmen's Compensation Act of the same year provided the sort of social legislation that had been impossible before 1900.

Foreign policy was more difficult. Just as imperial powers like Britain had developed the idea of 'Informal Empire', so the U.S.A. had encouraged businessmen to invest money in Central and South America and in the Caribbean, thereby gaining influence as well as an excuse to intervene in the affairs of other nations in order to protect the investments. This 'Dollar Diplomacy' had led to considerable American meddling in many lands touching the Gulf of Mexico and the Caribbean, especially those where no stable government had grown up to replace the sterile remnants of former Spanish colonial government.

Wilson and the First World War

Although more Americans identified themselves with Britain and her Allies than with the Central Powers in 1914, there was no desire to get involved in the war. Wilson immediately proclaimed American neutrality, thereby honouring the isolationist Monroe Doctrine, and at the same time leaving business interests to develop freely. In practice, this gave a great advantage to the Allies, because the British blockade of Germany cut American trade with Central Europe to nothing, while munitions, food and other vital supplies funnelled through to Britain, helping the war effort and at the same time stimulating the American economy out of a slump. The principle and the practice of the blockade was bitterly resented by some Americans (there had been a war in 1812 and a threat of war in 1861 between England and the United States because of such a situation), but far more powerful in moulding public opinion was the German decision in 1915 to use submarines to sink merchant ships. This policy was particularly frightful because there was no chance of submarines picking up survivors of the torpedo or gun attack. Innocent neutrals were thus condemned to a ghastly death.

The sharpness of the American reaction to the sinking of the *Lusitania* stayed the German hand for well over a year. During this time Wilson tried hard to arrange a peace conference, and fought the 1916 election successfully as the man who had correctly represented the American desire to stay out of the war. But already, a change of opinion which he had to interpret was on the way. 'There may at any moment come a time,' he said in 1916, 'when I cannot preserve both the honour and the peace of the United States. Do not exact of me an impossible and contradictory thing.' Congress passed laws in 1916 to increase the size of the Army, and provided for more naval vessels than Wilson's government actually wanted. In early 1917, when the Germans reopened unrestricted submarine warfare against belligerents and neutrals, Congress overwhelmingly supported Wilson and made the declaration of war which only they and not the President could do.

The man of peace was a great war leader. Wilson was able to preside over the transformation of a laissez-faire government and economy into an efficient and well-controlled war machine. The railways and the telegraph lines were taken over by the government; food and fuel were strictly rationed while their production increased; new laws were made about strikes in essential industries; a vast effort went into building merchant and fighting ships – destroyers could be launched less than three weeks after having their keels laid. Money was lent to the Allies, and, most important of all to English and French morale, American troops appeared in Europe.

Wilson and the Peace

Even before the American entry into the war, Wilson was calling for 'peace without victory', and after April 1917 he continued his diplomatic efforts. It was to Congress that he made his 14 Points in January 1918. He reinforced them in speeches in February and September 1918 which referred to 'the Four Principles' and 'the Five Particulars', ideals which in his view had to play a dominant role in the improved post-war world. He commanded the world stage: his vision was acknowledged and acclaimed.

But in Europe in 1919, the vision became obscured (see Chapter 3). The secret dealings of the Allies, before America had entered the war, and the desire for revenge and absolute security destroyed the trust and hope on which Wilson worked. By the time the Treaty of Versailles was ready for signature, with the League of Nations woven into its fabric, Wilson had been forced to compromise some of his ideals, and make concessions which antagonized various groups of American citizens, especially those with ties with Germany and Italy. Wilson returned to Congress to get the Senate's approval for the Treaty and the League, to discover powerful opposition to all his aims. The Senate's approval had to be indicated by a two-thirds majority, but it could not be obtained. Some Senators vowed to oppose every aspect of the Treaty; others, led by the Republican Henry Cabot Lodge, demanded 14 reservations to be added to the treaty, including one which would deny Article 10 of the Covenant of the League of Nations, which guaranteed the territorial integrity of all member nations by binding all other nations to help to preserve it, i.e. by committing them to a form of alliance which might well involve military or economic sanctions. This was too much for the traditional isolationists, and their opposition was too much for Wilson. In the autumn of 1919, he set out on a speaking tour to whip up public support for the League, but in rapid succession he suffered a nervous breakdown and a paralyzing stroke from which he never recovered. His aims suffered with him. In 1920, the Senate failed to produce the two-thirds majority for the Treaty, and therefore it could not be ratified. America could not join the League of Nations, even though it seems that a majority of the people, and a *simple* majority of the Senate, wished to do so. America eventually made a separate peace with Germany in 1921.

The Return of the Republicans

Reaction to the war with its increased governmental powers and rejection of isolationism spurred a revival in the fortunes of the Republican party, who were also able to take the political initiative when Wilson was crippled. In the 1920 election campaign, the Republican candidate Warren Harding pledged 'Less government in business and more business in government', and, a 'Return to normalcy' which appealed to most Americans. An overwhelming majority put Harding in the White House, from 1921 until 1923 when his sudden death from a heart attack (or suicide) brought Calvin Coolidge, his Vice-President, into office until 1929.

This was a period of economic boom, and the Republicans were popular because it seemed that their policies had brought it about. Despite clear evidence of scandalous corruption in high places, which was coming to light just as Harding died, the effects of higher tariffs and lower taxes on those with large incomes built up the strength of the big trusts again. Production and profits rose; the increased dividends paid to shareholders came back in fresh investment in new companies. Wages crept up more slowly, but unemployment was low, and new credit schemes made it possible for workers to buy cars, refrigerators and electric gadgets of all sorts even though they had not yet earned the money to pay for them. The American Dream of a good life for everyone seemed to be coming true: as Coolidge said 'The business of the United States is Business'. But despite the 42 per cent increase in salaries and 76 per cent increase in profits between 1922 and 1929, some sections of the community were having a very difficult time, most notably the farmers and the textile workers, and there were considerable social tensions. Concern about the quality of American life picked out four groups of scapegoats.

The first victims were the immigrants, restricted in 1917, 1924 and 1929 by Acts of Congress. Next were 'the Reds', rather pathetic groups of Socialists who were deported in 1919, most of them being recent immigrants. The blacks were victimized too by the vicious actions and propaganda of the Ku Klux Klan, a re-creation of the nineteenth-century racist secret society which became very powerful in local politics in the 1920s. But the last and strangest group were those who wanted to drink alcohol. By Act of Congress and by the 18th Amendment to the Constitution, the manufacture, sale and transportation of drinks containing more than half a per cent of alcohol in the U.S.A. was prohibited in 1919 and was not made legal again until 1933. But all these over-reactions to admitted social difficulties came from a society that then tolerated proven

Paradise regained? Alcohol returns to New York after the end of Prohibition in 1933.

The confident smile of a successful man: Al Capone, the gangster who dominated Chicago from 1925 to 1931, until sent to prison for income tax offences.

business corruption in the Cabinet, illicit drinking at every level of society, and a growth of gangsterism of unprecedented efficiency (Al Capone in Chicago and similar bosses). 'Normalcy' in the disturbed 1920s is very hard to discern.

Hoover and the Wall Street Crash, 1929

The Republican candidate Herbert Hoover was overwhelmingly elected President in 1928, winning support from the businessmen, the 'dry' (anti-alcohol) lobby and the anti-Catholics, (his Democrat opponent Alfred Smith was a 'wet' Catholic, and Governor of New York). Hoover was an experienced politician, with a good record of wartime administration, who had served as Secretary of Commerce from 1921–29. He looked forward 'to the final triumph over poverty' in America, and faced his term of office with understandable confidence. Within 12 months of his election victory, however, a financial disaster of huge proportions had struck America and stripped away all the magic appeal of 'rugged individualism' that he and the Republicans stood for.

Looking back, it is easy to see why the American Stock Market on Wall Street 'collapsed' in October 1929, but at the time it was unexpected. The prosperity of the preceding years had encouraged more and more people to invest their savings in stocks and shares, and the numbers of shares and their prices had steadily spiralled upwards. Confidence in the economy became over-confidence; care was thrown to the winds when speculators started to buy 'on margin', i.e. by producing only 10 per cent of the purchase price and getting the rest on credit. The increase in shares far exceeded the increase in the real wealth that they were meant to represent, and in October 1929, the bubble burst. Just a year after shares had gone up by 25 per cent in value in three months, somebody started to sell, and prices went down. In the past, somebody else would have bought up the cheaper shares, and stability would have been restored. When the selling began on 21 October, there was no one willing to pay the high price, and prices dropped generally, stimulating more selling, and more falls in value. By the end of the month, $15,000,000,000 had been knocked off share values. Nearly seventeen million shares changed hands on 29 October alone, and rich men were discovering overnight that they were poor. Hard cash on a large scale virtually disappeared; debtors could not pay their debts, and their creditors were sometimes forced into bankruptcy. 5,000 banks were to go out of business in the next three years, and over a hundred thousand other firms. One worker in four lost his job, while industrial production was cut by half..The disaster was total.

Hoover did what he could to meet the crisis, although in 1930 the Democrats won control of the House of Representatives. He persuaded them to help establish the Reconstruction Finance Corporation, which in 1932 lent $3,800,000,000 to banks, firms and relief projects, but Republican ideas did not really support much government intervention in the economy. The man who caught the eye with his positive actions in New York, where he was Governor, was Franklin D. Roosevelt, distant cousin of Theodore Roosevelt but a Democrat and one-time follower of Wilson.

The Depression

The Wall Street Crash and the Depression are not the same thing, nor did the former cause the latter. But they were closely linked, and shared several features in their origins, which go back at least to the First World War.

The Great Depression was a world-wide phenomenon, though it was first apparent in America, because there the economy was turning over fastest, and there the signs of strain showed first.

The earliest sign, to which no significance was attached at the time, was the agricultural depression of the 1920s. While the business community grew fat on profits, the farmers, employing 20 per cent of the work-force, were faring badly. Food production had expanded so much during the war that when it was over, prices fell throughout the world. With Australia and Canada, even Russia and Argentina all exporting food, American wheat prices dropped from $1.82 a bushel in 1920 to 38 cents in 1932; maize went from 61 cents to 32 cents a bushel, cotton from 16 cents to six cents a pound. Farm values dropped, and farmers experienced desperate financial difficulty. The only apparent solution was to produce more, in an attempt to earn more money. This had the effect of depressing prices further. The Republican government's answer was to put higher tariffs on foreign farm products, which had no effect because the home market was flooded by home production anyway. Coolidge vetoed the suggestion that the government might buy up farmers' surpluses at a decent price and sell them overseas at a loss just to keep American agriculture viable.

There were signs of over-production in industry too. Many men were laid off in the summer of 1929 because there was no market for their production. This was not uncommon – even the purchase of cars rises and falls according to the time of year – and no-one paid much heed to it. But the deeper significance of the 1929 cut-back was that it reflected the basic inequality of incomes in America, which affected purchasing power.

The more money you have, the higher is the proportion that you can save, and saving it takes it right out of the economy (unless someone borrows your savings and 'invests' them (see Chapter 1)). In the U.S.A., five per cent of the people received 35 per cent of the national wealth, and saved most of it, while 60 per cent of the people had small incomes and no savings to use when their incomes dried up. They lived, *and provided work for others*, by spending their income immediately. But when over-production caused firms to sack workers in 1929, the loss of those incomes, and of that purchasing power, meant that others had to be sacked because there were still too many unsellable goods. So the downward spiral continued.

There are three major ways of putting money into an economy: by wages, salaries, profits and rents paid to individuals; by investment by companies; and by government spending. In 1929 the *world* situation was one of static or declining wages and profits, in industry and in agriculture. The *American* situation was one of a sudden end to investment (significantly, the selling of shares on Wall Street started in the Wheat section) and a loss of confidence and credit. This was coupled with a Republican government whose policies throughout the 1920s had created international circumstances which made the Crash harder and the Depression more widespread. Each of the three sources of money, which a modern cash economy needs, was restricted in 1929.

How America affected the World

After the war, America was a 'creditor nation', i.e. she was owed money by other countries, which could only repay her by making a healthy profit in their trade. But the Republican isolationists, wanting to stimulate and protect American industry, put tariffs on imports, (by the Fordney-McCumber Act of 1922 and the Hawley-Smoot Act of 1930) which reduced world trade and led to retaliatory tariffs from other nations. Therefore their trade and their circulation of money slowed up. When the Americans started to withdraw their former generous loans in order to save their own system, they made matters worse. Reclaiming money lent in 1924 to Germany made the Germans remove investments that they had made in London. There, a run on gold developed in 1931, which nothing could stop until Britain came off the Gold Standard, thereby devaluing the pound; in 1932 Britain at last abandoned Free Trade (see Chapter 6). This hit not only France, but trading partners like the Commonwealth and Latin America. The Depression spread like a contagious disease wherever trade, investment or debt brought countries into contact. (Australia, Brazil, Japan, Poland, France and Canada all suffered a drop of 30 per cent or more in their export trade in the period 1929–30, and with the loss of that income, their own employment, production and consumption dropped accordingly. It was not that there was no economic wealth in these countries: they had lost the means of developing it because the money system of the world had gone wrong.) Only Russia, in its Communist seclusion, seemed immune to the capitalist disease. An advertisement for 6,000 skilled workers to go to Russia to assist in the Five Year Plan brought 100,000 applicants to the New York office of the Russian organizing agency in 1931.

Franklin D. Roosevelt, the man who was to lead the U.S.A. out of the Depression.

Franklin D. Roosevelt and the New Deal

Roosevelt offered to Americans in 1933 what Churchill was to offer to Britons in 1940: courage, hope, and resolution. 'The only thing we have to fear is fear itself,' he proclaimed at his first Inauguration in March 1933. He was not afraid of his responsibility, and he asked a willing Democrat Congress to give him power 'as great as the power that would be given to me if we were in fact invaded by a foreign foe'. What was new about the 'New Deal' he promised the people was the unprecedented use of the money, power and institutions of the government to rebuild (and interfere with) the economy of a country that had always previously been left to private enterprise. His measures offered immediate relief, a more extended recovery programme, and some long-term reform.

The Relief Programme

In his first 'Hundred Days' in office, Roosevelt tackled immediate human problems with furious energy. Banks were shut for several days to make the necessary arrangements, and then reopened with government funds to back them under an emergency Banking Act. An Economy Act cut federal pensions and salaries in an effort to balance the Budget, but legalizing the sale of beer, and providing jobs for the unemployed, mortgages for debtors and help for the farmers outweighed any unpopularity that came from it. The Federal Emergency Relief Administration gave out $500,000,000 in direct aid – food, clothing and shelter rather than work. Jobs came from the Civilian Conservation Corps which used young men in the national forests, or the Civil Works Administration (scrapped in 1934 and replaced by the Works Progress Administration in 1935), using money often provided by the Reconstruction Finance Corporation which Hoover had set up. The Farmers' Relief Act of 1933 set up the Agricultural Adjustment Administration (A.A.A.), which paid farmers for *reducing* their output of seven basic commodities (like corn and cattle), so attacking the problem of overproduction at the source. The Farm Credit Administration provided mortgages to farmers who were in danger of losing the ownership of their land, and the Home Owners Loan Corporation did the same for about one sixth of all home-owners in America. The immediate effect of the Hundred Days was to restore confidence: there was food for the hungry, security for the home-owners and farmers, an increased chance of getting at least a temporary job, but above all, there was a government which was doing something.

Recovery

The major aid to recovery was the National Industrial Recovery Act (N.I.R.A.) of June 1933, which set up the National Recovery

American street scene in 1933. Despite the apparent prosperity, 14,000,000 Americans were unemployed at the beginning of the year.

Administration (N.R.A.). This worked out a series of codes of agreement in any industry, about hours, prices, wages, production figures and conditions, so that the economy was more balanced and not torn apart by unfair competition. By February 1934, 765 separate codes had been produced – too many, in fact, for clarity. But the regulations of the N.R.A., and the practical help of the Public Works Administration (P.W.A.) which spent $3,000,000,000 on roads, hospitals, dams, houses and other community facilities, helped to put money into the pockets of ordinary working men, and their natural spending stimulated the economy and made more opportunities for others to work. Roosevelt was 'priming the pump'. Having understood the downward spiral of the Depression, he was working to create the conditions for an upward spiral.

He was not always successful. Unemployment did not drop below five per cent until after the war had broken out in 1941, and many firms and banks never recovered from the Depression. Spectacular dust-storms in the Great Plains played havoc with areas where bad farming had hastened erosion, and the A.A.A. could not stop the devastation. There was human opposition too, from conservatives who believed that he was abusing the freedom of others by making so many regulations, from socialists who wanted complete nationalization and social security, and from the Supreme Court, which challenged his constitutional powers.

From 1934 to 1936, in a series of well-publicized court cases and appeals, the Supreme Court declared that all or parts of the National Recovery Act, the Guffey Coal Act, the Agricultural Adjustment Act, the Railroad Retirement Act, the Municipal Bankruptcy Act and a few others were unconstitutional and could no longer be enforced. Roosevelt, bitterly frustrated, tried to alter the personnel of the Supreme Court by asking Congress to allow him to appoint six new judges, one for each existing judge over the age of 70 who would not retire on full pay. Congress refused to let Roosevelt interfere with appointment procedure, but one judge who had been opposed to Roosevelt now started to see things his way. Instead of a five to four majority against him, Roosevelt now enjoyed five to four majority support when the New Deal was questioned in the Courts.

Reform

Some aspects of the New Deal had long-term implications. The Tennessee Valley Authority (T.V.A.) of 1933 took over five dams on behalf of the government, and built a further 20 in the next 20 years. It provided electricity, controlled irrigation, replanted forests, and dominated planning in an area of 41,000 square miles. To critics, this was a dangerous, un-American, socialistic scheme, but the Supreme Court allowed it to survive. The Securities and Exchange Commission (S.E.C.) of 1935 made the Stock Market more manageable. The Wagner Act of 1935 set up the National Labour Relations Board which strengthened the power of the Unions in wage bargaining, and the Social Security Act of 1935 was the first effective guarantee of relief for the unemployed and the aged that America had seen.

The New Deal marks a watershed in American politics. From 1861 to 1933, there were Democrats in the White House for only 16 years. From 1933 to 1980, there have only been 16 years when Democrats have not held the Presidency.

Roosevelt's Foreign Policy

The old idea of Isolation suited Roosevelt when all his attention was being demanded by the troubles inside the U.S.A. He believed in a 'good neighbour' policy towards Latin America, but was aware of Japanese expansion on the other side of the Pacific, and growing tensions in Europe. The Neutrality Acts of 1935 and 1937 were attempts to define what America would and would not do in the event of war elsewhere: she would not export arms to either side, and any other goods sold must be paid for in cash, and not carried in American ships. This 'cash and carry' rule was to prevent both the lending of money, which might need an armed follow-up to protect it, and the use of American ships which might be attacked if carrying useful materials to a belligerent. In 1939, the Neutrality Act was revised to allow sales of anything to anyone subject to the 'cash and carry' rule, but in 1941, when Britain could afford to buy no more, Roosevelt arranged to 'transfer or lend' any articles needed. This 'Lend-Lease' programme saved Britain and later Russia. It was a total reversal in practice of the 1935 Neutrality Act, but it enabled Roosevelt to make his stand against Fascism and Nazism without declaring war.

The Japanese militant regime posed much more of a threat to the U.S.A. Despite the Washington Conference of 1922 which restricted Japan's naval expansion, Japan invaded Manchuria in 1931 and set up the puppet kingdom of Manchukuo. This abuse of Chinese territory put the Americans in an awkward position as they supported the 'Open Door' policy (see Chapter 8), and when Japan left the League of Nations in 1933, and in 1934 broke the London Naval Treaty on building warships, the Americans felt they had little choice but to strengthen their navy. (As in all other countries, this rearmament reduced unemployment significantly.) Anti-Japanese feeling grew considerably stronger when they launched another attack on the heart of China in 1937, and clearly had ambitions to dominate Eastern Asia and the islands of the Pacific. In 1940, this tension produced the Burke-Wadsworth Act, introducing peace-time conscription for the first time in American history, and in 1941, America and Japan were so aware of the possibility of war that the spring was spent in diplomatic nego- tiations, which dragged on intermittently for the whole year. They were still going on in December when Japanese planes dived out of the sun onto the American naval base at Pearl Harbor near Honolulu, and in a two-hour raid caused 3,500 casualties and destroyed 150 planes and six ships.

On the next day, the United States entered the Second World War.

6 Britain in Transition 1900-39

It is often said that Edwardian England (1901–10) enjoyed an 'Indian Summer', a last spell of peace and calm prosperity before the coming of world war and economic depression. Certainly the sun shone on many aspects of life. Food was cheap, and though wages were low, prices were stable. Unemployment was not a problem; most industries were expanding (agriculture was an exception), and there were plenty of jobs 'in service', working in the private houses of the middle and upper classes. New inventions added almost daily to the comforts of life, many of them based on the increased use of electricity. On a world scale, British pride in the Empire was brimming over, despite the recent Boer War: 'God, who made thee mighty, Make thee mightier yet,' declared Edward's Coronation Anthem.

The reality was less golden than the image, for Britain, *Great* Britain, with 0.2 per cent of the land area of the world, could no longer justify or maintain the predominance that she had enjoyed for much of the nineteenth century. Certain basic economic truths had to be acknowledged. In the light of foreign competition and increasing costs at home, the patterns of work and wealth had to be redrawn. Inevitably, social and political life had to evolve to keep in touch with the industrial structure and the demands of a more aware electorate. Finally, the 'Splendid Isolation' which was a part of the Edwardian atmosphere had to give way to the cold facts of international tensions and imperial restlessness. This chapter is therefore divided into three sections, concentrating respectively on the economy, political development, and those international changes involving Ireland and the Empire. Foreign policy relating to Europe and the rest of the world is considered in Chapters 3 and 11.

THE BRITISH ECONOMY

The Staple Industries and the Pattern of Trade

In 1873, at the height of a trade boom, Britain dominated the economic world. Fuelled by all the earliest advances in techniques of machinery and steam power, financed by experienced businessmen in the City of London, based on ample natural resources at home or in the Empire, and at that time supported by efficient food production in Britain itself, the British economy was thriving and confident. The stability of government was reflected in a lack of ministerial interference in economic matters: 'laissez-faire' ('let it happen') was the overriding philosophy. After 1873, although production figures still rose and the wealth of the nation continued to grow, the growth rate was slower (averaging less than two per cent per annum for the rest of the century) and foreign competition undercut the profitability of British firms. Although dividends were still paid handsomely to the shareholders, they were often achieved by cutting the wages of the workers.

Agriculture fared badly after the 1870s. Cheap wheat from abroad amounted to one million tons in 1860 and to nearly four million tons by 1880, largely because of the opening up of the American prairies and the 'feeder' railway lines. By 1914, more than five million tons a year arrived in Britain, three times more than British farmers were producing, and 35 per cent cheaper than the price in the 1880s. Refrigerated ships and railway wagons were responsible for huge imports of meat from the U.S.A., Argentina, Australia and New Zealand: again, prices dropped by a third in the face of this competition. Wool from Australia, cheese from Canada, butter from Denmark, eggs from Holland, even tinned milk from Switzerland – these all challenged the prices and the profits of the British producer.

Textiles also suffered from foreign competition, though the number of people employed in the cotton industry increased right up to the outbreak of the First World War. This was partly a bad sign; having stimulated much technical advance and invention in the eighteenth and early nineteenth centuries, the textile industry in Lancashire failed to keep up with developments in America and elsewhere. Automatic looms and electricity as a power source were only slowly adopted, which was a bad omen for the 1920s and 1930s.

Ship-building, on the other hand, looked very healthy before the First War. Technical changes (from sail to steam, from iron hulls to steel, from coal-firing to oil) stimulated demand, as did the steady growth of world trade which required plenty of merchant tonnage, some of it of specialist design (the first oil-tanker was launched in 1886). British shipyards, already flourishing because of Britain's island position, her exploitation of her overseas Empire and her belief in the Two-Power standard (see Chapter 1) supplied all British requirements in 1913 and a quarter of the demand from the rest of the world. It was a fluctuating business, but a good one. 580 berths and 200,000 workers in British estuaries depended on it.

Steel and iron production was greatly stimulated by ship-building, which used up 30 per cent of the record output of 1913, but, as in the textile industry, inevitable trouble was looming. A healthy steel industry which can compete in the world market needs helpful geology. The costs of transporting iron ore, coal and finished materials are a major factor in the market price; the closer together the mineral deposits and the market, the cheaper the steel. By 1900, Britain had used up her cheapest and easiest resources, while America and Germany were just getting to the heart of theirs, helped further by the fact that new techniques (especially the Gilchrist-Thomas converter) were more suited to their qualities of ore than to Britain's. America and Germany therefore were producing more iron and steel than Britain, and the gradual movement of the industry towards the coasts in Britain indicated that it was becoming more dependent on foreign ores and foreign markets in the early twentieth century. The manufacturers would have liked protection from competition by means of tariffs (duties which made imported goods more expensive) but the government would not consider it: Free Trade, meaning a total lack of government interference in the economy, was sacred.

Coal was *the* basic industry, employing 1,128,000 men in 1913 and producing 287 million tons in 1913, one third of it for export. It filled the merchant ships as well as fuelled them; it ran the railways and the electricity generating stations; it provided work, warmth and wealth. While world demand was growing at 4 per cent per annum, and Britain could keep supplying at that rate, it seemed not to matter that each ton got more expensive to mine, each man produced less in a year (403 tons per man in 1881, 309 tons in 1911). It would be a different story when the price on the world market fell.

Trade Unions and Syndicalism

The concentration and development of industries inevitably encouraged the growth of trade unions to protect and represent the work force. Successful strikes by the London match-girls and the dockers in 1888 and 1889 increased union membership. From 750,000 members in 1888, they rose to 1½ million in 1892, 2 million in 1900, 2½ million in 1910, 4¼ million in 1913 and nearly 8½ million in 1920. The restrictive law relating to unionism was clarified and in the long run eased. Gladstone's Criminal Law Amendment Act of 1871 and Disraeli's 1875 Conspiracy and Protection of Property Act legalized unions, protected their funds, and allowed peaceful picketing. By 1913, the right to strike was secure, as was the right to collect funds for political purposes.

From 1911 to 1913, the number of working days lost per annum through strikes reached the unprecedented height of 20,000,000. This partly reflected the strength of the unions and the new Syndicalist philosophy, an international movement aimed at obtaining workers' ownership of industry. It also partly reflected the gradual drop in real wages from which some workers were suffering as profits shrank. The miners and the railwaymen were the most exposed: in 1913, they formed a 'Triple Alliance' with the dockers, in order to increase the bargaining power of their members.

War and Post-War

The war had three broad effects on the economy. Firstly, it stimulated certain parts of it, like steel, ship-building, munitions and coal, while dampening down demand for luxury goods (the McKenna Duties of 1915 put a price increase of 33 per cent on most of them). Secondly, it changed the patterns of employment, as many women took over the jobs vacated by men who had gone to the Front. Even without counting those in uniform, there were more people employed in November 1918 than there had been in September 1914. Thirdly, it introduced an unprecedented measure of government interference, and dug the graves of laissez-faire and Free Trade, though neither was dead yet. The railways were requisitioned and brought under government direction early in the war; so were coal mines and all merchant shipping as the struggle progressed. The government secured the passage of laws about trade in wheat and sugar, about direction of labour and compulsory call-up, and about rationing of specified foods (though this was largely a voluntary scheme). The Ministry of Munitions set the example of employing women in large numbers, and government regulations about factory conditions sprang from that contact. The

Signs of the times: this First World War scene shows the acceptance of women in factories, a mark of their social and political progress. Their job was to stitch canvas to the frames of aeroplane wings, which emphasizes the unsophisticated technology of the period.

economy coped better with the war than its German rival.

After the smoke of war had lifted, a bright spotlight focussed on the weaknesses of Britain's position, following a brief boom in 1919 and 1920, when everyone drew breath and restocked after the restrictions of war. Ship-building fell away in the face of over-production all round the world, now that the U-boat sinkings were over. Iron and steel, textiles and coal all felt the lack of huge war requirements, and with unemployment high and wages already low, there was no way in which manufacturers and mine-owners could cut costs in order to keep prices competitive and profits attractive to the sources of capital. Unemployment affected 23 per cent of the work-force in June 1921, and it never went below seven per cent between May 1924 and the outbreak of the Second World War.

Coal and the General Strike of 1926

The coal industry was the most exposed and the most concentrated victim of the changed circumstances. The Sankey Commission of 1919 had proposed government subsidies and shorter working hours to keep the pits going in the face of foreign competition, the development of the internal combustion engine, and worked-out seams. The Samuel Commission of 1925 had another look at the problems, while the miners demanded 'Not a minute on the day, not a penny off the pay', despite the fact that the market price of

A civilian volunteer drives a bus during the General Strike of 1926, with a policeman to protect him, and barbed wire to protect his engine.

coal had dropped from 85 shillings a ton to 24 shillings in 1920 to 1921 alone. The government, however, could not continue the subsidies which it had been paying since the war. The owners could not avoid bankruptcy or wage cuts. The miners could scarcely exist on reduced pay.

The failure of prolonged negotiations led to the General Strike of 1926, which lasted for nine days. The 'Triple Alliance', which in 1921 had avoided this degree of confrontation, now called out its members and asked for sympathetic action from other trade unionists. Short of revolution, it was the strongest action that a working class movement could take. It failed.

It failed because the government and people stayed calm and waited for further developments. It failed because volunteers, mostly students and middle-class groups, kept essential supplies and services going. It failed because it lacked real leadership – the official Labour Party was embarrassed by it. Most of all, it failed because the fault lay deep in the economic structure and history of Britain rather than in one group of men exploiting their position. Although the miners themselves stayed on strike until November, when near-starvation drove them down the pits again, they gained nothing from their efforts.

The Wall Street Crash and the 1930s

After 1926, the British economy improved, on the strength of German recovery from massive inflation, French expansion and American confidence, but it was still vulnerable to anything which upset the export trades on which it depended. The 1929 Wall Street Crash (see Chapter 5) exposed the shallowness of the improvement and of the general confidence.

In 1929, British exports were worth £729 million, and there were just over one million unemployed in the country. The withdrawal of American funds from Europe led to a general reduction of European trade as well as a big drop in new investment, and by 1931 British exports were worth only £391 million, and unemployment had soared to 2½ million. Britain's future looked perilous, and those who held sterling for trade purposes or as savings decided to exchange their paper money for gold, a practice which had been possible ever since Winston Churchill had put Britain 'on the Gold Standard' in 1925. The reluctance of the Labour Government to cut unemployment benefits in order to balance the budget made foreign apprehension worse, and gold reserves dwindled. In August 1931, the government split and resigned, but the emergence of a National Government under Ramsay MacDonald restored international confidence, and negotiated a loan of £80 million from American and French bankers, in response to a promise to cut the pay of people employed by the state and the unemployment benefits.

This seemed to be enough to stabilize matters, but a mutiny in the Atlantic Fleet at Invergordon about the pay cuts upset the money markets again. The borrowed gold disappeared at a faster rate than ever, until Snowden, the Chancellor of the Exchequer, took Britain 'off the Gold Standard'. The value of the pound dropped by more than a quarter, but nothing else happened. The right remedy had been found in the nick of time, and it was to be of permanent benefit. Britain's exports were made cheaper by the fact that British pounds were cheaper, and after a low point of £365 million in 1932, they recovered slowly, and pulled up the numbers in employment (the unemployed numbered just over three million in the winter of 1932–33). In early 1932, Neville Chamberlain, the new Chancellor of the Exchequer, introduced 'Protection' for home industries by setting a general tariff of 10 per cent on imports, which also helped the recovery.

The 1930s showed that several lessons had been learned. The government increased its activities in the economy to a degree unprecedented in peacetime, and there was a fundamental move away from the old, over-producing, primary industries towards new consumer goods. Cars, electrical goods, household-fittings, sophisticated machine-tools, chemicals, clothing and synthetic materials all appeared in far greater volume, and the government, by means of financial grants to Depressed Areas (more tactfully called Special Areas) encouraged the mopping-up of the worst unemployment. The Unemployment Act of 1934 rationalized the system of benefits (now called 'Assistance', and, since 1931, based on a Means Test), and although individual hardship was still often great, the structure of a welfare state looking after its unemployed had been built. The 'Hunger Marches' of the 1930s were inspired by frustration more than by starvation.

Rearmament after 1936, as well as the rise of the new industries, brought the Depression to an end. By 1937, the official plan was to spend £1,500 million on ships, aeroplanes, tanks and guns over the next five years, which gave a huge boost to the steel, coal and ship-building industries. From a low point in 1932 when 35 per cent of coal-miners, 48 per cent of steelworkers and 62 per cent of ship-builders were out of work, the total of unemployed dropped steadily. By the spring of 1940, it fell below a million for the first time since 1920.

POLITICAL DEVELOPMENT 1900–40

Three interrelated themes dominate British political history in this period. The first is the increased importance of the widening electorate, and therefore of the House of Commons as contrasted to the House of Lords. The second is the decline of the Liberal Party and the rise of the Labour Party. The third is the growth of government powers and responsibilities, marking the end of laissez-faire and the 'self-help' policies of the Victorian era.

The Voters

At the beginning of the century, the right to vote was enjoyed by every male householder over the age of 21, a total of nearly seven million men. The law required that they were consulted at least once every seven years; their votes usually went to either the Liberal or Conservative Parties, although the issue of whether Ireland should have Home Rule turned the Conservatives into the 'Unionist' Party until the early 1920s (see end of Chapter).

The leaders of both parties were largely aristocratic, yet they believed that they could represent the wishes of the whole electorate. The Conservatives based their philosophy on a belief in the British Crown, the Church of England, the natural importance of land-owners and the strength of the Empire. The Liberals believed more in the rights of Parliament, the Non-Conformist church, the strength of industry and the principle of Free Trade. At the turn of the century, however, they were losing the support of the richer businessmen, who were tending towards the Conservatives, and gaining the support of the workers. In the 1906 election, after the Conservatives had been disastrously split by Josph Chamberlain's suggestion that they should agree to Free Trade, the Liberals took power with an unprecedented majority of 84 seats over all other parties combined (Unionists 157, Irish Nationalists 83, Labour Representation Committee 29, Trade Union-sponsored members 24).

In response to the obvious hopes of the electorate, the Liberals introduced an era of social reforms: in 1906, free school meals; in 1907, a school medical service; and in 1908, an Old Age Pensions Act which at the time was fairly generous in its provision of five shillings (25p) a week for anyone over 70 who had an income of less than 10 shillings (50p) a week.

Commons v. Lords – The People's Budget, 1909

In 1909, the Chancellor of the Exchequer used the annual Budget not only to pay for social reforms (and new Dreadnought battleships) but also to further the cause of reform. By taxing cars, petrol, and other luxuries, and by raising income tax and creating 'supertax' on incomes over £3,000 a year, he deliberately 'robbed the rich' to help the poor. His whole approach offended the Unionists, weak in the Commons but firmly entrenched in the hereditary House of Lords. Breaking the conventions of centuries, the Lords rejected the Budget by 350 votes to 75. Without money, the Liberals could not govern. Asquith asked the King to let the electorate resolve the issue. In January 1910, the Liberals were returned to power with a majority of just two over the Unionists

(275 to 273) but with the further support of 82 Irish Nationalists and 40 Labour members.

Asquith reintroduced the People's Budget, and alongside it, a Parliament Bill proposing cuts in the powers of the House of Lords. The Budget was passed (without a vote being taken in the Lords). The Parliament Bill, delayed by the death of Edward VII, was submitted to the test of public opinion at another General Election in December 1910, after the new King, George V, had secretly promised to support the Liberal plan by creating extra Liberal peers if deadlock continued. The election result showed hardly any change from the January position. In 1911, the Parliament Act became law, with 131 members of the Lords voting for it and 114 'diehards' voting against. Its provisions removed all power of the Lords over any 'Money Bill' (the Speaker of the Commons defines what is a Money Bill), and removed the power of absolute veto over any other bill, except one altering the Constitution. Instead, the Lords were allowed to reject a bill in two successive sessions, a weapon which was rendered useless if the Commons passed that bill in three successive sessions (as happened to the Irish Home Rule Bill of 1912–13–14). Only one limitation was put on the power of the Commons: it was to be re-elected at least every five years, thereby having to make more frequent reference to the voters.

Votes for Women, 1918 and 1928

Pressure for political rights for women can be traced back to the eighteenth century, but the Victorians thought little of the idea, and Mrs Emmeline Pankhurst's 'Women's Social and Political Union', founded in 1903, seemed at first an eccentric organization. But from a quiet start in their campaign for the 1906 election, they built up the practice of embarrassing politicians (all male, of course) and thus drawing attention to their cause. From the early days of interrupting meetings and displaying banners, the 'Suffragettes' developed tactics of breaking the windows of well-known buildings, setting fire to the contents of pillar-boxes, chaining themselves to railings (Buckingham Palace, Downing Street and Westminster were favoured sites for this) and slashing famous pictures, all to draw attention to their demands. Humiliation, fines and imprisonment strengthened their resolve (and their support). By 1913, they were using the hunger strike while in prison as another weapon to win publicity and sympathy, and the government certainly tarnished its own image when it passed the so-called 'Cat and Mouse' Act, the Prisoner's Temporary Release Act, which allowed the authorities to release hunger-striking prisoners until their friends had fed them back to health, and then re-arrest them. It was also in 1913 that Emily Davison, wearing the white, green and purple of the Suffragette movement, threw herself under the

King's horse in the Derby at Epsom, dying a few days later of her injuries.

But it was not the drama of protests that won votes for women; it was the sense of responsibility that they conveyed in the war. In July 1915, Mrs Pankhurst's daughter Christabel led the greatest of all Suffragette demonstrations in London, when 30,000 women in procession demanded 'the right to serve'. Encouraged by the example of Lloyd George at the Ministry of Munitions, employers took women into the vacancies left by men who had gone to the war. As factory workers, secretaries (replacing the male 'clerks'), agricultural labourers, transport workers, and even in posts attached to the fighting services, the women earned respectability and responsibility with a calm that would scarcely have been anticipated five years before. In 1918, the Representation of the People Act gave the vote to all adult males (this was taken to include those over 18 if they had actually *fought* in the war) and all women over 30 who were householders or married to householders – about eight million women in all. In 1928, when male worries about the dangers of female voters had been set aside, all women over 21 were given the vote. The granting of universal suffrage turned out to be a remarkably painless process.

The Troubles of the Liberal Party ...

The sweeping Liberal victory in 1906 was never repeated, and in retrospect was more a reflection of the troubles of the Conservatives than of Liberal strengths. Quite apart from the emergence of the Labour Party, formed a few months after the 1906 election, the Liberals had troubles of their own. Gladstone's obsession with the problems of Ireland had overshadowed any other real policy within the Party, and had caused a number of 'Liberal Unionists' to transfer to the Conservative Party. 'Free Trade' was another Liberal ideal which had less practical appeal to businessmen as foreign competitors challenged Britain's position. The Conservatives seemed more likely to adapt to modern conditions. Although the 1906 Cabinet had most of the brilliant politicians of the age in it – Asquith, Lloyd George, Grey, Churchill, Haldane – it was not held together by agreement on common policies but by the Prime Minister, Campbell-Bannerman. Lloyd George's social reforms, especially the 1908 Pensions Act and the 1911 National Insurance Act, seemed dangerously socialist to some of the more old-fashioned Liberals, and the destruction of the absolute veto of the House of Lords in the Parliament Act of 1911 could be interpreted as opening up the way for Labour Party government. This could never have been seriously considered while the Conservatives held unlimited power in the Lords.

The First World War dealt two more blows to the Liberals, by requiring 'un-Liberal' policies and by exposing a division between

Lloyd George: Liberal Chancellor of the Exchequer 1908–15; Minister of Munitions 1915–16; Secretary for War 1916; Prime Minister 1916–22.

personalities. The powers taken by the government, involving tariffs, conscription, the direction of labour and requisition of resources, were contradictory to true Liberalism as they involved considerable intervention, and even though Asquith shared the responsibility by taking the Conservatives into coalition in 1915 (thereby closing the last Liberal ministry that this country has seen), he was still reluctant to mobilize the full potential of government to run the war effectively and in a modern framework. In 1916, Lloyd George, the firebrand ex-Chancellor of the Exchequer, ex-Minister of Munitions and ex-Secretary for War, staged a political coup and was asked by the King to form a ministry. With a War Cabinet of five men, Lloyd George redesigned Britain's administration. Messages and commands streamed out from daily Cabinet meetings through a new Cabinet Secretariat; new men were brought into government for their business experience, not because they were career politicians; new powers to control broad policies and small details were taken under the provisions of the Defence of the Realm Act, which had been passed in 1914 but was scarcely used by Asquith.

An attempt to discredit Lloyd George in 1918, by claiming that he had lied to the House of Commons about the number of troops in France, backfired. The 'Maurice Debate' split the party between the followers of Asquith ('Squiffites') and the followers of Lloyd George, and this breach was never really healed. Lloyd George won the debate and the majority of Liberal support, which he kept while he was 'the man who won the war', the 'Welsh Wizard'. But in 1922, his wizardry looked tawdry. Heavy hints of corruption, in the selling of peerages for payment into Lloyd George's political Fighting Fund, and a war scare in Chanak destroyed his reputation. The Conservatives left the coalition which they had maintained since 1915. The Liberals, having deserted Asquith in 1916 or 1918, now deserted Lloyd George for a new political scene.

... and the Rise of the Labour Party

Working men had sat in Parliament in the nineteenth century under the protection of the Liberal Party. In 1892 Keir Hardie and John Burns were elected as 'Socialists'. In 1900 the Labour Representation Committee was founded to aid socialist candidates for Parliament, and when the 1906 election returned 29 L.R.C. men and 24 Trade Union-sponsored candidates, a new organization was created to co-ordinate and develop the left wing bid for political influence. This was the Labour Party.

From the beginning, the Labour Party took care not to be *too* radical or revolutionary, and certainly not to be considered similar to the Bolsheviks in Russia. In the elections of 1910, it attracted about seven per cent of the total votes cast. In the Coupon Election of 1918, after a difficult period in which the patriotism of some men was brought into question by their pacifism, the Party won 22 per cent of the votes, and 63 seats in the Commons. In 1922, when the Lloyd George coalition ministry was dissolved, and when growing economic pressures were making working-class men wary about their future, the Labour Party under Ramsay MacDonald gained 142 seats (compared with the Conservatives' 345, the Lloyd George Liberals' 62 and the Squiffites' 54). As the second largest party, they became the official opposition.

The Conservative period in office was an uneasy one. Bonar Law resigned with cancer of the throat in 1923, and his successor, the little-known Stanley Baldwin, divided his party by raising once more the issue which had split the Conservatives in 1903–05, namely Free Trade or Protection. Late in 1923, Baldwin called for the opinion of the country through a General Election. The Conservatives won 258 seats, the Labour Party 191, and the Liberals (superficially re-united under the magic banner of Free Trade) 159. The majority of the elected members of the Commons (i.e. the Labour and Liberal members) supported the continuation of Free Trade; Baldwin resigned in January 1924, and Ramsay MacDonald, illegitimate son of a poor Scottish crofter, was invited by George V to form a ministry.

This first Labour ministry (1924) was dependent on Liberal support, and therefore on its image in the country. An attempt to make a trade treaty with Russia and clumsy handling of a law case dealing with a Communist (the Campbell Case) destroyed the thin layer of trust on which MacDonald depended. In the autumn of 1924, the loss of Liberal support caused him to call another election.

The 1924 General Election campaign was dominated by the

Ramsay MacDonald, Britain's first Labour Prime Minister (1924, 1929–31) and leader of the National Government (1931–35).

Stanley Baldwin, Conservative Prime Minister (1923–24, 1924–29) and leader of the National Government (1935–37).

Zinoviev Letter, a strange directive allegedly sent by the head of the Comintern, encouraging revolution in Britain. 'Exposed' in the British press, the letter certainly affected the election result: the Conservatives won an overwhelming 419 seats, Labour won 151 and the Liberals 40. The victims were *not* the Labour Party, despite their apparent loss of seats; they gained an extra million votes. It was the Liberals who lost votes *and* seats. 'Middle road' politics were too indecisive for the electorate who now chose between Right or Left, Conservative or Labour. In the 1929 Election the Labour Party won more seats than any other party (Labour 288, Conservatives 260, Liberals 59) and MacDonald formed his second ministry, again depending on Liberal goodwill.

The Crises of 1926 and 1931

Twice in five years, governments were severely tested by circumstances arising from economic stresses. The second Baldwin ministry (1924–29) is remembered chiefly for Britain's only General Strike, which was precipitated by the difficulties of the coal industry. The inevitable decline of this industry was accelerated by Winston Churchill's Budget of 1925, which put Britain back on the 'Gold Standard' for the first time since the war, making her currency instantly exchangeable for gold. The Budget was designed to show – and to create – confidence, but it also had the effect of raising the price of British exports, and therefore of reducing their volume. When the Samuel Commission reported in 1926 that it could see no way of avoiding wage cuts for the miners, Baldwin's government accepted the consequences.

When the T.U.C. called out two and a half million workers, including those in transport, electricity, gas, mines, docks and printing, on 3 May 1926, the government stood firm: the police preserved law and order and good humour; troops were used to set up a food depot in Hyde Park and to bring a convoy of supplies from the docks in London; volunteers drove trains and trams and buses, and carried essential goods and messages. The right-wing Home Secretary Joynson Hicks was restrained from provocative action by his Cabinet colleagues. The most forthright government activity was the publication of *The British Gazette* by Churchill. The government's calm response and the lack of leadership among the strikers made the whole confrontation rather muted. As George V wrote 'Our old country can well be proud of itself, as during the last nine days there has been a strike in which four million men have been affected; not a shot has been fired, and no-one killed; it shows what a wonderful people we are...'. Nonetheless, the government tried to ensure that it could never happen again. The 1927 Trade Disputes and Trade Union Act banned 'sympathy strikes' designed to pressurize the government, forbade civil servants to join unions attached to the T.U.C., and insisted that any union member who wanted to make contributions to a political fund must 'contract in' to do so. Previously a union member automatically made contributions unless he specifically 'contracted out'.

Although the 1926 crisis was resolved by a lack of immediate government action, the economic crisis of 1931 required decisive handling and fundamental changes. It was ironical that the 1929 election should bring to power a party based on opposition to capitalism just before capitalism suffered its greatest ever setback: MacDonald and his party were ill-equipped for the Wall Street Crash and the Depression. Only the deep foundations of constitutional monarchy and parliamentary democracy enabled an all party 'National' Government to emerge and cope with the crisis and yet not demand the permanent and total powers that were handed to men like Hitler or Mussolini. There was pressure for such an approach: Sir Oswald Mosley, first a Conservative M.P. and then a brilliant junior minister in the 1930 Labour Cabinet, proposed a series of strong economic measures, which became the programme of his 'New Party', created when the other parties would have nothing to do with them. The New Party later became the British Union of Fascists (1932) and was responsible for considerable racial violence in 1934 and 1936, but it always had a very limited political appeal.

But the National Government which MacDonald formed in August 1931 (without the support of most of his own Labour Party) did what was necessary: it cut unemployment benefits and salaries paid by the government; it borrowed money and balanced the budget; it took Britain off the Gold Standard; it appealed to the electorate and in October 1931 received massive approval for its policies: 521 seats in the Commons against 52 for Labour and 33 for Liberals led by Sir Herbert Samuel. In 1932 it introduced a general tariff of 10 per cent on imports, the 'Protection' that had been considered since 1903.

In 1935, the Conservative Baldwin succeeded MacDonald at the head of what was still called a National Government. Another election confirmed public approval (National Government 432; Labour 154; Liberals 21). Before Baldwin resigned in favour of Neville Chamberlain (Prime Minister 1937–40), he faced the other major political question of the 1930s, the abdication of Edward VIII (see below).

Throughout these political changes, British public opinion in the 1930s remained solidly behind peace efforts until 1939. In 1933 a by-election in East Fulham turned a Conservative majority of 14,000 into a Labour majority of 5,000. Because it took place just after Germany had walked out of the Disarmament Conference, and because the Labour candidate was a 'Peace' candidate, this result was used by politicians as 'proof' of the country's hatred of war, as was the Oxford Union Society's passing of the motion 'This House will never again fight for King and Country' in the same year. Thus re-armament was undertaken only in 1936, and then with genuine reluctance. Those who cried 'War' – most notably Winston Churchill – were kept from public office, and British Foreign Secretaries (with the exception of Eden, who resigned early in 1938) favoured personal negotiations which would contribute to peace, even though they might involve concessions over details.

The Abdication Crisis, 1936

When George V died in January 1936, public sorrow was consoled by the knowledge that his successor, Edward VIII, was the most able and best prepared heir to the throne in modern British history. His personality, energy and experience promised a distinguished reign. Unknown to the public, Edward became convinced that he could not reign 'without the support of the woman I love', an American divorcee, Mrs Wallis Simpson. The fact of her divorces (one in 1925 and one in October 1936) made her socially unacceptable as a possible Queen of England. It was Baldwin's role to confirm this opinion in the top circles of England and the Dominions, and transmit it to the King, while the general public, suddenly aware of the difficulty, waited on events in dismay. On 10 December 1936, Edward abdicated the throne to his brother George VI, and left the country, never to reside in England again. He died in 1972.

A Royal walkabout in 1926. Edward, Prince of Wales, (later Edward VIII) was immensely popular with working people, and his abdication in 1936 shocked and disillusioned them.

The Growth of the Welfare State, 1900–39

Whichever one of the three parties was in power in this period, the government accepted an increasing amount of responsibility for the welfare of its citizens. The main beneficiaries were children, widows, the unemployed and the elderly, but the firm establishment of the principle of state aid was in itself an important change.

By 1900, an English child was compelled to go to school (free of charge) up to the age of 12, but the standard of education received was very variable. The 1902 (Balfour) Education Act created Local Education Authorities based on county and county borough councils, which not only improved primary schools, but provided more secondary schools, usually charging some fees but providing 'scholarship' places free for the brightest pupils from the primary schools. In 1918 the school-leaving age was raised to 14, and arrangements were made for further education between the ages of 16 and 18.

Pensions for the over-70s were introduced by the Liberals in 1908 and increased in 1919. In 1925 the Conservatives introduced a further contributory scheme for widows and orphans as well as the elderly. National Insurance also dated from the Asquith ministry (1911); starting from a contribution of four old pence a week by the employee (made up to nine old pence by further contributions from the employer and the state), a fund was established to provide medical benefits and, for certain categories of workers, unemployment benefits. In 1920 Lloyd George's Coalition extended unemployment provision to all wage-earners (thereby wrecking the

balance of the budget in the ensuing years of depression and high
unemployment). In 1931, the Means Test was introduced to help
to make the government's scarce funds go further, but the
principle of help for the most needy was not questioned.

Housing was another area of government involvement. Addi-
son's Act of 1919 authorized central government grants to local
authorities to help to provide the promised 'homes fit for heroes to
live in'. 200,000 council houses came from this policy. Chamberlain's Housing Act of 1923, Wheatley's Act of 1924 and Greenwood's Act of 1930 all provided money and planning to get rid of
bad housing and to build new estates, especially in the major cities.
With electricity being planned on a central grid system (1926), and
with the government becoming more involved in the planning of
transport (the Ministry of Transport was set up in 1910), there was
a more even spread of amenities over the country. From 1909,
'Labour Exchanges' helped to direct the unemployed towards
available jobs all over the country. In 1942, Sir William Beveridge
published a report on Social Insurance, and called for full
protection against 'Want, Disease, Ignorance, Squalor and Idleness'. The fact that the report was commissioned at all indicates
that an important start had been made before the Second World
War was declared.

IRELAND

In 1900, the whole island of Ireland was part of Great Britain, as it
had been since the Act of Union 100 years before. Gladstone's
belief that giving Home Rule to Ireland again would 'pacify
Ireland' had not been put into effect because many 'Unionists',
some of them from the Liberal Party, believed that Home Rule
would not work, and also that it would undermine the whole
principle of Empire. Most English politicians would have preferred
to forget the whole Irish issue at the beginning of the twentieth
century – even the Liberals dropped it from their programme in the
1906 election and the first election of 1910 – but in Ireland itself
pressure mounted for self-government and freedom from English
domination. Centuries of racial, religious, economic and political
frustration were funnelled into the Irish Nationalist Party, and,
after 1904, into the 'Sinn Fein' movement led by Arthur Griffith,
and the 'Irish Citizen Army' led by James Connolly and Michael
Collins.

The parliamentary events of 1910 and 1911 reactivated Irish
tensions more strongly than ever, for the election results placed the
fate of the Liberals in the hands of the Irish Nationalists (see
p.86). But the Parliament Act of 1911 also took away the last
insurmountable barrier in the way of Home Rule, the absolute veto
of the Unionists in the House of Lords. In 1912, Asquith
introduced a Home Rule Bill into the House of Commons very

similar to that of Gladstone in 1893. The Lords predictably rejected it, as they did again in 1913 when it returned to them having been passed by the Commons again. By the terms of the new Parliament Act of 1911, if it passed the Commons in the next session of Parliament, it could go to the King for signature, and thence onto the statute book. By this time, however, a new complication had developed: the role of Ulster.

Ulster

Ulster, the north-east province of Ireland, had evolved differently from the remainder of Ireland. In Ulster the majority were of English and Scottish extraction and of the Protestant faith; they identified with England far more than with Ireland, and the prospect of 'Home Rule' meant for them not freedom but 'Rome Rule'. English Unionists supported the Ulstermen's protests to the hilt. 'There are things stronger than Parliamentary majorities,' declared Bonar Law, leader of the Conservative and Unionist Party in the Commons. 'I can imagine no length of resistance to which Ulster can go in which I should not be prepared to support them and in which, in my belief, they would not be supported by the overwhelming majority of the British people.' Civil war was not impossible; Sir Edward Carson, leader of the Ulster Unionists, had already taken the salute at a march-past of 100,000 'Ulster Volunteers' who, while pledging their loyalty to the Crown, made it clear that they would fight English troops or laws in order to stay attached to England. In 1914, 58 officers at the Curragh, the main English army camp in Ireland, resigned their commissions rather than face the possibility of having to fight against Ulster loyalists. 1914 was a year of growing tension as the Home Rule Bill made its way through the Commons for the third time, while the statesmen tried to work out a plan to partition Ireland, and the Irish and Ulstermen armed themselves for a fight. But the fight that came first was the war between England and Germany. The Home Rule Bill, although it had passed the Commons, was suspended for the duration of the war.

The Easter Rising, 1916

Frustrated in their aims, Sinn Fein ('Ourselves Alone') were not as prepared to accept the postponement of Home Rule as John Redmond and the Irish Nationalist Party at Westminster. They planned a rebellion against English rule for Easter 1916, which might secure their aims: it depended on arms from Germany, support from the Irish people and a lack of determination in the English, but in the event, none of these conditions was forthcoming. The Germans did not send arms, and Sir Roger Casement, Irish-born British diplomat who had gone to Germany to win support,

Devastation in Dublin after the Easter Rising of 1916. Shells from 18-pounder guns and consequent fires destroyed 34 houses and 62 shops, as well as gutting the General Post Office.

was captured by the authorities as he came back to Ireland just before the Rising. He was tried and executed for treason in August 1916. The Irish people did not rebel in large numbers; perhaps 1,250 took some part, but their reckless courage could not make up for their scarcity. The English, although taken by surprise, did not crumble. The siege of the General Post Office, where the rebels had established their Headquarters and their 'Provisional Government', was undertaken with steadfast severity. Heavy artillery was used to reduce the building, and the rebels were court-martialled (15 of them were executed) as soon as they were captured. Connolly, already dying from his wounds, had to be propped up in a chair to face the firing squad; Collins escaped; Eamonn de Valera was sentenced to life imprisonment rather than the firing squad because his American passport made him diplomatically difficult to deal with, and Britain was anxious for American support in the World War.

Home Rule Achieved, 1922

The suppression of the Easter Rising left its legacy of hatred, and Sinn Fein candidates were successful against the more moderate Irish Nationalists in all but six of the constituencies outside Ulster in the Coupon Election of 1918. (Their 73 elected M.P.s included the first woman to be elected to Westminster, Countess Markiewicz. She, like the rest, refused to come to London. They all set up an 'Irish Parliament' (Dail) in Dublin.)

Sinn Fein now turned to terrorism; the English retaliated by recruiting the 'Black and Tans' (1920), a police force consisting of volunteer ex-soldiers who, with the Royal Irish Constabulary, were prepared to meet violence with violence. Undeclared war raged between the two sides, with some 1,500 killed before Lloyd George got Parliament to pass the Government of Ireland Act of 1920. This partitioned Ireland into six Ulster counties and the rest, and gave each section Home Rule, plus the right to keep their representation at Westminster. Ulster accepted the Act and the representation; the South did not, and fought on until a peace treaty was evolved in 1921, which was approved by a narrow majority in the Dail in 1922. The Irish Free State, the whole of Ireland except the six counties of Ulster, was born at last, though it still had to suffer civil war until April 1923 as the Irish Republican Army tried to incorporate Ulster. The Black and Tans were disbanded in 1922, and all British troops left Ireland. The I.F.S. became a self-governing Dominion within the British Commonwealth, with the same status as Canada, but in 1936 a revised Constitution placed more emphasis on its independence, and changed its name to 'Eire'.

INDIA

Most problematic of all Britain's imperial possessions was the subcontinent of India, peaceful since the end of the Indian Mutiny in 1858 but anxious for advance and development. In 1909, the Morley-Minto Reforms allowed elected Indians a small share in government by allocating them places on legislative and advisory councils. In the 1914–18 War, Indian loyalty and courage earned warm praise from English generals and politicians: Indian troops fought on the Western Front, in Africa, in Egypt and in Mesopotamia. In 1918 followed the Montagu-Chelmsford Report, which was implemented in the India Act of 1919. This established a central all-Indian elected parliament (albeit with little real power), and in eight provinces, the principle of 'dyarchy', rule by two bodies. External, financial and judicial matters were left in British hands, but other aspects of day-to-day administration like education were transferred to Indians.

This experimental Act did not work well, for apart from its own failings, it had to tackle the antagonism of Mohandas Gandhi and the increasing tension in India after 1919. Gandhi, a trained lawyer, spearheaded the opposition to British rule by the inspired use of passive resistance. His belief, backed up by his own experiences in South Africa, was that massive disobedience by the civilian population was the most effective pressure that could be applied. He was totally opposed to violence (he once apologized for kicking away a snake that bit his ankle), but was determined to organize the Indian people so that the continuation of the British presence was impossible. He was leader of the Indian National Congress party, a largely Hindu body.

In 1919, the Amritsar Massacre arose indirectly out of Gandhi's call for a General Strike, when anti-European violence flared up in the Punjab. General Dyer, commanding a force of 50 Indian troops, fired on a huge restless crowd, killing 400 unarmed men, women and children and injuring 1,200 more. Unrest diminished thereafter; the European will was ruthlessly enforced again, and many argued that Dyer's violence had been justified. Yet Gandhi worked on non-violently. His followers boycotted British goods, schools, law courts, titles and salaries. He was sent to prison in 1922, and again in 1930 following his much-publicized 'Salt March' to Dandi Beach, which challenged the government's salt monopoly. The British government could find no way to diminish the disruptive effect of Gandhi and his determined supporters.

In 1930, the Liberal Sir John Simon presented his Report to the government on the administration of India, and several Round Table Conferences followed, to discuss a greater degree of Indian self-government. In 1935, the India Act became law, establishing a new form of federal dyarchy, with a number of provinces run by their own elected parliaments. 40,000,000 Indians were given the right to vote. A British viceroy had the final say until the constitution was running properly.

It never did run properly. Though elections were held in 1936, the results were confused by the fact that the Congress Party (which won 716 seats out of 1,585) was not agreed on whether it should cooperate with the British scheme, while the new Muslim League (109 seats) would not cooperate with Congress. The coming of the Second World War temporarily patched things up, but once it was over, racial and religious division was more obvious than ever, and total self-government could not be delayed much longer (see Chapter 20).

EMPIRE AND COMMONWEALTH

The main principle of British Imperial policy ever since the Durham Report of 1839 was that colonies should eventually be granted their own governments. In 1867 the British North American Colonies became 'the Dominion of Canada', Australia became a Dominion in 1901, New Zealand in 1907 and South Africa in 1910. The Irish Free State took the same status in 1922. Definition of Dominion status was unclear: Lord Durham had never intended 'responsible government' to include matters of defence, foreign policy and tariffs. But before the end of the nineteenth century, Imperial Conferences in London and Ottawa were discussing such issues with great frankness. Though Britain's declaration of war in 1914 automatically took the Dominions into battle against Ger-

The British Empire and Commonwealth, 1931

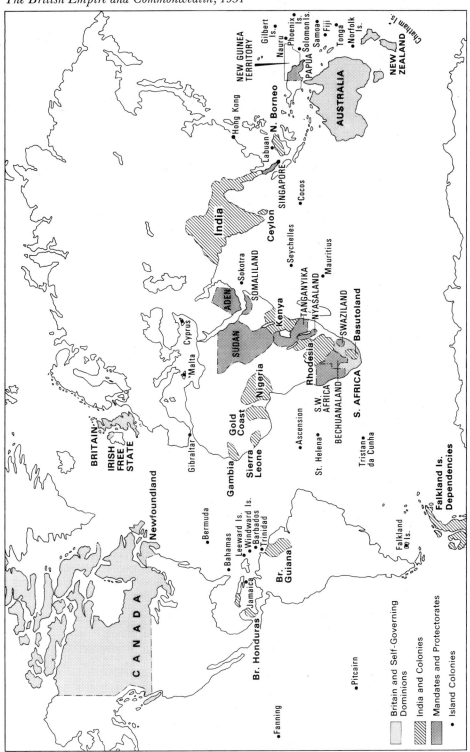

Chatham Is.

Gilbert Is.
Phoenix Is.
Nauru   Solomon Is.
PAPUA
NEW GUINEA TERRITORY

Fiji
Tonga
Samoa
Norfolk Is.

NEW ZEALAND

Hong Kong
N. Borneo
Labuan
SINGAPORE
AUSTRALIA

Cocos

India
Ceylon

Sokotra
SOMALILAND
Seychelles
Mauritius

ADEN
Kenya
TANGANYIKA
NYASALAND

Cyprus
SUDAN
SWAZILAND
Basutoland

Malta
Nigeria
Rhodesia
S.W. AFRICA
S. AFRICA
BECHUANALAND

Gold Coast
Ascension

BRITAIN
IRISH FREE STATE

Gibraltar
Gambia
Sierra Leone
St. Helena
Tristan da Cunha

Newfoundland

Bermuda
Leeward Is.
Windward Is.
Barbados
Trinidad

Bahamas

Br. Guiana

Falkland Is.
Dependencies

Falkland Is.

CANADA

Br. Honduras
Jamaica

Pitcairn

Fanning

Britain and Self-Governing Dominions

India and Colonies

Mandates and Protectorates

• Island Colonies

many, by 1919 they were able to insist on signing the peace treaties separately, becoming founder members of the League of Nations, and taking responsibility for mandates of their own (New Guinea for Australia, South West Africa for South Africa and Western Samoa for New Zealand).

Disagreements over the wishes of the dominions and Britain's declared policies (as over Chanak in 1922 and Locarno in 1925) made some clarification of their mutual relationship urgent. In 1926 an Imperial Conference in London declared that Britain and the Dominions were 'equal in status though united by a common allegiance to the Crown' and in 1931 the Statute of Westminster confirmed this in law, adjusting as necessary all previous legal statements. On this basis (which was in fact a recognition of what had existed before), the Ottawa Conference of 1932 set up the system of 'Imperial Preference', a new form of economic partnership, in which colonies and dominions were subjected to lower rates of tariffs in their trade with Britain or with each other, or in some cases were exempt from trade duties altogether.

The Statute of Westminster brought equality of status to the white-populated Dominions, but Britain still had a large dependent Empire comprising, as well as the Indians, some 60 million people in roughly 50 separate territories. On the whole, Britain exercised a benevolent dictatorship over these territories, ruling where possible through local chiefs and institutions, but setting up Governors who supervised the areas on behalf of the Colonial Office. The word 'colony' is a description and not a definition. Southern Rhodesia was called a 'self-governing colony' after 1923; other colonies were termed 'protectorates' or 'trusteeships'; each had its own arrangements tailored to its, and Britain's, requirements. (For British policies towards Europe, see Chapters 3 and 11.)

Europe Old and New 1918-39

7

The First World War was not merely a war fought all round the world; it was also a war which accelerated awareness of the rest of the world. The introduction of conscript armies did more for the education of the masses than all the previous good intentions of churches and charitable institutions. The need to deliver armies and supplies at the right time and place stimulated all forms of road, rail, air and sea transport, as well as communication by telephone, telegraph and 'wireless'. Mass industrialization changed the role of women, of trade unions, of governments and therefore of voters. The unselective nature of death, disease and despair mocked at barriers of class or race. The world that emerged from the drubbing of the First War could not therefore rely on old political systems to sustain the new society. In the face of vastly enlarged awareness and expectations, the politicians had to pick their way through a minefield of practical problems.

FRANCE

Basic Weaknesses of the Third Republic

From 1875 until 1940, France endured the Constitution of the Third Republic. In those 65 years, 98 ministries held the reins of power, indicating that whereas other countries ignored or forbade opposition to the established government, in France it was the government itself that was deprived of the means of responsible existence. The fragmentation of French politics into numerous small parties and the distrust of a strong executive produced a system where the Chamber of Deputies (the equivalent of the House of Commons) was elected every four years and was not dissolved even when a Cabinet fell. But the Senate, the upper house, was elected every nine years (one third of the Senators retiring every third year), on a more regional basis. The two houses, with equal law-making influence, seldom agreed with each other or with whichever coalition government was trying to produce generally acceptable policies. The President of the Republic was elected for seven years by both Houses meeting together, and although he had the authority to dissolve the Chamber of Deputies and call new elections, no President did so after 1877. All this, coupled with a persistent French dislike of paying taxes to the central government, reduced politics to a first-rate career for second-rate men. Few real statesmen emerged.

Political Patterns, 1919–39

With no two-party tradition, French politics became a matter of 'blocs', coalitions of deputies with overlapping views on some, if not all, issues. In the post-war elections of 1919, it was the right-wing group of parties led by Clemenceau who captured the Chamber with 433 seats to 104 Socialists and 86 Radicals. They represented the desire to punish Germany, to rebuild France on the money which reparations would bring, and to guarantee national security in the future. They were conservative and largely Catholic, and vehemently anti-Communist, but their forcefulness was not enough to bind them together for long. They deserted Clemenceau when he ran for the Presidency in 1920 because they believed he had not taken a strong enough line over Germany at Versailles, and he retired from office. The foreign policy of this 'Bloc National' was only patchily successful (see below), and when the occupation of the Ruhr, ordered by Poincaré in 1923, was unproductive, their financial policy was in ribbons too. They had relied too much on the magic of reparations payments from Germany.

In 1924, a Socialist and Radical coalition took over, the 'Cartel des Gauches'. The National Block had only 211 seats to the Cartel's 289, but the Cartel was hamstrung by attacks from Communists on one side, and near-Fascist organizations on the other. Afraid to tax the rich and unwilling to tax the poor, the government watched helplessly as the franc's value fell until the rate was 243 to £1 in 1926. A strong, centre-based coalition was required, and it was found in Poincaré's Government of National Union, 1926–29.

Firm financial handling restored confidence, and Briand (Foreign Minister 1925–1932) established a strong sense of security by his relationships with Stresemann of Germany and Austen Chamberlain of Britain. Locarno, Germany's admission to the League and the Kellogg-Briand Pact all allayed French fears, and with the construction of the Maginot Line on the eastern frontier, France felt safe at last. When Poincaré retired in 1929, he could be well satisfied with his work. Plans were even being made to end the French occupation of the Rhineland.

Within 12 months, the golden picture was badly tarnished. The Wall Street Crash took away the American money that had been underpinning the European banking system, and the Nazi Party announced its threatening presence by returning 107 members to the German Reichstag. Between 1930 and 1936, France suffered a

An anti-Popular Front poster from the 1936 French General Election. It warns that the Communists will swallow up the other left-wing parties. The Popular Front won the election nevertheless.

major crisis of political and national tensions. Ministries came and went; the Stavisky scandal (see below) of 1933–34 brought violence and threatened civil war; unemployment was high and production low; foreign policy brought humiliation with incidents such as the exposure of the Hoare-Laval Pact (1935) and the German occupation of the Rhineland (1936) (see Chapter 11).

In 1936 a new left-wing coalition, the Popular Front, gained 380 seats in the Chamber, and took power. Leon Blum (April 1936–June 1937) pushed through a number of economic reforms which improved labour relations and production, but from 1938 to 1940, it was the more orthodox Daladier and Reynaud who put up the last struggle to make the Third Republic work, before Hitler's invasion brought it to an end.

The Stavisky Scandal, 1933–34

In December 1933, millions of francs' worth of bonds, issued to float a business in Bayonne by a Russian-born financier Alexandre Stavisky were shown to be worthless. Stavisky, a man with many friends among politicians and in high society, fled to another part of France, but in January 1934, he committed suicide to avoid arrest. Anti-Republican groups used the incident to draw attention to what they claimed was deep-seated corruption in the government, and when the police officer in charge of investigating the affair was found poisoned and tied up on a railway line, it looked as if a

clumsy government cover-up was taking place. Anti-government
agitation in Paris reached the point of riot on 6 February 1934,
when 15 rioters were killed by armed police, and 1,500 people were
injured. Two prime ministers, Chautemps and Daladier, resigned
within a month, and a former President, Doumergue, eventually
restored calm with a centre block government. In the event, the
absence of an inspiring leader of either the extreme Right or the
extreme Left saved the Republic from its threatened overthrow.
The Communists tried another violent uprising on 9 February
1934, but they won no substantial support.

Principles of French Foreign Policy, 1919–39

Above all, France sought security after the First War. Having
incurred a death toll of nearly 2,000,000 soldiers and civilians, the
French population statistics still show not one gash but two, for the
generation of sons and brothers killed in 1914–18 never lived to
father a new generation. In 1935–39, the number of recruits
coming into the French armed forces was half the normal total
because of the slaughter 20 years before. This human reminder, as
well as the vast material damage on the 'Western Front' (i.e. in
north-eastern France), created the pressure for revenge and
repayment.

The Versailles terms which Clemenceau accepted disappointed
many hard-line Frenchmen, although the occupation of the Rhineland in three zones for five, 10 and 15 years respectively while
Germany paid the reparations was one consolation, and an Anglo-
American pledge of immediate assistance if France were ever
attacked again was another. However, the renegotiation of repara-
tions by the Dawes and Young Plans (see Chapter 10), and the
American failure to ratify the Treaty of Versailles increased French
disillusionment, and sent them scurrying to seek their own security.
A Treaty with Poland in 1921 and the 'Little Entente' with
Czechoslovakia, Yugoslavia and Romania not only put a ring of
French allies round Germany, but also built up a 'cordon sanitaire'
around Bolshevik Russia. The Geneva Protocol of 1924 and the
Locarno Treaties of 1925 ushered in the Briand era, and France felt
secure enough to cut her compulsory military service to 12 months
in 1928, to propose a European Union in 1929, and to evacuate the
Rhineland five years early, in 1930. But their sense of suspicion
remained strong. In 1929, the French Assembly voted money for a
new defensive system, the Maginot Line, designed to stretch from
Switzerland to the frontier with Luxembourg and Belgium, and in
1930 they rejected the tonnage ratio allocated to them by the
London Naval Conference.

Hitler's rise to power in 1933 resurrected the spectre of a
vengeful Germany, and French confidence evaporated further. In
October 1934, Foreign Minister Barthou met King Alexander of

Yugoslavia at Marseilles as part of the revival of the Little Entente. Their assassination by a Croat fanatic increased the feeling of vulnerability, and in 1935 the new Foreign Minister Laval cast around in all directions for support and cover. The Stresa Front, the Franco-Soviet Pact and the Hoare-Laval Pact (see Chapter 11) were all attempts to avoid confrontation in the year in which Germany announced her rearmament, while the condemnation of the Italian invasion of Ethiopia, also in 1935, was a hollow gesture.

Internal disagreements made French participation in the Spanish Civil War impossible, although Blum, while in office, wanted to help the Republicans, the only other Popular Front representatives in Europe. He also opposed the continued appeasement of the Fascist powers, but French guarantees to Czechoslovakia and Poland, separated geographically from France by Hitler's Germany, were shown to be worthless in military terms because France was geared to her own defence rather than to international police action. In practice, French foreign policy after 1936 was uncomfortably dependent on Britain's lead. Daladier went to Munich in 1938 as an appeaser.

The Nazi takeover of Czechoslovakia in 1939 stiffened French resolve once more, and once again Paris guaranteed the independence of Poland. On 3 September 1939, Daladier committed France to a new war in response to the German 'Blitzkrieg'.

AUSTRIA

The Hapsburg family had ruled Austria since 1292, but their power was declining before the assassination of the Archduke Francis Ferdinand, heir to the throne, at Sarajevo in 1914. Racial tensions, economic weaknesses and outdated institutions took their toll, and the last Austrian Emperor, Charles I, abdicated on 11 November 1918 without waiting to hear the verdict of the forthcoming Peace Conference. The Treaty of Saint-Germain in 1919 established a democratic republic, which was to be called 'Austria' and not 'German-Austria', which its inhabitants wanted. Union with Germany was expressly forbidden without the permission of the League of Nations. The population was reduced to six million (one third of them in Vienna) as land was stripped away and given to Czechoslovakia, Yugoslavia, Hungary, Poland, Italy and Romania, and most sources of natural wealth were lost in this share-out. With no parliamentary tradition, no money and no distinctive feature except largely German origins, the new Austria was a pathetic shadow of its former self.

Two major political parties emerged, each with its own 'defence forces'. The Social Democrats, left-wing reformers, held power only from 1919 to 1920, but they retained a strong influence in some areas, and they were the largest single party in 1930. They ran a private army, the 'Schutzbund', which clashed regularly with the

'Heimwehr', the 'home defence force' of the right-wing Christian Socialists. The 'Heimwehr' looked more and more like a Fascist brigade, and the Christian Socialists always pressed for the strengthening of central government, to the point of amending the constitution in 1929.

The world Depression of the early 1930s had its effect on Austria. The government tried to propose a Customs Union with Germany in 1931 to ease the problem, but protests from France and the Little Entente countries secured a veto of the union from the International Court at The Hague. The bankruptcy of the Kreditanstalt, the biggest banking house in Austria, in 1931 precipitated a new political crisis, and in the elections of 1932, the National Socialists (Nazis) ominously increased their proportion of the vote. With an overall majority of only one seat in Parliament, the Christian Socialist leader Dollfuss found effective government almost impossible, but in March 1933 he took advantage of a parliamentary stalemate to set up a virtual dictatorship, supported by the arms of the 'Heimwehr' and the obvious goodwill of Mussolini in neighbouring Italy. Attacks on the Social Democrats increased, but Dollfuss had no sympathy for the Nazis in Austria and Germany – where Hitler was now in power – who were campaigning for Austro-German union.

In February 1934, Dollfuss and the Heimwehr took to arms and after four days of fighting abolished all parties except their own 'Fatherland Front', establishing a new Fascist constitution. In July 1934, a group of Nazis murdered Dollfuss and attempted a coup, but their failure in Vienna and the rapid mobilization of an Italian Army in the Brenner Pass dissuaded Hitler from any plans that he may have had for a German Nazi military takeover. Kurt von Schuschnigg, another Christian Socialist, took over the Chancellorship of Austria in 1934. Less forceful than Dollfuss, he seemed to accept the gradual rise of Nazi influence in Austria, and in 1936 he signed a vague treaty with Hitler, acknowledging Austria as a 'German state' while Hitler guaranteed Austrian sovereignty. (See Chapter 11 for later developments.)

CZECHOSLOVAKIA

Czechs and Slovaks are two different races, from two different areas. In the 600 years of the Austrian Hapsburg Empire, they moved and mingled with other racial groups (Germans, Slavs, Magyars and Ruthenes) in the belt of land on the northern edge of the Empire, which used the names of Bohemia, Moravia and Slovakia at different times. The idea of a unified, independent Czechoslovakia grew only during the First War, in the mind of Thomas Masaryk, a Czech member of the Austrian parliament.

Three things brought Masaryk's dream to fulfilment. The first was his organization of a Czech Legion out of the prisoners of war in Russia who were prepared to fight for an independent homeland (see Chapter 4). The second was the support of President Wilson, in his 14 Points, for the self-determination of the peoples of Austria-Hungary. The third was the recognition by Emperor Charles I that his Empire had broken up into independent fragments before he abdicated in November 1918.

By patient negotiation, Masaryk defined the geographical and political structure of the new land. Boundaries were agreed with Germany, Austria, Hungary and Poland (following a dispute with Poland, Teschen was partitioned in 1920), and a democratic constitution was adopted in 1920. Rich mineral deposits and agricultural self-sufficiency gave Czechoslovakia economic and financial stability (the country was both richer and bigger than Austria, its former overlord), and in the first 10 years of his Presidency, Masaryk looked likely to overcome the three disadvantages of the Republic. First, it lacked a centralized communication system, because its roads and railways all fed out from the Austrian capital, Vienna. Second, it was not easily defensible, especially in the west, and it lacked allies except for France and the flimsy Little Entente powers. Third, it was still a mongrel nation, a fact that was emphasized when in October 1933, just after Hitler's accession to power in Germany, a young teacher, Henlein, launched the Sudeten German Patriotic Front.

The Sudetenland was a mineral-rich mountainous area on the Czech-German frontier, populated largely by Germans. Henlein's party, renamed the Sudeten German Party in 1935 and showing distinct Nazi tendencies, initially wanted self-government for the area. Masaryk resisted the claim, and when he retired from the Presidency in 1935 and was succeeded by his life-long friend and supporter Edvard Beneš, the Czech government continued to negotiate on a cooperative and friendly basis with the Sudetens, aiming to find a peaceful settlement.

The Anschluss with Austria in March 1938 changed the whole position. Western Czechoslovakia now stuck deep into Greater Germany. The British and French governments, busy preserving peace at all costs, in keeping with the wishes of the majority of their electorates, urged the Czechs to take notice of the increasingly vociferous demands of the Sudeten Germans and their strident support from the Reich.

POLAND

The Re-establishment of the Old State

At its greatest extent, Poland stretched from the Baltic almost to the Black Sea, but that was in the sixteenth century. In the eighteenth century, Prussia, Austria and Russia had plucked

Poland right off the map in three massive Partitions. But the defeats of the three Empires of Russia, Austria-Hungary and Germany in 1917 and 1918 opened a real vacuum in north-eastern Europe, into which Poland was triumphantly reinserted.

Poland, like Czechoslovakia, contained a mixture of races, but the greater problem was to find its true frontiers. Wilson's 14 Points called for 'independence', 'indisputably Polish populations', and 'a free and secure access to the sea'. These requirements made it logical that Danzig, a predominantly German city, should not be submitted to Polish rule but administered by the League of Nations, while to the west of Danzig, Poland reclaimed a strip of her own former territory from Germany in order to establish a 'Corridor' to the sea. The southern boundary with Czechoslovakia was not disputed except for the Duchy of Teschen which was partitioned in 1920; Upper Silesia was partitioned in Poland's favour after plebiscites in 1921. The most difficult frontier to establish was that with Russia. War between the Red Armies and the Poles (1920–21) ranged east and west. An armistice line suggested by Lord Curzon, British Foreign Minister in 1920, was rejected by the Poles, and by the Treaty of Riga (1921) they achieved a frontier 100 miles further east, at Russian expense. Like the Polish Corridor in the west, this was to be a source of friction and complication later. Not only did they bring minorities under Polish rule – Germans in the west and Ukrainians and Byelo-Russians in the east – but they offered pretexts for German and Russian aggression in 1939.

Politically, Poland established a parliamentary system, though the presence of the minorities and the lack of previous democratic experience produced too many parties and too little agreement. The first Prime Minister was Ignacy Paderewski, composer, pianist and renowned Polish patriot. But even his reputation could hold a ministry together for only 10 months in 1919. Real power lay in the hands of Roman Dmowski and Josef Pilsudski, the politician and the soldier who had fought hardest for Polish independence.

Marshal Pilsudski was to Poland what Masaryk was to Czechoslovakia. Always a focus of national resistance to the occupying power, in this case Russia, he used the First War to build a military force (the Polish Legion) and reputation, and was invited to become 'Head of State' within days of the end of the war. This he remained until the end of 1922, appointing ministries and conducting the war against Russia. He then retired, but in 1926, alarmed at the lack of effective government, he marched on Warsaw at the head of a few regiments. From then until his death in 1935, he ran a thinly disguised dictatorship (his own post was Minister of Defence) with moderate support in the country but with sufficient opposition to require a harsh purge in 1929 and 1930, when 70 leading politicians were locked up. The world depression of the 1930s hit Poland hard – its production in 1938 barely reached the level of 1913 – and neither Pilsudski nor his successors had any answer to it.

Aware of its international vulnerability, sandwiched between Bolshevik Russia and a disgruntled Weimar Germany, Poland made alliances with France (who helped to save Warsaw from Russian attacks in 1920) and Romania in 1921. The Locarno Pact of 1925, and the Russo-German Neutrality Pact of 1926 negotiated by Chicherin and Stresemann, worried the Poles rather than reassured them, and Pilsudski instructed his Foreign Minister Josef Beck to ensure Polish security. Non-Aggression Pacts with Russia in 1932 and Germany in 1934 achieved this, and from 1934 to 1938, Poland, though economically poor, seemed strategically safe and politically stable.

HUNGARY

The collapse of the Austro-Hungarian Empire and the principle of self-determination cost Hungary more dearly than any other land. With Romania, Yugoslavia and Czechoslovakia claiming 13 million of the former Hungarian inhabitants, (leaving Hungary with a mere seven million), and grabbing 70 per cent of the former Hungarian Crown lands, Hungary seemed to be no more than a reservoir of assets for adjusting other people's claims. The Treaty of Trianon (1920) confirmed this feeling – over three million Magyars were transferred to other countries and six nations were awarded land from Hungary. The creation of a Little Entente between Romania, Yugoslavia and Czechoslovakia added to the Hungarian sense of isolation and persecution.

Internally, the largely peasant population had no political tradition. The attempt by a nobleman, Count Karolyi, to form a liberal progressive government was thrust aside by a 'soviet republic' led by Bela Kun, a Bolshevik and former associate of Lenin. Kun lasted only from March to August 1919. His nationalization of everything, including a takeover of private bathrooms for public use, and his disorganized 'Red Terror' were not impressive enough to hold the people's credibility, and a military takeover led by Admiral Horthy followed. A single-chamber Parliament was elected, and Horthy was declared Regent in March 1920, pending the return of the monarchy. This never took place, despite an attempt by King Charles in 1921, and Horthy remained Head of State until he was abducted by German troops in 1944. Hungary's antagonism towards her immediate neighbours found her support in Italy (pacts in 1927 and 1934), on whom she did not try to impose sanctions at the time of the Ethiopian invasion.

Relations with Germany were more difficult; half a million Germans living in Hungary formed an influential minority. Until the Anschluss with Austria, the rise of the Nazis in Germany posed only a small threat, but after 1938, and the receipt of part of

Southern Czechoslovakia following the Munich agreement, Hungary's policies became increasingly pro-German. In 1939, Horthy signed the Anti-Comintern Pact, allowed the passage of anti-Jewish laws, and gained the eastern end of Czechoslovakia (Carpatho-Ruthenia) when Hitler marched into Prague in March. By the time war broke out, in September 1939, Hungary was considered to be in the German camp.

THE BALKANS

The nineteenth-century decline of Turkey and of Austria-Hungary turned the future of the Balkans into 'the Eastern Question': which power would predominate in Eastern Europe? Would Russia gain unrestricted access through the Dardanelles and the Bosphorus? Which naval power would control the eastern Mediterranean? How would the relationships between Western European powers be altered by the Balkan pattern? Not least, how would the Balkans themselves develop, economically and politically?

The Balkan Wars of 1912 and 1913 removed most of the Turkish influence from the region, and established new frontiers. The First World War, exploding out of the pistol-shots at Sarajevo, shook up all previous arrangements and produced, after the Treaties of Saint-Germain, Neuilly, Trianon and Sèvres, five independent countries with very similar problems. The five were Albania, Bulgaria, Greece, Romania and Yugoslavia. National self-determination was extremely difficult to arrange where the racial groups were so mixed. 'Yugoslavia' (South Slav land) was a deliberate attempt to create a new nation out of the Serbs, Croats and Slovenes, and Greece, Turkey and Bulgaria had to resort to massive exchanges of population to rationalize the races within their boundaries. Furthermore, the economies were still feudal; peasants were tied to the land, but the increase in population meant that a land shortage was developing, and the new generations were unhappy with their lot. There were social pressures aplenty, but there was no political experience to balance them.

Against the pressures of both peasant revolutionary movements and Communism, deliberately fostered by the Communist International (founded in 1919), the five countries all produced monarchies of a sort with some parliamentary backing. In Albania, Ahmed Zogu spent two years as Premier and three as dictator before declaring himself King Zog. In Greece, the monarchy came and went, George II (uncle of the Duke of Edinburgh) being its most capable representative. Romania witnessed a power struggle between Michael and Carol II, while a Fascist movement, the Iron Guard, waited to pick up power, and in Bulgaria Boris III took over from a succession of military dictatorships.

Relationships between the Balkan powers were stiff with mutual suspicion. Romania and Yugoslavia joined Czechoslovakia in the Little Entente of 1921, to prevent Hungarian expansion. Similarly, the Balkan Pact of 1934 linked Romania, Yugoslavia, Turkey and Greece against Bulgaria. Both Communism and Fascism had hopes of expansion in the Balkans, but in 1939 it was Fascism that had secured the better position. Albania had become a virtual Italian protectorate under King Zog despite his resistance, and in April 1939, Mussolini took advantage of the world's preoccupation with Hitler's seizure of Czechoslovakia to invade and take over the country. From Albania he invaded Greece in 1940. The Germans invaded Yugoslavia in 1941. The Bulgarians were more willing allies of the Axis powers: as allies of Germany in the First War, they had lost the war, and with it, their access to the Aegean Sea. A revision of the 1919 Treaties would almost certainly work in their favour, and so they joined the Axis in March 1941, taking part in the occupation of Greece. The Romanians found themselves being forced to cede territory to Russia, Hungary and Bulgaria in 1940; the humiliation cost King Carol his throne, and his successor, the dictator General Antonescu, invited the Germans to enter and protect the country in October 1940.

TURKEY

The Sultan Abdul Hamid II (1876–1909) earned his nicknames: Abdul the Damned and Unreformed, and Abdul the Old Spider. After succeeding his mentally ill brother, he offered the Ottoman Empire a constitution, but within two years (1878) had withdrawn it. Henceforth, sitting in the middle of a web of intrigue and oppression, whose outward sign was the extension of telegraph wires over the Turkish Empire, he presided over 40 years of decadence and often atrocity. Foreign capital was attracted from Germany, largely for the building of the Kaiser's dream, the Berlin to Baghdad Railway, which at the outbreak of the First War was just over 200 miles short of completion.

By 1908 a Committee of Union and Progress consisting of Turks educated in Western Europe was calling, from the safety of Paris, for revolution. In 1908, an Army mutiny in Macedonia produced the required momentum, and the Young Turk Revolution of that year led to the re-establishment of the constitution, and, in 1909, the deposition of Abdul the Damned. His brother Mehmed V succeeded him. The Young Turk Revolution brought with it new attitudes to education, censorship, the role of women, the encouragement of modern industry and the updating of the administration, but all these improvements tend to be obscured by simultaneous disasters in foreign affairs.

The Balkan Wars of 1912 and 1913 stripped Turkey of 83 per cent of its European territory and 69 per cent of its population there, and the hasty decision to join the Central Powers in the First World War, encouraged by the dramatic arrival of the *Goeben* and

Breslau, proved costly during and after the war. The Turks fought hard at Gallipoli, in Palestine and Syria, and in Mesopotamia, and tied down many Allied troops, but Russia, France, Britain and Italy circled like vultures over the battlefields, waiting for the diplomatic pickings. The London and Istanbul Agreements of 1915, the Sykes-Picot Agreement of 1916, and the Agreement of St-Jean-de-Maurienne of 1917 all prepared the way for the dismemberment of the Ottoman Empire.

In the Treaty of Sèvres (1920), the Allies believed they had found a working answer to the Eastern Question. The Bosphorus and the Dardanelles were to be internationalized (with British, French and Italian supervision); Eastern Thrace and the area around Smyrna were given to Greece, the latter for five years; Arabia was to be independent, while Syria came under a French mandate and Palestine and Mesopotamia became British mandates; Italy gained Rhodes and the Dodecanese.

The comprehensive nature of this dictated treaty stung the Turks into renewed nationalistic action. General Mustafa Kemal (later called Kemal Atatürk, the 'Father of Turks') rebelled against the feeble government of Mehmed VI (1918–22). Starting in Samsun, Asia Minor, in 1919, he established a new capital at Ankara in 1920, and finally removed not only the Greeks and British from Smyrna and the Straits (the Chanak Crisis of 1922) but also the last of the Sultans who for 600 years had ruled the Ottomans. The renegotiated Treaty of Lausanne (1923) returned control of the Straits to Turkey, restored Eastern Thrace and the area around Smyrna, sending 1,300,000 Greeks back to Greece, but acknowledged the loss of Arabia and the lands to the east of the Mediterranean.

Kemal's Reforms, 1922–38

In 1923 Kemal became the official President of the new republic; in 1924 the Republican constitution was published, and the Caliphate, the Islamic religious hierarchy, was abolished. But Kemal's reforms started before this, and were carried out in the same spirit as the Young Turk ideas of 1908, but more effectively, because of his autocratic position.

There were six clear principles behind his reforms. Republicanism opened up new avenues of opportunity for all, and guaranteed the fundamental rights of the people. Populism and Statism were socialist ideals, encouraging popular participation in schemes based on government investment, like housing projects and industrialization. Nationalism was a straightforward appeal to national pride which involved not only the eradication of foreign-based words from the Turkish language, but also a careful re-writing of some of the recent history of Turkey. Secularism had huge social significance, for by cutting out the control of Islam, Kemal made

*Mustafa Kemal (left) in 1922,
dressed in the Western style he was
introducing into Turkey.*

possible the reform of laws relating to education, family life, the system of courts and clothing habits. The Koran was translated from Arabic into Turkish, and Latin script was adopted to make education easier, and more in keeping with Western influences. The final principle was Revolution, the constant stirring and reactivating of Turkish life to create a modern, integrated state.

Kemal Atatürk was highly successful. His revolution had strength but lacked much of the violence of other dictatorial revolutions. He was not hard-pressed by other powers after 1923 – in that sense, the Eastern Question had been resolved and the focus of tension moved back to central Europe. Turkey joined the League of Nations in 1932, and the Balkan Pact with Greece, Romania and Yugoslavia in 1934. At the outbreak of the Second World War, she remained neutral despite some popular sympathy for Germany. Only in February 1945 did she elect to join the victorious Allies.

8 China and Japan to 1941

CHINA

China was an empire, a mixtures of races and tribes rather than a single nation. Life at the top was cultivated, sophisticated and luxurious. But for the vast majority of the 400 million subjects in the middle of the nineteenth century, life was organized on an economically backward feudal system. Only the strong tradition of obedience and submissiveness which came from Confucianism and Buddhism held the huge empire together. Human life was cheap, and human expectations were not high.

Into this complicated situation 'foreign devils' introduced two new ingredients which flavoured Chinese history in the middle of the nineteenth century and thereafter. The first was opium and the second, in an unlikely combination, was Christianity.

Foreign Influences

The opium trade, supervised by the British East India Company, twice led to war (1839–42 and 1856–60); twice the Chinese were defeated and subjected to the 'unequal treaties' of Nanking and Tientsin. They lost Hong Kong to the British, and allowed foreigners to have special trading rights in a number of other ports. British subjects in China no longer came under Chinese law, and any privilege given to one nation was to be enjoyed by all foreign countries.

The importation of Christianity led to the Taiping Rebellion from 1851 to 1865. The importance of this was that it raised the power of the 'Warlords' in China. 'Warlords' were what the West would have called feudal barons, men with their own armies and their own territories, whose real power exceeded that of the Emperor.

In addition to this, the foreigners also nibbled at the edge of the Empire. The Russians claimed Amur province in 1858 and Manchuria in 1900; the French took Annam (Vietnam) and Laos in 1885 and 1893, and the British annexed Burma in 1886. Formosa and Korea were lost in 1895 to the hated Japanese, who also took over Manchuria in 1905. The valleys of the Yangtse and Yellow

Rivers had Europeans settling in increasing numbers at their eastern ends, and more and more 'treaty ports' were opened to Western traders. The only advantage to the ruling Ch'ing dynasty was that the Chinese people were more angered by the foreigners than they were by their own old-fashioned and corrupt rulers.

The Dragon Empress

In 1861, the Emperor Hsien-fung died at the age of 30. He named his son as his successor, but the boy was only five years old, and power was snatched by the child's mother, the Empress Tz'u-hsi, who for the next 47 years dominated China and its policies and personalities, in peace and in war. When the Emperor T'ung-chih died of smallpox in 1875, she enforced the acceptance by the court of her three-year-old nephew as the new Emperor Kuang-hsu. In name at least, he ruled until he died in 1908; in fact, the 'Dragon Empress' ruled, until she died less than 24 hours after him, having already appointed a new child-Emperor through whom she obviously intended to continue her grip on the reins of power. That boy's name was P'u Yi. He was destined to be a puppet ruler for others, not for T'zu-hsi who, by courage and corruption, by bribery and brilliance, presided over the competing courtiers and generals, and kept at bay anyone who might disturb her power. The biggest threat to her were the 'Boxers'.

The Boxers and The Siege of Peking

The 'Boxers' were members of a Chinese nationalist secret society, whose full name, 'Righteous and Harmonious Fists', indicated their belief in the religious purity of their movement. They were so fanatical that they believed that they were immortal, and they had a strong hold over many superstitious minds. They came to prominence after the economic disasters in Shantung province in 1898, when flood, famine and locusts devastated the area, and they spread wherever there was hatred of the Christians. When Yuan Shih-k'ai, Governor of Shantung Province, executed some Boxers to prove their mortality, the local populace was not impressed. If they stayed dead, then they were not true Boxers: if they were true Boxers, they would return. More and more Chinese joined the movement; missionaries and merchants were attacked, and slowly ribbons of red-robed Boxers wove their way towards Peking, looting and burning anything which was contaminated by foreign contact. The Empress appeared to support them, and the foreign ambassadors, having protested vigorously, summoned troops from their home countries.

On 21 June, 1900, the Empress declared war on Great Britain, the United States, France, Germany, Italy, Austria, Belgium, Holland and Japan. The three acres of ground that included the

A building in Peking's Legation Quarter, sandbagged against the attacks of the Boxers in 1900.

foreign legations of these countries in Peking was immediately besieged. The siege lasted 55 days, during which time about 1,000 Westerners and 3,000 Chinese Christians waited for relief from whichever national forces could get through to them. In England, the *Daily Mail* ran an exclusive story which described the fall of Peking to the Boxers, and the atrocities which they committed. A memorial service in St. Paul's Cathedral was planned for the alleged victims, but before it was held, the truth was known. Russians, Japanese, and Indians with English officers had fought their way through to the legations to find that, miraculously, only 66 Europeans had been killed – they did not bother to count the number of dead converts. The Empress disowned the Boxers and fled from her capital, but in 1901, she was forced by the presence of 45,000 foreign troops in China to accept the ruinous terms of the 'Boxer Protocol'. Ten officials were to be executed and 100 more punished. In 45 cities, examinations were to be suspended, which meant that no more Chinese could win promotion within their own Civil Service. Finally, an indemnity of 450 million taels (£67 million in those days) was demanded, to be paid before 1940. The effect was to discredit the Ch'ing dynasty even further in the eyes of the Chinese, and of the outside world.

Provincial viceroys arriving at Shanghai under military escort, seeking safety during the 1911 Revolution.

The Revolution of 1911

In 1911, the Ch'ing dynasty was overthrown. Having withstood years of pressure, it crumpled to nothing following an accidental explosion in the Russian quarter of Hankow, the treaty port on the Yangtse River. Because police investigations into the explosion would have shown that it happened in the local headquarters of a revolutionary group, the rebels, including several army officers, decided that they must come out into the open. Their example was followed all over China. In some areas Manchu officials were savagely slaughtered, but for the most part there was little resistance to the revolution, and within a month all but three of China's 18 provinces were in rebel hands. The man most responsible for the revolution, Sun Yat-sen, was not even in China. The man entrusted with its suppression, Yuan Shih-k'ai, former Governor of Shantung and an Imperial General, started to put it down and then decided to steer events in a different direction. These two men created the Chinese Republic, but with very different motives.

Sun Yat-sen and The Three Principles

Sun Yat-sen was the son of a Cantonese farmer. At the age of 12 he had been sent to Hawaii to join his emigrant brother, and so had received a Western education and been converted to the Christian religion. He qualified as a doctor in Hong Kong, and practised medicine in Macao, and then in Canton. He despised the Manchu dynasty, and in 1895 was lucky to escape arrest for plotting the

Sun Yat-sen (1867–1925), the main inspiration of the national revolution against the Manchu dynasty.

overthrow of the government. He fled from China, travelling to country after country to enlist support from Chinese people who had emigrated. In London in 1896, he was melodramatically kidnapped by members of the Chinese Legation, who had orders to ship him home for execution. Freed only by the intervention of Lord Salisbury, the British Prime Minister, Sun received such publicity from that incident that his task was much easier. With a philosophy based on his 'Three Principles of the People', Sun continued to tour the world, raising money and preaching his belief in Nationalism, Democracy and Socialism.

These ideals were for Sun Yat-sen the only way in which China could be raised from chaos and cruelty to a system of justice and efficiency. He knew that the vast majority of Chinese people were illiterate, resistant to change, and unaware of most issues of national importance, and he planned three distinct phases for China's future. The first, Nationalism, aimed at the expulsion of foreigners and foreign influence from China, and the creation of a new national pride which acknowledged one central *Chinese* government. This phase would have to be introduced by a near-military government. The second phase, of Democracy, would follow when Sun's political party would educate the masses in the ways and responsibilities of self-government. This would lead to the setting up of an elected parliament and president, and an understood code of rights and duties, all laid out in a written constitution. Finally, economic democracy, Socialism, would follow, when control of the land and the factors of production passed to those who did the work or to their representatives, the government. Sun was not a Communist, but he planned to destroy the power of the landlords, and to use the state to modernize the economy.

In 1905 he founded the T'ung Meng Hui, a new revolutionary society, and it was this organization that inspired most of the rebels in 1911. It had already been responsible for 10 unsuccessful revolts, but this time, the Manchus could hold on no longer. In late December 1911, Sun landed triumphantly at Shanghai, and at Nanking four days later he was elected provisional President of the Chinese Republic.

Yuan Shih-k'ai

At this point, the initiative lay with Yuan Shih-k'ai, who held all the military power. Having been appointed Commander-in-Chief and Prime Minister by the child-Emperor P'u Yi and his Regents, Yuan wanted total control. On 12 February, 1912 P'u Yi abdicated, in return for his title for life, a large pension, and possession of the Summer Palace in Peking, and on 13 February, Sun accepted that Yuan was more experienced in government, and so resigned his provisional Presidency. The Revolution and the Republic were now in the hands of a former Manchu official.

Yuan Shih-k'ai faced an almost impossible task. Parliamentary government was unknown in China, but a new Nationalist party, the Kuomintang, was rapidly organized by a follower of Dr. Sun, Sung Chaio-jen, advocating advanced ideas of democracy and reform. Yuan organized a 'Republican Party' in opposition, but the Kuomintang easily won the first, very corrupt, election in 1913. Sung Chaio-jen, the obvious candidate for Prime Minister, was assassinated afterwards by command of Yuan. Parliament was thus leaderless, and before the end of the year, Yuan had banned the Kuomintang, and was negotiating loans with foreign powers by himself.

In 1914 he got rid of Parliament altogether, and in 1915 he arranged for the return of the monarchy, to be proclaimed officially in January 1916. This backward step provoked revolt once again. Yuan was universally detested, and distrusted by Provincial Governors and Army Generals. His bid to set up his new Empire failed, and in June 1916 he died, leaving China in a deepening political crisis. Not only was there a clear split between the South of the country, where the Kuomintang were strong, and the North, where Warlords predominated. There was also a spate of new political and economic ideas like Sun Yat-sen's 'Plans for the Building Up of the Realm'. The ideas of Marx, and, increasingly, Lenin were known, and Western capitalists argued that China could become an area of intense and profitable business activity. To add to China's problems, the outbreak of the First World War complicated her international relationships. Even before Yuan died, Japanese troops had firmly established themselves on Chinese soil.

China, Japan and the First World War

In 1914, when the Western European powers and Russia marched into war, China declared its neutrality, and asked that the war should not be fought within Chinese frontiers between German, British, French and Russian nationals. But Japan had different intentions. Having gained less territory after the Sino-Japanese War of 1894-95 than she had hoped, she now declared war on Germany and occupied the German-leased area of Kiaochow and its capital Tsingtao, and took control of the German-built railways in Shantung province. In January 1915, Japan sent a list of 21 Demands to Yuan, demanding such rights as a share in the policing of certain Chinese towns, mining and railway rights, territorial advantages in treaty ports, harbours, bays and islands, and a favoured status in any diplomatic negotiations. This would have turned China into a satellite of Japan. Yuan tried to dilute the terms, but in May 1915 he signed an agreement with the Japanese which was generally considered a total humiliation. This was one reason why his attempt to declare himself Emperor failed: he had 'lost face'. 7 May was for three years a day of student demonstrations, marking China's degradation.

In 1917, the U.S.A. declared war on Germany, and President Wilson invited the Chinese to sever diplomatic relations with Berlin. In the North of China, the Warlords and the Prime Minister wanted war while the President was uncertain. In the South the Kuomintang were against war. For six months, the interested parties battled it out, their allegiances changing as it suited them. For a period of 10 days in July 1917, one Warlord even tried to restore the boy-Emperor P'u Yi, unsuccessfully. In August 1917 the Warlord Government of the North declared war on Germany. The Kuomintang declared that the Peking Government was illegal, and set themselves up as a provisional parliamentary government in Canton, led by Sun Yat-sen. When the First World War ended, both regimes, Peking and Canton, were represented at Versailles in the Peace negotiations, a fact which probably halved rather than doubled their effectiveness. Although the U.S.A. had promised support to China, it had more interests in Japan, and eventually all the former German spheres of influence in China were awarded to Japan. The Chinese refused to sign the Treaty with Germany, though by signing a lesser agreement with Austria they qualified for membership of the League of Nations. Anti-Japanese feeling became intense, as did contempt for their former allies America, Britain and France, who had failed them in the negotiations.

International Relations

One former ally which did not earn Chinese contempt was Russia, for in 1917 the collapse of the Tsarist regime meant a change of policy. The Bolsheviks, struggling to establish themselves in Petrograd and Moscow and the west, had neither time nor troops to claim privileges in the East previously held by the Tsars, and so in 1920 the Russians cancelled their share of the Boxer indemnity, returned to the Chinese full control of the Chinese Eastern Railway and renounced all imperial rights once exercised by the Tsars in Manchuria. It was a gesture which cost the Russians very little, but won them considerable favour in China itself, and it is no coincidence that the Chinese Communist party was founded shortly afterwards.

In 1921 and 1922 the Chinese improved their international position by positive negotiations at the Washington Conference, called by the Americans to reduce friction between themselves and the Japanese, and attended by a total of nine powers. Although the Conference strengthened Japan's naval control of the maritime approaches to China, it also guaranteed China's independence and sovereignty, took away foreign postal agencies, radio stations and armed forces from the Chinese mainland, and agreed an increase in Chinese tariffs which gave the government more money. The Japanese also returned the disputed Shantung areas and Kiao-chow, while retaining certain business interests there. The worst features of the 21 Demands of 1915 were thus remedied.

The Warlords and the Kuomintang

But internally, there was no corresponding improvement in the situation. The Warlords were growing increasingly treacherous as they found it difficult to establish themselves; might was the source of right, and even a Christian Warlord, Feng Yu-hsian (it was said that he baptized all his troops by spraying them with a firehose) controlled Peking from 1923 until 1926, appointing puppets to the position of Chief Executive until he in turn was ousted. During this period there was an attempt to link up with the Kuomintang in the South, but they too were changing their stance.

Sun Yat-sen had little real power in the South. He too was dependent on the goodwill of a Warlord, but he was the acknow-ledged leader of a great nationalist revolutionary movement. Thus he attracted the attention of Lenin and the Russian Bolsheviks, and of the Chinese Communist Party, founded in 1920. In 1923 Sun signed an agreement with a Russian diplomat, Joffe, by which the Kuomintang were to receive Russian advice, money and training in return for friendship with Russia, and co-operation with the Communist Party. Shortly afterwards, one of Sun's aides, Chiang Kai-shek, went to Moscow for military and administrative training, and on his return was put in command of Whampoa Military Academy, where a young Communist, Chou En-lai, was in charge

Chiang Kai-shek (1887–1975) on the right, standing alongside the Christian Warlord Feng Yu-hsian, the man who was supposed to have baptized all his troops with a firehose.

of political education. Meanwhile, with the help of Borodin, a Russian adviser, Sun was reorganizing the Kuomintang. Henceforth it was to be based on local party units, as was the Communist Party. Each cell was to be part of a pyramid of power, carrying orders down from the top. Policy was not to be debated by ordinary people, because all decisions would be made by a small group at the head of the Party. In 1924, the first 'National Congress' of the Kuomintang approved the new arrangements, and in the same year Sun Yat-sen went north to Peking to see if he could establish positive links with the Warlords. Within a few months (March 1925) he died of cancer in a Peking hospital, a hero whose very death increased his status and reputation. Knowing that he was dying, Sun wrote his will in the form of a message to the people of China: 'For 40 years I have devoted myself to the cause of the National Revolution, the object of which is to raise China to a position of independence and equality.' His death made his objectives more attainable, for he was a man of vision rather than of organizational or military skill. His successor as leader of the Kuomintang was the tougher, more ruthless Chiang Kai-shek, who staged a coup in Canton in March 1926.

Chiang Kai-shek

Chiang Kai-shek was first and foremost a military man, but he was also concerned about the increasing influence of the Communist Party. In 1926 he led the Kuomintang's 'Northern Expedition' against the Warlords, with impressive success, so that by January 1927 the Nationalist capital was moved from Canton to Hankow in the centre of the country. In March, Nanking fell to Chiang, and in April Shanghai succumbed too. But relations between Chiang and the Communists were very strained, and mutiny in Nanking caused

Chiang to purge his forces of Communist elements. From April until September 1927, he hunted down his enemies amongst the Nationalists, executing many and forcing others to flee. Chu Teh, a full general, and Lin Piao, an officer in his corps, led a 'Red Army' which was quickly chased into desolate areas on the borders of Hunan and Kiangsi provinces. There they linked up with the rough and ready forces of an assistant librarian from Peking who had become a political organizer in Hunan, Mao Tse-tung. Having expelled the Communists from all influential positions, Chiang further strengthened his own reputation by marrying the sister-in-law of Sun Yat-sen. No-one had a purer, stronger claim to lead the Nationalists than Chiang, and in 1928, with help from some of the former Warlords, he captured Peking and thus, outwardly at least, unified the Chinese Republic. Peking was renamed Peip'ing ('Northern Peace'), but the government was now based at Nanking, in the lower Yangtse valley. It is fair to say that it was only in the Yangtse valley that Chiang's government had any real control, for former Warlords were acting as governors in the distant provinces, and their efficiency and loyalty could not be guaranteed. Furthermore, from 1928 until 1937, Chiang faced two threats which allowed him no chance to consolidate his power: the Communists and the Japanese.

The Communists

After the Shanghai massacres of 1927, most surviving Communists withdrew to the mountains and wildernesses of rural China to rethink their position and their policy. Russian Communist theory was that revolution must be based on the urban working classes, the unskilled factory workers and the railwaymen, the last-named being a vital element in spreading messages. Li Li-san, hiding in Shanghai, was the chief exponent of this 'traditional' Marxist ideal. But many felt that China's urban workers were too few and too weak. The economy was even more primitive than Russia's back in 1917, and there was no escaping the fact that 97 per cent of the Chinese were rural peasants. If Communism could free these peasants from the exploitation of their landlords, if it could bring about a more equal sharing of wealth, and if it could hold off the Nationalist troops by guerilla warfare, then a new form of revolutionary Marxism would be established. Mao Tse-tung, who was stuck on the Chinghanshan plateau in the mountains of Kiangsi, was joined by Chu Teh, with the battered remnants of the 'First Red Army'. They established between them the Kiangsi-Hunan Soviet, which immediately posed a far greater threat to Chiang and the Nationalists than did Li Li-san.

By December 1930, 100,000 troops were moving against the Soviet, in Chiang's First Extermination Campaign. By January 1931, they admitted defeat. The peasantry gave no support to the

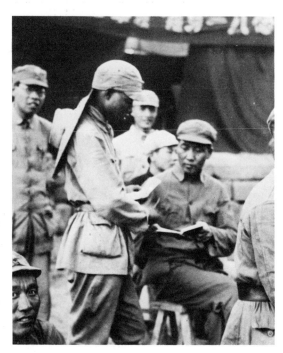

Mao Tse-tung (1893–1976) seated among members of the Red Army in the 'Cave University' in the mountains of Yenan, 1937. The face in the foreground is believed to be that of Chu Teh, who with Mao led the First Front Army on the Long March.

Nationalists, while the Red soldiers put into practice the new tactics which Mao had worked out, 'When the enemy advances, we retreat; when the enemy camps, we harass; when the enemy tires, we attack; when the enemy retreats, we pursue'. The tactics proved highly effective. Three thousand of the prisoners taken by the Reds changed sides; six thousand rifles were captured, and two radio sets. In the Second and Third Extermination Campaigns, both in 1931, Chiang's efforts (and his losses) were greater each time. In 1933, the Fourth Campaign led only to the capture of 13,000 Nationalists in one battle, and the sacking of Chiang's field commander, but in October 1933 Chiang launched the Fifth Campaign, with nearly a million men mobilized against the Reds, and with a new strategy suggested by his German advisers. This was to starve out the Reds by a programme of getting between them and the peasants who were supplying them with food, and building lines of temporary forts, one every mile or so, around their mountain strongholds. By the autumn of 1934, the lines were complete, and with winter approaching, the Reds had to come down, or die. In October 1934, they came down, and started on an epic journey which might not be believed in a work of fiction, but for which the evidence is irrefutable.

The Long March

The Red Army, 100,000 strong, broke out of the south-west corner of their Soviet, and battled their way through four separate lines of

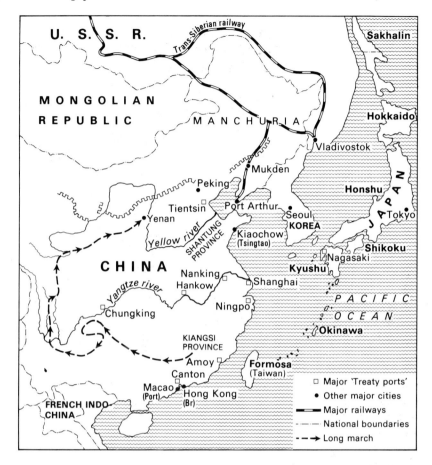

Map legend:
□ Major 'Treaty ports'
• Other major cities
━━ Major railways
--- National boundaries
-·-→ Long march

fortifications, fighting nine battles within a month and losing perhaps a third of their men. Their objective was to reach Shensi province, in the north west of China, but the Nationalists had anticipated this, and were determined to keep the Reds south of the Yangtse River, pushing them, if need be, into the wastelands of Tibet. All crossing points were heavily defended, all boats ordered to the northern bank. The Reds seemed trapped, victims of aerial reconnaissance and regular bombing, but speed and courage got them across the rivers and past the Nationalist armies. Thereafter the main obstacles were physical barriers: more rivers, the Great Snowy Mountain, five more mountain ranges, then the Great Grasslands of eastern Tibet. In Kansu Province, the Reds turned towards the north-east, and after more fighting at last entered Shensi, where Mao established a permanent headquarters at Yenan. Probably about a fifth of the original refugees from Kiangsi completed the journey.

The statistics of the Long March are difficult to comprehend. It lasted 368 days, of which 253 were devoted to marching and 15 were spent in major pitched battles. The total distance covered was at least 6,000 miles, which meant a daily march of about 24 miles across some of the worst terrain in the world: 18 mountain ranges, 24 rivers, 12 provinces passed beneath their feet. 62 towns were occupied, 10 Warlords defeated. It is hard to remember that the Long March was actually a retreat.

It was also a triumph which guaranteed the survival of Communism in China, for it spread the message of Marx and it established a sole leader in Mao Tse-tung. The Marchers tramped spectacularly through provinces where 200,000,000 people lived. They left behind them small groups ('cadres') of highly trained organizers and propagandists, who were able to take full advantage of the goodwill which the Marchers often earned by their confiscations and redistributions of goods and money along the route. Taking the supplies and belongings of the rich, the Reds gave away their surpluses – ham, salt, even ducks – and wherever possible they paid for goods taken from peasants with bullion and silver dollars from Kiangsi banks. They destroyed rent rolls, land ownership deeds, tax records. Most peasants understood little of what was happening, but knew that it was intended for their benefit.

The determination and brilliance of Mao was the mainstay of the Marchers. There were other leaders: Chu Teh led the First Front Army with Mao; Ho Lung led the Second Front Army, which travelled further to the west, but he accepted Mao's leadership when he arrived at Yenan; Chang Kuo-t'ao led the Fourth Front Army on another route, but he eventually defected to the Nationalists. But no-one achieved the dominance over men's minds that Mao won. He was part Moses, part Lenin, part Napoleon, in all ways a challenger to Chiang Kai-shek and the Nationalist regime. But Chiang had a second challenge to face, from the Japanese, and, paradoxically, this brought him into unwilling partnership with Mao in 1936.

JAPAN

Like China, Japan was an empire, a mixture of clans and traditions, and more divided than China because of its geography: in 1890 it consisted of four major islands with over 500 lesser ones. But in 1895, after the First Sino-Japanese War, it added Formosa and the Pescadores as well as informal control of Korea, which it officially annexed in 1910, and in 1905 it was also given title to half the island of Sakhalin, in the Treaty of Portsmouth. That territorial expansion around the turn of the century was one outward sign of the enormous growth that was taking place internally, in the reign of the Emperor Meiji (1868–1912).

Meiji means 'Enlightened Government'. While the Dragon Empress in China suppressed change and perpetuated obsolescent systems, Meiji got rid of the old 'Shogunate' (military dictatorship), introduced parliamentary government, permitted Christian-

A French cartoon of 1904 portrays the flimsy figure of Japan challenging the mighty Russian bear. The cartoon was prophetic: the clumsy bear overreached itself, and the Japanese won the war of 1904–05.

ity and foreign travel, and established such innovations as steamships, vaccination, western dress and post offices. Harnessing nationalism to his cause, he overcame complaint and even revolt, and victories in battle against the Chinese (1894–95) and Russia (1904–05) secured his own position and advertized Japan's emergence as a world power. So impressive was the capture of Port Arthur (1904) and the destruction of the Russian Baltic Fleet at Tsushima (1905), that President Theodore Roosevelt was moved to mediate between the Russians and the Japanese. In 1902, indeed, Britain astoundingly broke away from her 'Splendid Isolation' to commit herself to an alliance with this new naval power.

Japan, China, and the Post-War Treaties

The annexation of Korea in 1910 inevitably brought Japan into diplomatic conflict with China, and the outbreak of the First World War temporarily diverted the attention of the Western powers from the true significance of what was happening in the Far East. Japan declared war on Germany in August 1914 as a pretext for moving onto the mainland of China, and in 1915 presented the Peking government with the 21 Demands (see p.120). Early in 1917, Britain, France and Russia made secret agreements with the Japanese to support them in their claims to the formerly German areas of China in exchange for further naval help. The Japanese gladly supplied this in the Mediterranean, convoying a total of 788 ships from port to port, giving protection from German submarines. Those secret agreements were sufficiently binding on the Powers at Versailles to maintain the Japanese presence in China for the time being, though there was an understanding that China would eventually receive the territory again.

The Washington Conference of 1921–22 represented a diplomatic defeat for Japan. Britain was now in debt to the U.S.A., and so gave up the Anglo-Japanese Alliance in exchange for a Four Power Agreement (the powers being Britain, Japan, America and France). This meant that Japan had no major power prepared to argue or vote on her behalf, and so she returned the disputed Kiaochow and Shantung areas to China. She also accepted a naval agreement which established 5:5:3 as the ratio of British, American and Japanese fleets. The only positive gain that the Japanese seemed to make from the Conference was a promise that the Western powers would not increase their naval bases in the Western Pacific, thereby guaranteeing Japanese supremacy in that area.

Internal Developments

The 1920s were a grim time for the Japanese in many respects. Their Emperor Yoshihito was increasingly ill, and his son Hirohito had to become Regent in 1921, succeeding to the full title when Yoshihito died in 1926. Their politicians changed frequently, some assassinated, some retiring, some rejected by the uncertain behaviour of the elected representatives in Parliament. In 1925, all men over 25 were given the vote, even though no democratic tradition had been established, and bribery and corruption began to flourish.

In 1923 Tokyo and Yokohama were devastated by the greatest earthquake in Japan's recorded history. 107,000 people died. But such disasters and loss of life made only a minor difference to Japan's most significant trend, the growth of the population. The birth rate dropped from 35.1 per 1,000 in 1921 to 32.3 per 1,000 in 1931, partly because the government allowed instruction in birth control; but in the same period, the death rate dropped even faster, and ended at 18.2 per 1,000. The annual rate of population increase reached nearly a million, and the total population of 64 million in 1930 was crammed into an area a little larger than Italy, of which only 15 per cent could be cultivated. Nonetheless, so efficient were the Japanese farmers that they managed to supply six-sevenths of the rice requirement of this huge population. They provided barley too, and a little wheat, but the next most important crop was the mulberry bush, on which silkworms flourished. In 1928, Japan produced more than two-thirds of the silk crop of the entire world; four-fifths of all the raw silk produced was exported, and more than 96 per cent of that went to the U.S.A. The textiles industry was of great importance to Japan, for although she grew little cotton, she imported large quantities from the U.S.A., and was the third biggest consumer of raw cotton in the world. So, like Britain a century and more before her, Japan in the early twentieth century was experiencing an industrial revolution spearheaded by agricultural efficiency, a growing population providing a cheap labour force, and a textiles industry which stimulated the iron and steel industries, railways and ship-building. The lateness and the speed of this industrial revolution is indicated by the fact that the first railway in Japan was not opened until 1872 (it was 18 miles long, and built by English engineers); by 1906 there were 4,746 miles of track, and by 1927 10,884 miles. By 1929, Japan had built for herself the third largest merchant shipping fleet in the world, and had established a strong naval tradition in both peace and war.

But this remarkable development could not be sustained indefinitely. The expansion of the population was bound to bring about at least one of three different consequences: more and more industrialization; massive emigration to receptive countries; or forcible expansion into new areas. Increasing industrialization strained the financial resources of Japan (there was a serious banking crisis in 1927) and made her increasingly dependent on other countries for her imports of raw materials. By 1930, 100 per cent of her aluminium, cotton, wool, rayon and rubber needs were supplied from overseas, as was 93 per cent of her lead, 85 per cent of her iron and steel, 79 per cent of her petrol and 74 per cent of her tin. When the international market collapsed after the Wall Street Crash of 1929, the import-export trade which was the life-blood of the Japanese economy ebbed away. Prices dropped to less than a third of their 1925 level, and hundreds of thousands of Japanese workers accepted jobs which provided no pay, but merely food and shelter supplied by the employer. Poverty was extreme, and many young men joined the army, because it represented security of employment.

Foreign Attitudes

Ten years before, many would have emigrated to start new lives elsewhere: the main areas of resettlement were China, the U.S.A., the Hawaiian Islands, and, unexpectedly perhaps, Brazil. But in 1924, the United States passed a new Immigration Law which excluded Japan from the list of countries from which America would accept a limited number of immigrants. Political pressure in California had already stopped President Wilson from supporting a declaration of racial equality which the Japanese had wanted the League of Nations to accept in 1919, and it was the Californians who pressed for this new law. The Japanese were deeply offended. There was already discrimination against them in Australia and Canada, and the extremists in Japan's infant parliamentary system could now appeal not only to those who were suffering economically because of the plight of 'Western' capitalism, but also to those whose nationalistic feelings were affronted. Anti-Western propaganda grew rapidly with the power of the militarists in government.

The appeal of the Shinto religion, which involved ancestor-worship and especially reverence for those who had given their lives in service to the Emperor, also grew considerably.

The Manchurian Incident, 1931

All these tensions and needs vented themselves in the 'Manchurian Incident' of 1931. Manchuria was a logical area for Japanese expansion because of its position and its recent history. Not only was it just to the north of Korea; it was also adjacent to China and contained the Chinese Eastern Railway (which linked up with the Trans-Siberian Railway), and the South Manchurian Railway, which since 1905 had been administered by Japan. The Liaotung peninsula, which lay at the southern end of the Manchurian Railway, and which included the vital ports of Dairen and Port Arthur and the Kwantung territory, had also been taken over by the Japanese after their victories in 1904–05, and a large amount of investment in coal, steel and soya beans had been poured into Manchuria because of its proximity. The Chinese and the Russians resented Japan's increasing influence in the area, but were not ready for what occurred in September 1931.

Japanese soldiers were expressly forbidden to take part in politics, but throughout the 1920s, they clearly resented the 'weak-kneed diplomacy' of the politicians, and began to involve themselves in various plots. By 1931 there was a definite split between the military General Staff and the government in Tokyo. In September 1931 a bomb exploded on the railway line near Mukden, provoking the Japanese Kwantung Army to seize the whole town within six hours. Meanwhile a major-general, carrying an order from the Emperor expressly forbidding such violence, was deliberately staying out of the way in a local tea-house. After capturing Mukden, the Japanese Army went on to capture the whole of Manchuria, despite protests from all other parties, including the Tokyo government, until public opinion brought a more aggressive ministry to power. In 1932, the Japanese declared that Manchuria was the independent state of Manchukuo, and produced its new ruler, the Emperor Kwang-teh, previously known as P'u-Yi, the last Manchu emperor of China. The United States announced that it still supported an 'Open Door' policy in China, whereby all nations had equal influence and rights and no single nation should be allowed dominance in that area. The League of Nations produced the report of the Lytton Commission, also in 1932, which called upon Japan to withdraw and allow the League to administer a neutral settlement. When the League formally adopted this report as policy, Japan announced the end of her membership of the League.

To many observers, the Manchurian Incident is the effective beginning of the Second World War. Naked aggression had gone virtually unchallenged, and certainly unpunished; the League of Nations was shown to be totally ineffectual in the face of deliberate violence. Japan had antagonized America, Russia and the League of Nations, and now posed an even bigger threat to China. The militarists became increasingly powerful in the government, and Japan was conspicuously the only major power to be building up a large navy *and* a large army in the period 1930–35, and this had its own effect on Chinese politics.

The Japanese in China, 1937

Mao Tse-tung's 'Long March' had brought him and his troops to the north of the country, where the Japanese were threatening, and although Chiang Kai-shek still hoped to exterminate the Communists, the Warlord whom he appointed to do the job was more concerned to fight a patriotic war against Japan than a civil war. In December 1936, the Warlord mutinied, captured Chiang, and compelled him to listen to a Communist proposal of a united Chinese front of Nationalists and Reds against the common enemy, the Japanese. Chiang had no choice; in 1937 the Sian Agreement was made public (Sian was the small town in Shensi province where Chiang met the Communist emissary, Chou En-lai) and Japan wasted no time in testing its strength. In July 1937, a few shots exchanged by a Chinese garrison and a Japanese force on illegal night manoeuvres near Peking heralded the beginning of the 'China Incident'. Although no declaration of war was made, battles started that were to merge into the Second World War and the phenomenal expansion of the Japanese Empire. Peking fell within three weeks, Nanking and Shanghai within six months. Chiang Kai-shek retreated to Hankow, but that strategic Yangtse port was captured by the Japanese in October 1938. Thereafter Chiang set up his capital in Chungking, far up the river, and held his ground, knowing that his Communist allies were doing the same in Shensi. This situation remained virtually unchanged until 1941, when the Japanese attack on Pearl Harbor altered the whole perspective.

9 Italy and Spain to 1939

The Totalitarian Spirit

In the words of President Woodrow Wilson, the Great War was fought 'to secure democracy'. But within 15 years of its conclusion there were totalitarian governments in Russia, Germany and Italy, and militant regimes in Japan and China which were quite prepared to use force against opposition opinions. Even in democratic America itself, the new President, Franklin D. Roosevelt, was taking such power to himself that the Supreme Court questioned its legality and blocked some of his executive actions.

The totalitarian spirit was therefore widely established. Its aim was total control for total efficiency. A totalitarian government claimed the right to do whatever it felt was necessary, and therefore the views or the rights of private citizens were relatively insignificant. As Mussolini explained in 1922, 'My desire is to govern if possible with the consent of the majority, but in order to obtain, to foster and to strengthen that consent, I will use all the force at my disposal.'

The pressures of the First World War had stressed the need for efficient, interventionist governments, and so did the complicated workings of the modern national economies. But what gave the various totalitarian governments the chance to establish themselves was the popular desire for distinct change and quick, clear-cut results rather than fumbling democratic evolution. Part of the appeal of the Bolsheviks in Russia was the absolute clarity of their slogans and programme: part of the appeal of Hitler in Germany was his uncompromising challenge to the Versailles settlement.

But Russia and Germany were both beaten and humiliated in the First World War before they accepted the rise of totalitarian governments. This chapter looks at two Western European countries, one on the side of the victorious allies and one which remained neutral in the war, which both turned to totalitarianism from ineffective 'democratic' monarchy rather than from defeat.

ITALY

The Inadequacies of Unification, 1861–1918

Until the year of the first Italian Parliament, 1861, the area that we know as Italy had been a patchwork of separate states and not a unified country. Through the inspiration, courage and skilled diplomacy of Mazzini, Garibaldi and Cavour, a nation was forged under King Victor Emmanuel II out of the states of Sicily, Naples, most of the Papal States, Parma, Modena, Tuscany, Romagna, Lombardy and Piedmont. To these Venetia was added in 1866, and Rome in 1870. But Italian unification worked better in theory than in practice. A kingdom with 78 per cent illiteracy, massive poverty, less mineral resources than any other Western country, and a tradition of Church-dominated conservatism did not live up to the heroic vision of the 'Risorgimento', the movement that had 'resurrected' Italy. It is common to compare the shape of Italy with a human leg in a high-heeled shoe: one could add that the circulation of the blood (meaning money, people and ideas) was very weak, leaving the foot almost lifeless, while septic spots of urban poverty, crime and corruption speckled the thigh.

There were no parliamentary traditions. The aristocrats who had held power before unification were replaced by self-seeking civil servants and haggling politicians. Ministries lasted for months rather than years: Crispi's second ministry (1893–96) was relatively successful because he played up Italian pride, and began to acquire an Empire. The Italians took over Eritrea on the Red Sea, but in 1896, 20,000 Italian troops were humiliatingly defeated at Adowa by the forces of Emperor Memelik of Abyssinia.

This was a significant failure. Not only did it leave the Italians thirsting for revenge and for an Empire in Africa like other European powers. It also emphasized the complete failure of Italian armies throughout the nineteenth century, even in the glorious period of unification. Every gain had been achieved by Italy's *allies*. Without Britain, France or Prussia, Italy would still have been patchwork.

Giolitti, five times Prime Minister between 1892 and 1921, did something to salve Italian pride by annexing Tripoli in 1911 and winning Libya, Rhodes and the Dodecanese from Turkey in a brief war (1911–12). When in 1914 Italy deserted the 1882 Triple Alliance with Germany and Austria-Hungary, and then in 1915 joined the Western allies, it was because it seemed that in this way she could acquire most land. The secret Treaty of London promised to pass Trentino, Trieste, South Tirol, Istria and the North Dalmatian coast to the Italians in return for their intervention against Austria-Hungary. The disaster of Caporetto in 1917 (see Chapter 2) magnified the Italian military inferiority complex, and not even Vittorio Veneto in 1918, when French and British troops stiffened the Italian assault, could wipe out the sense of failure.

The Roots of Fascism

Italy's governmental problems after the war were even more serious than before, for although it had been on the winning side as far as military matters were concerned, it made virtually no diplomatic gains at the Peace Conference of 1919. Trentino, Trieste and South Tirol passed to Italy, but Fiume and Dalmatia became part of the new Kingdom of the Serbs, Croats and Slovenes (later Yugoslavia). No former German territory was granted to Italy as a mandate.

Resentment over foreign affairs thus caused deep distrust of the Liberals who had dominated politics for the past 50 years, and gave a strong advantage to any party which could appeal to Italian nationalism. But internal affairs also provided a seed-bed for Fascism. Among the destitute peasantry of the South and the exploited workers of the North, among those who hated the power of the Catholic Church and the corruption of the aristocrats, and especially among those who came from the lower middle classes and who could see no prospect of an enriching future for themselves or for their country, there grew an overwhelming desire for a new start.

Ironically, there were certain advantages in a dictatorial system which appealed also to the aristocrats and the Churchmen and the landlords, the very groups whose activities sparked off the search for a new political philosophy and a new leader. Aware of the political dissatisfaction in the country, and afraid that it might give rise to Bolshevism, these influential upper levels of Italian society were prepared to give their backing to a movement which stood for discipline, Italian nationalism, economic efficiency and strong leadership from the top.

Thus Fascism was always contradictory. On the one hand, it appealed to the down-trodden and the poor, to whom it promised organization, a job and a future, while on the other it appealed to those whose economic and political power seemed threatened, for it promised them a disciplined control of the workforce and protection against the uncertainties of unchecked democracy. Fascism was therefore an economically modernizing force, but a bulwark against democratic political modernization.

The Emergence of Mussolini

The Italian elections of 1919 were the first to be held on the basis of universal suffrage and proportional representation. They resulted in a massive defeat for the hitherto dominant Liberals. The Socialists took 30 per cent of the votes and 156 seats in the

Chamber; their sworn enemies, the Catholic 'Popular Party', took 20.5 per cent of the votes and 100 seats. At the other end of the scale, the Fascist Party which had been in existence for only eight months took less than two per cent of the votes.

Three years later, the Fascist Party was in total command, and its leader Benito Mussolini, the son of a blacksmith, was Prime Minister. Mussolini was a journalist who rose to become the editor of *Avanti!*, Italy's leading socialist newspaper. He had supported Italy's entry into the war, on the Allied side, because he saw that it could lead to major social change. The Socialist Party expelled him. Wounded in the war, he returned advocating the need for a dictator to oversee the changes that must come; in March 1919, he formed his first 'Fasci di Combattimento' in Milan. 'Fasci' means 'groups' or 'bundles'; in Latin the 'Fasces' were the bundles of rods which symbolized Roman authority and justice, and Mussolini's Fasci were gangs of men, originally ex-servicemen, who were determined to cure Italy's ills by taking authority and justice into their own hands.

Mussolini was an impressive leader in contrast to the ineffective politicians and the King. Victor Emmanuel III was so short that the minimum height for an Army recruit had to be reduced so that he could qualify to be Commander-in-Chief. Mussolini had something tangible to offer: 'Today, with a fully tranquil conscience,

Benito Mussolini (1883–1945) in full flow.

I say to you that the twentieth century will be a century of Fascism, the century of Italian power, the century during which Italy will become for the third time the leader of mankind.' He was not afraid of power and its implications, 'I do not believe in perpetual peace; not only do I not believe in it, but I find it depressing and a negation of all the fundamental virtues of men.'

The March on Rome, 1922

In the elections of 1921, the Fascists claimed 35 seats out of 535 in the Assembly, but their power in the land was far stronger than that implies. Organized squads of blackshirted Fascists terrorized Socialist newspapers and took over factories, local government and policing activities wherever they could. 'Punitive expeditions' wiped out opposition; murder became a normal political weapon. But in 1922, when moderates hoped that the Socialists and Fascists would destroy each other, the Socialists called for a General Strike. Mussolini demanded that the government – or the Fascists – should prevent it. His call for a 'March on Rome' precipitated panic: the King accepted the resignation of his government, and invited Mussolini to become Prime Minister. (Mussolini came to Rome by train and the 'marchers' arrived *after* he had taken power.) With four Fascists in his government, Mussolini now began the ordering of Italy. In 1923, a new law gave a majority of the seats in the Assembly to the biggest single party, whether they had a majority over all other parties or not. Another new law established the Voluntary Militia for National Security. In 1924 most of the opposition to Mussolini decided that it was wiser and safer to withdraw from the Assembly, and in 1926 a new law provided that Mussolini, 'Il Duce', could govern by decree without limitation. Dictatorship was thus firmly established, with a legalized internal army to enforce it. Little Victor Emmanuel was still King, but was almost entirely obscured by Mussolini.

The Corporate State

The firmness of Fascism did produce some economic benefits by forbidding strikes, lock-outs and 'class warfare'. A Ministry of Corporations divided the economy into 22 sections (the Corporations themselves were not officially set up until 1934) and regulated wages, hours, conditions and therefore trade unions by law. Investment too came from the government, and government contracts, mostly for roads, railways and armaments, reduced employment. New forests were planted; tourism was keenly encouraged, partly by the 'restoration' of what Mussolini believed to be the classical atmosphere conferred by rapidly built 'ancient' buildings. Everyone had a role to fulfil, a duty to perform. Women

*Groups of ex-servicemen gather in the Roman Forum to listen to Mussolini.
The ancient buildings in the background served to remind them of the grandeur
the Fascists were planning to restore.*

were proclaimed to be inferior to men; civilians were inferior to
soldiers; non-party members were inferior to Fascists. A barrage of
propaganda reinforced the claims, in schools, on the radio, on wall
posters and at Party meetings. To begin with, Fascism used the
slogan 'Me ne frego' – 'I don't give a damn'. By the 1930s, the cry
was 'Believe. Obey. Fight.' which captured the spirit of the
movement equally well. So did 'Il Duce is always right', festooned
over every wall.

The Lateran Treaties, 1929

One very positive result of Fascist rule was the agreement made
between the Pope and the Italian state, the first such agreement
since the French garrison had withdrawn from Rome in 1870,
leaving the Pope to the mercy of the government. For 59 years,
successive Popes had remained 'prisoners of the Vatican', but now
their independent Vatican State was recognized by Italy, and
Catholicism was acknowledged to be the national religion. The
Church also received cash compensation for Church lands taken
during or since 1870. In return, the Pope (Pius XI, 1922–39)
officially recognized the Italian State and its government, thereby
reducing the tension between Catholics and Fascists, but also
appearing to give some measure of support to the Fascists. In the
Second World War this rebounded against the reputation of
the Catholics.

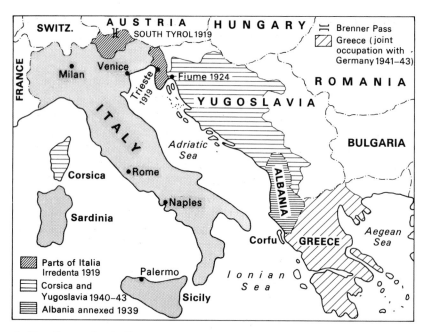

Italian Expansion in Europe

Corfu and Fiume

Italian foreign policy in the interwar years is considered in Chapters 3 and 11, but two incidents involving territorial claims stand apart from Mussolini's general European and Imperial policies.

In 1923, an Italian General and some of his staff were shot while they were helping to determine the new border between Greece and Albania: the incident gave Mussolini a chance to demonstrate Fascism's firm front when Italy appeared to have been insulted. Not content with a demand for financial compensation from Greece, he ordered the occupation of the Greek island of Corfu. Appeals to the League of Nations achieved little, although Mussolini withdrew his forces, pending a settlement arranged by the Council of Ambassadors, a relic of the Versailles Conference rather than an organ of the League. Greece eventually paid up, giving victory to the side that threatened and used force.

Fiume was a port on the Adriatic Sea claimed by both Italy and the Kingdom of the Serbs, Croats and Slovenes when the Austro-Hungarian Empire was being dismembered at the Versailles Conference. In 1919 it had been seized by the eccentric Italian war-hero D'Annunzio, who held it for Italy until January 1921, when Giolitti's Liberal Government sent a naval task-force to expel him in order to try to establish Fiume as a Free City, according to the wishes of the League. Such a concession did not fit in with Mussolini's policies. After he came to power in 1922, it was merely a matter of time before he announced the incorporation of Fiume into Italy. The announcement was made in January 1924.

SPAIN

Spain remained neutral in the First World War, already a victim of its own internal difficulties. In the eighteenth and nineteenth centuries, this once great imperial power had been dogged by financial disasters and by royal deaths and madnesses to the point where it could no longer provide adequate administration of either its own territory or its colonies. In 1820, revolution in Madrid led to further revolutions in the Spanish American colonies in 1823, at the end of which Spain retained only the islands of Cuba, Puerto Rico and the Philippines as the remnants of a world-wide empire. Another revolution in 1868 and a short-lived Republic in 1873 illustrated the fickle nature of domestic politics, while in 1898 Cuba, Puerto Rico and the Philippines were lost, leaving Spain with only its nineteenth-century acquisition, Spanish Morocco.

King Alfonso XIII (1902–31) alternated liberal and conservative governments, but there was never sufficient agreement among the politicians for stable government to develop. Between 1902 and 1923, 33 different governments held office, and the King was the object of many attempted assassinations. Although he attracted some popularity by his personal courage, Alfonso became increasingly reliant on the support of the Army, but even the Army proved fallible. In 1921, a rebellion in Spain's last colony, Morocco, was mishandled: the Army lost badly at Anual, when a dramatic victory was expected, and neither the King nor Spain could do much about it.

Primo de Rivera

In 1923, a coup d'état by General Primo de Rivera rescued Alfonso from his embarrassment, and introduced to Spain a system of government which looked very similar to that which Mussolini was building in Italy. His motto of 'Country, Religion, Monarchy' was not far removed from Mussolini's 'Believe. Obey. Fight.', and Primo de Rivera tackled his problems in a fascist manner. The Cortes (Parliament) was dissolved and the country was put under martial law. The Press was censored and political parties were strongly discouraged, especially those who gave any support to the Catalans, a group who had always resented rule from Madrid and who now sought independence. The Moroccan War was brought to a successful conclusion in 1927 with the defeat of Abd-el-Krim, the rebel leader. The economic situation was improved by putting tariffs on imports, encouraging investment in such capital as dams, irrigation projects, hydro-electric schemes and the transport system. By giving support to one large union, Primo de Rivera reduced the number of strikes and disputes significantly, and rooted out much inefficiency.

Yet this first dictatorship did not succeed. Unrest grew, especially after 1926, as the middle classes refused to give unqualified support, and the agricultural labourers pressed for land reforms which the General could not produce. Three times in 1926, Primo de Rivera had to use force to quell trouble, and as his health began to deteriorate, Alfonso steadily withdrew his support from him. In 1929, as the peseta started to lose its international value, it became clear that the Army had also lost confidence in Primo. In January 1930, the King forced him to resign, and within six weeks he was dead.

The Second Republic

Elections called in 1931 by the King after the dismissal of Primo de Rivera showed strong support for moderate republicanism. The vote had been extended to all Spaniards over the age of 22, and, in the cities especially, the result indicated that the King had no more authority. In an attempt to save his country from civil war, Alfonso left Spain in 1931, settling in Fascist Rome until his death in 1941, and always entertaining the hope that he would be recalled to his throne.

The Constitution of the Second Republic, which was adopted at the end of 1931, received most of its support from the Left Republicans, Socialists and Radicals. This moderate left wing coalition led by Prime Minister Azana ruled until 1933, but fell victim to a number of internal disagreements over such issues as the amount of autonomy to be granted to Catalonia, the strength of certain anti-clerical laws, the inadequacy of its land reforms and the harshness of its Law of Public Order. Violence escalated steadily, from both the right and the left wings, and in late 1933 power passed to an equally uncomfortable but more right wing coalition led by Lerroux's Radicals and the Catholic confederation of conservative parties led by Gil Robles.

In October 1934, the Second Republic was threatened by a further revolution. The Socialists in the mining districts of Asturias set up Revolutionary Councils and called for a general strike, while in Barcelona the Catalans took arms against the Madrid Government because they feared that their autonomy was being eroded by recent laws. The Revolution was firmly put down by the Army acting under orders from the Lerroux-Robles government, but the crushing of this left wing popular movement was decisive in establishing Spain's future political pattern. On one side, the right wingers felt that they had seen evidence of 'Red Revolution', a deliberate uprising against the legally elected government; on the other side, the left wingers were convinced that they had witnessed true 'Fascism' in the brutal way in which the 1934 Revolution was suppressed, and they determined to mobilize all possible electoral support against the right wing in the 1936 elections. At the suggestion of the small Communist party, the splits in the old Azana coalition were healed, and a new 'Popular Front' movement of Communists, Socialists and Republicans narrowly won control of the Cortes. Within months, following the murder of a monarchist member of the Cortes, the right wing formed the 'National Front', a combination of monarchists, Catholics and military men, focussed around the Falangist Party, a Fascist organization which had been founded by Primo de Rivera's son, Jose Antonio, in 1933.

The Spanish Civil War, 1936–39

The Spanish Civil War broke out because neither left nor right would accept the democratic decision of the ballot box if it went against them. The poverty and backwardness of Spain called for vigorous and radical changes, but the vested interests of Churchmen, land-owners and aristocrats were too strong and too traditional to allow the necessary modernization. In 1936, deeply conscious of the apparent chaos in Bolshevik Russia (see Chapter 4), the right wing put its faith in the Army when it rebelled against the Popular Front Government from its bases in Spanish Morocco. Morocco (where Franco was in command), the Canaries and Majorca fell to the Nationalists in July 1936, as did most of the

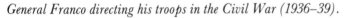

General Franco directing his troops in the Civil War (1936–39).

north-western quarter of Spain. The big cities of Madrid and Barcelona, the Basque and Catalan areas that had been granted some degree of autonomy by the Republicans, and the prosperous south-eastern quarter stayed loyal to the elected 'Popular Front' Republican Government. There could be no compromise between the two sides. Even without the pressures of external ideological forces, the 1934 Revolution and its suppression had destroyed the possibility of reconciliation.

By the end of 1936, General Franco had brought his troops over from Africa, and appeared to be about to capture Madrid, but the city was saved and the war was prolonged by the arrival of International Brigades, organized by the Communist International out of volunteers from many nations. The role of foreigners in the Spanish Civil War was considerable, despite the establishment of a Non-Intervention Committee in London which hoped to prevent interference in the war. The International Brigades added 60,000 men to the ranks of the Republicans, and won several victories, most notably at Guadalajara over an Italian motorized column in 1937. But, also in 1937, it was Fascist 'volunteers' who bombed the Basque capital of Guernica, horrifying the rest of the world. Germany provided Franco with 100 military planes (the 'Condor Legion'), and it was soon apparent that the German pilots were practising and perfecting a new technique, dive-bombing, on luckless Spanish civilians as well as the Republican forces. Italy

The Spanish Civil War, 1936–39

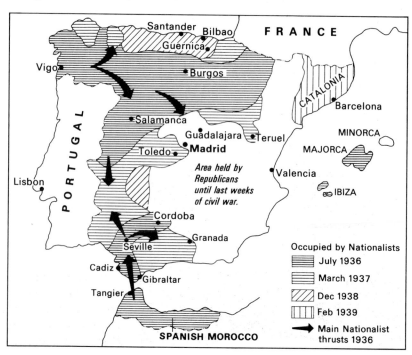

also supplied some 50,000 troops as well as aircraft, tanks and guns, although there was no official commitment by Mussolini to Franco.

The Course of the War

The war had four distinct phases. The first was in the autumn of 1936, when the Nationalists made rapid advances from Morocco into the southern province of Andalusia and then northwards into the heart of Spain, eventually linking up with other rebels fighting southwards from Galicia and Asturias in the north-west. This put the entire Portuguese frontier into Franco's hands, thereby restricting Republican trading possibilities.

During the second phase, in 1937, the Nationalists captured the Basque area around Bilbao, but suffered a defeat at Guadalajara and lost the recently captured town of Teruel. In 1938, the third phase of the war followed Franco's recovery of Teruel, when he turned against Valencia, only to be attacked by the Republicans across the River Ebro in July. This, the bloodiest of the battles, exhausted the Republicans, and by early 1939 they had started to fight amongst themselves, making the fourth and final phase of the war brief and emphatic. They lost control of Barcelona, Valencia and Madrid, and surrendered. 750,000 lives had been lost in the three years of fighting, 100,000 of them in cold-blooded executions.

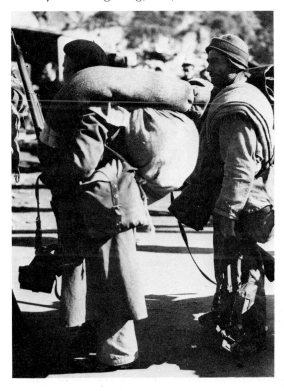

Men of the International Brigade fleeing from Spain into France, early in 1939, as Franco's troops closed in on the last centres of Republican resistance.

Franco, who as 'Caudillo' had taken an iron grip on both the Army and the Falangist movement, remained in power until his death in 1975.

The Spanish Civil War was the first clash of ideologies in the twentieth century. Whereas the First World War had been fought between similar but competing nations, the Spanish Civil War provided the battleground for Communism to challenge Fascism. Young men of the 1930s were invited to choose between these two creeds: in Britain, for example, it was not uncommon to find in school and university magazines articles and advertisements encouraging students to join Oswald Mosley's British Fascist movement, while at the same time many left-wing students were persuaded to join the Communist party.

In 1939, Franco signed the Anti-Comintern Pact created by Germany and Italy, but he attached little importance to it. In September 1939, he declared Spain neutral in the Second World War, and devoted himself to the painful, gradual process of unifying his country.

Inside Germany 1918-39

10

The Impact of Defeat

In September 1918, the German historian Meinecke wrote 'A fearful and gloomy existence awaits us ... Though my hatred of the enemy, who remind me of beasts of prey, is as hot as ever, so is my anger and resentment at those German power-politicians who have dragged us down into the abyss.' He spoke for all Germany. No country was more torn by internal division, more humiliated by defeat and more spurned by other nations, except perhaps Russia. But Russia already had a new government with a positive philosophy, and its isolation on the fringe of Europe gave it a chance to lick its own wounds in a way which the central position of Germany would not allow. Victorious enemies with their vindictive peace treaties were only one form of danger. The wild, conflicting ideas of those who wanted to take the place of William II's Reich and rebuild Germany were another.

Kiel, Communism and Kapp

In the final month of the First World War, fearing an ignominious surrender of his High Seas Fleet to the British, Admiral von Speer ordered the ships to sea, but sabotage and strikes by the sailors at Kiel made this impossible. On 5, 6, and 7 November 1918, Kiel, Hamburg, Hanover and Cologne all passed into the hands of workers, sailors and soldiers; northern Germany seemed lost to the Kaiser, and on 8 November a socialist leader, Kurt Eisner, proclaimed a Republic in Munich, capital of the southern state of Bavaria. On the next day, the Kaiser fled to Holland, and a German Republic was proclaimed under the rule of Friedrich Ebert, leader of the Majority Socialists (the S.P.D., or Social Democratic Party). Ebert was no revolutionary, though this transition is called the 'November Revolution'. The real left-wing extremists broke away from the S.P.D. in December 1918 and formed the K.P.D., the Communist Party, led by Karl Liebknecht and Rosa Luxemburg. In 1916 these two had published a magazine called *Spartacus Letters*, and the name 'Spartacists' became attached to their followers, an emotive echo of the days when Roman slaves rebelled under the leadership of an escaped gladiator, Spartacus. Like Spartacus, Liebknecht and Luxemburg came to a violent end, after a fortnight of street-fighting in Berlin in January 1919.

The Spartacists were the sort of urban Communist group on whom Lenin and the Bolsheviks had rested their hopes of German (and then World) Revolution just a year before, when they were considering the Treaty of Brest-Litovsk. With the same thought in mind, German right-wingers reacted very strongly against the Workers' and Soldiers' Councils and the Spartacists, and raised the 'Free Corps', a semi-military force of ex-soldiers and volunteers which was violently anti-Communist. The repressive tactics and unrestrained brutality of the Free Corps, many of whom turned up later in Hitler's S.A. and S.S., broke up all the genuine and constructive working class movements, and nearly produced a successful right-wing coup in the Kapp Putsch of March 1920. When the government ordered two brigades of the Free Corps to disband, they took over Berlin, led by Kapp, a right-wing politician and Ludendorff, the former Chief of Staff. A general strike paralysed the movement and caused its collapse, but not before the helmet-badge of one brigade, the swastika, had been prominently displayed in the nation's capital.

The Weimar Constitution

The troubles in Berlin in early 1919 deflected the first meeting of

Paul von Hindenburg (1847–1934), hero of the First World War and second President of the Weimar Republic.

the National Constituent Assembly to the little town of Weimar on the Elbe. Although the Assembly returned to Berlin in 1920, the name 'Weimar Republic' had become attached to the Constitution devised there, and to Germany itself until 1933.

The Constitution was republican, federal and democratic. It was to be headed by a President elected for seven years (Ebert held this post from 1919 until his death in 1925, and Hindenburg from then until 1934), whose main task was to appoint the Chancellor, who in turn would appoint the Cabinet Ministers who would be responsible to the Reichstag (the lower house of Parliament). The other major role of the President was defined in Article 48 of the Constitution: 'He may, if the public safety and order of the country are considerably disturbed and endangered, take such measures as are necessary to restore public safety and order. If necessary, he may intervene with the help of the armed forces. For this purpose, he may temporarily suspend, either partially or wholly, the Fundamental Rights...'.

The Fundamental Rights were clear and basic to the Constitution, having been based on those in other Western democracies. Voting rights were given to women; there was proportional representation in the Reichstag, where most legislation was argued and enacted, while the Reichsrat (the upper house) had the power to hold up the passage of a proposed law. The Reichsrat was elected on a federal basis, for like the Empire before it, the Weimar

Germany after Versailles

Republic respected the differing desires and attitudes of the separate states that Bismarck had brought together to form a united Germany. The central government was strong, with more power over the states than William had held, but it was not empowered by the Constitution to control the economy by the nationalization of major industries or the establishment of corporations as was about to happen in Italy.

The moderate Socialists of the S.P.D. held the balance in Weimar politics for a little over a year, but they were never unchallenged. The humiliations of the Treaty of Versailles tainted them with the defeat for which they had not been responsible. It was their representatives who signed the Treaty with its hateful Article 231 which seemed to accept 'war guilt': 'The Allied and Associated Governments affirm, and Germany accepts, the responsibility of Germany and her allies for causing all the loss and damage to which the Allied and Associated Governments have been subjected as a consequence of the war imposed on them by the aggression of Germany and her allies.' It was easy to hate the Socialists and Republicans, and to suggest that, since there had been no true military defeat in 1918, it was a 'stab in the back' by certain politicians that had brought the Empire down. In 1921 Erzberger who had signed the Treaty was murdered; in 1922, Walter Rathenau, the Minister of Reconstruction, was also killed. By that time, elections were showing distinct swings towards the extremes of left and right, so that the political fabric of the centre was becoming increasingly stretched. Uneasy coalitions of Centre and Catholic politicians still held office, but power was passing to those with economic or political ruthlessness.

Reparations and the Ruhr

In 1921, the Allied Reparation Commission announced that Germany would be expected to pay 132,000,000,000 gold marks (£6,600,000,000 in sterling at that time) to the victorious Allies in order to atone for the damage they had caused. Such a burden was also intended to weaken Germany permanently. France was to receive the major share. 1,000,000,000 gold marks were to be paid within 25 days, a target which was achieved by the German government by the simple expedient of printing paper marks, and then selling them for gold and other 'hard' currencies on the foreign exchange market. The effect was to drive down the international value of the paper mark from 60 to the dollar in May 1921 to 310 to the dollar in November. The Wiesbaden Agreement of October 1921 authorized the Germans to pay off more in kind and less in money, but even so, it was clear by early 1922 that the German economy could not stand the strain of the reparations target. It was also clear that the French right wing, led by the Prime Minister Raymond Poincaré, intended the Germans to pay up, in cash, and not in goods which might compete with French products.

By late 1922, the weak coalition government of Cuno in Germany was claiming that without ruining the value of the mark and destroying the Weimar economy, 20,000,000,000 gold marks was all that could be offered. In January 1923, French and Belgian troops began to occupy the Ruhr, the major industrial area on the east bank of the Rhine, in an attempt to force the Germans to produce 'productive pledges' of reparations payment. Rather than working harder, the Germans of the Ruhr started a campaign of passive resistance and sabotage. Strikes and go-slows were called; machines broke down; trains were derailed; productivity dropped.

This resulted, as intended, in the frustration of the French, but Germany suffered heavily too. The Ruhr was supposed to supply 85 per cent of German coal; without it, German industry slowed up all over the country. Unemployment rose; demands for government aid rose (at a time when the costs of war pensions were already high) and taxes fell. Industrialists and bankers would not permit the government under Cuno to make radical changes in the economic structure. The Dawes Commission later reported that 'the wealthier classes have escaped with far less than their proper share of the national burden.' In August Cuno resigned the Chancellorship with obvious relief. The political atmosphere in Germany was like that of 1918, with a tattered economy and rock-bottom morale. The amount of reparations demanded; the passive resistance in the Ruhr; the incompetent handling of the economy by politicians who were surrounded by self-interested advisers; the damage done by four years of blockade, war and disruption: all these rushed Germany to spectacular ruin in 1923.

Inflation in 1923 and the Dawes Plan of 1924

Between 1920 and 1923, the German governments overspent their income by 31,771 million marks. They made up the deficit in the same way that they paid their reparations in 1921: by using the printing press. By the end of 1923, 1,783 presses were running night and day to try to keep up with the demand for paper money, which was so plentiful that it lost its value before it got from the press to the bank. The American dollar, which in July 1914 had been worth 4.2 marks, had increased in value to 8.9 marks by the end of the war. Thereafter the mark slipped away dramatically. To buy one dollar on the international exchange in July 1920 cost 39.5 marks; in July 1922, it cost 493 marks; in July 1923, it cost 353,412 marks, and in the four succeeding months the price rocketed up to 4,200,000,000,000 marks. Monthly salaries were paid in hundreds of billions of marks. Special work-breaks were created for people to go out and shop, because massive price-rises occurred several times a day. People took their money around in wheelbarrows; the wheelbarrows were more valuable than the load of money, and therefore more likely to be stolen. Life became a hysterical farce, so painful and disrupted that people passed beyond worry. Prices were meaningless; the savings of a lifetime were not worth a spent match; there was no more stability, and no way of planning individual businesses, let alone the whole economy. By December 1923, more than 70 per cent of the workforce had been sacked by employers unable to pay the spiralling wages.

Two sets of policies dragged Germany out of chaos. The first was the internal work of Gustav Stresemann, who as Chancellor for three months only, persuaded the people of the Ruhr to end passive resistance, and launched a new controlled currency (Rentenmark) which restored hope and then confidence. Although unable to calm the political volcano for long, Stresemann did manage to refashion the economy, and thus open the way for constructive help from the Allies over the question of reparations. This second set of policies incorporated the Dawes Plan of 1924 and the Young Plan of 1929.

The Dawes Plan was the result of a report made by an international commission on the payment of reparations. It acknowledged all the difficulties that the Germans were facing, and proposed a scaling down of payments; they were to start at 1,000,000,000 gold marks per annum, rising to 2,500,000,000 in 1928 and thereafter. But to make these repayments possible, the French were to evacuate the Ruhr, and the Americans were to lend substantial amounts to German industry. In 1929, this Plan was further amended by the Young Plan; the total amount payable was cut to 121,000,000,000 marks, and the instalments were to be spread over 59 years, making the final payment due in 1988. In practice, President Hoover suspended the payments of all war debts in 1931, and they were never resumed; ironically, Germany received more in loans and aid than she actually paid out in reparations after the war.

The Stresemann Era, 1923–29

Gustav Stresemann founded the German People's Party (D.V.P.) in 1919 out of the old right-wing National Liberal Party. Never a keen republican, he nonetheless wanted to see Germany make the best possible recovery from her humiliation in 1918, even if that meant first accepting all the terms of the Treaty of Versailles, and then having them revised by international consent. After a brief spell as Chancellor leading a 'Grand Coalition' in the heart of the 1923 crisis (see above), he became Foreign Minister until his death in 1929. His policy of 'national realism' was not always popular in Germany, even within his own party, but he kept office through several changes of coalition government, and gained an international reputation which won him the Nobel Peace Prize in 1926, in symbolic partnership with Briand of France.

His achievement was to make Germany acceptable again in the diplomatic corridors of the world. The Dawes Plan of 1924 was a sign of international sympathy and understanding for German problems; the Locarno Pact in 1925 (see Chapter 3) subtly increased German bargaining power while accepting the new Franco-German borders. In 1926, Stresemann achieved the admission of Germany to the League of Nations, a Neutrality Pact with Russia and the evacuation of much of the Rhineland by the Allies, who had been there since the war. In 1928, he signed the Kellogg-Briand Pact, and in 1929, he was negotiating the Young Plan and the final Allied evacuation of the Rhineland before his death at the age of 51.

Stresemann's death occurred in October 1929. Just three weeks later, the American Stock Market on Wall Street collapsed. The financial depression that followed was the primary cause of the collapse of the internal political and economic structures that had been built up in the preceding six years, and of the international understandings that Stresemann had forged. It also catapulted Adolf Hitler upwards towards power.

Adolf Hitler's early years

Born in 1889, the son of a minor Customs official, Hitler's early career was undistinguished. He failed to obtain the normal school-leaver's certificate; he failed twice to get into the Vienna Academy of Fine Arts; he failed his army medical test in early 1914 in Austria. But he volunteered successfully for a Bavarian regiment in the German army as soon as war broke out, and achieved promotion to the rank of corporal, and two decorations. The second, the Iron Cross, First Class, was rarely earned by a non-commissioned officer, and was therefore a real tribute to his bravery in the front line, where he ran with messages for Headquarters. He was once wounded, once gassed. After the war, having enjoyed more success and comradeship in the Army than in civilian life, he stayed in his regiment until 1920, acting from 1919 onwards as army political agent for the German Workers' Party in Munich, a party of which he was Member Number Seven. In 1920, the party changed its name to National Socialist German Workers' Party (abbreviated to 'Nazi') and by 1921, Hitler had so established himself by his fiery oratory, and his fanatical devotion to the cause of the party, that he became its 'Führer', its dictatorial leader.

What did the Party stand for? Its first programme appeared in 1920, and among its 25 points it called for the creation of a Greater Germany, the expulsion of Jews from office or citizenship or in some cases the country, the takeover of much of the economy by the State, the destruction of the Treaty of Versailles and the massive strengthening of central government. These points never substantially changed.

The Munich Putsch of 1923 and *Mein Kampf*

In the hectic days of 1923, especially after the end of passive resistance in the Ruhr, extremist groups sprouted like weeds in the fertile soil of hyper-inflated Germany. Only the loyalty of the Army saved Stresemann's government on several occasions, but by November only Bavaria (which had always resented being tied to northern, Protestant Germany) looked likely to declare independence from the Weimar Republic. It was therefore the natural place for Hitler's bid for power. On 8 November 1923, he invaded a political meeting in a Munich beer hall where 3,000 people were listening to Kahr, the State Commissioner. 'The National Revolution has begun,' he proclaimed, after getting attention by firing his revolver at the ceiling. The meeting was less convinced, although the inclusion of General Ludendorff in Hitler's forces was impressive. On the next day, the Nazis set out to capture the centre of Munich with 3,000 brown-shirted storm troopers; Hitler and Ludendorff led the column. Stopped by a volley of rifle fire from 100 policemen, the Nazis fled. Ludendorff marched proudly forward, to inevitable arrest; Hitler dislocated his shoulder as he fell prostrate for safety. Sixteen Nazis were killed, and the 'putsch' collapsed in ignominious failure.

The trial of the ten men who were held responsible for the attempt was, however, a triumph for Hitler's oratory. 'The court (of History) will judge us as Germans who wanted only the good of their own people and Fatherland, who wanted to fight and die.' Sentenced to five years' imprisonment instead of the possible life sentence, and released less than nine months later, Hitler had obviously struck a chord of sympathy in his judges and gaolers. In prison, he dictated to his later deputy, Rudolf Hess, the first chapters of *Mein Kampf*, the book which became the Nazi bible. First published in 1925, it expanded on the points made in the

An English cartoonist makes fun of Hitler's famous powers of oratory, and at the same time points out his untrustworthiness.

Party programme of 1920, but was more specific. Germany needed living room ('lebensraum'), which it would seek in the east. France must be destroyed. The purity of the Aryan race must be emphasized, and those who had diluted or opposed it must be eradicated; he specified the Jews and the Slavs. Strong leadership would make pure Germans 'lords of the earth'.

Mein Kampf is a dull, rambling book. Few people read it until Hitler had come to power. For his opponents, by then it was too late.

1924–33

For five years after Hitler's trial, the Nazi party quietly consolidated its ideas and organization without expanding significantly. The brown-shirted S.A. ('Sturmabteilungen' – assault division) were reorganized in 1925 under Röhm, and attracted many thuggish ex-members of the right-wing Free Corps which had exercised irregular power in 1919 and 1920. The S.S. ('Schutzstaffeln' – protection squads) were hand-picked, zealous supporters of Hitler, led by Himmler who was later to become Head of the Gestapo (secret police), Head of Reich Administration and Minister of the Interior. Hermann Goering, wounded in the 1923 putsch, brought military distinction to the early Nazis, being an air ace and former commander of 'the Red Baron' Richthofen's Squadron. He became Speaker of the Reichstag in 1932. Joseph Goebbels was another early Nazi with a dramatic flair for words; appointed leader of the Berlin Nazis in 1926, he went on to take charge of Nazi propaganda, and in 1933 became the youngest minister in the history of the Republic, his post being the ominous-sounding Minister of Enlightenment and Propaganda. Frick became the leader of the few Nazis in the Reichstag in 1924, while Streicher, another veteran of the Munich putsch, became known as a vehement Jew-baiter.

In the Reichstag, the Nazis had little power and only 12 seats in 1928. But in 1929 came negotiations over the Young Plan, a tightening of American credit to Europe, and then the Wall Street Crash. Hitler's tough economic and nationalist attitudes attracted the support of industrialists like Hugenburg, and the use of their newspapers. In 1929, 800,000 people voted Nazi; in 1930 as the Depression hit Germany and unemployment soared, 6,000,000 votes gave the Nazis 107 seats in the Reichstag. Dark memories of the economic chaos of 1923 stirred the middle classes who had been ruined by the loss of their life-savings; the spectre of hopeless unemployment haunted the workers; the fear of Communist exploitation of capitalism's disaster drove businessmen to seek strong allies. Like the Fascists in Italy, Hitler's uncompromising Nazism seemed to offer security to each insecure group in German society. The tensions generated could be released against scapegoats like the Jews or the American bankers, while the Nazis guaranteed a solution to each class's specific problems.

In 1932, Hitler's share of the poll for President of the Republic was 37 per cent (as opposed to Hindenburg's 53 per cent): in the Reichstag elections, the Nazis became the largest party with 230 seats. Hitler's attempt to force his way into office as a result of this was very clumsy, and led to fresh elections in which the Nazis lost two million votes. This reduced the threat of his power, and in a series of complicated intrigues, his main political rivals, von Papen of the Catholic Centre Party and von Schleicher, one-time Minister of Defence and briefly Chancellor of the Republic, persuaded the aged President Hindenburg to appoint Hitler as Chancellor. Each man thought that Hitler, inexperienced at this level, would need his support and might therefore become manageable. They were both mistaken.

The Reichstag Fire and the Nazi Revolution

Hitler became Chancellor on 30 January 1933, with two other Nazis (Frick and Goering) in his Coalition Cabinet. Claiming that he did not have enough support to govern properly, he persuaded Hindenburg to dissolve the Reichstag and call fresh elections. On 27 February 1933, just a week before the end of a bitter campaign, especially between the Nazis and the Communists, the Reichstag building was burnt to the ground. A half-witted Dutchman, van der Lubbe, was arrested and shot for the crime of arson, though it is unlikely that he had the intelligence or the equipment to start such an effective fire in a public building. The most 'incriminating' evidence against him was his membership of the Communist Party. Eventually in 1942 Goering claimed responsibility for the fire; in 1933 the discrediting of the Communists was an important part of the Nazis' campaign to attract electoral support.

The election result did not show the swing to the Nazis that Hitler expected. His 288 seats in the Reichstag added to the 52 of Hugenberg's National Party gave him a small overall majority in the 647-seat Chamber, but to gain power independent of the control of President or Reichstag, he needed an Enabling Act passed by a two-thirds majority. By arresting or banning 81 Communist deputies, locking up 12 Socialists and promising the Catholic Centre Party a written guarantee of all fundamental rights, Hitler arranged an impressive majority of 441 to 94 in favour of the Enabling Act. He was now *legally* dictator for four years. The Third Reich thus began in 1933.

There followed a programme of 'national awakening' and 'co-ordination'. State Parliaments were re-formed, without elections, to have the same proportion of parties as in the Reichstag. Thus Nazism predominated everywhere. In February 1934, the Reichs-rat (the upper, federal house of Parliament) was abolished, bringing everything under the control of Hitler's Berlin Government. All other political parties had already been banned (July 1933); trade unions were suppressed and merged into a National Labour Front in May 1933. Within a year of the Enabling Act, only two organizations could possibly challenge Hitler: the Armed Forces, or his own supreme Nazi Party.

The risk was real. The Army generals resented the meteoric rise of this Austrian corporal with his political thugs of the S.A. and S.S. The S.A., on the other hand, were frustrated not to have been given more power and freedom; their leader Röhm was unwise enough to put it into words: 'I'm the nucleus of the new army.' On 30 June 1934, 'the Night of the Long Knives', Hitler solved both aspects of his problem by dozens of cold-blooded murders. Röhm and all other significant leaders of the S.A. were shot; General von Schleicher disappeared, as did Kahr, the State Commissioner of Bavaria at the time of the Munich putsch, and other men who stood in the way of Hitler's political ambitions. By protecting the Army as well as himself from Röhm's challenge, Hitler won the support of the Army. When Hindenburg died in August 1934, Hitler became President, and Commander in Chief of the Armed Forces. He was already Chancellor and Führer of the Party. Totalitarianism was complete.

The Nazi Economy

Hitler had ridden to power on a wave of economic troubles; the maintenance of his position depended not only on a Stalin-like purge of rivals, but also on an economic policy like Roosevelt's New Deal. Hitler too 'primed the pump'. The unemployed were organized into building the autobahnen (Europe's first motorways), canals, public offices and new factories; a billion Reichsmarks of government funds were made available. Private industry took heart and expanded also, and the government took special interest in the development of synthetic materials, notably alloys, fuels, artificial rubber and certain foodstuffs. Farmers were given high status in laws from 1933 onwards. From the outset, the Nazis wanted to reduce Germany's reliance on strategic imports of raw materials and food. In 1936, a Four Year Plan was announced, to be directed by Goering, and in a secret memorandum, Hitler demanded that the economy 'must be capable of supporting war in four years'. By a narrow margin, this was achieved.

Rearmament started seriously in 1935, when Hitler rejected the Versailles Treaty which limited his Army, and when he made a Naval Pact with Britain which allowed him to expand his Navy. With a million young men being sucked into the Armed Forces, Hitler had no unemployment problem (only 34,000 in August 1939). German workers were economically secure while the rearmament programme lasted, and their lack of trade unions was

Hitler won popularity by giving work to the unemployed. In return, they gave him power, and support.

compensated for by the 'Strength through Joy' movement, which provided holidays and recreations of all sorts for good workers. The 'People's Car' ('Volkswagen') was in mass production, and as the general standard of living rose, most families could realistically plan for the day when they might own such a car. Considering the plight of Germany in 1932, when the number of unemployed was just under six million, some sort of economic miracle had been achieved, though a dangerous and a costly one. It was dangerous because it was badly financed and its continuation was dependent on a war economy and territorial expansion; it was costly because it had been built by a regime which dealt ruthlessly with the rights and lives of innocent people, particularly the Jews.

Life in a Police State

From its earliest days, the Nazi Party used violence. After the suppression of the S.A. in 1934, the S.S. under Himmler took complete control of 'security'. Individual rights became meaningless. All children went through the regimentation of the 'Hitler Youth' movement, to 'National Labour Service', then to the Armed Forces. Children were encouraged to spy on their parents, to put the state and the Führer before everything. The Ministry for Propaganda and Enlightenment censored books and broadcasts, while Nuremburg became the centre of fanatical, emotional rallies. By glorious stage-management and by terror, the Nazi code of intolerance, aggression, inequality and distrust was forced onto a population that had voted for Hitler in good faith in 1932, and had confirmed his power in plebiscites pressed on them in 1934 and 1935.

The people who suffered most were the Jews. Hitler did not create German anti-Semitism, but he channelled it. From early days he blamed the collapse of Germany in the First War on 'November criminals and Jews'. Within six weeks of becoming Chancellor, he weeded Jews out of Civil Service posts, and fostered a poisonous campaign of anti-Jewish propaganda which called for the isolation and punishment of Jewish 'profiteers and speculators' (i.e. shop-keepers and businessmen). Jews were forbidden entry to most universities and the professions, and in the Nuremberg Laws of 1935, Aryan blood became a necessary qualification for German citizenship. Jews could neither be, nor marry, German citizens. Notices in public parks said 'No Jews wanted here'; any Jew was dogged by physical, economic and psychological persecution. On 9 November 1938, a new climax was reached on 'Krystallnacht', so named because of the hundreds of thousands of panes of glass in Jewish property which were smashed deliberately. Synagogues were burnt to the ground; 7,000 businesses were destroyed and thousands of Jews were beaten up, some losing their lives. Goering added to the attack by confiscating their insurance payments so that they could not repair their houses, and by passing a Decree on Eliminating Jews from German Economic Life. Other Nazis were beginning to talk of a 'final solution', the total elimination of the Jews. In the end, by means of forced labour, concentration camps and open murder in the ghettos, the Nazis were responsible for the deaths of perhaps 6,000,000 Jews out of just over 8,000,000 who lived in Central Europe in the early 1930s.

The Nazis eventually built over 30 major concentration camps,

Even beer mats became vehicles for propaganda. The slogan reads: 'Whoever buys from a Jew is a traitor to his people.'

some with the main purpose of exterminating their victims, like Auschwitz and Treblinka, and others for imprisoning, punishing, enslaving and eventually liquidating the victims, like Dachau and Ravensburg, Buchenwald and Sachsenhausen. Not only Jews were brought there. Official Gestapo records for April 1939 show 112,432 people convicted of 'political crimes' and another 162,734 people in 'protective custody'. Among them were Communists and Socialists, and representatives of all Christian Churches. Pastor Niemoller of the Lutheran Church was an outspoken opponent of the Nazis who suffered for his courage but survived, but thousands of other pastors and priests perished. The Catholic Church had made an agreement (Concordat) with the Nazis in 1933, but it did not protect it from constant harassment. In 1937 Pope Pius XI published *Mit Brennender Sorge* (*With Burning Anxiety*), accusing the Nazis of breaking the agreement and practising hateful racialism. (For German Foreign Policy in the 1930s, see Chapter 11.)

The Thirties: Years of Depression and the Road to War

11

In the 1920s and 1930s, there was plenty of talk of ideals (internationalism, democracy, justice, 'peace in our time') and of positive ideologies (Communism, Fascism, Socialism, Nazism). But the facts of the 1920s, and even more of the 1930s, show that national security was more important than anything else.

In the last resort, nations threatened by unemployment, economic depression, military insecurity or political instability trusted only themselves, thereby stimulating others to do the same.

For most of the 1920s, the atmosphere was nonetheless optimistic (see Chapter 3). Yet in October, economic confidence in the West collapsed following the Wall Street Crash (see Chapter 5), and the last six months of 1929 witnessed the disappearance of several characters whose presence was essential for stability. In Britain, the assured, comfortable government of Stanley Baldwin gave way to a new Labour Ministry (dependent on Liberal support) under the relatively inexperienced Ramsay MacDonald. In France, Prime Minister Poincaré retired through ill-health, and his former Foreign Minister Briand took over the cares of domestic affairs, only a few months before his German opposite number in much of the reconstruction of the 1920s, Gustav Stresemann, died. In 1929 also, Trotsky was expelled from Russia as Stalin cemented himself into an unchallenged position; Herbert Hoover was inaugurated as President of the United States.

In spite of these changes, and the growing economic hardship, there was still some international optimism on the subject of disarmament.

Disarmament

Disarmament was one of Woodrow Wilson's 14 Points. Only one of the major negotiating powers at Versailles expressed reservations about the principle of disarmament, and that was the power that had been the victim of the strategy of the Schlieffen Plan, France. The French argued that, rather than disarmament leading to greater security, the plan should be for greater security by means of alliances, which must precede any serious attempt at disarmament. Whereas most countries interpreted security as being security against war, the French preferred to think of it as security against defeat. In 1923, the Assembly of the League considered a Draft Treaty of Mutual Assistance which was designed to reassure French worries, but the British and the Scandinavians rejected it. In 1924, the Geneva Protocol was another attempt to allay French fears, again squashed by Britain (see Chapter 3), but in 1925, the Locarno Pact was accepted by France, Britain, Germany, Italy and Belgium. This web of alliances and guarantees, which led also to German admission to the League, made the quest for disarmament worth pursuing once more.

The main Disarmament Conference opened in Geneva in 1932, with some 60 nations attending, including several who were not members of the League, like Russia and America. The opening ceremony was delayed for a few hours because of the news that the forces of one of the represented powers, Japan, which was also a permanent member of the Council of the League, were attacking Shanghai, the territory of another. It was an ominous start to the Conference, for which a Preparatory Commission had been planning for the past six years, but it was characteristic of the way in which the selfish intentions of one country often blocked the universal ideal. In 1927, Britain firmly indicated her reluctance to cut her number of cruisers; in 1928, nineteen out of the 24 powers in the Preparatory Commission flatly rejected the simplest of all ideas – complete disarmament by every power, suggested by Russia. In 1930, France and Italy refused to accept a formula for relative strengths suggested at the London Naval Conference, and in 1932, at the main Conference, Britain declared itself not prepared to ban aerial bombing in future wars.

The Conference sat for five months in 1932, and eight months in 1933, but its discussions in each year ran into difficulties because of German and French attitudes. In 1932, Germany withdrew from negotiations on the grounds that, as she did not have equal status in armaments anyway, she was at a diplomatic disadvantage in a *Dis*armament Conference. In 1933, she argued that she should at least have the prototypes of any weapons maintained by other powers, despite being expressly forbidden to have tanks, guns and aircraft by the Treaty of Versailles. Meanwhile France pursued her line towards security by proposing that all continental powers should be allowed conscript armies. In the light of Hitler's accession to power in Germany, this proposal fitted in with the growing feeling that rearmament should be controlled rather than forbidden, but in October 1933, Hitler withdrew Germany from the Conference and from the League. The Conference broke up in despair, and apart from a fortnight's effort in 1934, it never met again.

The Aggressors

Once the Disarmament Conference had collapsed, diplomatic initiative passed into the hands of three powers, Italy, Germany and Japan, though it was not until 1936 that their aims and activities were in any way coordinated with each other.

The Italian policy of the early 1930s was aimed at the renegotiation of the Versailles settlement so that Italy could dominate central Southern Europe and the heart of the Mediterranean; it depended on a weak Weimar Republic, a weak Austria, and the goodwill of France and Britain. Thus the rise of Hitler threatened Mussolini's position. 'He is quite mad ... a silly little

Areas of League of Nations activities

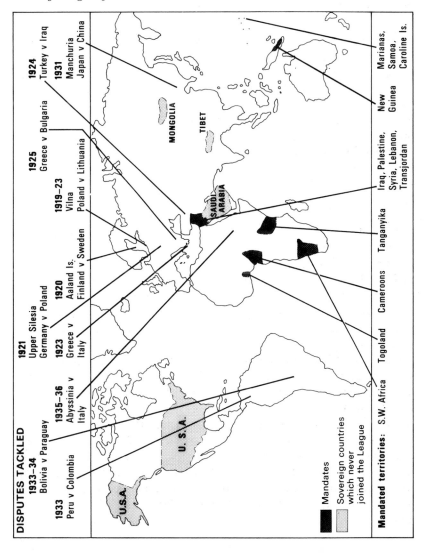

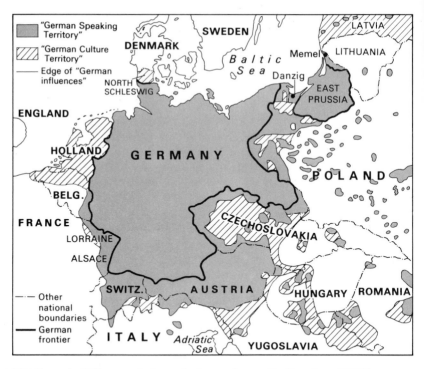

The Spread of 'German Influence', drawn from a Berlin atlas of 1936

clown' was his personal opinion, and in July 1934 he rushed Italian troops to the Brenner Pass on the Austrian frontier when it looked as if Hitler might try to take advantage of a Nazi revolt in Vienna (see Chapter 9). Although in 1935 Mussolini maintained his friendly relationship with France and Britain in the Stresa Front, his attack on Ethiopia indicated his real ambitions and brought him into closer harmony with Hitler, who offered his support to Italy when the League of Nations voted to use economic sanctions against Mussolini. In 1936, the 'Rome-Berlin Axis' was established to provide joint military help for Franco in Spain, and in May 1939 the 'Pact of Steel' bound Italy and Germany together in an agreement that was both defensive and aggressive.

Germany's aims in the 1930s were crystal-clear, for they were laid down in *Mein Kampf*, and were a major part of Hitler's appeal to the German electorate in 1932 and 1933. They entailed a total rejection of the humiliations of the Versailles settlement, and the establishment of German control over Central Europe, followed by a search for 'Lebensraum' ('living space') to the east. Having left the League of Nations in 1933, Hitler took no part in any other international plan for European resettlement. He worked by playing off one nation against another, making a 10-year non-aggression pact with Poland in 1934 and a naval agreement with Britain in 1935 while mounting an increasing challenge to the

Versailles Treaty by reintroducing conscription (1935), reoccupying the Rhineland (1936) and then embarking on three massive stages of expansion involving Austria, Czechoslovakia and Poland. He was not challenged before 1939 because Britain and France could not accept that such aggressive intentions could or would be carried out. They believed that sweet reason and appeasement would in practice restrict Hitler's demands.

The Japanese had no interest in Europe, but like Hitler and Mussolini had been condemned by the League, in their case for their invasion of Manchuria in 1931 and the consequent creation of the puppet state of Manchukuo in 1932. They withdrew from the League in 1933, but as they looked for further expansion on the Asian mainland to absorb their rising population and to fulfil their economic demands, they faced possible hostility from Russia. For this reason they signed an Anti-Comintern Pact with Germany in 1936, which Italy joined in 1937, and in 1940 all three aggressors signed a pact which was intended to discourage American interference in any of their selfish ambitions.

The Critical Year – 1935

After the shock of Germany's withdrawal from the Disarmament Conference and the League in October 1933, 1934 witnessed a scramble by France and by Italy to clarify their standing with Poland and Austria respectively. But 1935 opened with the completion of one of the Versailles arrangements, to the total satisfaction of Hitler and the chagrin of the French.

Under the terms of the Treaty of Versailles, the Saarland and its coalmines had been administered by France on behalf of the League for 15 years, after which a plebiscite was to be held in which the Saarlanders themselves would decide whether they wanted the arrangement to continue, or preferred union with France, or reunion with Germany. The vote was held in January 1935. 8.8 per cent of the electorate wanted the existing arrangement; 0.4 per cent wanted union with France; an overwhelming 90.3 per cent opted for reunion with Germany. The obvious hopes of the French (and to a lesser extent the British) were rebuffed by their own treaty. The Saar became part of Germany again on 1 March.

Before the month was up, Hitler had pressed home his psychological advantage by announcing that Germany already had a new Luftwaffe (expressly forbidden by the Treaty of Versailles) and that he was introducing conscription so that Germany could raise an army of 36 divisions, five times larger than the Versailles limit. This explicit challenge to the diplomats of Europe posed different threats to each country. For the French, their own security was at stake; for the British, more trusting, the balance of power; for the Italians, their secret ambitions in Africa. A hasty meeting at Stresa in April 1935 produced a formula from the leaders of these three countries that they would collaborate by all practicable means against any repudiation of treaties by any other country that might endanger peace.

To the British, the Stresa Front did not rule out the making of new agreements which might accommodate Hitler's Germany, provided that such agreements did not threaten peace. In June, an Anglo-German Naval Treaty agreed that Germany could have a surface fleet equivalent to 35 per cent of the tonnage of the Royal Navy, and a submarine fleet equal to 45 per cent of that of Great Britain. The French, fearful of any German rearmament, were aghast.

To Mussolini, the Stresa Front meant that Britain and France would ensure that Hitler would take no aggressive action against Austria while Italy made a deliberate bid to enlarge her reputation and her Empire. In 1934, a clash between Ethiopians and Italians near the borders of Somaliland led to the death of 30 Italian soldiers, and a steadily escalating dispute. Early in 1935, Ethiopia, one of only two independent countries in Africa, appealed to the League for arbitration, but the Italians continued a steady build-up of troops in Eritrea and Somaliland, and in October 1935, without declaring war, invaded Ethiopia from north and south. Within four days, the Assembly of the League had branded Italy as an aggressor by 50 votes to one (Italy) with two abstentions (Austria and Hungary). Over a month later, it was agreed to apply economic sanctions against Italy, but excluding oil because France and Britain would not use their navies to prevent its shipment. Britain and France were not fully agreed on how to treat the Ethiopian crisis: Britain was prepared to be stern with Italy, but France preferred to try delicate handling in order to keep Italian support against Germany. In November the British Foreign Secretary, Sir Samuel Hoare, met the French premier, Pierre Laval, and devised a scheme whereby Ethiopia would surrender

Ethiopian equipment was primitive. An oil embargo imposed by the League of Nations would have held up the Italian invasion without hindering Ethiopian resistance.

virtually two-thirds of its area in exchange for a guaranteed corridor to the sea. When the Hoare-Laval Plan leaked out, a massive public protest forced the resignation of Hoare, and his replacement by Anthony Eden. But the damage was done; it was clear that neither France nor Britain would readily make a stand on a point of principle, and that neither Germany nor Italy would miss a chance of self-aggrandizement.

1936 and 1937 – The League Defied

In May 1936, the Italians captured Addis Ababa, capital of Ethiopia, and solemnly declared Victor Emmanuel III as Emperor. The three areas of Ethiopia, Eritrea and Italian Somaliland were united as Italian East Africa, and Marshal Badoglio was appointed Viceroy. Much pride was taken in the new Empire, and much faith placed in it as a possible area for economic development. In July, the Council of the League acknowledged its defeat, in that it advised the abandonment of the sanctions policy. It had failed at its first and only full attempt, and it was clear that with America, Germany and Japan all outside the League, a successful sanctions policy would be most unlikely, even if the League itself could agree to enforce one. In December 1936, the League significantly changed its strategy, and in the instance of the Spanish Civil War passed a resolution that no other states might intervene in any way. This too was quickly shown to be an unenforceable policy as the Germans and Italians, non-members of the League, created the 'Rome-Berlin Axis' with the avowed aim to give military help to General Franco, while also recognizing him as the official Head of State. (See Chapter 9.)

Sanctions had a final airing after Japan had launched its attack against China in 1937 (see Chapter 8). This time, the Council of the League suggested that individual members of the League should apply their own sanctions against Japan. It was feeble advice, offered in 1938 and 1939, and universally ignored.

In March 1936, Hitler's troops occupied the area of the Rhineland that had been demilitarized by the Treaty of Versailles. It was his first territorial aggression. It has since been confirmed that his officers carried sealed orders to withdraw if any major resistance was encountered, but the German population greeted the soldiers as liberators (a plebiscite gave 98.8 per cent approval of the move) and the French government, uncertain of how much support it might get from Britain, was not prepared to risk another humiliation. The reoccupation of the Rhineland broke not only the Versailles arrangements, but also the 1925 Locarno Agreement, into which Germany had entered in the Stresemann era. Hitler's claim was that Locarno had already been broken by a Franco-Russian agreement in February 1936, making the whole Pact null and void. Belgium, victim of the 1914 dispute between Germany and France, quickly asked to be released from its Locarno commitments, and to be considered a totally neutral country once again.

With soldiers back in the Rhineland, Hitler could now build his line of fortifications to oppose the Maginot Line. The 'Siegfried Line' was constructed immediately, and was defensively powerful enough to make it obvious that France would be able to do very little to help Poland or her Little Entente allies in an emergency.

1938 – Anschluss with Austria (See also Chapter 7)

The union of Germany with Austria is proposed on the first page of *Mein Kampf*; it was a natural ambition for an Austrian who, as dictator of Germany, had always promised to recreate a Greater Germany.

In and after 1936, Italian protection of Austrian interests diminished as Mussolini became involved in Ethiopia and then Spain; German influence strengthened proportionately, and a pro-German Nazi party was soon in evidence. In January 1938, after the Austrian Nazis had attempted a 'putsch' which failed, Hitler intervened directly. Summoning the Austrian Chancellor Schuschnigg to his Bavarian reatreat at Berchtesgaden, he blatantly bullied him into appointing the leader of the Austrian Nazis, Seyss-Inquart, to the post of Minister of Public Security and the Interior. Schuschnigg agreed, but early in March he proclaimed that Austria was 'a free, German, independent, socialist, Christian and

During the 30s, the German swastika became a symbol to be feared and hated. But it merely attracted curiosity when it was displayed on this March of European Nazis in London, 1934.

united country', and invited the Austrians to register their support for it in a plebiscite, to be held four days later on 13 March. Hitler could not afford to wait; he demanded that Seyss-Inquart be appointed Chancellor in place of Schuschnigg, and under intense pressure, Schuschnigg resigned on 11 March. Seyss-Inquart took power, simultaneously inviting German troops to restore order. On 13 March, Hitler was in Vienna, proclaiming the Anschluss in front of crowds who divided clearly into the delighted and the distressed. Nevertheless the plebiscite held a month later throughout the new enlarged Germany gave a 99.7 per cent vote of approval. France, struggling from one ministry to another, made no resistance to the Anschluss; Britain took the line that if Germans wanted to be united, it was in the long run unreasonable of the Treaty of Versailles to prevent it.

Austria was immediately totally absorbed by the German system. Not only did the Nazis take over the government and the economic resources, at once purging them of Jews and soon of Catholics; they also had German troops in the Brenner Pass, where in 1934 Mussolini's men had safeguarded Austrian independence, and along the southern border of Czechoslovakia.

1938 – Czechoslovakia and Munich (See also Chapter 7)

The takeover of Czechoslovakia began as the Anschluss had begun, with a political party inside the country suggesting some sort of link with Germany. Czechoslovakia's territorial independence was better secured than Austria's had been, because she was the lynchpin of the Little Entente of 1920–21 (Czechoslovakia, Yugoslavia and Romania), further supported by mutual assistance treaties with France (1925) and Russia (1935). But when Henlein, leader of the Czech German (i.e., Nazi) Party stepped up the violence of his Party's demands for self-rule for the 3,000,000 Germans living in the Sudetenland (the western fringe of Czechoslovakia), the French and the British governments became deeply concerned. Early in August 1938, Neville Chamberlain, the chief exponent of Britain's policy of appeasement of the dictators, sent Lord Runciman to Prague as his special emissary, to give advice to the Czechs on what reasonable concessions they might make to Henlein. His advice amounted to virtual independence for the Sudeten Germans, but at that point Henlein refused to negotiate any further, while Hitler took up the cry that the Sudetenlanders had the right to determine their own future.

As riots increased in Czechoslovakia in early September, and German troops appeared to be massing on the borders, Chamberlain decided that only personal diplomacy at the highest level could preserve peace. After rapid consultation with Daladier of France, he flew to meet Hitler at Berchtesgaden. Three days later, in London, Chamberlain drafted a plan which was in keeping with

Hitler's intention of self-determination for the Sudeten Germans: the Czech government was to cede to Germany all areas containing more than 50 per cent German inhabitants. On 19 September Chamberlain and Daladier tried to persuade President Beneš of Czechoslovakia that this was a necessary sacrifice, a task that took 48 hours. On 22 September, Chamberlain undertook his second flight to Germany, and to his horror he discovered at Godesberg that Germany would not accept the '50 per cent' formula. Instead, Hitler presented an ultimatum demanding the immediate cession of all Sudeten areas, announcing that military occupation by the Germans would follow between 26 and 28 September. Neither the Czechs, nor their allies the French, nor the British, could accept this.

On 24 September the Czechs mobilized their army, while the French called up their reservists, although Hitler announced that the date for his occupation of the Sudetenland had been moved to 1 October. War seemed inevitable; on 28 September, the British fleet was mobilized, and at home civilians prepared for hostilities by building air-raid shelters and issuing gas-masks. Chamberlain still sought compromise, and a message to Hitler brought in return an invitation to a Four Power Conference in Munich.

The 12 hours of bargaining at Munich (29 September 1938) changed little of the terms of the Godesberg Memorandum, but Hitler and Mussolini persuaded Chamberlain and Daladier to accept them, in the interests of peace. The Four Powers agreed to act together as an international commission supervising the transfer of the Sudetenland, and guaranteeing the revised frontiers of Czechoslovakia. The Czechs were not consulted, but informed of the decision on 30 September; they were also told to hand over to Poland the part of Teschen which they had held since 1920. On 5 October, as German troops swarmed over the strategic points of the Sudetenland, President Beneš resigned, knowing that his

Munich, September 1938. From the left, N. Chamberlain, Daladier, Hitler, Mussolini, and Mussolini's son-in-law, Count Ciano, who was Italy's Foreign Minister.

country could not last long.

Chamberlain, apparently less aware of the implications of Munich, had already returned to England promising 'peace in our time'. To a population who three days before had been filling sandbags in the sad expectation of war, he was a deliverer, a statesman of the highest degree, despite Churchill's bitter comment: 'The German dictator, instead of snatching his victuals from the table, has been content to have them served to him course by course.'

1939 – Prague, Albania and the Russo-German Pact

The strategic significance of the Sudetenland which Chamberlain had yielded to Hitler was that the defence of all Czechoslovakia depended on it. Not only was the frontier with Germany aligned along the natural barrier of the Bohemian mountains, but it was further strengthened by a Czech version of the Maginot Line, which was manned by an efficient army backed by a strong armaments industry. All this was rendered useless by the Munich agreement. In March 1939, the Czechs had no way of stopping the Germans as they imposed a Protectorate over Bohemia-Moravia, the entire western half of Czechoslovakia, while Hungary simultaneously seized the eastern quarter, Ruthenia. The remaining chunk, Slovakia, retained nominal independence, but the country of Czechoslovakia had vanished. Within a week, Hitler had seized Memel from Lithuania, and was demanding his next course: German occupation of Danzig, and the establishment of a German land-link with East Prussia which would cut the Polish corridor. Since 1933 Danzig had been ruled by the local Nazi Party, which had actively encouraged links with Hitler's Reich.

In April 1939, taking advantage of the diplomatic concern over

The Disintegration of Czechoslovakia, 1938–39

Poland and Germany, Mussolini launched an army of 100,000 men against the tiny state of Albania, just across the Adriatic from the 'heel' of Italy. In less than a fortnight, Victor Emmanuel III had added it to his Empire. Europe was not prepared to make an issue of its fate.

But by the end of March 1939, even Chamberlain and Daladier were prepared to make a stand if the dictators threatened Poland, Greece, Romania and Turkey. In that order, Britain and France offered 'all the support in our power' to preserve the independence of these states. It was a new, tough approach to Hitler, but in real terms it was unlikely to mean much, unless it was further strengthened by an alliance with the Russians.

Since 1931, the Russian Foreign Secretary Litvinov had pursued a policy of supporting the League of Nations and the idea of collective security, while at the same time aiding the creation of Popular Front (socialist-communist coalition) governments in Europe. In 1933 Russia had been recognized by America; in 1934 she joined the League; in 1935 she made defensive alliances with France and Czechoslovakia; in 1936 she sent help to the Popular Front Republican Government in Spain. But German aggression in 1938 and the Munich Agreement between Germany, Italy, Britain and France made the League and collective security look like shadows. In May 1939, Stalin dismissed the Jewish (anti-Nazi) Litvinov and replaced him with Molotov, an uncompromising champion of Russian interests above all else. In the summer of 1939, Stalin and Molotov controlled the balance of power in Europe, as every national leader was aware.

The Poles, already hesitant about making an alliance with Russia (they had so recently been part of the Russian Empire), became even more tentative, despite encouragement from Britain and France. In August, while the Western powers were desperately trying to find a formula that would tie in the Russians while safeguarding the Poles, it was announced from Moscow that Russia and Germany had signed a Non-Aggression Pact. Molotov and von Ribbentrop had met in secret. What was not immediately revealed was their agreement to divide Poland and the Baltic provinces into distinct spheres of influence: Russia was to have Eastern Poland, Finland, Estonia and Latvia (and the Romanian province of Bessarabia); Germany would claim West Poland and Lithuania.

The End of Appeasement

Hitler presumed that the mere announcement of the Non-Aggression Pact would make Chamberlain abandon his pledges to Poland just as he had persuaded the French to abandon their commitment to Czechoslovakia in 1938. He was wrong. On 1 September German troops stormed into Poland following provocative rioting in Danzig. Hitler still assumed that Britain and France could and would do nothing, but he misjudged the House of Commons even more than he misjudged Chamberlain. Arthur Greenwood, acting Labour Leader, raised cheers all round the House when he declared, 'Every minute's delay now means the loss of life, imperilling our national interests.' On 3 September, Chamberlain announced to the House 'This country is at war with Germany ... Everything that I have worked for, everything I have hoped for, everything that I have believed in during my public life, has crashed into ruins.'

Appeasement was killed by the Polish invasion, but on the other side the 'Pact of Steel' was severely wounded. This military alliance between Italy and Germany which had been signed in May 1939 was now shown to be hollow. Mussolini had signed it believing that Germany would not risk major war for at least another three years, but as soon as the Russo-German Non-Aggression Pact was announced, he realized its full implications and was quick to declare that he would take no military action in the event of a war with Poland and her allies. Not until France was about to fall, in June 1940, did Mussolini fulfil his part of the 'Pact of Steel'.

12 The Second World War 1939-45

The Characteristics of the War

Having declared war on Germany on 3 September 1939, the British rushed to put on their gasmasks while the French sat smugly behind the linked fortresses' of the Maginot Line, stretching the length of the Franco-German border. Both countries believed they had learned a lesson from the First World War. They were both wrong; gas was not used in the Second War, and the idea of the strong, static defensive line was outdated.

The Second World War was a war of movement rather than of trenches, of aerial rather than artillery bombardment (one bomb at Hiroshima in 1945 had the explosive power of four million First

A group of bystanders in Downing Street catch up with the latest news on 3 September 1939. When Parliament met in the evening, Chamberlain announced, 'This country is at war with Germany'.

World War field guns). Military casualty figures were often less significant than the numbers of combatants taken prisoner (the French casualties were only about one third of their First War total; the British and Commonwealth numbers half) but there was a huge increase in civilian deaths which still cannot be assessed accurately. Estimates suggest 22,000,000 Chinese civilians killed in their eight-year war with Japan; Russia may have lost 7,000,000; Yugoslavia lost 1,200,000 civilians killed which was roughly the total of *military* casualties suffered by Britain and the Empire in the First War.

The dramatic changes in mobility and firepower which had been introduced since 1918 made the war more technical, and closely tied to economic potential. Up to 1942, the war reflected the advantages gained by Germany, Italy and Japan by their build-up of military supplies and experience. After 1942, the Allies began to enjoy the benefit of their later organization on a war footing. The manpower and mineral resources of the Soviet Union, the technical expertise of British designers and inventors, and the massive mechanization and capital of the United States came into full production when the Germans were becoming increasingly reliant on the slave labour of Jews and other subject races and the Japanese were suffering from a shortage of strategic materials. During the six years of war, the U.S.A. produced 87,000 tanks, 296,000 aircraft (one every five minutes in 1943), 315,000 guns and mortars, 2,434,000 lorries and 53,000,000 tons of shipping.

Organization and strategy therefore mattered as much as heroism in the face of the enemy. The cooperation of the British and Americans, from Churchill and Roosevelt downwards, pro-vided the springboard for victory. After the 'phoney war' of 1939–40 and a spell of desperate defence, the Allies brought together the men and materials for a series of combined or coordinated attacks that snatched back the territory taken earlier by the Axis powers, and at the same time drained the energy and initiative away from them.

Poland

Germany attacked Poland with 40 infantry divisions and 14 mechanized divisions. The Poles could match the infantry strength, but could back them up only with cavalry brigades, one of them armoured. 1,750 miles of frontier was too much to defend, and unlike Czechoslovakia, the Poles might have found a better defensive position well behind their frontiers. National pride however kept them forward, and vulnerable. The German 'light-ning attack' (Blitzkrieg), delivered by tanks and aerial bombard-ment, scythed through the defences. Within ten days Warsaw was surrounded (it finally surrendered on 28 September) and when the Russians also invaded from the east on 17 September, there was no place on which resistance could be focussed. A month after their

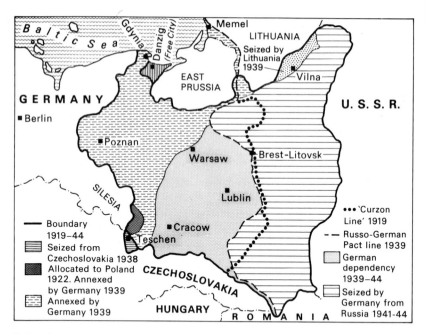

Poland, 1919–44

Non-Aggression Pact, Germany and Russia divided Poland among themselves, roughly along the line of the Bug river. Lithuania became part of the Soviet sphere of influence along with the territory that Russia had lost in the Polish War of 1921–22, while Warsaw, Central Poland and the Polish Corridor, which had been the original cause of the tension, were absorbed by Germany. This sharing of the spoils was different from that planned by Molotov and von Ribbentrop in August, but both sides were content.

The Northern Wars

Stalin now turned against Latvia and Estonia, as well as consolidating his position in Lithuania. In October 1939, they were forced to accept Soviet garrisons on their territory, and in June 1940 they were brought back under Russian political control by being declared Soviet Republics within the U.S.S.R. Finland resisted similar Russian infiltration and was invaded in November 1939, only to continue its resistance under Mannerheim. For three months the Russians were frustrated by the bitter hostility of the Finns and the weather in this 'Winter War', but an attack by tanks and sledgeborne infantry secured the Finnish surrender in March 1940, and the Treaty of Moscow conceded a large area of south-eastern Finland to Russia as well as the Hanko peninsula for 30 years. Briefly, the war was focussed on Scandinavia as the Allies considered helping Finland, thereby threatening Germany and her supplies of Swedish iron-ore.

Denmark, Norway and Sweden had all declared neutrality on the outbreak of war, and Norway and Sweden refused an Allied request to allow the transit of troops over their territory to help the Finns in February 1940. Nevertheless the Allies planned to mine Norwegian waters and capture the ports of Narvik, Trondheim, Bergen and Stavanger, a process which they started on 8 April 1940 unaware of the German plan to invade Norway and Denmark which started on 9 April. The Germans were significantly helped not only by the element of surprise (their paratroop landings at Oslo and Stavanger were the first in the history of warfare) but also by the cooperation of many Norwegian Nazis under Vidkun Quisling, who offered to form a government on 9 April. The Anglo-French landings were not effective, though Narvik was eventually captured and then conceded again. By early June, the Allies had evacuated Norway, leaving the whole of Scandinavia in German hands, because Sweden, though still technically neutral, was forced to allow the passage of German troops and supplies across her territory from 1940 to 1943.

The 'Phoney War' and the Fall of Chamberlain

In September 1939, Britain's declaration of war on Germany was followed by air-raid warnings, gas alerts, the digging of trenches and bomb-shelters – and no visible enemy action whatsoever. Hitler's attention was on Poland and then Scandinavia. Chamberlain's government could find no way to put into effect its guarantee of Polish independence. Rearmament, military training and the evacuation of children from the south-east quarter of England (including London) went ahead. Street-lighting was forbidden; car headlights were masked; emergency powers were granted to the War Cabinet if they were needed, but it seemed that they were not. Apart from damage inflicted by German submarines (one penetrating the main British naval base at Scapa Flow in October 1939) and pocket battleships, real warfare did not touch British affairs until the Norwegian landings in April 1940.

Chamberlain's War Cabinet included three men associated with the policy of appeasement (Halifax the Foreign Secretary, Simon the Chancellor of the Exchequer and Hoare the former Home Secretary) and three Service ministers, Hore-Belisha for the Army, Sir Kingsley Wood for the Air Force and Winston Churchill for the Navy. In the House of Commons, the Cabinet, and Chamberlain especially, came under attack following the failures in Norway and the losses of British shipping. L.S. Amery, himself a former Conservative First Lord of the Admiralty and Colonial Secretary, rounded on Chamberlain: 'Depart, I say, and let us have done with you. In the name of God, go!' Other Conservatives failed to support Chamberlain in the vital vote at the end of the debate on the Norwegian campaign. A majority which should have been 240 fell to 81, and Chamberlain accepted that he no longer commanded enough of the loyalty and confidence of the House. Within 48 hours he had resigned (he died six months later) and Winston Churchill had accepted George VI's commission to form a new government. 'I have nothing to offer but blood, toil, tears and sweat. You ask "What is our policy?" I will say "It is to wage war ...".' By his very words, Churchill offered one more ingredient than he listed: leadership.

The German Advance of 1940 and Dunkirk

On the day that Churchill accepted office (10 May 1940) German troops launched their long-expected attack against France, but by an unexpected route. Instead of throwing themselves against the defences of the Maginot Line, where 41 French divisions were waiting for the onslaught, they moved their Army groups due west into neutral and relatively undefended territory. Army Group B under General Bock moved into Holland, aiming for Amsterdam. Holland surrendered within four days. Army Group A under Runstedt thrust through the Ardennes into Belgium in parallel columns, heading across the Meuse (Maas) and round in a great

The Fall of France

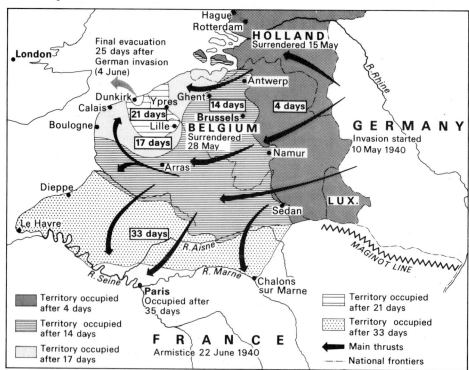

arc behind the British, French and Belgian troops that had faced north to resist Bock. Leeb's Army Group C remained facing the Maginot Line, holding the French in position.

Aided by the disruption caused by airborne troops deep behind the lines, the Germans reached the Channel in 11 days and turned north. The only escape for the British Expeditionary Force and their allies was by sea; they could not fight their way out. From 27 May to 4 June, they queued in the soft sand of the beaches at Dunkirk on the French-Belgian border for improbable rescue. The improbable was allowed to become fact by fine weather, brilliant R.A.F. fighter cover, a massive flotilla of privately owned pleasure craft acting as ferries home or to bigger Royal Naval craft, and German errors including a delaying order from Hitler himself. 198,000 British troops and 140,000 French and Belgians were plucked to safety at the cost of most of their equipment, the loss of six destroyers and 19 others damaged. A further 220,000 Allied troops were pulled out from other ports in the north-west of France, but Belgium had already surrendered on 26 May, and in the three week campaign, the Germans had taken over a million prisoners. On 10 June, Italy at last entered the war against France and Britain. The French government, led by Reynaud, having hoped to find safety in Bordeaux, resigned after Paris had been occupied. Marshall Pétain, hero of Verdun in 1916, took over and asked for an Armistice, which was granted on 22 June.

By the terms of the Armistice, the French government, which moved to Vichy, was to administer the whole of France, a part of which in the south-east was not occupied by German troops. The French were to pay the costs of occupation troops elsewhere, to cooperate in all ways with the German authorities, to demobilize their forces and to neutralize their navy and air force. This last clause was upset when Britain seized all French ships in British-controlled ports, and fired on the important force in Oran harbour in Algeria, an action which caused the Vichy government to break off diplomatic relations with Britain. Thereafter, Churchill treated General Charles de Gaulle's Free French movement as the rightful representatives of France.

'Operation Sea Lion' and the Battle of Britain

On 16 July 1940, Hitler gave orders for the planning of a sea-borne invasion of Britain, which, when complete, would free him from threat from the west and allow him to expand his Reich in the east. Knowing that Britain's army was ill-equipped and disorganized after Dunkirk, and that her navy was committed to convoy duties (and was in any case too vulnerable to shore-based artillery to be used in the confines of the Channel), the German plan was based on the destruction of the R.A.F. This would give them control of the Channel and the chance to bring 200,000 troops across the narrow seaway on huge barges. But this landing, 'Operation Sea Lion', was prevented at one of those very rare turning points in military history where the outcome of not just a battle but a whole war depends on the unpredictable mixture of skill, morale and courage among the fighting men themselves. The Germans had numerical advantage in July 1940, with 1,000 fighters (mostly Me. 109 and the twin-engined Me. 110) and 1,400 bombers challenging the defence of 820 fighters, mostly Spitfires and Hurricanes. (The loss of 474 R.A.F. aircraft over Dunkirk six weeks before now took on a new significance.) On the British side, there were the advantages of superior aircraft design in the Spitfire, a shorter range to the battle, friendly territory beneath for the parachuting pilot, superb organization by Air Marshal Sir Hugh Dowding (C-in-C Fighter Command) and energetic support from the newly created Ministry of Aircraft Production headed by Lord Beaverbrook. Most important of all, Britain had developed effective 'radar' (Radio Detection and Ranging) from scientific principles discovered by Robert Watson-Watt and pursued by the Committee for the Scientific Survey of Air Defence led by Henry Tizard. The early warnings provided by radar made possible the most economical use of men and machines, and thus neutralized the German numerical advantage.

The Battle of Britain was fought in three phases. For a few days in August 1940, Goering's Luftwaffe attacked British shipping in the Channel. Then the planes and airfields of Fighter Command became the target as up to 1,800 German planes crossed the Channel each day. Finally, German attention was concentrated on docks and centres of population, in an attempt to destroy civilian morale, a switch of policy that gave Fighter Command a vital respite. But British bombers were also attacking German supply routes and the waiting invasion barges while fighters took a heavy toll of the Luftwaffe. On 11 September, Hitler postponed 'Operation Sea Lion' until 24 September, but on 17 September he postponed it indefinitely. The Germans had lost 1,733 planes (not 2,700, as British sources claimed). The British had lost 915, but thanks to Beaverbrook could still put more than 600 into the air. 'Never in the field of human conflict was so much owed by so many to so few,' as Churchill told the House of Commons. 'The Blitz' – bombing raids on cities – went on until April 1941, London being attacked by an average of 200 bombers a night. But the danger of invasion was over.

The Balkans, 1940–41

Hitler's intention to expand in the east and turn against Russia was now delayed by an ally rather than an enemy. In October 1940 Mussolini invaded Greece from Albania, but was soon repulsed. Hitler, anxious for easy access to Romanian oil and Hungarian food as well as the Black Sea coast, made agreements with Romania and Hungary in November 1940, and with Bulgaria in March 1941. In April 1941 the Germans launched 'Operation Marita' against Greece and Yugoslavia. Nearly 60,000 Allied troops hastily brought from North Africa could not hold back the Axis forces. Late in April 1941 they began an evacuation from Greece to Crete. A month later they were forced out of Crete by a massive airborne invasion by the Germans, whose losses of paratroopers were sufficiently high to make them unable or unwilling to use this method of attack again. Once again, Hitler could look towards Russia.

'Operation Barbarossa'

On 22 June 1941 (one year to the day after the French Armistice) 120 German divisions advanced out of East Prussia and Poland onto Russian soil, fanning out as they did so, but occasionally concentrating the Panzer divisions of Guderian and Hoth to trap large pockets of Russian soldiers. 300,000 were captured between the frontier and Minsk, 200 miles away, largely because the German tanks covered the distance in five days. A similar 'bite' caught 200,000 men near Smolensk in mid-July, and when Guderian wheeled south to link up with Kleist coming north from Kiev, a further half-million prisoners were engulfed by mid-September. By October, Leeb was on the outskirts of Leningrad; Bock, having taken yet another half-million prisoners, threatened

The Russian Front, 1941–45

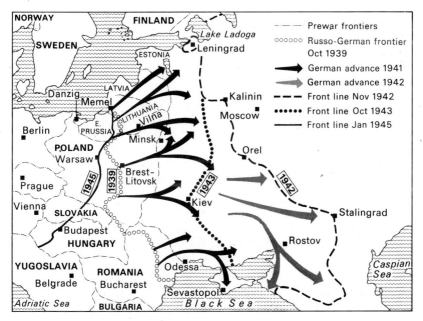

Moscow; Kleist and Runstedt were on the edge of the Caucasus. But the Russian winter was beginning to engulf the German vehicles and troops. The few weeks of delay caused by 'Operation Marita' had a catastrophic effect on the precisely-timed 'Operation Barbarossa'.

In December 1941, Marshal Zhukov began the Russian counterattack. Britain and Russia had been allies since August, and in mid-December Hitler added to his enemies by declaring war on America, but he was still confident of winning the Russian campaign before Britain and America could affect its outcome. The Germans held their positions through the winter of 1941–42 despite hunger made worse by the scorched-earth policy of the Russians, and in the early summer of 1942, they advanced again along the southern half of the front. Kleist's major target was the Caucasus, while General Paulus with the Sixth Army wheeled towards Stalingrad, a vital communications centre as well as a psychological symbol. The Russians clung to Stalingrad as they were clinging to beleaguered Leningrad (the new name of Petrograd) far in the north. With the winter of 1942 again exposing the stretched supply lines of the Germans, they launched their own counterattacking pincer movement. Paulus was surrounded just outside Stalingrad in a pocket 15 miles long, in contact with Germany by radio and through a few planes which brought in meagre supplies and ferried out 29,000 casualties. On 31 January 1943, Paulus surrendered; 91,000 Germans, including 24 generals, were

The hero of George Orwell's 1938 novel Coming Up For Air *spent a lot of time worrying about 'the streamlined men from Eastern Europe'. This photograph of Russian troops during the Second World War gives an idea of what he meant.*

marched away to the prison camps of Siberia, and only 5,000 survived to see Germany again. Two months earlier, the Sixth Army had consisted of 285,000 men.

The Germans still managed one last attack on the Dnieper in February 1943, and maintained their siege of Leningrad until early 1944, but from midwinter 1942–43, the Russians advanced until in April 1945 they were fighting one block away from Hitler as he took his own life in the Berlin bunker from which he was directing operations. The savagery of the Russian assault on Berlin was revenge for the '900 day' siege of Leningrad from 8 September 1941 to 27 January 1944, in which just under a million Russians died from enemy action, disease and starvation. Supplies were brought in across the ice of Lake Ladoga during the winter months, but the suffering of the Leningraders is vividly recalled today and is constantly referred to as a reason for the Russian dislike of (West) Germans.

North African Campaigns, 1940–43

The strategic importance of North Africa centred on Egypt. The port of Alexandria was a naval base; the Suez Canal was a supply route (or an escape route) for the Eastern Mediterranean, of increased importance after the fall of France and the loss of her naval power. From Egypt the oil of the Persian Gulf could be defended or attacked, as could East Africa. With an army of 300,000 men in Libya under Graziani, and a further 200,000 under the Duke of Aosta in East Africa (Eritrea, Somaliland, Ethiopia), Italy posed a major threat to Egypt and therefore to the whole direction of the war.

After declaring war on an already defeated France in June 1940, the Italians invaded Greece in October 1940 but took no immediate action in North Africa. General Wavell, British C-in-C in the Middle East, therefore took the offensive by sending Major-General O'Connor with 30,000 men westwards from Mersa Matruh in December. In a brilliant 10-week campaign, O'Connor broke out of Egypt, crossed Cyrenaica and threatened Tripoli, the most westerly Italian stronghold. 130,000 prisoners, 1,300 guns and 400 tanks fell into his hands.

But in the first week of February, a young German general arrived with two mechanized divisions to help the Italians, just as British troops were being hastily transferred for the defence of Greece. Within two months, General Rommel had chased the raw British replacement troops back to the Egyptian frontier, except for a garrison trapped in Tobruk. Wavell retaliated with an unsuccessful offensive ('Battleaxe'), in June 1941, and was then replaced by General Auchinleck as C-in-C, with General Cunningham leading the Eighth Army. Another offensive ('Crusader') under another general, Ritchie, saw the front line move 300 miles to the west

(November 1941-January 1942), only to be beaten eastwards again to Gazala by Rommel (February 1942), and then in May and June 1942 further east still to El Alamein, only 60 miles from Alexandria. Tobruk fell at last to the Axis on 21 June 1942.

Auchinleck held up Rommel's advance at El Alamein, but could regain no ground. Churchill replaced him as C-in-C with General Alexander. Command of the exhausted Eighth Army passed to General Montgomery who had a brusque and realistic brilliance similar to that of his opponent, Rommel, leading the Afrika Korps. After holding off one more German attack at Alam-al-Halfa in August-September 1942, Montgomery launched a break-out offensive from El Alamein in October 1942, opening with an artillery barrage of First War dimensions before thrusting his superior armour forward. In 18 weeks, the Eighth Army pushed Rommel, sick and unsupported by Berlin, 1,400 miles back across Libya and Tunisia to the Mareth Line. Meanwhile on 8 November 1942, 'Operation Torch' had brought three Allied landings to the coast of Morocco and Algeria, under the supreme command of the American General Eisenhower, and by February 1943 Americans, Free French and British were moving against the Germans and Italians from the west. In March, Rommel lost the battle for the Mareth Line and resigned his command. In May, all Axis resistance in North Africa ceased as the Allies took 250,000 prisoners, and prepared a jumping-off point to go north against Italy and Germany themselves. El Alamein and Stalingrad at the end of 1942 mark the turn of the tide of war: the three years of retreat were to be followed by three years of Allied advance in Europe, Africa and Russia.

The War against Japan

The Japanese military advance had begun well before any declaration of war. Manchuria had been engulfed in 1931 and much of northern and eastern China in 1937 (see Chapter 8). When the Netherlands and France fell in 1940, the Japanese took over much of French Indo-China as well as the oil supplies from the Dutch East Indies, and joined the Axis Pact with Germany and Italy. In 1941 Japan and Russia made a Neutrality Pact, while Japanese troops overran the rest of Indo-China and threatened Burma. With Britain deeply committed in Greece and North Africa, and struggling against German naval power (see below), only the United States could stand in the way of Japanese aggression in the Pacific.

While talking peace, the Japanese planned war. On 7 December 1941, their carrier-borne aircraft attacked the U.S. Pacific Fleet in its base at Pearl Harbor, Hawaii. 17 prime American ships were sunk or crippled; 140 American aircraft were destroyed and 80 more were damaged. The only miscalculation in the Japanese plan was the failure to sink the three Pacific Fleet aircraft-carriers, then at sea. On the same day, the Philippines, Hong Kong and Malaya came under attack, and within six months the Japanese had won a series of well-planned victories, despite the rugged resistance of the Americans under MacArthur at the Bataan Peninsula, which fell in April 1942, and Corregidor which fell in May. Most islands of the South Pacific within an arc 3,500 miles from Tokyo were soon in Japanese hands, as well as much of China, all Indo-China, Malaya, Singapore, and a large part of Burma. India and Australia were threatened. Only American naval victories at the Coral Sea and Midway relieved the gloom in May and June 1942. At Midway, the Japanese lost four heavy aircraft carriers, a huge strategic loss in the age when 'naval' battles were fought by planes from the decks of ships which never sighted the enemy.

In July 1942, the Japanese attacked Guadalcanal in the South Solomon Islands with a view to building an airfield for attacks on Australia. The Allies responded with vigorous defence which was slowly turned to attack: the Japanese lost the six-month battle for the island as well as several naval encounters. There followed two bloody years of bitter 'island-hopping', as MacArthur's Allied troops picked their way back through New Guinea and the

The War in the East

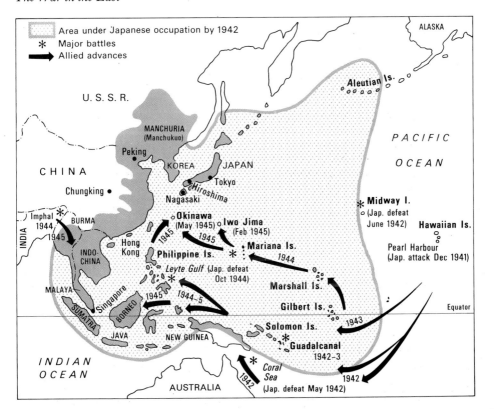

Philippines to Iwo Jima (captured March 1945) and Okinawa (attacked April 1945), the last steps before an attack on the main Japanese islands. Meanwhile in Burma, General Wingate's 'Chindits' (guerilla forces expert in penetrating deep into enemy territory) were disrupting Japanese communications and security by their unconventional attacks, easing the task of the British and Indian troops fighting under General Slim towards Rangoon, and encouraging Chiang Kai-shek in China to turn from defence to offence.

War at Sea and In the Air

Allied morale, particularly in Britain, was much affected by spectacular naval battles. In December 1939, the German pocket battleship *Graf Spee*, which had sunk nine ships on a voyage across the Atlantic, was challenged and damaged by three British cruisers in the 'Battle of the River Plate'. Retiring to neutral Montevideo to carry out repairs, the *Graf Spee* was unable to prepare herself adequately for a continuation of the battle with the cruiser squadron. On leaving harbour, she was scuttled by her crew. In February 1940, her supply ship, the *Altmark*, was captured in Norwegian waters.

The *Bismarck* went down in the Atlantic in May 1941; the *Tirpitz* was disabled by midget submarines in a Norwegian fjord in 1943 and the *Scharnhorst* was sunk in the same year. In the long run, these dramatic triumphs were less important than the regular courage and achievement of those who brought in the merchant convoys and the troop shipments. Germany started the war with only 49 serviceable submarines (as opposed to Russia's 235) and for 15 months lost more U-boats than she could launch. But by December 1941, the U-boat fleet had risen to 230, and Admiral Doenitz had devised the 'wolf-pack' tactic whereby the sighting of a convoy led to the summoning of a group of U-boats before an attack was started. Just over 7,000,000 tons of shipping were sunk by German submarines from December 1941 to May 1943, but total losses from all enemy action dropped from 1,665 ships in 1942 to 597 ships in 1943, 205 ships in 1944 and 105 ships in 1945. The biggest single disaster was the loss of 24 ships from the convoy PQ17 to Russia in June 1942.

Aerial warfare was an integral part of all fronts from 1939 to 1945. Bombers attacked population centres (London 1940–42, Dresden 1945, Hiroshima and Nagasaki, 1945) and industrial points (Essen and the Ruhr 1942 and 1943, the Mohne and Eder dams 1943, and English Midlands 1940–42); fighter-bombers and fighters strafed convoys on land and sea, especially in North Africa and after D-Day in 1944, and held off enemy air attack; reconnaissance planes also worked over land and water, seeking fleets, spotting submarines, checking on troop dispositions. The Japanese developed the kamikaze suicide attack and sank or damaged over 300 ships at the cost of 1,200 planes and pilots. The Germans and English developed airborne assaults with gliders and paratroopers; the English and Americans made the biggest advances in aerial navigation, the use of radar and the accuracy of bomb-aiming. Transport aircraft were so developed that the British Army in Burma in 1945 (300,000 men) was supplied entirely from the air by 23 squadrons.

As capacity increased, so did speed. Frank Whittle's jet engine led to the Gloster Meteor's appearance in 1944; the Germans tried several versions of jet aircraft, and a rocket-powered interceptor, the Me. 163, which reached a speed of 596 m.p.h. This was a clear step on the way to the V1 and V2 weapons (V for Vengeance) which rained terror on south-east England in late 1944 and 1945.

Sicily and Italy, 1943–44

The victorious Allies in North Africa (the British 8th Army under Montgomery and the American Seventh Army under Patton) returned to the mainland of Europe via an attack on Sicily in July 1943. The demoralized Italians showed little heart for the fight; Mussolini was summoned to an audience with Victor Emmanuel III after a meeting of the Fascist Grand Council and was removed from office and placed under arrest. The German C-in-C in Italy, Kesselring, evacuated 40,000 Germans and 60,000 Italians across the Straits of Messina, where they were followed in September by the Eighth Army. Although the new Italian government of Marshal Badoglio capitulated to the Allies, Kesselring resisted the secondary landings at Salerno, on Italy's shin, and established the Gustav Line south of Rome, hinged on Monte Cassino. Not until May 1944 did the multi-national forces of the Eighth and Fifth Armies (including Americans, British, Canadians, French and Poles and with Italian support) break through, entering Rome in June 1944, one day before the Normandy landings. Even so, Kesselring's retreat remained orderly. Florence fell in August, but a new defence line, the Gothic Line, was held until April 1945, when the Allied presence in the heart of Germany destroyed Nazi resistance in Italy. On 28 April 1945, Benito Mussolini, who had been rescued from house arrest by German airborne troops and set up as a puppet ruler of the 'Repubblica Sociale Italiana' in Salo in the north, was recognized by Italian partisans as he tried to flee. He and his mistress were shot. Their bodies were hung by the ankles from a shop-front in Milan, a savage humiliation by Italians who felt that *he* had humiliated *them*.

Allied Aims and Objectives

In September 1940, Britain and her Empire and Commonwealth

Allied co-operation early in the war. Winston Churchill, with the cigar, is flanked by General de Gaulle (left) and General Sikorski. Sikorski, the leader of the Polish government in exile, was killed in an aircrash in 1943.

stood alone against the Tripartite Pact of Germany, Italy and Japan. The sympathy of the U.S.A. was reflected in the 'cash and carry' ruling by which Britain could buy supplies, and in January 1941 Roosevelt's speech to Congress about Freedom from Want and Fear and Freedom of Speech and Worship was an obvious rejection of Fascism and Nazism. In March 1941, Congress approved 'Lend-Lease' by which America, 'the great arsenal of democracy' supplied first Britain, then China, then Russia with the necessary supplies of war materials and food to keep them in the war even though payment was not immediately forthcoming.

In August 1941, Churchill and Roosevelt met on board H.M.S. *Prince of Wales* off the coast of Newfoundland, and produced the 'Atlantic Charter', a statement of aims in the spirit of Wilson's 14 Points of 1918 but drafted largely by Churchill. It later became a foundation of the principles on which the United Nations Organization was built (see Chapter 13).

After Pearl Harbor, America was officially at war with all the Axis powers, and at a conference in Washington (December 1941-January 1942) agreed that the strategy of the Allies must be based on victory in Europe first. This was eagerly supported by Stalin who throughout 1942 pressed for the opening of a 'Second Front' in Europe which would take the pressure off Russia. For several months, 'Operation Bolero', an Anglo-American landing in France, was considered, but eventually 'Torch' was approved and in November 1942 initiated when the Anglo-American forces landed in North Africa.

At Casablanca in January 1943, Churchill and Roosevelt agreed on a 1943 attack on Italy and a 1944 invasion of Germany via France. At the final press briefing of the conference, Roosevelt referred to a demand for the 'unconditional surrender' of all the Axis powers, a phrase which surprised Churchill but which became an Allied objective thereafter. Further conferences in Washington (May 1943), Quebec (August 1943), Cairo (November 1943) and Teheran (November-December 1943) respectively clarified the plans for the landings in France, recognized de Gaulle as the leader of French Liberation forces, brought Chiang Kai-shek into direct contact with Churchill, and finally brought Churchill, Roosevelt and Stalin to their first face-to-face meeting. Russia accepted the principle of unconditional surrender, agreed to enter the war against Japan at some future time, and advocated the permanent division of Germany, a Russian policy that still exists today. The three leaders met only once more, at Yalta in February 1945; two months later Roosevelt died.

'Operation Overlord', 1944

The long-awaited landings in France started on D- (for Deliverance) Day, 6 June 1944. Under the supreme command of General Eisenhower and the immediate command of Montgomery, 156,000 men came ashore on five Normandy beaches in the biggest yet most minutely planned amphibious invasion in history. PLUTO (Pipe-Line Under The Ocean) carried fuel across the Channel. Two artificial harbours ('Mulberries') were created by linking prefabricated sections and sinking concrete-filled ships as breakwaters, and plans were made for 189,000 fighting vehicles and nearly a million men to come ashore there in the 20 days after the landings. 14,600 aircraft sorties were flown by the Allies in the first 24 hours of the attack. Even so, by 23 June the Allies had only reached the line planned for 11 June, held up by resistance in Caen. In July and August they broke out southwards and eastwards. Paris was liberated late in August while a new Franco-American landing on the south coast 'Operation Dragoon' quickly cleared the Rhône Valley of Germans. German difficulties were increased by the injury of Rommel (commanding the 'Atlantic Wall') in a strafing attack in July and by the tensions released by an unsuccessful attempt to assassinate Hitler which led to over 5,000 executions and enforced 'suicides', including those of the luckless Rommel and Kluge, German C-in-C in the west.

The Defeat of Germany on all Fronts 1944–45

By the end of September 1944, Allied forces stood along the western frontier of Germany: Aachen, the first German city to be captured, fell on 20 October, a month after the First Airborne Division had been badly mauled at Arnhem on the Rhine in Holland in an over-ambitious attack. In November the Germans mobilized every male between the ages of 16 and 60, and in December, Runstedt launched a surprise attack through the Ardennes which held up the Allies for a month. This 'Battle of the Bulge' was later said to have sapped most of Germany's remaining strength.

The Rhine was reached early in March 1945. After a cautious build-up Montgomery gave the order to cross the river on 23 March, and moved on to the Elbe, 60 miles from Berlin by 11 April. There his troops linked up with the Russians whose westward advance had started from Stalingrad, more than two years earlier.

Having established themselves firmly in Romania and the Balkans by October 1944, the Russians turned their attention to the Germans in Poland. Encouraged by their advance, the people of Warsaw rebelled against the conquerors who had sent more than 300,000 Jewish citizens to the gas chambers and killed another

Europe and North Africa, 1942–45

60,000 in suppressing the Jewish ghetto in 1943. Another 150,000 Poles died in the 1944 revolt against the Germans, while the Russian advance seemed to falter rather than accelerate to take advantage of the situation. By the time the Russians got to Warsaw in January 1945, it was in total ruin.

On 19 April the battle for Berlin started. Americans and Russians linked up on 25 April; on 30 April, Hitler committed suicide in his bunker, leaving Admiral Doenitz to surrender what was left of the Third Reich which Hitler had boasted would last for a thousand years. Montgomery accepted the first surrender at Luneburg Heath on 4 May; Eisenhower was granted the 'unconditional surrender of all German forces' three days later. 8 May 1945 marked V.E. Day, Victory in Europe.

Victory over Japan

In Burma, General Slim and his 'Forgotten Army' pressed south in 1944 and 1945, capturing Rangoon in May 1945. Meanwhile the Americans, despite having wiped out the Japanese fleet at Leyte in the Philippines in October 1944, faced increasingly fanatical defence as they advanced towards Japan. The siege of Iwo Jima cost 6,000 U.S. lives in March; Okinawa cost 12,000 dead and 36,000 wounded (and 100,000 Japanese dead) in April-July 1945. But two weeks after the surrender of Okinawa, American scientists tested the world's first atomic weapon in the heart of the New Mexican desert. Its ferocious power put a totally new tactic into the hands of the new American President Harry Truman, who had been in office for only three months. By using this weapon, he could

'Little Boy' – the atomic bomb which destroyed Hiroshima and took nearly 80,000 lives. It was 10ft long, weighed 900 pounds, and had the power of 20,000 tons of high explosive.

stun Japan into surrender and avoid the casualties (Japanese and American) that a full-scale invasion would inevitably entail.

The final Allied Conference of the War was held at Potsdam near Berlin. Stalin was told of the atom bomb and its potential, and the Allies discussed the unconditional surrender of Japan which they required. When Japan indicated that she would continue to fight, Truman gave orders for an atom bomb to be used. On 6 August, a single B29 bomber dropped its mysterious load over Hiroshima and banked away sharply. Within a minute, nearly 80,000 people were dead and a further 70,000 injured, quite apart from victims of radiation who still fall sick today or who have suffered genetic defects. On 9 August, a further bomb on Nagasaki added 40,000 more to the death roll, and on 14 August, Japan accepted the Allied surrender terms. This unthinkable reversal of policy by the nation that had invented the kamikaze philosophy had to be communicated by Imperial princes to some generals who had not seen the atomic devastation. It was the only way to get the message across to them.

Whether they liked it or not, the Second World War was over.

The Aftermath of War: 13
First Steps in a New Age

The End of European Dominance

When American and Russian forces linked up in April 1945 to begin the final assault on Berlin, they neatly symbolized the change that the Second World War had hastened. The fall of Europe's most heavily defended capital city to the troops of two major non-European combatants was a sign that the age of European dominance of the world was over.

Whereas after the First World War, American politicians had refused to ratify the Treaty of Versailles and had stayed out of the League of Nations, and whereas the Russian Bolshevik leaders had been cold-shouldered by the European powers and thus forced into a similar diplomatic isolation, now, in and after 1945, these two 'super-powers' held in their hands the strategic, economic and political future of Europe. Twice in one generation, Europe had been a battleground. On each occasion, a strong Germany had been thwarted in its planned expansion by an Anglo-French combination, with help each time from Russia and America. The two wars can be seen as parts of the same process: the settling of a contest for supremacy between various imperialistic, capitalistic and nationalistic countries within Europe. (See Chapter 1.)

Not only had this contest invited the intervention of Russia and America; not only had it exhausted European resources and devastated the countries over which it was fought. It had also been carried over into the colonies and dominions of the European powers, getting muddled up with a separate but similar contest between China and Japan, and it had clearly demonstrated that the white man was not infallible. The imperial powers were forced to beg or bargain with their colonies for support against the Germans or the Japanese, and in so doing they were acknowledging that self-determination, the principle over which Europe was fighting, could also apply to the people of their own overseas empires. Though the fighting in Europe and Japan ended in 1945, the continuing struggles in India, Indo-China, the East Indies and Africa were really part of the same saga, that of the ending of Europe's predominance.

Russia and America

A common hatred of Nazism bound Russia and America, but without the shared enemy, there was little else to keep the powers together.

Russia under Stalin was intensely suspicious of the West and its capitalist system. Believing in the Marxist theory of class war between the bourgeoisie and the proletariat (see Chapter 1) and in the inevitability of a revolutionary overthrow of the bourgeoisie, Stalin tended to support Nazism in its early days because he thought it too was an inevitable phase of political development, and one which came just before the workers' revolution. So until about 1935, the German Communist Party cooperated with the Nazis on Stalin's order. After 1935, most European Communists changed tack and devoted their energies to trying to set up Popular Front governments which opposed Fascism and Nazism. In the 1930s in Russia itself, Stalin was ruthlessly establishing his own brand of Communism and his own organization (see Chapter 4). He imposed on the Russian people a collective economy, State planning, the nationalization of all industry and control of the labour force, and ran the country by means of his iron grip on the official Party bureaucracy. He allowed no softening in the system, and as his forces moved westwards again after their desperate defence around Stalingrad in the winter of 1942–43, they imposed the Soviet way of life on all the territories that they liberated from the Nazis. Some 90,000,000 East Europeans were brought under the yoke of Communism, while Stalin remained so suspicious of capitalist attitudes that he executed or banished to distant labour camps many of his own troops who had spent too much time in contact with Western Europeans.

In contrast, the Americans had from a very early stage of the war pledged themselves to the democratization of the Fascist states of Europe and Japan, and to the principle of self-determination for all people. They therefore found it hard to agree with the compulsion which went with Russian 'liberation', while admiring the heroism of the Red Army in the face of incredible hardship. They believed in free elections, and in free enterprise in economic matters. As the indispensable 'arsenal of democracy' which had supplied nearly $50,000,000,000 worth of arms and other supplies to their allies (including Russia), the Americans were determined that their efforts should not be turned inside out and converted into support for a totalitarian system. Thus, well before the war ended, cracks began to appear in the wall of Russian and American partnership.

The End of the War – The Conferences

Roosevelt, Stalin and Churchill met for the first time at Teheran in late 1943. Their agenda included the opening of the Second Front in Europe, the possible entry of Russia into the war against Japan, and the need to set up some form of international organization after the war on the lines of the League of Nations, but with a greater authority for peace keeping.

The next time they met – and it turned out to be the last time – was at Yalta in the Crimea, in February 1945. By now victory was confidently expected over Germany, and Roosevelt's major concern was to secure Stalin's support against Japan, and his support for the United Nations Organization (about which, at an earlier meeting at Dumbarton Oaks in 1944, the Russians had seemed hesitant). These two matters were resolved satisfactorily. On the issue of Germany, all three powers agreed that she was to be disarmed, demilitarized, de-Nazified, democratized and divided into zones of occupation. Reparations would be expected, half of them to go to Russia. Countries which had been occupied by Germany were to be allowed democratic self-determination, but Poland (where Stalin promised to hold free elections as soon as possible) was to concede some land to Russia in the east in exchange for land from Germany in the west.

By the time the Three Powers met again, at Potsdam near Berlin in July 1945, much had changed. Roosevelt had died, and was replaced by Truman. Churchill was awaiting the delayed result of a General Election, and then had to give way to the new

The 'Big Three' at Yalta, February 1945. Churchill, Roosevelt and Stalin pose for formal photographs. Two months later Roosevelt died.

A brief break at the Potsdam Conference table, July 1945. On the far side sits Stalin. Churchill and Eden (left foreground) were replaced by Attlee and Bevin eight days after the Conference had started, as a result of the British Election.

British Prime Minister, Attlee. Only Stalin remained of the 'Big Three', and by now, Russia had improved its bargaining position by occupying not only Poland but the eastern half of Germany (including Potsdam itself).

The Potsdam Conference confirmed and clarified most of the Yalta provisions. Poland was moved bodily sideways as the Oder-Neisse line became its western frontier and the old Curzon Line divided it from Russia in the east. A puppet Polish government based at Lublin was given full support by the Russians and became more influential than the members of the Polish government in exile whom the Western allies supported. Reparations were agreed: Russia was to be allowed to claim up to 25 per cent of certain capital equipment in the Western zones of occupation, and 100 per cent in her own zone, provided that the Germans were not left dependent on foreign aid.

Germany was divided into four zones (the Americans had reduced theirs in size so that the French could be granted one). But it was agreed that the country should be run as one economic unit for the time being. Each occupying power, however, was responsible for the reintroduction of local government machinery which the Nazi state had totally suppressed; each occupying power was also responsible for dealing with former Nazis in its area, all of whom were liable to be tried. The German armed services ceased to exist. Finally, Germans living in Poland, Hungary and Czechoslovakia were to be sent back to Germany, so that these minorities would not cause a new 'Sudetenland' problem in the future.

On the first day of the Potsdam Conference, the Americans exploded the first atomic bomb in the deserts of New Mexico. The results were quickly conveyed to Truman, who informed Stalin that the Americans had 'a new secret weapon'. Nonetheless, the Western powers still expressed anxiety that the Russians were not helping to bring to an end the war against Japan. When, four days after the end of the Potsdam Conference, the first atomic bomb was dropped on Japan, it was clear that the West no longer needed Russian help. For that very reason, the Russians were quick to declare war on Japan and invade Manchuria, so that they could claim their 'rightful' place at that conference table when peace was discussed.

The End of the War – The Treaties

Neither Yalta nor Potsdam produced agreement on an overall plan as to what should happen to Germany. Russia wanted to divide and dismember the country that had twice invaded her in the twentieth century, while Britain, France and America were more concerned to find permanent peace by producing a more acceptable settlement than had been found at Versailles in 1919. This

Occupied Germany, 1945

absolute disagreement on the treatment of Germany became a primary feature of the 'Cold War' (see below) and prevented the making of any form of German Peace Treaty. Not until the 1970s and Willi Brandt's 'Ostpolitik' (see Chapter 16) did the two parts of Germany officially recognize each other (1972) and become members of the United Nations (1973), thereby in effect rounding off the diplomacy arising directly out of World War II.

Germany's former allies were more easily dealt with, by the Council of Foreign Ministers appointed by the Potsdam Conference (Byrnes from America, Bevin from Britain and Molotov from Moscow. France was not represented). The treaties relating to Italy, Finland, Hungary, Bulgaria and Romania were signed in Paris in 1947. Italy lost her African Empire (Libya, Ethiopia, Eritrea and Somaliland) and had to give up her claims to Trieste, which became a Free City, and to Albania. The Dodecanese Islands passed to Greece. Romania lost Bessarabia in the north to Russia, and Dobrudja in the south to Bulgaria, but regained Transylvania in the west from Hungary. Finland was forced to confirm Russia's hold on the border areas that had been lost in 1940 (see Chapter 12). Russia also held on to Ruthenia, once part of Czechoslovakia, until it was taken by Hungary in 1939 and then liberated by the Red Army in the winter of 1944–45. This Russian acquisition, together with her gains to the east of Poland, created common borders between Russia and Czechoslovakia, and Russia and Hungary for the first time ever, a fact that was to be of vital importance in the 1950s and 1960s.

Because of the 1938 Anschluss, from which she had been liberated by Russian troops, Austria came into a different category from other German allies. Subjected like Germany to Four-Power occupation, Austria was a further cause of disagreement over details between Russia and the Western powers, and a final settlement was delayed until 1955, when the Austrian State Treaty formally re-established the Austrian Republic with its pre-1938 boundaries. Union with Germany was forbidden, and, as if to emphasize this point, before the end of 1955 Austria declared itself to be permanently neutral. Russia was granted certain rights to reparations ($150,000,000) and to 10,000,000 metric tons of crude oil from Austrian wells and refineries. Austria was left with one major resentment against the Treaty: South Tirol, which had been taken from her by Italy in 1919, was still not returned, despite its German-speaking population.

Japan's major post-war treaty was also slow to emerge: it was finally hammered out at the San Francisco Conference of 1951 and came into effect in 1952 (see Chapter 18), while lesser treaties were made later still with Burma, the Philippines and Indonesia. Until 1952, the Japanese had to accept occupation by the Allies (in practice, by America), who supervised the appearance of a new constitution in 1947, tried and punished Japanese war criminals,

and organized Japan's diplomatic relationships. They also lost all
their conquests of the previous 50 years: they were expelled from
Korea, the Chinese mainland, the island of Formosa (Taiwan), the
islands that had been Japanese mandates since the First World
War, and various other Pacific islands which now came under the
U.N. Trusteeship Council.

The Birth of the United Nations Organization

After the First World War, the delegates at Versailles linked the
creation of an international organization, the League, with the
passing of the peace treaties themselves. For this reason, America
never became a member of the League (because she never ratified
the Treaty of Versailles), and the League always smacked of being
an organization set up for the benefit of the rest of the victors. It
was not until 1946 that the League invoked the last of the 26 clauses
of its Covenant and amended itself unanimously out of existence.
By then, a new international organization had been formed which,
it was hoped, would benefit greatly from the many sad lessons
learned by the League.

The 'United Nations' were originally those who had declared
war on the Axis powers and who subscribed to the statement of
aims made by Churchill and Roosevelt in the 'Atlantic Charter' of
1941. In 1942, 26 nations signed the 'Declaration of the United
Nations'. In 1944, more detailed planning of the new organization
was made at the Dumbarton Oaks Conference by representatives
from America, China, Russia and Britain, which was further
amended by the 'Big Three' at Yalta in 1945. Finally, the San
Francisco Conference of June 1945 produced the Charter of the
United Nations, and in October the United Nations Organization
was officially born, with 51 members.

The early membership had a Western bias, but, illustrating the
extent of the collapse of European dominance, by no means a
European one. 21 of the founder-members were American republics, seven were Near Eastern states, and six were independent
Commonwealth countries. The continent of Africa was badly
represented, with only four countries sending delegates. Initially,
nine 'enemy' countries were barred from membership: Thailand
(admitted in 1946), Italy, Japan, Hungary, Austria, Romania,
Bulgaria, Finland (all admitted in 1955), and Germany, ultimately
admitted separately as East and West Germany in 1973. By 1950,
membership had grown to 60, and by 1980 to 150. The change from
being an association of anti-Axis powers to being a truly international forum was achieved in the 1950s and early 1960s, when
many former colonies achieved independence and sovereignty. 15
new African nations joined in 1960 alone, swelling the 'Afro-Asian
bloc' to the point where small states, each with a vote as powerful
as that of a super-power like Russia and America, threatened to

unbalance world diplomacy. That they have not done so is due in part to their reliance on the economic and financial resources of the super-powers, although this pattern has changed with the growing shortage of oil and other vital raw materials.

Purposes and Organs of the U.N.

The main purpose of the U.N. is to save 'succeeding generations from the scourge of war'. This involves not merely preventing war in a time of crisis, but preventing the crisis as far as possible by previous action. The pressure for human rights and liberties, provision of a framework of international law and negotiation, and continuous care for the economic development of all areas of the world are the best guarantees that no political disagreement reaches the point where war is the only possible course of action. There are six major instruments of U.N. action as well as subsidiary agencies.

The General Assembly is the place where all member-nations meet on equal terms: one country, one vote, regardless of the size, power and previous history of that country. It controls almost every aspect of U.N. work including its budget and its membership, and it can discuss, and make recommendations on, almost any political matter in the world provided that it is not a purely domestic matter which is the concern of one country only. The General Assembly meets annually in New York, though it can call a special session at very short notice. Its debates are public, and instantaneous translation into five official languages (Russian, Chinese, French, Spanish and English) is always available. Decisions are taken either by simple majority or by a two-thirds majority depending on the issue at stake. Many committees and sub-committees are at work throughout the year on behalf of the Assembly. The U.N. is never 'off duty'.

The Security Council, as the name suggests, bears the main responsibility for peace in the world. Originally consisting of 11 members, it now has 15, five of them permanent (China, France, Britain, Russia and America) and ten chosen for two-year terms from specified parts of the world (five from Africa and Asia, one from Eastern Europe, two from Latin America, and two from Western Europe and elsewhere). Each member holds the presidency of the Security Council for a month at a time. Decisions are made by the agreement of nine members, but permanent members have a right of veto. This special privilege could destroy the effectiveness of the U.N. (as the League of Nations' experience showed). In the period 1945–50, Russia resorted to regular use of the veto, but the General Assembly took advantage of the Korean crisis of 1950 to pass the 'Uniting for Peace Resolution' which authorized the Assembly to take emergency action, even involving armed intervention, if the Security Council, 'because of lack of unanimity of the permanent members, fails to exercise its primary function'. The Security Council may consider any dispute brought to its attention, and can recommend courses of action ranging from negotiation to economic, diplomatic or even military sanctions in order to achieve peace and security. Delegates from Security Council countries are always at U.N. Headquarters, because of the possible need for speedy emergency action.

The Secretariat provides the U.N. with permanent administrators. Headed by a Secretary General who is appointed by the General Assembly for five years at a time, the Secretariat is based in New York but runs agencies around the world. The influence of the Secretary-General is so great that he is usually chosen from a smaller or non-aligned country: Trygve Lie (1946–52) came from Norway, Dag Hammarskjöld (1953–61) from Sweden, U Thant (1961–71) from Burma and Kurt Waldheim (1971–   ) from Austria. His personal standing and acceptability among the leaders of the world affects the reputation and usefulness of the U.N.

The International Court of Justice succeeded the Permanent Court of International Justice which the League of Nations had set up. Based at The Hague, and staffed by 15 judges, each elected by the General Assembly and each from a different country, the Court gives opinions of cases which arise between states. Many of the incidents and cases relate to aircraft and shipping, where the power of national laws is uncertain. The judgements of the Court are not

U.N. forces were first used in Korea (1950–53). Such military intervention proved that the U.N. was more positive and powerful than its predecessor, the League of Nations.

automatically binding on all members of the U.N. If necessary, the Security Council could be asked to enforce a decision, but to date only one country has failed to honour its obligation, (Albania failed to pay Britain some £843,000 following the Corfu Channel case of 1949) and no punitive action has taken place.

The Trusteeship Council acts for the General Assembly and looks after undeveloped territories that are no longer colonies but are not ready for total independence. It has taken over the role of the mandate system in the League of Nations, but its activity is rapidly declining as all areas gain independence. The Caroline, Marshall and Mariana Islands, and Namibia, are examples of recent trusteeship.

The Economic and Social Council is the sixth main branch of the U.N. It is a body of enormous importance, which receives little publicity in the Western world because its concern is mostly with economically backward countries, and it works through specialist agencies like UNICEF, UNESCO and UNRWA.

The Cold War

The creation of the United Nations Organization could not conceal the split between communism and capitalism already referred to on p.192. Even before the Second War had ended, there was a competitive tension between Russia and America with their respective satellites and supporters, which fell short of military war but was a distinct conflict. This 'Cold War' took the form of intense rivalry in political, economic and propaganda fields, as either side tried to convince as many people as possible that its creed, communism or capitalist democracy, was the better, stronger, more moral and more stable way of life. Both sides built up their military might and their web of alliances with the Cold War in mind, but neither side was seeking real war, for which there were plenty of opportunities, had any excuse for fighting been wanted.

Geographically, the first area of competition was in Europe itself. As Winston Churchill said in a speech to students in Fulton, Missouri in March 1946: 'From Stettin in the Baltic to Trieste in the Adriatic, an Iron Curtain has descended across the Continent ... All these famous cities and the populations around them lie in what I must call the Soviet sphere, and all are subject in one form or another, not only to Soviet influence, but to a very high and in many cases increasing measure of control from Moscow.' Fear of this possibility had conditioned Churchill's attitude to the Russians for many months before the end of the war. In negotiating the Peace Treaties in 1946 and 1947, the Western powers strongly resisted Russian ambitions as they appeared to stretch towards Western Europe. It was over Austria and Germany that they were most adamant, though they were also deeply concerned about potential Russian influence in the eastern Mediterranean and so chose to make a stand against Communism in Greece and Turkey. The most tense incident of the Cold War in Europe was the blockade of Berlin and the consequent 'Airlift' of 1948–49 (see below).

But the Cold War also spread beyond Europe, into the arena of the newly independent colonies of Africa, the Indian sub-continent, Indo-China and the East Indies. In Korea in 1950 and in Vietnam in the 1960s it bubbled over into a state of real, though contained, war between military forces, and since 1955 it has been an ever-present feature of the Russian and American handling of the 'Third World'. (For further discussion of the Cold War, after 1950, and of the 'Third World', see Chapter 19.)

The Truman Doctrine and Marshall Aid, 1947

In 1947, the American attitude to the Cold War was clearly defined by President Truman to Congress. Following Russian claims to parts of Turkish territory, and Russian support for Communists in Greece, Britain (which had been trying to establish stability in the eastern Mediterranean) appealed to America for diplomatic and material help. As Truman explained, 'At the present moment, nearly every nation must choose between alternative ways of life. One ... is based on the will of the majority and is distinguished by free institutions... The second ... is based on the will of a minority forcibly imposed on the majority. It relies on terror and oppression, a controlled press and radio, fixed elections and the suppression of personal freedoms. I believe it must be the policy of the United States to support free peoples who are resisting attempted subjugation by armed minorities or by outside pressures.' This 'Truman Doctrine' set the pattern of economic, political, military and psychological support not only for Greece and Turkey, but for any part of Europe that would stand up to Russian encroachment.

In June 1947, the U.S. Secretary of State George Marshall announced a plan whereby the United States would finance the recovery and reconstruction of Europe 'to assist in the return of normal economic health in the world, without which there can be no political stability and no assured peace.' Immediately, the British and French governments called a conference of 22 other European states to assess what Europe's needs really were. The Russians could have come to this conference. They did not, and they also forbade the attendance of the countries over which they had influence – Albania, Bulgaria, Czechoslovakia, Finland, Hungary, Poland, Romania and Yugoslavia. This group became 'the Eastern bloc', the group inside the Iron Curtain. But 16 other European nations, including former enemies like Austria and neutrals like Portugal, Sweden and Switzerland formed the Organization for European Economic Cooperation (O.E.E.C.) to administer the European Recovery Programme, usually referred to as

Marshall Aid. In the years 1948–52, America provided $13,150,000,000 in aid, usually in cash but often in goods, vehicles and machinery, distributed to those countries whose need was greatest. Britain received about a quarter of the early contributions, France about a fifth, but before the plan ended, the western zones of Germany had become a part of it, and they also received substantial help, much of it at the time of the Berlin Airlift.

The Berlin Airlift, 1948–49

The administration of Marshall Aid required European-based economic organizations. In Germany after the Second World War, such a body needed the agreement of all four occupying powers. In 1948, the Russians refused to cooperate in the setting up of a German Economic Council to cope with the application for aid and the currency reform that would be necessary for its implementation. They marked their disapproval by making access to Berlin uncertain and irregular, a pin-pricking policy used several times to indicate diplomatic displeasure in the Cold War.

In June 1948, the Western Allies introduced a revalued currency, Deutschmarks, into West Germany and West Berlin, having failed to reach agreement with the Russians and the East Germans about a new currency for the whole nation. The East Germans retaliated by introducing their version of the new mark, and by interrupting access to Berlin by painstaking and tedious inspections of all vehicles and people travelling there. An American troop train that refused to submit to inspection was shunted into a siding and left there until it was withdrawn by its commanders. But on 24 June 1948, the Russians stopped all traffic by rail, road and canal between Berlin and the West. Two and a half million people were being put under siege.

The West accepted the unspoken challenge. 'We are going to stay. Period,' announced Truman. A minimum of 4,000 tons of goods a day were required to supply the Berliners' needs, and an immediate airlift began from the Western zones, using Dakotas (whose capacity was only three tons of goods each), Yorks (capacity five tons) and a few Skymasters (11 tons). Round-the-clock flying was necessary. Planes arrived at and left Berlin every 30 seconds. 20,000 Berliners, men and women, built a new airport at Tegel and lengthened the runways at Tempelhof and Gatow largely by hand, since the necessary machinery did not exist in Berlin.

By December 1948, 4,500 tons a day were flowing into Berlin. By March 1949, the figure had gone up to 8,000 tons a day, and on Easter Day a record 13,000 tons arrived from the West. On 9 May 1949, the Russians lifted the blockade, without comment or explanation.

Neither side won or lost the confrontation. The Russians had

Unloading supplies during the Berlin Airlift. (In front of the aeroplane stands an early 'Volkswagen', the 'People's Car' first produced by the Nazis, which scarcely changed its styling for 40 years.)

proved how easily they could disrupt the West, causing vast expenditure of money and effort at very little cost to themselves. The West had proved its determination in this 'Cold War'; they would not easily be deflected by Russian awkwardness. But each side could do the same thing again at any time. That knowledge, and the intensification of the Cold War illustrated by the Berlin blockade, encouraged both sides to consider the need for military pacts and agreements for greater security.

Military Pacts since 1948

In 1948, the Brussels Treaty bound Britain, France, Belgium, the Netherlands and Luxembourg to provide 'all the military and other aid and assistance in their power' in the event of one of their number being attacked. Though this pact was expanded into the Western European Union by the addition of Italy and West Germany in 1955, it was less important in world strategy than the North Atlantic Treaty Organization (NATO) set up in 1949.

NATO combined the original Brussels Treaty powers with America, Canada, Denmark, Iceland, Italy, Norway and Portugal. The military commitment was less binding, but Article V of the Treaty stated that 'an armed attack against one or more of them in Europe shall be considered an attack against them all', requiring 'such action as the member deems necessary.' Aimed clearly at resisting any Russian threat, it was the first treaty to link America and Canada with European defence, though the wording did not commit them to automatic war if fighting were to break out. In

1952 Greece and Turkey joined NATO, and in 1955 West Germany became a member, to the alarm of Russia and the confusion of France, where there were many reservations about West German re-armament, especially in a force which had access to nuclear weapons. (Similar French worries had already wrecked a proposed European Defence Community in 1952.) Although NATO's Headquarters (SHAPE, Supreme Headquarters, Allied Powers in Europe) were originally in Paris, French objections had them moved to Brussels, and from 1966–70, French forces withdrew from all military commitments to NATO, although General de Gaulle still considered that France was part of the Atlantic Alliance. In 1974, Greece similarly withdrew from the military structure of NATO following her conflict with Turkey in Cyprus.

In 1955, the Communists responded to the Austrian State Treaty and the admission of West Germany to NATO with the Warsaw Treaty Organization. This set up a unified military command for Russia and her satellite countries, and allowed Russian troops to be stationed in Albania (which withdrew in 1968), Bulgaria, Czechoslovakia, East Germany, Hungary, Poland and Romania, for defensive purposes, a reason which the Charter of the United Nations specified in Article 52 as being perfectly acceptable. The presence of these troops restrained anti-Russian feelings in Poland in 1956, but in Hungary in the same year and in Czechoslovakia in 1968 they were called into violent action to suppress nationalist uprisings.

The Korean War of 1950–53 (see Chapter 19) indicated that the Communist threat was world-wide. In 1951 America, Australia and New Zealand formed the ANZUS Pact, which in 1954 became the nucleus of SEATO, the South-East Asia Treaty Organization, consisting of the ANZUS powers and Britain, France, Pakistan, the Philippines and Thailand. In 1955 the Baghdad Pact provided vague links between Iraq, Turkey, Persia (Iran), Pakistan and Britain, which were intended to be a defence against Russia encroachment in the Middle East. In 1958 Iraq withdrew, and the Baghdad Pact was refashioned as CENTO (the Central Treaty Organization) in 1959. Revolution in Iran in 1979 led to its collapse in that year, but for 20 years it was in every sense a central part of the containing wall around Russian and Chinese Communism.

Chapter 19 traces the developments in international diplomacy from the Korean War to the start of 1980, but before that the evolution of four international focal points must be considered: not merely Russia and America, but also Western Europe (including Britain) and the most populous nation on earth, China.

Russia and Eastern Europe since 1945   14

RUSSIA

Russia and the Second World War

Russian losses in the Second World War were vast. Between seven and 10 million civilians are estimated to have been killed. A further seven and a half million servicemen lost their lives (one Russian soldier for every 22 of the population; for Britain the figure was one for every 150 and for America one for every 450). The barbarous nature of 'Operation Barbarossa' had left 25 million people homeless, destroyed 17,000 towns and 70,000 villages, torn up 40,000 miles of railway track and rendered useless 31,000 factories. In the fields, 45 million head of stock had been killed. The cash value of all losses was put at 679,000,000,000 roubles, an amount that could be calculated but not imagined. The German occupation of the south and west of the country caused the relocation of much industry; in late 1941 nearly 2,000 factories were dismantled and moved eastwards to Siberia or beyond, in 15 million truck-loads.

Yet the war was not totally destructive. A year of chaos followed the German invasion of June 1941, but in 1943, the Russians were able to produce 19,500 tanks and 35,000 planes. The war economy was becoming feverishly efficient, spurred on by the patriotism unleashed by the Nazi presence. The war became 'the Great Patriotic War', 'the Great Fatherland War', and no sacrifice was too great. In early July 1941, Stalin, once the ruthless dictator but now the symbol of patriotism, had appealed to the Russian people on the radio, 'Brothers, sisters, I turn to you, my friends. . .'. Slowly he came to personify the struggle against Germany. 'Not a single step backward. You must fight to your last drop of blood to defend every position, every foot of Soviet territory.' As Molotov put it, 'For our country, for Stalin.'

Thus the indirect effect of the war was to strengthen Stalin's position, without continuing the Great Purges of the 1930s. His appeal to pure patriotism fell on more sympathetic ears than an appeal to pure Communism, and he won an international image for heroic national leadership ('Uncle Joe') as well as a new respect in Russia.

The war completely altered Russia's international role. In the 1930s Stalin had been concentrating on 'Socialism in One Country', and to protect this ideal had signed the Non-Aggression Pact with Hitler in August 1939. From this unlikely position (unlikely because of the outspoken hatred between Nazism and Communism), the German invasion of Poland, and, in 1941, of Russia stimulated Russia's emergence as a world power. A new framework of alliances was built with Britain and America; Lend-Lease agreements were signed, and convoys of ships brought arms and supplies from Stalin's capitalist friends. In 1944, described by Soviet historians as the 'Year of the Ten Victories', Russian forces thrust their way into the Ukraine and Poland, Finland and the Baltic Provinces, Romania, Bulgaria, Hungary and Yugoslavia. In 1945, Slovakia, Upper Silesia, Austria and East Prussia fell to the Russians, as well as the eastern part of Germany, including the city of Berlin, and a number of former Japanese possessions in the Far East. Stalin was now one of the 'Big Three', conferring at Teheran, Yalta and Potsdam with the British and American leaders. Then, because of the death of Roosevelt in April 1945 and Churchill's loss of office following the July election, Stalin suddenly became the most experienced and strongly placed statesman in the Western world. Russia entered the war as a likely victim of Hitler's expansion: she ended it as one of the two greatest powers in the world.

Home Affairs 1945–53

Economic recovery, at least to the level of the 1930s, was remarkably speedy. Planning had started as soon as the German retreat gathered speed in 1943, and in 1946 Stalin announced the Fourth Five Year Plan (1946–50). Its emphasis was on heavy industry, transport and power sources, but it also included the maintenance of four million men in the armed services. A Fifth Five Year Plan was outlined at the same time, again stressing major building projects and hydro-electric schemes. This was to be interrupted by Stalin's death in 1953.

The success of industrial reconstruction was based on the ruthlessness made possible by a planned economy. The Russian people were deprived of most consumer goods, and knew that none would be produced until basic capital requirements had been fulfilled. Long hours of labour with defined production targets earned very little money, but guaranteed adequate food and shelter. Some two million prisoners of war faced the choice of work or death, and many Soviet citizens suspected of 'treason' or lesser crimes found themselves in labour camps. From the eastern zone of Germany came reparations in the form of any and every machine that the Russians could strip down and move, and from Finland, Romania, Hungary and Manchuria came confiscated goods and 'voluntary contributions'. By 1948, overall industrial production exceeded that of the last full year of peace, 1940. By 1952, it was more than twice that figure.

Agricultural production on the other hand remained low, though this was concealed. In 1946 drought hit the Ukraine, followed by famine in 1947. Tractors and horses were in short supply, and in areas where the menfolk had been killed in the war, it was not uncommon for women to drag the ploughs. When Khrushchev was able to reveal the statistics after Stalin's death, they showed that in 1953 there were three and a half million less cows than in 1941, six million less horses, and significantly less grain, potatoes and vegetables to feed an increased population. Housing conditions were also awful. Russian couples were encouraged by allowances and tax concessions to have large families – 10 live children entitled a woman to be a 'Heroine Mother of the Soviet Union' – but they might find themselves sharing an apartment with another family if they lived in any of Russia's major cities.

Stalin and his Successors

In 1952 Stalin called the Nineteenth Party Congress, the first to be held since before the war. The Party membership had grown to nearly seven million (from about three million at the beginning of the war), but Stalin's control was still absolute. As he had been born in 1879, speculation about his possible successor was inevitable. But to be prominent was to be at risk, and Stalin deliberately encouraged a sense of insecurity and tension among the Politburo and the Party Central Committee. In 1945 Malenkov and Zhdanov, both Party Secretaries, seemed to be rivals for higher office, but when Zhdanov died in 1948, his friends were purged and it was Malenkov and Beria, the Chief of Police, who appeared to have control. In 1949 Stalin summoned to Moscow N. Khrushchev, chairman of the Council of Ministers in the Ukraine, thereby creating new doubts and rivalries. Molotov and Kaganovich, longstanding members of the Politburo, also held an undefined amount of influence, but at the Nineteenth Party Congress, Stalin announced the abolition of the Politburo and the establishment of a new Praesidium. It is possible that he now planned a new and massive purge of the top of the Party. In January 1953, it was announced that nine doctors on the Kremlin staff (most of them Jewish) had been charged with killing Zhdanov and other high officials. Two of the doctors died while 'confessing' their 'crimes', and further deaths were expected, among them those of Molotov and Malenkov. But it was Stalin who died, of natural causes. He had a stroke and lived on for only three days. Russian officials were so unprepared for this turn of events that they delayed the news for two days.

In the succeeding power-struggle, Beria was arrested in June

1953 and shot in December for 'seeking to set the M.V.D. (the Ministry of the Interior) above the Party and the Government'. Malenkov, having become Prime Minister and First Secretary of the Party immediately on Stalin's death, lost the latter post within a fortnight and the former in February 1955, when he resigned it because of his 'responsibility for the unsatisfactory state of affairs in agriculture.' Molotov lasted as Foreign Minister from 1953 until 1956; Kaganovich, who knew more about transport and industry than anyone, was steadily demoted. The two men who moved upwards were Khrushchev, who became First Secretary of the Party in September 1953, and Bulganin, who became Prime Minister after Malenkov. From his post at the head of the Communist Party, Khrushchev began to emphasize the need for collective decisions, and used all his influence to place in key positions men who would support him. By 1956, his power was increasing everywhere except in the Praesidium, and following the troubles in East Berlin, Czechoslovakia, Poland and Hungary, his opponents tried to force him out. In May 1957 a seven to four majority in the Praesidium demanded his resignation. Khrushchev appealed to the Central Committee of the Party, while the war hero Marshal Zhukov, who had been appointed Minister of Defence at Khrushchev's suggestion, assured him of military support. In June 1957, the Party voted for Khrushchev, and the 'anti-Party group' were forced to resign. They were not executed but sent off to strange and separate fates: Molotov became Ambassador to Outer Mongolia; Malenkov became manager of a power station in Kazakhstan; Shepilov became a schoolmaster. Khrushchev was now supreme, but he did not take over the office of Prime Minister until January 1958. Until October 1964, he ran Russia.

The Twentieth Congress, 1956, and De-Stalinization

In February 1956, the Twentieth Party Congress was held in Moscow. It was the first since Stalin's death, the first ever that Stalin had not attended. On the final day, the Congress went into secret session to hear a speech by Khrushchev 'On the Cult of Personality and its Consequences.' It was a dramatic condemnation of Stalin, his policies and his methods. It revealed Lenin's worries about Stalin, as written in his Testament; it contained damning evidence of injustice and brutality taken from M.V.D. files; it condemned the arrogance with which Stalin had given his name to countless towns, streets, farms and factories. It destroyed the reputation of the man who had led Russia for 30 years, tore him down from his near-sacred position alongside Marx, Engels and Lenin as a creator of Communist ideology, and later led to the removal of his body from the mausoleum in Red Square for reburial elsewhere.

Khrushchev's speech stunned the Communist world. Those

Khrushchev (left) visits Tito in Yugoslavia, 1963. Khrushchev's friendly approval of Tito's brand of Communism not only failed to bring Yugoslavia into the Russian bloc, it also unsettled other Communist leaders inside and outside Russia.

who had worked for Stalin felt condemned with him, and therefore unsafe. Those who had sacrificed so much under his leadership felt cheated. Those who believed in him still (and many Russians had no other political memories or allegiance) felt unsettled and angry. History and political theory were being rewritten, past judgements were being turned inside out. Tito of Yugoslavia (see below) was now praised for resisting Stalin's pressures, and Khrushchev announced that there were many different and acceptable roads to true Communism, including Tito's. He also said that war against imperialist and capitalist states was not absolutely inevitable, implying that even Lenin had made mistakes. Although the speech was probably intended to make Communism more attractive and less rigid, and at the same time secure Khrushchev's own position in the Party, it had the opposite effect. In the satellite countries discontent and disillusionment welled up into violence in the autumn of 1956 (see below), while Khrushchev himself came under attack in the Praesidium in 1957 (see above).

Khrushchev's Economic Policy, and his Fall from Power

The Fifth Five Year Plan (1951–55) had contained many grandiose projects which after the fall of Stalin looked suspiciously like parts of his 'personality cult'. It was therefore modified, and from 1953 to

1955 the Russian people were treated to the 'New Course', which concentrated on food, clothing and household goods. The Sixth Five Year Plan (1956–60) swung back towards heavy industry (coal and steel), but its targets were badly assessed, and in 1959 the Seventh Plan took its place. Khrushchev's intention was to boost secondary industries like chemicals, fertilizers and plastics, which would support his agricultural policy, as well as a huge housing programme. He announced in 1961 that Russia would 'catch up and overtake the U.S.A. in per capita output by 1970', and the people were led to expect massive improvements in their living standards. A new education policy was instituted in 1958, requiring school attendance until the age of 15.

Once again, agriculture wrecked Russian ambitions, and helped to bring down Khrushchev, who was directly responsible for agriculture from 1953 until his fall in 1964. His failure was not caused by lack of effort: he reduced the central Party's control over farms in the hope of encouraging local organization. Collective farms became fewer but larger, and the Machine Tractor Stations with their political commissars were abolished, their tractors being sold to the farms. But although the guaranteed price paid by the state for dairy products went up by 150 per cent, and that for meat by 400 per cent, production was not stimulated by all these changes. The only real gain came from the cultivation of the 'virgin lands', vast areas of Kazakhstan, South and Central Siberia and the Southern Urals which totalled as many acres as the entire cultivated area of Canada. From 1953 to 1958, these lands more than justified the huge investment of machinery, money and skilled labour by producing an annual growth rate of 8.6 per cent. But in the period 1959–61, production totals fell back because the virgin lands had been farmed too intensively and without proper rotation of crops. In 1963, drought struck Russia. The virgin lands produced five million tons of grain instead of the 14 million of 1958; total production was 20 per cent below that of 1962, and Russia found itself back in the humiliating position of having to import grain from North America.

The failure of the agriculture policy contributed to the fall of Khrushchev; so did his foreign policy (see below) and his 'Programme' of 1961, in which he tried to bring Communist philosophy up to date. He stressed that up to that point only Socialism had been achieved: true Communism would come in the 1980s, when gradually the state would wither away, as Marx had forecast. The ideal of 'From each according to his ability; to each according to his needs' would be carried out without strict governmental supervision. A golden age would follow the tyranny of Stalin. Khrushchev was much more liberal than Stalin had been. He personally authorized the publication of Solzhenitsyn's *One Day in the Life of Ivan Denisovich*, a story of life in a labour camp. Censorship of all sorts diminished, and literature, art and music all displayed a daring which had not been experienced since the Revolution.

In October 1964, the Soviet press announced that Khrushchev had resigned 'in view of his advanced age and deteriorating health'. In fact he had lost a crucial vote in the Central Committee of the Party, and was found guilty of 'harebrained schemes, half baked conclusions and hasty decisions' as well as 'bragging and bluster'. His post as Prime Minister was taken by Kosygin. Brezhnev succeeded him as Party Secretary.

Brezhnev and Kosygin – Domestic Affairs

Brezhnev and Kosygin exercised 'collective leadership', along with men like Podgorny (Chairman of the Praesidium 1965–77), Kuznetsov and Chernenko. Brezhnev came nearest to being the sole ruler of Russia when in 1977 he combined the post of Head of State (Chairman of the Praesidium) with that of Party Secretary, but his poor health prevented him from establishing any form of dictatorship.

Policies in the 15 years after Khrushchev's fall changed gradually, becoming 'safer' and more predictable, but less tolerant of internal disagreement and outside criticism. Rash promises and optimistic targets gave way to practical achievements of all sorts. Agricultural production improved again in 1966 after Brezhnev granted higher prices for grain and livestock from State farms and Collectives, and doubled the investment in farm machinery. Good

The Moscow Metro, a cheap, efficient and spotlessly clean Underground system. Certain public facilities in the U.S.S.R. are lavishly built, in marked contrast to the state-owned apartment blocks and ordinary shops.

harvests were brought in in 1968, 1970 and 1976, and the 1977 harvest was the fourth biggest in Soviet history. The household plots which collective farmers had been given to grow produce for their own use were partly responsible for the higher level of production. Although representing only four per cent of the country's arable area, they contributed a third of the country's meat, milk, vegetables and eggs.

In the late 1970s, Russia possessed more than half the world's known energy sources (oil, natural gas and coal), and the economy therefore expanded more steadily than those of Western nations, and without the rapid rate of inflation. Industrial production rose by 50 per cent between 1970 and 1976 (comparative figures for Britain and the U.S.A. are two per cent and 22 per cent respectively), and the economy was able to sustain not only a new housing initiative but also an ambitious space programme, the hosting of the Olympic Games in 1980, and an increase in consumer goods for the man in the street.

The organization under which these advances were made was similar to that which had existed before Khrushchev's rise to power. 'Gosplan' ran the central planning of the economy, while individual ministries were responsible for specific sections. A State Committee for Material and Technical Supplies took charge of the distribution and allocation of the machines and resources needed for production. The 1966–70 Five Year Plan concentrated on agriculture; the 1970–75 Plan was geared towards 'the welfare of the masses', and for the first time aimed at a faster growth of consumer goods than of producers' goods. This was not achieved, and it was not attempted again in the Tenth Plan (1976–80), which stressed heavy industry, 'efficiency and quality', and a more gradual growth rate.

After the fall of Khrushchev, criticism of the regime became more dangerous. Solzhenitsyn was expelled from the Writers' Union in 1969, following the publication abroad of his books *Cancer Ward* and *The First Circle*. Although awarded the Nobel Prize for Literature in 1970, he did not leave Russia to collect it, lest he was not allowed back into his homeland. In 1974, he was expelled from Russia following the publication in Paris of the first part of *The Gulag Archipelago*, which returned to the theme of Russian labour camps. Other dissidents like Sinyavsky and Daniel were sentenced to hard labour in such camps in the 1960s. In the mid-70s, there were frequent indications that dissidents were being committed to psychiatric hospitals.

In 1977, Brezhnev presented a new Soviet Constitution to the Central Committee, to replace Stalin's Constitution of 1936. It stressed the duties and rights of Soviet citizens, emphasized the role of the Party, and reaffirmed the Russian belief in 'peaceful coexistence' and the end of 'aggressive wars'. Foreign policy had thus changed greatly since 1945.

Brezhnev and Fidel Castro in Havana, 1974.

Foreign Policy after 1945

The Second World War ended with Russian troops occupying much of Germany, the east of Austria and all of Poland and Czechoslovakia, as well as Hungary, Bulgaria and Romania. Communist influence was strong in Albania and Yugoslavia, and growing significantly in Greece and Turkey. Russia was a major member of the Atlantic Alliance, and as such, a founder of the United Nations Organization, with a permanent seat on the Security Council. Its foreign policy was therefore very different from that of Russia in the 1930s, when Stalin struggled for 'Socialism in One Country' and Britain and America focussed their attention on the right-wing dictatorships. Russia now had to take up the leadership of the Marxist world revolution, holding its position in Europe while also supporting its Communist allies in the Far East. Russian post-war foreign policy therefore has three main threads, sometimes interwoven, sometimes distinct. The first, the relationship with China, is discussed in Chapter 18. Russia's relationship with the Western powers is discussed in Chapter 13 and 19. The third thread, the development of Eastern Europe, is considered below.

RUSSIA AND EASTERN EUROPE

When Stalin wanted Eastern Europe to become and remain Communist, he meant 'Russian' Communist, not nationalist Communist. For this purpose he created the Communist Information Bureau ('Cominform') in 1947, with headquarters in Belgrade (and after 1948 in Bucharest), and the Council for Mutual Economic Assistance ('Comecon') in 1949. Cominform was dissolved in 1956, but Comecon expanded to include Outer Mongolia, China and Cuba as full or associate members. The idea of Comecon was to provide long-term economic planning, like Western Europe's Organization for European Economic Cooperation (1948) and Organization for Economic Cooperation and Development (1961). In 1962 it produced a Basic Plan, and in 1971 it agreed to the 'Complex Programme for the Development of Socialist Economic Integration', which is still operative. The Warsaw Pact of 1955 was a third unifying feature.

But Eastern Europe has not remained tightly united and strictly loyal to Russia. Stalin's grip failed to hold Yugoslavia, which was expelled from Cominform in 1948 for following the independent line of Marshal Tito, while other nationalistic leaders were quickly eliminated: Xoxe, Deputy Premier of Albania, was executed; Dimitrov of Bulgaria was invited to Russia for a 'cure'; Gomulka of Poland was dismissed for 'insufficient appreciation of the role of the U.S.S.R.', but was later reinstated. But each communist country of Eastern Europe has developed in a different way since 1945.

Albania

Since the end of its occupation by Italians in the Second World War, Albania has maintained a stubborn and sometimes confusing independence of spirit. It has been led throughout that time by one man, Enver Hoxha, wartime resistance leader and First Secretary of the (Communist) Party of Labour. Geographically isolated from all other Warsaw Pact countries (it joined the Pact but was expelled in 1961), Albania has the smallest population and the poorest economy. Hoxha accepted Russian aid until 1961, when he swung his allegiance towards China, with whose leaders he declared 'unbreakable friendship'. This policy lasted until 1977. During the 1960s, more than 50 per cent of Albania's trade was with China, but when the Chinese reduced their aid, Hoxha attacked the 'arbitrary, insidious and hostile' acts of the Peking government while still criticizing the Russian 'social-imperialists', thus leaving himself totally isolated. Albania's relationship with Yugoslavia, its only Communist neighbour, was always stormy after 1948, perhaps because of the similarities between their dictators Hoxha and Tito. Albania is a 'People's Democracy'. Of the

1,436,289 people entitled to vote in 1978, all but one did so, and except for three spoiled papers, every vote was cast for the Communist-led Democratic Front.

Bulgaria

Bulgaria, also a People's Republic, stayed firmly and contentedly in the Russian sphere of influence after Soviet troops ousted the Nazis in 1944. The 'Fatherland Front', a coalition of Communists, Agrarians and Social Democrats, abolished the monarchy in 1946. The Communists under Dimitrov then worked their way to total power. Russian pressures squashed the idea of a Balkan Federation under Yugoslav domination in 1948, and the Bulgarians were quick to put 'Titoists' on trial. Dimitrov, who died in Moscow in 1949, was replaced by a steadfast Stalinist, Chervenkov. A regular pattern of Five Year Plans has followed since, with 51 per cent of all imports coming from Russia, and 55 per cent of all exports going there.

Czechoslovakia

The Communist party under Gottwald organized much of the Czech resistance to the Nazis, and was therefore in a strong position in 1945. Despite the presence of Beneš as President and Jan (son of Thomas) Masaryk as Foreign Minister, the Communists took 38 per cent of the votes in the 1946 election, and dominated the National Front, which governed until 1948. The non-Communists wanted to accept Marshall Aid in 1947, but the Communists outmanoeuvred them, and early in 1948 started to pack the security forces with Party members only. In February 1948, the ailing Beneš accepted Gottwald's Cabinet list which was clearly Communist controlled. The only possible prominent opponent, Masaryk, was found murdered in March.

Under Gottwald until 1953, Zapotocky until 1957, and Novotny until 1968, Czechoslovakians frequently showed moderate resistance to the Communist plans and a succession of churchmen, poets and politicians were hauled before 'people's courts' by security police. But neither purges nor planning on the Soviet model gave the authorities the confidence of the people, and in 1968 economic discontent mingled with Slovak-Czech racial rivalry to produce a demand for policies which were more liberal and more locally varied. Alexander Dubček, Secretary of the Party from January 1968, was prepared to be sympathetic: he and Cernik, the Prime Minister, called for an extra meeting of the Party Congress in September 1968 to discuss 'Socialism with a Human Face'. His 'Action Programme' promised immunity for victims of past purges, economic reforms, the abolition of censorship, and a more broadly-based democracy than the existing one-party system. But before it

could be put into effect, Warsaw Pact manoeuvres brought troops
and tension to the Czech frontiers. Dubček consulted Tito of
Yugoslavia, Ulbricht of East Germany and Ceausescu of Romania,
but could find no solid support. In August the Pact troops, with
units from East Germany, Hungary, Poland, Bulgaria and Russia,
invaded: Dubček was whisked away to Russia for a week, and
resistance evaporated. When a student, Jan Palach, set himself on
fire in January 1969 in protest against the loss of freedom in
Czechoslovakia, he became the new national martyr, but few others
were prepared to sacrifice their lives to express their opposition. In
1969 Dubček was eased out of office by Husak. Cernik fell in 1970.

Husak, a moderate, added the post of President of Czechoslovakia to his General Secretaryship of the Party in 1975. His
concern was to restore the 'normalization' of relations with
Moscow after Dubcek's year in office, but he faced attacks from
both wings. In Party Congresses Vasil Bilak constantly produced
'hard-line' policies, but among the people the desire for liberalization was still strong. In January 1977, 'Charter 77' appeared for the
first time, a series of documents appealing to the Czech government
to abide by its own laws on human rights. 242 people signed the
Charter, a number which grew to 1,000 by 1978, even though
signing inevitably cost jobs, freedom and sometimes lives. Professor
Patocka, one of the first spokesmen for the Charter, died in March
1977 after 10 hours of police interrogation. The Charter, which
grew month by month, concentrated on specific charges against
government oppression: illegal house searches, arbitrary arrest,
police violence, cultural censorship (including cutting the number
of pop musicians from 60,000 in 1968 to 3,000 in 1978) and
victimization of churchmen. Too well-publicized and too deep-
rooted to be destroyed quietly, Charter 77 was as embarrassing to
the government in the late 1970s as the rapid and resented rise in
consumer prices.

East Germany

The Russian-occupied zone of Germany was recognized as the
German Democratic Republic (D.D.R.) in 1949, following the
West's creation of the German Federal Republic out of their three
zones of post-war occupation.

At first the Russian attitude to East Germany was markedly
oppressive and punitive. All bank accounts were blocked so that
everybody had to work in order to live; all estates of more than 250
acres were taken over without compensation. The only political
parties allowed were the 'Anti-Fascist' parties, which since 1946
has meant the dominance of the Socialist Unity Party, which is a
combination of the Communists and a few Social Democrats. The
1949 Constitution set up two legislative houses, but the upper
house was abolished in 1952.

In 1953, Russian policies provoked a series of strikes which ended in a violent uprising, requiring Russian troops to suppress it. The East Germans resented the shortage of food and consumer goods, the anti-religious policy of the Russians, and the constant political and economic interference by Moscow. Having crushed the trouble, the Russians tried to win the support of the Germans by stopping the collection of reparations in 1954, announcing that the D.D.R. was a sovereign state in 1954, and allowing it to be a founder member of the Warsaw Pact in 1955. They failed: the trickle of refugees from East Germany moving towards the West became a flood, despite the creation of a three-mile wide control zone along the dividing frontier. Between 1945 and 1961, 3,500,000 people arrived in the West, most of them through the divided city of Berlin. In 1961, this gap was suddenly closed by the Berlin Wall (see Chapter 16).

After 1961, partly because it was no longer losing skilled men to the West, the East German economy picked up and became very important to Russia and the Eastern bloc, supplying coal, iron ore, steel, cement and machinery. Renovation of its own ruined cities followed: East Berlin, Dresden, Magdeburg and Leipzig received much-needed attention, and the East German resentment of Russia diminished but has by no means disappeared.

In December 1972, a treaty between East and West Germany removed much of the uncertainty that had existed since 1945. This mutual recognition led to their admission to the United Nations in 1973, and East Germany has now established diplomatic relations with all major Western countries.

From 1945 until 1971, East German politics were dominated by Walter Ulbricht, a tough Stalinist and efficient organizer whose control of the Socialist Unity Party during those years made him more important than Grotewohl and Pieck, who were Prime Minister and President in the early years. In 1971 Erich Honeker became Party Chairman and First Secretary, to which he added the Chairmanship of the Council of State in 1976. As in Russia, Party rank carries more power than State titles.

Hungary

Soviet troops were in occupation of Hungary at the end of the Second World War. Their presence was enough to lever the country into accepting a Communist government in 1949. Free elections in 1945 had produced an overall majority for the Smallholders (non-Communist) Party, but open intimidation reduced their share of the vote to 15 per cent in the 1947 elections and turned them into Communist puppets by 1949. The Workers' (Communist) Party under Rakosi gradually took power and produced a new constitution in 1949, though there was considerable political infighting, and many 'National Communists' were imprisoned or executed on charges ranging from spying for the Gestapo during the war to supporting Tito in Yugoslavia. Rakosi was a 'hard line' supporter of Moscow's policies. Through his control of the Hungarian Communist Party he set up a police state, pummelling the people into acceptance. His most outspoken opponent, Cardinal Mindszenty, Head of the Roman Catholic Church in Hungary, was sentenced to life imprisonment in 1949 for 'treason' (opposing the State's takeover of Catholic schools), but there was always an undercurrent of resistance to Rakosi, and in 1953 he handed over the Premiership to Imre Nagy, who tried to establish more trust and cooperation in the country. He released political prisoners, reduced the demands of heavy industry, slowed down the move towards collective farming, and tried to improve the standard of living.

The change of direction proved very unsettling: Nagy was replaced by Rakosi again in 1955, but in July 1956 he was in turn sacked from all his State and Party posts, being replaced by his deputy Gero, another hard-liner. In October 1956 (just three days before the Suez Crisis gripped the attention of the entire non-Communist world) a student demonstration asking for a redress of all grievances turned into a full-blooded revolution when the police fired on the demonstrators. The secret police were hunted down; Hungarian Army men turned against their Russian 'advisers', and Russian troops and tanks called in by Gero quickly retired from Budapest. Cardinal Mindszenty was released from prison by

Humiliation of a 'Head of State'. When the Hungarians rose against Russian domination in 1956, Stalin's huge statue in Budapest was an obvious target.

cheering crowds, and popular pressure brought Nagy back to power, along with representatives of all those political parties that had disappeared in the previous 10 years.

Nagy tried to create an independently Communist Hungary by leaving the Warsaw Pact, but his position was impossible: he could control neither the demands of the people nor the reactions of the Kremlin. Early in November Russian tanks ringed Budapest; on 4 November they blasted their way back to control. Nagy fled to the Yugoslav Embassy until he was offered a guarantee of safety by the government of Janos Kadar. He came out and immediately disappeared; his execution was announced two years later. Mindszenty took refuge in the U.S. Embassy and remained there until 1971, when he agreed to move to the West, remaining a bitter critic of Communism and of those who tried to come to terms with it. 150,000 Hungarians fled to the West, but the official figures of 3,000 dead and 13,000 wounded indicate the ferocity with which this shortlived freedom had been defended.

Kadar proved to be a loyal Communist and follower of Khrushchev's general philosophies, trying to find a road to true Socialism acceptable to both Moscow and the Hungarians. By taking the line that those who were not against him could be assumed to be for him, he enabled most Hungarians to lead their own lives without the element of fear that Stalinism had provoked. Although twice Prime Minister (1956–58 and 1961–65), his greater source of power came from being First Secretary of the Communist Party. Patient planning and sensitive regulation over a period of more than 20 years have stabilized Hungary again without cementing it too firmly into a Russian pattern, and Kadar has been careful to cultivate his country's image as a loyal satellite country yet with a life of its own.

Poland

When the Second War ended, Poland had two potential governments. One, based in London, had been formed by General Sikorski but had lost all Russian support in 1943, when it accused Stalin's regime of the mass murder of several thousand Polish officers at Katyn, near Smolensk, in 1940, when Russia was still allied to Germany. The other, with strong Russian support, had established itself in Lublin in 1944 and claimed the right to govern those parts of Poland liberated by the Russians. Although representatives from each group made up the Polish Government of National Unity in June 1945, it was not Mikolajczyk from London but Gomulka and Bierut from the Lublin Committee who had most influence.

Gomulka was Secretary-General of the Polish Communist Party from 1945 until 1970 with the exception of the years 1948–56, when he was considered too nationalistic by Stalinists, and was accordingly stripped not only of political office but also of Party membership, and was imprisoned. Less liberal than Dubček of Czechoslovakia, less nationalistic than Tito of Yugoslavia, less rigid than Kadar of Hungary, Gomulka tried like these men to find a Communist 'middle way' between the demands of the Stalinists and the desires of the people. In 1956, when workers in Poznan rioted in support of their economic demands and the Russians threatened to reimpose order by force, the evident strength of Polish feelings brought about not confrontation but the reinstatement of Gomulka (not long after Khrushchev's de-Stalinization campaign had begun) and a number of reforms. The persecution of Catholics ended; press freedom increased; collective farms were disbanded; living standards were improved. Nevertheless in 1970 bad harvests and a widespread frustration with the government caused a threat of more riots. Gomulka resigned and handed over to Gierek, a more conciliatory leader. Nevertheless, frustration over Russian interference, and economic failure, produced in 1980 the Communist world's first independent Trade Union, 'Solidarity'.

Amidst the economic and political gloom of Poland in the 1970s, the election of Cardinal Wojtyla, Archbishop of Cracow, as Pope John Paul II in October 1978 provided a beacon of nationalistic pride and religious fervour which the Communist authorities did not try to extinguish. The first non-Italian Pope since 1522, and the first Pole to hold the office, John Paul returned to his country for an official visit in 1979, voicing thoughts about the independence of the human spirit which are not often heard behind the Iron Curtain.

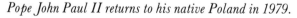

Pope John Paul II returns to his native Poland in 1979.

Romania

Romania was occupied by Russian troops in 1944. In 1945 King Michael appointed a Communist Prime Minister, Groza, but after rigged elections in 1946, the monarchy was forcibly suppressed in 1947 and a 'People's Republic' proclaimed, under Communist leadership. Romania provided the headquarters for Cominform from 1948 until 1956, and is a member of Comecon and the Warsaw Pact, though in 1964 the Romanian government complained that it was being expected to contribute too many agricultural products to the Eastern bloc when it wanted to expand its own industrial production. In 1965, following the death of Gheorghiu-Dej, who had run the country since 1945, Ceausescu became First Secretary of the Communist Party and in 1974, he assumed the newly created position of President of the Republic. Under his guidance Romania has appeared to steer an increasingly independent course, but the country remains committed to Russia for financial investment in several major canal and hydro-electric projects which were launched in the 1970s.

Yugoslavia

Josip Broz (known as 'Tito' since 1934) stands supreme as the most stubborn, the most successful and the most long-lived nationalist Communist leader since the Second World War. A committed Communist since the early 1920s, he led the Partisan resistance to the Nazis in Yugoslavia with such brilliance that by the end of the war he held considerable political power. In 1945, he became President of Yugoslavia, after King Peter had been formally deposed.

A tough administrator, Tito rapidly fell out with his former allies in the West by supporting the Communist rebels in Greece, shooting down two American planes over Slovenia and trying to gain control of Trieste, but he also fell out with Stalin over his ambitious plans to set up a loose Balkan Federation, which at first received enthusiastic support from Albania and Bulgaria. In 1948 Yugoslavia was expelled from Cominform, and its neighbours hastened to prove – by holding public trials of Titoists – how loyal they were to Moscow. Tito pursued his independent course unabashed, even accepting economic aid from America. When Stalin died and was condemned by Khrushchev at the Twentieth Congress in 1956, Tito's way of Communism was given official Russian approval, but Soviet support had as little effect on his policies as Soviet opposition. Throughout the 1960s Tito kept up the 'non-aligned' stance, which he clearly proclaimed at a conference in Belgrade in 1961. He travelled all over Africa, Asia and Latin America in order to make the 'Third World' conscious of its power and its rights (see Chapter 19), and he was secure enough to condemn vigorously the Russian invasion of Czechoslovakia in 1968. Throughout the 1970s, Tito's age (he was born in 1892 and died in 1980) inevitably influenced the policies of friend and foe alike as they waited to see what would happen after his death. Thus, relatively unchallenged, Tito was able to broaden contacts with other countries, not least by increasing tourism in Yugoslavia, and to further decentralize his government's economic controls, as a way of stimulating the economy. Nevertheless, Yugoslavia remained economically vulnerable, the one major drawback of its hard-won independence.

America since 1941 15

America and the Second World War

In August 1941, the American Congress was called upon to renew the Burke-Wadsworth Act which had set up 'the draft' (compulsory service in the armed forces) in peacetime for the first time in American history. After a blistering debate, the Act was renewed by 203 votes to 202. Four months later, after the Japanese attack on the US Navy base at Pearl Harbor, American opinion was not divided: 'Modern warfare ... is a dirty business. We don't like it; we didn't want to get into it; but we are in it and we are going to fight it with everything we've got,' said President Roosevelt in a broadcast to the people. It was his idea that America should be 'the arsenal of democracy', and his policies won so much support that even as a visibly sick and drained man, he won the Presidential Election of 1944 by 432 Electoral College votes to 99, a handsome and unprecedented fourth election victory.

America's material contribution to the war was enormous: 87,000 tanks, 296,000 aircraft, 64,500 landing craft, 6,500 fighting ships, 5,400 cargo ships and troop transports. Eleven and a half million Americans went overseas to fight; 300,000 were killed.

America bore the brunt of the Japanese war. U.S. planes won the crucial 'naval' battles of 1942 at the Coral Sea and Midway. U.S. submarines destroyed 4,000,000 tons of Japanese shipping, thereby strangling the island economy; American marines spearheaded the island-hopping advance towards Japan itself in 1943–45, and America produced the two atom bombs which forced the Japanese to speedy surrender in 1945, saving perhaps 250,000 American lives, which any other attack on Japan would surely have cost.

In the war for control of Europe, America provided four-fifths of the troops that invaded Morocco and Algeria in 1942 ('Operation Torch'); Patton's Seventh Army shared the invasion of Sicily, and went on to Italy, while in 1944, 73,000 Americans were involved in the first assaults on the Normandy beaches on D-Day, and the Seventh Army appeared again in August, invading the south of France ('Operation Dragoon'). The U.S. Air Force protected Atlantic convoys and bombed Germany; U.S. shipping supported the Royal Navy in the Atlantic.

At home, the war caused huge dislocation as men and women went off to fight, but there was no fighting on American soil, no bombing of industry nor destruction of civilians' homes. The overall effect was to stimulate the economy and the general level of production. By the beginning of 1944, American production was double that of all the enemy countries put together, and the efficiency was such that a 'Liberty Ship', a very basic standardized cargo ship, could be built in four days: the first one in 1942 had taken 245 days. Agricultural production went up by a sixth; the number in employment increased by six and a half million (apart from the 15 million in the armed services) and gross wages increased (on average) by 72 per cent, while prices went up by 29 per cent. Taxes were increased to pay for the war and to minimize inflation, and the National Debt increased five-fold between 1941 and 1945. The effect was to create a thriving, bustling economy, on which most of the non-Axis world came to depend for armaments, food, fuel and finance, all acquired by 'Lend-Lease' or by direct purchase. That same dependence was even more in evidence after the war.

FDR – the Presidency and the People

In April 1945, as Allied troops closed in on the centre of Berlin, where Hitler was living out his final frantic days, President Franklin Roosevelt had a stroke while posing for a portrait, and died without regaining consciousness. Having been crippled with polio since 1921, his health had always been a cause for concern. But 'In the days of peace he had broadened and stabilized the foundations of American life and union,' Churchill recalled. 'In war he had raised the strength, might and glory of the great Republic to a height never attained by any nation in history.' But Roosevelt's greatness was not universally appreciated. His 'New Deal' philosophy had saved the economy and shored up American society, but had also angered many conservatives who feared the growth of state control, centralized powers and creeping socialism in 'the land of the free'. His sympathy for Britain in 1939, and his gradual swing from the Neutrality Act of 1935 to 'Lend-Lease' in 1941 angered not only those Americans of German and Italian descent, but also the traditional isolationists. His fearless prosecution of the war brought more criticism, though not enough to prevent his fourth election and inauguration as President. Such agencies as the War Production Board, the Office of War Mobilization, the Office of Price Administration and the National War Labor Board were regarded by some as threats to American democracy because of the powers which they brought to the President and his administration. The locking-up in special camps of 112,000 American-Japanese in 1942 is an example; many of them were deprived of their rights as citizens. On very rare occasions, in 1942–44, the government interfered in industrial strikes and labour relations, though

FDR greets a wounded sailor in Washington, 1942. His informal style made him one of the more popular Presidents of the century.

Roosevelt was less keen than Congress to do this. In 1943, the Smith-Connally War Labor Disputes Act, which required unions to give 30 days' notice before a strike, was passed in spite of the President's veto.

Roosevelt's period in office certainly raised the power and prestige of the Presidency. He was the first Head of State to use the radio as a medium to explain things regularly to 'his' people; his gentle, fatherly style ('the fireside chat') was more informal than that of the British monarchs who used the radio to address their subjects in Britain and the Empire and Commonwealth, especially at Christmastime. But the fear arose that Roosevelt was almost a monarch, and the Republicans felt threatened. In 1947, Congress proposed the 22nd Amendment to the Constitution, ensuring that no-one could be elected to the Presidency more than twice; it became law in 1951. Congress also challenged Roosevelt's successor, Truman, but they were not altogether successful.

Harry S. Truman, President 1945–53

Truman was a Midwesterner, from Independence, Missouri. His early adult life, when he was too poor to go to college and too poor-sighted to get into the army, saw him in numerous unskilled jobs and tentative business ventures. His early political life was slightly marred by contact with 'machine politics' (where voters are heavily influenced by self-interested party 'bosses'). But after he entered the U.S. Senate in 1935, he established a reputation for honesty, common sense and devotion to the public interest which won him a new term in office starting in 1941.

Early in 1941, he was appointed Chairman of the Committee to Investigate the National Defence Program, usually known as 'the Truman Committee'. Aware that the First World War ended with 112 government committees investigating frauds and failures after they had happened, Truman's Committee was to check immediately on the use or abuse of government funds. He estimated that his checks saved $15 billion of taxpayers' money. The respect he earned brought him to the Vice-Presidency when Roosevelt was re-elected President in the 1944 elections.

Truman had been Vice-President for only 82 days, and had talked to Roosevelt twice in that time, when Roosevelt's death automatically raised him to the vacant office. Inexperienced and unprepared, he made a series of rapid, fateful decisions. He lent his weight to those forming the new United Nations; he went to Potsdam to confer with Stalin and with Churchill, then Attlee; he decided on the dropping of the atom bombs only a few months after he had first become aware of their existence. On his desk he put a much-quoted notice: 'The buck stops here.' Less publicized is the second sign, a quotation from Mark Twain: 'Always do right. This will gratify some people and astonish the rest.' This combination of decisiveness and matter-of-fact awareness and endeavour characterized the man.

Home Affairs 1945–53

Truman had supported Roosevelt's New Deal. In 1945, faced with the demobilization of some 12 million Americans and the changeover from a war economy to the different demands of peace, he produced his own 'Fair Deal' proposals. These were 21 points of reform relating to social security, slums, health insurance and public works programmes. None became law in his first term of office, as the Republican majority in Congress rejected them in favour of their own more repressive Acts, many of which were passed despite Truman's use of the Presidential veto. The Taft-Hartley Act of 1947 restricted trade unions' rights, doubling to 60 days the 'cooling-off' period before strikes could occur, forbidding 'closed shops' and unions' financial contributions to political parties, and making unions liable in law for the actions of their officials. Truman could not prevent its passage into law.

Despite some periods of rapidly rising prices which aggravated industrial relations in the towns but pleased the farmers, the American economy avoided the dangers of a post-war slump. Most problems arose from shortages of goods (or of housing) and too much 'demand' (i.e. more money available than goods to buy with it), rather than from too little demand, which had been the pre-war pattern. The main items of Truman's Fair Deal which did get through Congress were a low-cost housing project, passed in 1949 by the Democrat-dominated 81st Congress, and the 1950 Social Security Act which increased the number of people entitled to old-age pensions.

The difficulties which Truman experienced with the 80th Congress turned to his advantage eventually. When the 1948 Presidential Election was approaching, Truman seemed certain to lose. Not only had he achieved little of his 'Fair Deal'; he had also caused a split in the Democrat Party by championing Civil Rights for American blacks, and the Southern Democrats nominated Strom Thurmond as a States' Rights candidate (they became known as Dixiecrats). Former Democrat Vice-President Henry Wallace also stood for election, proposing a softer line with Russia. Against these three Democrat candidates squabbling for the voters' attention, the Republicans nominated Thomas Dewey, experienced campaigner and Governor of New York. Contrary to all expectations and to the predictions of Dr Gallup who 'invented' the public opinion poll, Truman won the election by two million votes. An eye-catching whistle-stop tour, in which he roundly condemned the 'Do-nothing' Republican-dominated 80th Congress and offered the Fair Deal afresh to the people, culminated in his triumphant return to the White House.

The group in America for whom Truman tried to do most were the negroes, who in the Southern states especially, suffered constant

Robin Day of the B.B.C. interviewing ex-President Truman (right) when he visited England in 1956.

discrimination and humiliation. In 1946 Truman set up a committee to investigate ways of guaranteeing Civil Rights to all citizens.
In 1947 and 1948, following the report of this committee, entitled
'To Secure These Rights', he made numerous direct demands that
Congress should change certain laws. His only success was to start
to de-segregate the armed services (until 1954 there were separate
black units and white units) and, to a lesser extent, Federal
Government jobs. But his concern also initiated greater consciousness of the racial problems in America which previous politicians
had tended to brush aside.

Truman's Foreign Policy, 1945–53

Truman's foreign policy established the pattern of the post-war
world and the 'Cold War', just as his decision to use the atom bomb
in 1945 established the perils of modern warfare. At Potsdam in
July 1945 he seemed insignificant after his predecessor Roosevelt;
after Hiroshima and Nagasaki, he was the most powerful man on
earth.

Truman's policies fall into distinct phases. From 1945 to 1947,
the level of American involvement in world politics was uncertain
and untested. Some observers felt that Isolationism had returned
when Lend-Lease ended a week after the Japanese surrender, and
the American troops went home. But diplomatically the U.S.A.
was already involved in a struggle against Russia. Within the
United Nations, the two super-powers argued about who could join
that organization, and about what powers it should have. The
Russians vetoed the 1946 Baruch Plan, whereby America would have
voluntarily surrendered all its nuclear knowledge on condition that no
other country tried to develop such techniques and weaponry, and the
Americans considered this veto to be a sign of hostility. From 1947 to
1949, the 'Cold War' centred on the 'Truman Doctrine' and Marshall
Aid (see Chapter 13). But in 1950, the outbreak of the Korean War
(see Chapter 19), brought an extra internal problem to Truman, that
of General Douglas MacArthur.

General MacArthur

MacArthur was an outstanding soldier. He won the highest marks
ever at West Point Military Academy (an *average* of 98.14 per cent
over four years); he was the youngest divisional commander in
France in 1918; the youngest major-general in the U.S. Army, the
youngest Chief of Staff and the youngest full general – the only one
to win the Congressional Medal of Honour. Called out of retirement in 1941, when war against Japan threatened, he became
Commander of the Allied Forces in the South West Pacific, and
later Commander of all American forces in the Pacific. He
masterminded and inspired the island-hopping campaign which

thrust back the Japanese, and, after Nagasaki, he accepted the Japanese surrender. From 1945 to 1951, MacArthur was Supreme Commander for the Allied Powers in Japan (see Chapter 18), Commander in Chief of all American Far East forces, and from 1950 until 1951, Commander of the United Nations force in Korea. He had become, in one way and another, the controller of two countries (Japan and Korea) and the leader of an international army. Although he had not been back to America between September 1945 and the outbreak of the Korean War in June 1950, he had many American supporters, whose number increased after the Inchon landings of 1950 and the invasion of North Korea. MacArthur was known to favour invasion of China, and his tough provocative attitudes led Truman to dismiss him from all his posts in April 1951. MacArthur returned to a hero's welcome in several American cities – but Truman had made the wise and more popular decision. In an interview in 1954, MacArthur admitted that he would have used '30–50 atomic bombs' and a belt of radio-active cobalt to beat the Chinese. A Senate Investigating Committee approved of the President's action and agreed with General Bradley, who felt that MacArthur would have started 'the wrong war at the wrong place at the wrong time and with the wrong enemy.'

McCarthyism

Senator Joseph McCarthy from Wisconsin made his mark on American domestic politics in the early 1950s when General MacArthur was affecting foreign policies. Their common enemy was Communism. The 'Cold War' of suspicion and the 'hot' war in Korea coincided with a 'Red Scare' in America, a phobia which was made worse by Russia's explosion of an atomic bomb in 1949 and by the Communist takeover of the whole Chinese mainland in the same year. In 1948, leaders of America's Communist Party (which had a small and declining membership) were tried and convicted under the Aliens Registration Act. To add to the hysteria, Alger Hiss, a member of Roosevelt's State Department, was tried for being a member of the Party in the 1930s and passing secret information to the Russians. In 1950 he was found guilty of lying under oath, though not of the main charges, and was therefore disgraced. One of his prosecutors was a rising lawyer and politician, Richard Nixon.

In this atmosphere, the virtually unknown McCarthy claimed in February 1950 that there were 57 'card-carrying' Communists in the State Department and a total of 205 members of the Party employed there, all with the knowledge of the Secretary, Dean Acheson. With the coincidental arrest the next day of Klaus Fuchs, a British physicist who had passed atomic secrets to the Russians, America was ready to believe McCarthy. For the next four years, as Chairman of the Senate Committee on Government Operations and its subcommittee on Investigations, McCarthy waged war on Communism real or imagined. Government figures (Acheson and Marshall), scientists (Oppenheimer, the man responsible for the making of the first atom bomb), army officers, public servants, religious minorities, Hollywood stars (Charlie Chaplin) and writers all were said to be Communists or suffered actual investigation. Ultimately not a single 'card-carrying Communist' was produced, and McCarthy became the victim of his own weapon, a Senate investigation. In 1954 he was formally censured by a vote of 67 to 22 in the Senate for 'conduct contrary to Senate traditions'. He lost influence, and died in 1957, unmourned.

The McCarthy 'witch hunts' had had a political impact. They had attracted support to the nationalistic Republican Party in the 1952 elections (which Eisenhower won), and only when Republican popularity was diminishing again was McCarthy 'disowned' by his party. They also had the effect of reducing civil liberties, leaving two major Acts on the statute book: the McGarran Act of 1950 requiring all Communists to register with the Attorney-General, and the Communist Control Act of August 1954, outlawing the Communist Party altogether. Senator John Kennedy was one proposer of the latter act.

Eisenhower, 1953–61 – Domestic Politics

The Truman era was tense. By 1952, the America voter wanted reassurance. Against the original wishes of their right wing, who would have supported the isolationist Senator Taft, the Republican Party invited General Eisenhower to resign his post as Supreme Commander of NATO and become their Presidential candidate. The idea was supported by history as well as by observation: Washington, Jackson, Harrison, Taylor and Grant were all military men with reputations for success – some undeserved – who became President of the United States. Eisenhower, a courteous, honest, unostentatious soldier, was a national hero without obvious political affiliations: he could have represented moderate Democratic policy as easily as moderate Republican policy. With Nixon as his more professional Vice-Presidential partner, he trounced the Democrat candidate Adlai Stevenson in all but nine states in 1952 and all but seven in 1956. He promised calm, moderate policies, with a balanced budget, less government intervention and experienced statesmanship in foreign affairs.

Although he held the Presidency for eight years (despite three heart attacks while in office), Eisenhower was not a 'strong' President, partly by intention, and partly because three of the four Congresses which served with him had Democrat majorities, the other having only a small Republican majority. Being used to his military role of taking the major decisions and leaving the details to others, 'Ike' did the same in the White House. His special assistant

Sherman Adams, former Governor of New Hampshire, dealt with most domestic issues until he resigned in 1958, and there was less change in political emphasis than had been expected. The economy prospered under the guidance of the 'eight millionaires and a plumber' in his Cabinet (the 'plumber' was Durkin, a member of the Plumbers' Union who became Secretary of Labor). A new Department of Health, Education and Welfare indicated that the Federal Government would not shirk its social responsibilities, though some of the New Deal projects, notably the T.V.A., were reduced in scope. By the 'Soil Bank' scheme, farmers were paid increased subsidies, not for increased production, but for taking land out of production, thereby reducing the surplus on the market and increasing the prices for those who were producing. As a result of this, and increased overseas aid, there was a budget deficit in five of Eisenhower's eight years in office, reaching a record level of $12,900 million in 1959.

More significantly for the future, Eisenhower took a firm line against racial discrimination (see below). He also set up NASA (the National Aeronautics and Space Administration) in 1958 in response to the public dismay when Russia became the first country to launch an earth-orbiting satellite in October 1957.

Foreign Affairs, 1953–61

From 1953 to 1959 John Foster Dulles, steel-nerved and stubborn, was Secretary of State, a declared opponent of Communism who once wrote 'If you are scared to go to the brink, you are lost' and once said that 'massive nuclear retaliation' would follow any aggression by Russia. But he was not reckless. In 1953–54, he refused to allow the U.S. to be drawn into the defence of Quemoy and Matsu for the Chinese Nationalists, though he was happy to promise support for their main base in Formosa (Taiwan), and he threatened to 'unleash' Chiang Kai-shek on the Communist regime in China itself (see Chapter 18). Similarly he avoided entanglement in the fall of the French empire in Indo-China in 1954 and the subsequent Geneva Conference, but he was the main influence in setting up SEATO in 1954 and the 1955 Baghdad Pact (see Chapter 13).

In Europe too, deeds were less dramatic than words. In 1953 Dulles had announced 'to all those suffering under Communist slavery' that 'you can count on us.' Hard bargaining over the details of the Austrian State Treaty of 1955, and pressure for the admission of West Germany to NATO (resulting in the defensive Communist Warsaw Pact of 1955) turned to relatively mild protest when Russian tanks crushed the Hungarian uprisings of 1956.

In the Middle East, America condemned the Anglo-French invasion of the Suez Canal zone in 1956 (see Chapter 22), but in January 1957 the Eisenhower Doctrine was announced: a promise to send American troops to the Middle East to hold off Communism. In 1958 a contingent was sent to Lebanon.

In 1955, personal diplomacy began again for the first time since Potsdam, with a summit meeting for Heads of State at Geneva. Eisenhower's 'open skies' policy was not accepted by the Russians, and in 1960 the shooting-down of an American U2 spy-plane over Russian territory led to the stormy break-up of a new summit in Paris.

The Eisenhower administration's last act in the field of foreign affairs, in January 1961, was to break off diplomatic relations with Fidel Castro of Cuba, a man whom America had once supported when he overthrew the old Batista dictatorship in 1958, but whose acceptance of Communist aid made him a suspect neighbour.

The Kennedy Magic, and LBJ, 1961–69

In November 1960 the Democrat John F. Kennedy won the Presidential Election with a majority of popular votes of only 118,000 over Richard Nixon. Kennedy's two and a half years in office were energetic, exciting and, for many people, inspiring. He was the youngest man to be elected President and the first Roman Catholic to hold the office. His style was new, personal and forceful.

J. F. Kennedy shakes hands with Khrushchev in Vienna, 1961. Within two years, the youngest American President was dead.

He promised a struggle against 'tyranny, poverty, disease, and war itself' and set a series of tasks to be completed by his own administration within '100 days', a tactic later copied by Harold Wilson in England.

On the home front, Kennedy's Presidency had more promise than achievement. Although the Democrats controlled both Houses of Congress, many Southern Democrats resented Kennedy's pledges to improve blacks' Civil Rights, and they resisted some of his changes in this and other spheres. In 1963, bills for the reduction of income tax and for better Civil Rights were being dealt with by Congress when Kennedy was assassinated while visiting Dallas, Texas. His alleged killer, Lee Harvey Oswald, was himself shot by a strip club owner, Jack Ruby, although Oswald was in police custody at the time. Were the killings masterminded and if so, by whom? Chief Justice Warren investigated, and his Report (1964) could produce no evidence of a conspiracy. But rumours persisted about Communists, or Cubans, or the C.I.A., or the Ku Klux Klan. Kennedy's foreign policy (see Chapter 19) achieved more than his domestic policy, but he was succeeded by Lyndon Johnson, whose five and a half years in office saw through many of the policies Kennedy had wanted in his 'New Frontier' programme. Having been leader of the Democrats in the Senate for eight years before becoming Vice-President, Johnson knew how to bully and cajole Congress into passing his Civil Rights Act of 1964, the Economic Opportunity Act (1964), and then, following his landslide victory over the Republican Goldwater in the 1964 elections, the Acts which made up his 'Great Society' programme. This 'war on poverty' included the creation of another government department, Housing and Urban Development (1965), and Acts relating to social security for the disabled (1966), medical care for the elderly (1966), a new Civil Rights initiative (1965) and other measures which increased the control of the Federal Government on day-by-day issues, hitherto the concern of state and local government.

Johnson's foreign policy was dominated by the Vietnamese issue (see Chapter 20) which lost him more support than his practical liberalism won. He therefore decided not to run for re-election in 1968, in which campaign Senator Robert Kennedy, a leading Democrat, fell like his brother John to an assassin's bullet.

Nixon, 1969–74

Richard Nixon's Presidency mixed triumph (mostly in foreign affairs) with disaster and personal humiliation; his undoubted political skills were outweighed by his self-justifying, arrogant and finally dishonest use of power, which caused him to be the only man to resign the Presidency.

His election in 1968 was his first triumph, for after four years as Vice-President to Eisenhower, he had been written off as a 'loser' when Kennedy beat him in the 1960 election, and Goldwater won the Republican nomination in 1964. But his attachment to 'Law and Order' and his determination to reduce the American role in Vietnam won him 301 votes in the Electoral College. The Democrat candidate Hubert Humphrey won 191 votes, after his campaign had been marred by bitter wrangles and violence at the Party Convention in Chicago. The presence of a third candidate, Governor George Wallace of Alabama, representing the reaction against Federal interference in Civil Rights matters, indicated a general swing to the right in American politics. Wallace won 46 votes.

Nixon's main achievements were in foreign affairs. In 1971 the United States agreed to the admission of China to the United Nations, to the position held until then by Nationalist China (Formosa/Taiwan). In 1972 Nixon visited Peking and had long discussions with Mao Tse-tung and Chou En-lai, but also managed to keep positive contact with Moscow despite the bad relationship between China and Russia. Nixon visited Moscow in 1972 (signing SALT 1 as well as various trade agreements) and Brezhnev visited the United States in 1973. Meanwhile Nixon was continuing his policy of Vietnamization (whereby South Vietnamese were made increasingly responsible for their own defence), and a cease-fire was

'Nixon had earned himself an international reputation for statesmanship.' The first U.S. President to visit Communist China, he nevertheless maintained contacts with Russia. Here he greets Brezhnev (left) at the White House, 1973.

arranged for January 1973 (see Chapter 20). Nixon had earned himself an international reputation for statesmanship, and his Secretary of State Henry Kissinger earned another for 'shuttle diplomacy' in the trouble-spots of the world, especially the Middle East, Southern Africa and the Far East.

At home, Nixon faced the problem that had dogged his Republican predecessor Eisenhower, a Democrat majority in Congress which remained even when in the 1972 Presidential Election Nixon won every state of the Union except Massachusetts and the District of Columbia. Domestic violence over Civil Rights and student protests over war in Vietnam and Cambodia gradually diminished in the early 1970s, but the American economy was badly unbalanced by the cutback in war expenditure on top of inflation and high unemployment (around six per cent in 1970, rising to nearly nine per cent in 1975). The cost of living, having averaged a three per cent per annum rise in the 1960s, rose to five per cent and six per cent in the early 1970s and to 10 per cent in 1974. The dollar lost value internationally, and a balance of payments crisis in 1970 led to the imposition of a 10 per cent import surcharge as well as attempts to freeze prices and wages. The 'affluent society' had clearly started to live beyond its means, and Nixon had to cut back on the poverty programmes as well as on overseas aid.

'Watergate'

It was 'Watergate' that dragged Nixon from office. During the 1972 Election campaign, Republican Party workers broke into the offices of the Democrat Party in the Watergate building in Washington to plant a bugging device. After the election was over, suspicions grew that there had been a deliberate cover-up of links between the accused men and the Campaign to Re-Elect the President. Searching newspaper coverage revealed increasing numbers of irregularities in White House behaviour including illegal behaviour by security officers, perjury by members of the Justice Department, tax evasion by the Vice-President Spiro Agnew, and above all, a deliberate cover-up of the deliberate cover-up of the original break-in. 'There will be no whitewash at the White House,' Nixon promised the nation on television, but his assurance was inadequate. In July 1974, the Supreme Court ruled that he must produce relevant material, including tape recordings of conversations in the White House, and the Judiciary Committee of the House of Representatives voted to recommend the impeachment of the President. In August 1974, Nixon resigned from the Presidency, admitting to some irregularities and suspected of many more.

His successor Gerald Ford reached the Presidency of the West's biggest democracy without ever being elected to an executive post. He had been appointed Vice-President by Nixon after Agnew had resigned in late 1973; he now automatically filled the Presidential vacancy. His honesty and sincerity were unquestioned, but as he himself punned (referring to types of car or Presidents) 'I am a Ford, not a Lincoln.' His most demanding task was to reunite the nation and restore its pride, but he lacked the special style of a Lincoln, and the people resented almost any use of executive power after Nixon's abuse of it. Ford pardoned Nixon even before formal charges had been made against him, though all the lesser figures in the Watergate Affair, including John Mitchell (former Attorney General) and Nixon's top aides Erlichman and Haldeman, were sent to jail. The pardon was not popular, nor was his economic policy WIN ('Whip Inflation Now'). Discontent grew. Although the Vietnam war at last ended in April 1975, Ford won no credit for it; his one dramatic gesture, the rescue by American marines of merchant seamen illegally held by Cambodia, went sour when several lives were unnecessarily lost. The C.I.A. and the F.B.I. came under Congressional scrutiny; the Lockheed Aircraft Corporation admitted bribing members of foreign governments. America lost confidence in itself and its image, despite the celebrations of the Bicentennial of its Declaration of Independence of 1776.

The Presidential Election of 1976, and Jimmy Carter

Ford narrowly won the Republican nomination as Presidential candidate in 1976 over the right-wing former film star and Governor of California, Ronald Reagan. But he equally narrowly lost the Presidential Election itself to the Democrat candidate, former Governor of Georgia, Jimmy Carter. Carter won most of the eastern states and all the 'solid south'; Ford captured every western state. The campaign was dull, despite T.V. debates between the rivals, and only 55 per cent of the eligible voters bothered to turn out. Although Carter had been virtually unknown outside Georgia two years before the election, he won many votes because he was in no way tainted by Watergate or by the pardon of Nixon, and because he promised 'open government' and less Federal interference in daily life: 'I'll never tell you a lie.'

Carter's declared foreign policy supported the Helsinki Agreement of 1975: 'Our moral sense dictates a clear-cut preference for those societies which share with us an abiding respect for individual human rights.' This statement, clearly aimed at the Communist powers, briefly strained relationships with Russia and China, but the American commitment to the SALT 2 talks remained strong. Elsewhere in the world, the Carter administration worked for peace or the reduction of tension. In 1977 America signed a treaty handing control of the Panama Canal to Panama by 1999, despite considerable resistance from some Senators. In 1978, Carter offered to mediate between President Sadat of Egypt and Prime Minister Begin of Israel, and invited them both to Camp David near Washington in September. From the resulting 'framework agreements' a formal peace treaty was negotiated and signed in Washington in March 1979. Although the problems of the Palestinians remained, Israel was at last recognized by a major Arab neighbour (see Chapter 22).

In the last days of 1979, the occupation of Afghanistan by 50,000 Russian troops, (theoreticaily at the request of the Afghan President) seriously threatened the diplomatic balance of the world. To underline his condemnation of this move, Carter called for a boycott of the 1980 Moscow Olympic Games by the 'free' countries of the West. In 1980, tension was further increased by the actions of Iranian students in Teheran, who took as hostages the staff of the American Embassy there.

At home, Carter was trapped between the conflicting desires of the American people, who sought leadership and inspiration and yet were reluctant to follow. Carter's Energy programme, first announced in 1977 and strongly reiterated in 1979, received little sympathy from Congress, especially the proposal for a tax on petrol. But by 1979 Americans had accepted the unwelcome truth that they were too dependent on imported oil, and must therefore face a phased reduction of overseas supplies (25 per cent over 10 years). Even so, Carter's image was that of an honest but gullible amateur, who meant well but lacked the qualities of real leadership.

Civil Rights

Some 12 per cent (24 million) of the total population of America are black. Although many have entered the country in the past 50 years, most are descendants of the slaves who were set free by Lincoln's Emancipation Proclamation (effective 1 January 1863) and yet have had to struggle for genuinely equal status with whites ever since. Despite the 13th, 14th and 15th Amendments to the Constitution (abolishing slavery, establishing citizens' rights, and protecting voting rights respectively), black equality was legally put out of reach by the 1896 *Plessy v. Ferguson* judgement in the U.S. Supreme Court, which said that 'equal and separate' accommodation on railway trains for blacks and whites was within the Constitution. Soon changed in emphasis to 'separate but equal', the judgement was widely applied to housing, public services, army units, and above all, education, thereby passing on the existing inequalities to each new generation. Roosevelt in the 1930s and Truman in the late 1940s began to acknowledge that separate facilities were almost certainly not equal, and in 1954, Eisenhower's new Chief Justice, Earl Warren, declared in *Brown v. Board of Education of Topeka* that 'In the field of public education, the doctrine of "separate but equal" has no place. Separate educational facilities are inherently unequal.'

This ruling, like *Plessy v. Ferguson*, was applied widely. In 1955 blacks in Montgomery, Alabama began to boycott buses on which the seats were reserved for whites. Their leader was a Baptist minister, Martin Luther King, who stressed non-violence but who was prepared to organize 'civil disobedience' in order to publicize the blacks' plight. The boycott led on to 'sit-ins' in 1960 in cafés and hotels hitherto reserved for whites, and to 'Freedom Riders' in 1961 on supposedly segregated public transport. Liberal opinion supported the blacks. In the north, east and west of America (except in the big cities where black ghettoes increased racial tensions), discrimination gradually diminished.

In the south, the old issue of States' Rights emerged in 1957 to challenge the progress being made. In Little Rock, Arkansas, when 17 black children attempted to join the all-white High School, the State Governor, Orville Faubus, stationed National Guardsmen outside 'to prevent violence', in effect preventing black admission. Eisenhower eventually used his powers as Commander-in-Chief, took the same troops under *his* command, and ordered them (and 1,000 paratroopers) to carry out the integration. Civil Rights legislation in 1957 and 1960 encouraged blacks to register to vote, but the pattern repeated itself. In 1962 and 1963, Federal troops had to supervise the admission of blacks to the University of Mississippi and the University of Alabama, and in 1964 President Johnson succeeded (where Kennedy had failed) in getting Congress to pass an Act outlawing discriminatory behaviour in trade

Martin Luther King (1929–68).

unions and as many other specific organizations as could be covered by such a law. In 1964 also, the 24th Amendment to the U.S. Constitution plugged another loophole used by southern segregationists, the application of a Poll Tax to discourage blacks from registering to vote. In 1965 and 1968 Congress passed new laws to try to ensure black Civil Rights, the latter in the wave of horror that followed the assassination of Martin Luther King (April 1968), whose personal courage and non-violence had been marked by the award of the Nobel Peace Prize in 1964.

In the 1960s, violence was close to the surface of the racial problem. The 'respectable' N.A.A.C.P. (National Association for the Advancement of Coloured People) and Dr King's S.C.L.C. (Southern Christian Leadership Conference) were too mild for those who joined CORE (Congress of Racial Equality), or, more militant still, the Black Muslims. From these groups came the proud cry 'Black is Beautiful', and then 'Black Power'. Riots in Philadelphia (1964), the Watts district of Los Angeles (1965), Chicago (1966), and Newark (1967) threatened more urban violence than America had ever known. Under men like Malcolm X (assassinated 1965) and Stokely Carmichael, extremist blacks began to call not for equality but for control. At the Mexico Olympics in 1968, many white Americans were deeply offended by the clenched fist 'Black Power' salute of some of their medal winners, but in the 1970s, the tensions took new and less dramatic

Black America

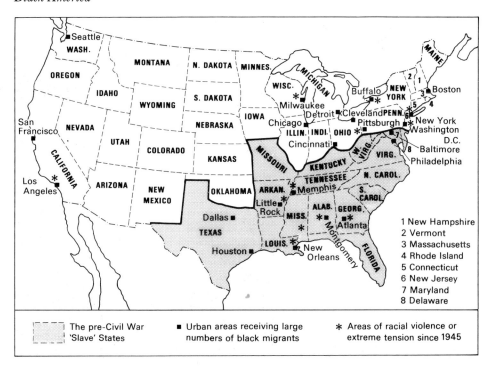

The pre-Civil War 'Slave' States	■ Urban areas receiving large numbers of black migrants

* Areas of racial violence or extreme tension since 1945

forms. Whites became much more upset about the fact that
children were being compulsorily 'bussed' out of their neighbour-
hood to attend schools where blacks predominated and vice versa,
and in a flourish of irony, complaints reached the Supreme Court of
'reverse discrimination', which stopped people from being able to
go to university because the only places available were being
reserved for underprivileged members of minority groups. In such
circumstances, to be an intelligent white American was a distinct
disadvantage.

LATIN AMERICA SINCE THE WAR

The continent of South America was strangely isolated from
developments in the rest of the world until well into the twentieth
century. This was partly because of its geographical position;
partly because, until this century, it had a relatively small
population (43 million in 1900) in a vast area; partly because that
population was mostly rural and poor, with only a few landowners
and businessmen trading with overseas countries and importing
direct the luxury goods that they required; and partly because the
Monroe Doctrine of 1823 had warned off all European powers from
making a bid for an empire in Latin America.

Three things have shaped the events of the last half-century in
South America. One is the massive increase in population, from
43,000,000 in 1900 to 303,000,000 in 1975. (Brazil's population is
currently twice that of any European nation, and whereas European populations are relatively static, those of South American are
doubling every 25 years.) This increase in population has broken
up the old social patterns and led to a huge increase in urban
settlement, even where there is little industry or other employment.
The second feature of the past 50 years has been the exposure of the
underlying weakness of most South America economies, by the
Great Depression and then by the Second World War. Most of the
countries lived by subsistence agriculture plus the export of one or
two primary commodities, which paid for the supremacy of a small
land-owning or business-owning élite. The commodities ranged
from ores like copper and silver to agricultural produce like cattle,
coffee or bananas. When international trade dwindled in the
Depression and the War, South America had to develop its own
resources more fully, and immediately came up against the
inadequacies of its social structure (with no real middle class,
backward systems of agriculture, almost universal illiteracy, and
often a repressive Church).

The third feature of the past 50 years stems from the previous
two, and is the conspicuous failure of democracy to cope with the
extreme social and economic variations in any country for very
long. Further complicating these three pressures has been the
varied policy of the United States of America, which, having

established its dominance in the Western Hemisphere in the nineteenth century, has conducted a 'love-hate' relationship with the regimes of Latin America ever since. During and after the First World War, the U.S. interfered directly in the affairs of most Central American states (Mexico, Cuba, Panama, Nicaragua, Haiti) and was involved in considerable 'dollar diplomacy' in the bigger countries further south. But Franklin Roosevelt and his Secretary of State Cordell Hull changed all this and undertook a 'good neighbour' policy in the 1930s, for instance repealing the 'right' to interfere in the politics of Cuba and of Panama which was actually written into American law, and establishing instead an Import-Export Bank, specifically to lend capital to governments, and reducing tariffs which seemed harmful to South American interests.

In the absence of any firm base on which economic, social and political stability seemed likely to grow, South American politics became at first the prerogative of the 'natural' leaders of each society: the land-owners and the (under-occupied) Army. Dictatorship was thus common, and dictators were reasonably secure from challenge except from rivals of their own class. But in the post-war period especially, the growth of education and of communication has led to greater popular involvement in politics, and the emergence not only of dictators protecting the interests of a privileged minority, but also of dictators representing the desires of moderates, of extremists of the left and of large 'democratic' factions.

16 Western Europe since 1945

Between the First and Second World Wars, Europe was the focal point of international tensions. While America remained isolationist and Russia, China and Japan were preoccupied with their own internal problems and patterns of development, the rise of Mussolini and Hitler provided the most obvious threat to the Versailles settlement, and demanded the urgent attention of the statesmen of France and Britain, as well as the leaders of the new European countries (see Chapter 7). In the years 1939–45, Europe was the primary battleground – though by no means the only one – but when the war was over, it was clear that the focus had shifted to 'the super-powers', and that the age of the European nation-states was past. If Europe was to count for anything in world politics hereafter, it would be as a combined unit and not as a collection of divided countries. This chapter therefore traces not merely the individual progress of each nation after the Second World War, but, more importantly, the steady growth of cooperation and interdependence which marked Europe's acknowledgement of the new balance of power.

GERMANY

The Aftermath of War

In 1945, the Germans signed not an armistice but an unconditional surrender. Invading armies settled into zones of occupation which had been outlined at Yalta, and 'demilitarization, denazification, decentralization and democratization' followed on their command. Economic conditions were primitive; the massive destruction of bridges, railways, factories and offices made supply and distribution almost impossible, and production in 1945 ran at less than one-third of the 1938 total. Refugees from Poland, Russia, Austria and Czechoslovakia streamed in ahead of the Red Army tide and stood workless, homeless and leaderless in the rubble. The humiliation of defeat was made worse by enforced acknowledgement of the atrocities committed by the Third Reich. The

In the dock: 20 lesser officials of the German Third Reich listen to the case for the prosecution at Nuremburg, December 1947. After the original trial of 24 leaders of the Reich, many other trials were held in the same courtroom.

Nuremburg Trials of 24 of the most infamous and influential members of Hitler's regime revealed the hideous truth of the concentration camps. In October 1946, 10 of the accused were hanged for war crimes. Goering committed suicide before his sentence could be carried out. Himmler had also committed suicide after being captured, while Goebbels and Hitler had taken their own lives before the Allies reached them. The remainder were sent to Allied or to German prisons.

The Russians were determined that there would never again be a strong Germany dominating central Europe. At their insistence, Poland was moved bodily sideways (see Chapter 13). By this means the Russians gained, and the Germans lost, strips of territory about 100 miles wide. The Russian zone of occupation was a further block some 180 miles wide which included Berlin. The city was put under four-power control, but access to it was controlled by the Russians. The Russians, and to a lesser extent the French, demanded reparations from Germany. The British and Americans, mindful of the problems of reparations after the First World War, were more concerned to rebuild Germany and avoid bitterness. It was therefore over Germany that the 'East-West split' first became clear. From 1946, when Britain and America suspended all claims to reparations and suggested amalgamation of their zones, until 1949, when the Berlin Airlift finally overcame the Russian blockade of Berlin, the Cold War focussed on Germany (see Chapter 13). As the U.S. General Clay wrote to Truman, 'If we mean to hold Europe against Communism, we must not budge.' As a result, the West resolved that if Germany could not be unified, *Western* Germany should be created as soon as possible.

Germany Divided

In 1948, a Parliamentary Council produced a Basic Constitution for West Germany, henceforth known as the German Federal Republic. Accepted in 1949, this constitution avoided all the weaknesses of the Weimar Republic. The President was to be elected by the two houses of Parliament, and there were to be no referendums. The upper house, the Bundesrat, had considerable power to amend or delay laws passed by the lower house, the Bundestag, but the Bundestag, chosen by universal suffrage, had the right to choose the Federal Chancellor (the equivalent of the Prime Minister). Local affairs were in the hands of the governments in each Land (province), and the Bundesrat had the special role of representing the views of each Land rather than the political parties. It was a balanced, well-conceived constitution, and the Chairman of the Parliamentary Council that produced it was elected Federal Chancellor in 1949 by one vote. His name was Konrad Adenauer.

In October 1949, East Germany also produced its new constitution. Despite its name, the German Democratic Republic (D.D.R.) immediately became a one-party state dominated by the Socialist Unity Party and its leader, Walter Ulbricht. (See Chapter 14 for the later history of the D.D.R.) Not until 1972 did the two sections of Germany give each other official diplomatic recognition.

An East Berlin policeman supervises the building of part of the Berlin Wall in 1961. In 1957, more than 250,000 refugees fled through Berlin to the West. In 1960, the monthly totals were still around 17,000, a loss of manpower which had to be stopped.

But even then, the Wall, built in 1961 across Berlin as well as along the whole Eastern bloc frontier with the West, remained to prevent the free movement of Germans from East to West, unless they were too old to work usefully for the state.

The Age of Adenauer, 1949–63

The 1950s were the age of the German 'economic miracle'. Between 1950 and 1960, West Germany's unemployment fell from 1,600,000 to 270,000. The growth of real G.N.P. per head was 6.5 per cent per annum (compared with Britain's 2.2 per cent). Foreign currency reserves trebled and the German share of the world export market doubled, while the cost of living went up by an average of 1.9 per cent per annum compared with Britain's 4.3 per cent. In the 12 months after currency reform, industrial production shot up 63 per cent, partly because there was reorganization of the sixteen major trade unions, with six million members, into a disciplined and cooperative body, the 'Deutsche Gewerkschaftsbund'. There were also psychological reasons for the miracle, as the German people worked to salvage their pride and dignity as well as their economy. The Marshall Plan 'primed the pump' at the critical moment in 1948, and the Adenauer government, with Erhard as Minister of Economics, guided and planned the expansion, mobilizing the plentiful manpower and material resources with confidence. With the advantage of 'starting from scratch', the Germans (like the Japanese) could build a post-war society based on hard work, fair reward and social justice. One further cause of the German success was its central role in the Coal and Steel Community and the Common Market (see below).

Politically, the new constitution proved to be very stable. Adenauer founded the Christian Democrat Union (C.D.U.), a moderate conservative party, which ruled for 20 years with assistance from smaller parties like the Free Democrats and the German Party. The opposition until 1966 centred on the Social Democrats, who started as a strongly left-wing party but who in 1959 gave up their absolute commitment to Marxism and offered a programme of moderate socialism. In 1965 and 1966, a new Nazi party, the National Democratic Party, appeared in Bavaria and Hesse, causing considerable tension, but not gaining enough support to win any power.

Adenauer retired in 1963 at the age of 87, handing on power to his colleague Erhard, who held the Chancellorship until 1966. Erhard became the victim of the first real slackening in the pace of German expansion. His coalition fell apart when the Free Democrats withdrew their support, and it was replaced by an unprecedented alliance between Christian Democrats and Social Democrats. Kiesinger (C.D.U.) became Chancellor, but Brandt (S.P.D.) became his deputy and Foreign Minister.

The Socialist Chancellors, Brandt (1969–74) and Schmidt (1974–   )

Willy Brandt was elected Mayor of Berlin in 1957. An ardent anti-Nazi (he had fled to Norway in 1933 and adopted the name by which he was known thereafter), he also stood up to Communism with courage and clarity, especially at the time of the building of the Berlin Wall (1961). In 1969 he had a reputation for being firm, fair and positive, and a coalition between his S.P.D. and the Free Democrats brought him to the Chancellorship. Less afraid of the Russians than most politicians, he concentrated on *Ostpolitik*, ('Eastern policies'), i.e. coming to terms with the Communist bloc. It was a controversial policy, but in 1970 he signed treaties with Russia and Poland confirming existing frontiers, and in 1971 he arranged a series of talks with East German leaders (and was awarded the Nobel Peace Prize). In 1972, he achieved the formal mutual recognition of the two Germanies, and in 1973 he signed a border agreement with Czechoslovakia and saw both Germanies become members of the United Nations. He had thus achieved some sort of diplomatic conclusion to the Second World War, though many people on either side of the Iron Curtain could not accept that Germany was to be partitioned for ever. In 1974, his career was ruined when he accepted responsibility for one of his aides who was accused of spying for the Communists. He was succeeded by Helmut Schmidt, whose experience as S.P.D. Minister for Defence (1969–72) and for Finance (1972–74) admirably suited him for the main tasks ahead. In 1976 the S.P.D.-Free Democrat coalition lost some ground in the Federal Elections but remained in office. In 1977 and 1978, Schmidt's popularity rose again, partly because of his handling of the problems of terrorism.

Urban Terrorism

One side-effect of the 'economic miracle' was the contempt felt by some people for the constant pursuit of money and material progress. Ulrike Meinhof, a left-wing political journalist, turned to violence in the 1968 student riots. In 1970, she founded the 'Red Army Faction' with Andreas Baader, and declared war on the values of modern society. The 'Baader-Meinhof Gang' soon alienated a small amount of sympathetic moderate opinion by its indiscriminate policies of murder, arson, robbery and violence. In 1972 many of the gang were arrested, including the leaders. Meinhof committed suicide in 1976, Baader in 1977, after the failure of his supporters to hijack an airliner to obtain hostages for his release. The violence of the terrorists provoked a series of new laws and police procedures, and worries about the role of the state. Did the refusal to employ Communists in any civil service or teaching post, or the interpretation of laws about distributing

leaflets, breach the Basic Law of the Federal Republic? West
Germany's dread of being or seeming extreme, either on the left or
the right, was very apparent in the late 1970s.

ITALY

Constitutional Problems

Italy's monarchy was too closely identified with the Fascist regime
of Mussolini to be welcomed after the war. In 1946 Victor
Emmanuel III abdicated in favour of his less compromised son
Umberto II, but a referendum showed a majority (54 per cent) in
favour of republicanism, and Umberto also abdicated. A new
Republican Constitution was approved by the Italian people in
1947, and took effect from 1 January 1948. Through the 1960s and
1970s, it showed itself to be increasingly incapable of solving the
numerous problems which Italy faced.

The main problem arose from the existence of too many parties,
lacking discipline or distinctive philosophies. Although the Christian Democrats were usually the largest single party, the Socialist
Party of Proletarian Unity and the Italian Communist Party
regularly challenged them, and each side relied constantly on
splinter groups and small parties ranging from the extreme right to
the extreme left. De Gasperi, leader of the Christian Democrats and
Prime Minister from December 1945 until July 1953, had to form
eight different coalition cabinets during those years, and even when
the elections of 1949 gave him an absolute majority in the Chamber
of Deputies (304 seats out of 574), he still found it advisable to
share his power. Between 1958 and 1963, the Christian Democrat
Fanfani was Prime Minister four times and between 1963 and 1976
Aldo Moro held the office five times. However this constant
shuffling of coalitions achieved little in the way of reform. Although
Moro worked for an 'opening to the left', i.e. cooperation with
Socialists and even Communists, power remained mostly in the
hands of conservative, middle-class, Catholic politicians whose
own life-style depended on minimum change.

'The Strategy of Tension'

This immobility at the top was increasingly challenged. The years
1952–62 saw rapid economic advance in Italy, as many of the
population previously involved in agriculture moved into manufac-
turing industries, thereby stimulating the doubling of the national
income in ten years. The general standard of living therefore
improved noticeably, at a time when Italy's entry into the Common
Market also stimulated more investment and modernization of
factories. But after 1962, inflation and balance of payments crises
caused recession and higher taxation, which re-emphasized the

split between the rich north and the poor south of the country. Strikes and lock-outs in the late 1960s gave encouragement to terrorist organizations of the left and right wings, and the trade unions and Communist Party gained considerable strength. At the same time, the Catholic Church lost some of its control over the faithful voters of Italy. In 1970 a bill to legalize divorce was introduced, and after four years of bitter struggle was accepted. Then in 1978 the Chamber of Deputies and the Senate passed a law legalizing abortions, despite strong criticism from the Church.

By the late 1970s, Italy was limping from one crisis to another. The kidnapping and murder of Moro in 1978 by the 'Red Brigades' horrified moderate opinion, but produced no real political change. The 'strategy of tension' was employed by extremists on both wings, and although Andreotti, the Christian Democrat Prime Minister in 1977, made a political pact with the Communists which granted them considerable power in Italy's 20 regional administrations, there were still 280 left-wing terrorists and 300 right-wing terrorists in Italian prisons at the end of the year. The lira remained one of the weaker European currencies, and Italy was widely regarded as 'the poor man of Europe'.

SPAIN

The Spanish Civil War ended with Franco's Nationalists occupying Madrid in March 1939 (see Chapter 9). Although his sympathies were clearly with Mussolini and Hitler, Franco kept Spain clear of the Second World War and devoted himself to trying to improve the economy. Shortage of capital, of skilled labour and of a reliable bureaucracy made recovery slow. It was not until the 1950s, when other countries' improved conditions brought tourists' money into Spain, that there was a significant increase in Spanish wealth in the coastal areas and the big cities. Elsewhere, poverty remained.

Franco retained supreme control until his death in 1975, but as early as 1947 he had decreed that Spain was officially a monarchy, reserving to himself the right to be regent. In 1969, he appointed Juan Carlos, grandson of King Alfonso XIII, as his legal heir, and in preparation for this transfer of power he steadily reduced the influence of the Falange Party and of the army and accepted more advice from the most successful businessmen. The Cortes remained subservient to him, and when Juan Carlos became King in November 1975, he found it difficult to break the pattern of the dead dictator's power. In July 1976, he managed to dismiss Arias from the post of Prime Minister and appointed the more liberal Suarez. A referendum in December approved complete political reform: the Cortes became totally democratic in its lower house and at least 80 per cent democratic in its upper house (the King retained the right to appoint up to 20 per cent of its members). Political parties were legalized by being allowed to register with the authorities. In April 1977, even the Communist Party was fully recognized, a change that Franco could never have permitted.

FRANCE

Vichy, and the Fourth Republic

In July 1940, the final Parliament of the French Third Republic met at Vichy, and having authorized Marshal Pétain to draft a new constitution, it voted itself out of existence. Pétain's deputy, Laval, was convinced that collaboration with the Germans would avoid defeat and humiliation, and would assure France of an independent future. He arranged a meeting between himself, Pétain and Hitler at Montoire in October 1940, but he could not win over his countrymen. A Resistance movement grew steadily, encouraged by the appeals of the Free French, led by de Gaulle, and by the support of the Allied military command. In 1942, Hitler ordered the total occupation of Vichy France by German and Italian forces. Thereafter the Vichy regime had no reason for existence, though the Germans permitted it to remain. In 1944 Laval fled to Spain, returning in 1945 to face charges of treason. His excuse that his 'limited collaboration' had protected France from total subjection was not accepted: he was executed in October 1945. Pétain was also condemned to death, but his 89 years and his First War reputation turned the sentence into one of solitary confinement. He died in prison in 1951, aged 95.

The Vichy Government was ousted by de Gaulle's Committee of National Liberation, the General becoming provisional President, while a new political framework was worked out. In 1946, he resigned in an attempt to persuade the people of France that the proposed Constitution of the Fourth Republic would be inadequate. He failed; so did the Constitution. Dogged by too many parties and too few loyalties, by a failing economy and a resentful empire, the Fourth Republic staggered from crisis to crisis from 1946 until its final collapse in 1958.

In 1954, the French withdrew from Indo-China, leaving the states of North and South Vietnam, Laos and Cambodia to work out their own destiny (see Chapter 20). Other places were affected, including France itself, for almost immediately Algeria burst into revolt, and Tunisia and Morocco threatened the same. These last two were granted independence in 1956, but Algeria, with nearly a million settlers claiming French nationality, could not be calmed so easily. By 1958, half a million French soldiers were unable to keep the peace in Algeria, and civil war in both Algeria and France seemed likely, when right-wingers seized power in Algeria, demanding the continuation of 'Algérie francaise'.

The Coming of the Fifth Republic, 1958

At this point de Gaulle offered himself as the man to sort out French problems. A fortnight of complicated negotiations followed, until de Gaulle was appointed Prime Minister and given full emergency powers for six months by the National Assembly, which then dissolved itself. By September he had produced the Constitution of the Fifth Republic, which was overwhelmingly approved by the people. In November, a new National Assembly was elected with Gaullists as the biggest group, and in December, de Gaulle was elected President.

The role of President in the Fifth Republic was the most significant change from the Third and Fourth Republics. Chosen by a large number of local dignitaries, and after 1962 by the whole electorate, the President had the power to appoint the Prime Minister, suggest legislation to the Assembly, run foreign policy and act as final court of appeal. He was no longer a figurehead, but an active, involved politician, with the right to use his own initiative at any time, and with considerable extra powers in emergencies. Not the least of these powers was a direct appeal to the people in a referendum over the heads of the National Assembly. No longer would the legislature make executive action impossible, as it had done for the past 80 years. There were still two houses of Parliament (the National Assembly and the Senate). The Prime Minister and his Cabinet were still responsible to the Assembly. But both on paper and by the strength of his personality, power belonged to de Gaulle. He remained President until 1969. His Prime Ministers, Debré, Pompidou and Couve de Murville, worked loyally under him, but his greatest asset was his understanding of the French people. His television and radio broadcasts, his personal appearances, his choice of subjects on which referendums were held, all these combined to hold in check the destructiveness of French political attitudes. When a deputy of the National Assembly asked him what the future would be, his reply was 'You will have to find another de Gaulle.' Until 1969, such arrogance pleased more people than it alienated.

The Algerian crisis which had catapulted de Gaulle to power continued for four more years. De Gaulle appeared at first to support 'Algérie francaise', and then some loose link between the two countries. When in 1960 he raised the possibility of 'Algérie algérienne', two of his former colleagues Soustelle and Bidault turned against him, and in 1961 the O.A.S. (Organization de l'Armée Secrete) was formed by colonists and high-ranking army officers to keep Algeria French by any means. The terrorism of the O.A.S. and the cost of keeping order in Algeria turned French opinion in favour of granting independence. In March 1962, de Gaulle negotiated this, at Evian, by which time virtually all the rest of France's African colonies had also asked for, and gained, self-

government while retaining a specially favoured status with the
European Economic Community.

France under de Gaulle

The French economy moved ahead swiftly under de Gaulle, though
it required the stimulus of his unpopular policies of lower
government spending and higher taxes. In December 1958, he
devalued the franc and then issued a new currency (one new franc
for every hundred old ones), thereby restoring confidence; he also
urged the adoption of two National Plans which between 1958 and
1965 more than doubled France's exports of manufactured goods
and produced an average growth rate of five per cent, higher than
that of the United States.

In 1963, de Gaulle vetoed British entry to the Common Market,
after 18 months of negotiation, on account of Britain's links with
America and the Commonwealth. In 1967, he refused to allow new
negotiations to begin (see below and Chapter 17). With similar
stubbornness he withdrew the French fleet from NATO in 1959,
and in 1966 withdrew all French forces while insisting that France
was still part of the Organization.

In May 1968, de Gaulle's Republic faced its greatest crisis
when student unrest, especially in Paris, erupted into riots and,
some tried to say, revolution. Police repression won support for the
students; 10,000,000 men went on strike as the street battles raged,

*Riot police confront Parisian students in 1968, during the violent upheaval
which contributed to de Gaulle's downfall in 1969.*

but de Gaulle's reply was to consult all the French people in a new election, offering a choice of his continued authority or chaos. He won a landslide victory, though he found it wise to grant concessions to both the students and the trade unions.

In 1969 the referendum, the democratic weapon on which much of his authority was based, turned against de Gaulle. He asked for support in policies of decentralization and changing the powers of the Senate, but 53 per cent of the voters voted against him. He resigned at once, and withdrew to his country estate at Colombey-les-deux-églises, where he died in 1970, respected rather than loved. Twice France had looked to him for salvation in political crises; twice he had voluntarily stepped down from power, a rare move for any national leader.

France since de Gaulle

Georges Pompidou, de Gaulle's Prime Minister from 1962 until 1968, was elected to the Presidency in 1969 and held the office until he died in 1974. He was succeeded by Giscard d'Estaing, who narrowly defeated the left-wing candidate Mitterand, and became a vigorous President in the Gaullist tradition, but one who steadily broke free of the restrictions of the Gaullist party (called the U.D.R. until 1976 and the R.P.R. since then). After seven government shuffles involving Gaullist and 'centre-right' coalitions, Giscard appointed Raymond Barre Prime Minister in August 1976. A man of no party affiliation, Barre had been a professor of political economy, and he met his task of straightening out France's economy by producing the 'Blois Programme' in January 1978. This list of 30 objectives and 110 specific proposals created greater confidence in the government and in the international value of the franc. The National Assembly elections later in 1978 confirmed Barre in power at the head of an able and broadly-based government. The left wing, which had threatened in the mid-70s to form an effective coalition, seemed to be in disarray once again.

THE EUROPEAN MOVEMENT SINCE 1945

In 1944, the governments-in-exile for Belgium, the Netherlands and Luxembourg agreed to set up a Customs Union when the war was over. This 'Benelux' agreement was the first tangible result of a widespread determination to keep alive the advantages of international alliance and commitment which had won the war. Churchill had a wider vision when he said in 1946, 'We must recreate the European family in a regional structure called the United States of Europe ... France and Germany must take the lead ... Great Britain, the British Commonwealth of Nations, mighty America and, I trust, the Soviet Union must be the friends and sponsors of

Chancellor Adenauer of West Germany (left), President de Gaulle of France (centre) and President Lubke of West Germany, pictured together in 1962. The diplomatic alliance of France and Germany was the keystone of the European movement.

the new Europe...'. The Cold War dashed any genuine hopes that he might have had on this last point, but the actions of statesmen like de Gasperi of Italy, Adenauer of Germany and particularly Schuman and Monnet of France kept the European ideal moving forward when Churchill himself was out of office. Cooperation on defence and economic matters was attempted first. But the difficulties in establishing agreement on these destroyed any immediate idea of a United States of Europe.

Defence Agreements

In 1947, Britain and France signed the Dunkirk Treaty, agreeing to act together against any indication of aggression by Germany. By 1948, however, it was clear that the real threat to European peace came from the Soviet Union, and while Berlin was still being blockaded by the Russians, Britain, France and the Benelux countries signed the Brussels Treaty (1948), pledging 'all the military aid and assistance in their power' if any one of them was attacked. Significantly, further agreements were made about the abolition of visas, the mutual recognition of social insurance benefits and matters which had nothing to do with defence. In 1955, Italy and the Federal Republic of Germany joined the organization, which was renamed the Western European Union.

In 1949 the five powers in the Brussels Treaty Organization became part of NATO (see Chapter 13). Though NATO's creation has not been followed by any further advance of Communism in Europe, its conventional forces on the continent are considerably weaker than those of the Warsaw Pact. In 1977 NATO could mobilize just over a million men in Europe, to the Pact's one and a quarter million; the Pact had 16,000 medium tanks to NATO's 6,600, and 2,500 tactical aircraft to NATO's 1,800. NATO's aircraft were of over 130 different sorts, creating the same problem as NATO's 31 types of anti-tank weapon, that of coordination. On the credit side, NATO in the 1970s has collaborated on research and development of new aircraft and missiles, thereby sharing the huge costs of modern weapon technology.

Economic Agreements

In 1947, the American Secretary of State announced the European Recovery Programme, to which he gave his name: Marshall Aid. This massive injection of goods and money was administered by representatives from each recipient country in the Organization for European Economic Cooperation (O.E.E.C.). This administrative body encouraged further consultation on the subject of European unity. In 1948 a 'Congress of Europe' met at The Hague, and from its deliberations emerged the 'Council of Europe' (1949), a specifically non-military assembly which, full of ideals, lacked the power to do anything very eye-catching or practical.

Practical planning came from Robert Schuman and Jean Monnet of France, Foreign Minister and Finance Minister respectively. In 1950, they proposed the pooling of French and German coal and steel production, a move which would make war between those two powers impossible and which would rationalize the production of the most fundamental materials in Europe. Enthusiastic support came from Italy and the Benelux countries; in 1951 a treaty was signed, and in 1952 the European Coal and Steel Community came into being, six countries in harness under a High Authority which was supra-national, and which was presided over by Monnet.

In 1955 Benelux began to press for a new stage in European unification. Britain remained unconvinced of the value of supra-national organizations and was prepared to talk only about free trade areas. 'The Six' pressed ahead with plans for a more structured 'Common Market' and for the sharing of atomic energy. In 1957, France, West Germany, Italy, Belgium, the Netherlands and Luxembourg signed the Treaty of Rome, which set up the European Economic Community with effect from 1 January 1958. The same six countries also joined together in 'Euratom'.

Britain has never been singleminded about entry into the Common Market. Here Conservative M.P. Sir Derek Walker-Smith (left), joins forces with Labour's Renee Short and Michael Foot to oppose the pro-European movement.

In 1959, Britain, Austria, Switzerland, Portugal, Norway, Sweden and Denmark ('the Seven') signed a European Free Trade Association (E.F.T.A.) Convention which became operative in 1960. Aiming simply at reducing tariffs and trading restrictions, it was less effective and imaginative than the Common Market idea, and by 1961 Britain was announcing its intention to apply for E.E.C. membership. Negotiations were stopped abruptly by de Gaulle in 1963, and in 1967 he refused to let further negotiations start because he still felt that Britain was unready to play its proper part. In 1973, after 18 months of negotiation and a year of preparing the necessary legislation, Britain at last gained admission to the E.E.C. Eire and Denmark joined at the same time, but Norway turned down the chance because of a narrow majority for the 'No' vote in a referendum.

The Common Market – Institutions

The administration of the Common Market rests in four bodies, which since 1967 have also served the E.C.S.C. and Euratom. These are the Commission, the Council of Ministers, the European Parliament and the Court of Justice.

The *Commission* consists of 13 permanent officials appointed by their member governments: France, Germany, Italy and Britain have two Commissioners each, the other countries one each. The Commission has a staff of about 3,000 civil servants to help them, based in Brussels. The purpose of the Commission is to make proposals to the Council of Ministers, to prepare the budget, to run the agricultural market, to supervise industrial and commercial policies, and to coordinate the application of the rules of the Treaty of Rome. The Commission is a 'super-Cabinet', sworn to work for the Community and is therefore supra-national. Roy Jenkins, former British Chancellor of the Exchequer, became President of the Commission in 1976. The Commission is not a dictatorship because it is limited by its responsibility to the other institutions.

The *Council of Ministers* consists of one politician from each member state, to discuss and make policy decisions (which may well have been recommended by the Commission). Usually foreign ministers attend the Council, but others (agriculture ministers or heads of government) may be the national representative. Voting is 'weighted': France, Germany, Italy and Britain have votes worth 10 points, Belgium and the Netherlands five each, Denmark and Eire three each and Luxembourg two. 41 votes is the usual minimum before a decision is considered agreed, and this provides some protection for minorities.

The *European Parliament* which sits alternately in Strasbourg and Luxemburg consisted originally of politicians delegated by their own Parliaments, but in June 1979 the world's first international elections for a legislature produced a total of 410 Members of the European Parliament, elected for five years. The 'big four' countries returned 81 members each, the Netherlands 25, Belgium 24, Denmark 16, Eire 15 and Luxembourg six. Most countries used a system of proportional representation for the vote, but Britain, to the disgust of the Liberals who were not represented, used its normal single-member constituency system. The job of the Parliament is to exercise democratic control on the Commission and the Council, though it does not have to pass laws to authorize every action taken by them. It is a consultative body, which in emergencies could force the resignation of the Commission. In 1979 it rejected the Commission's budget, an unprecedented use of its power.

The *Court of Justice* has one judge from each member-country, whose task is to decide, by majority verdict, the legality of actions committed by the Community or by a member state, according to the Treaties which members have signed. It is the final court of appeal, but not of criminal law.

The Common Market – Policies and Achievements

The nine countries of the E.E.C. abolished the last of their internal customs duties on 1 July 1977 after a series of 20 per cent cuts started in 1973. This provided a free market of about 260 million people, compared with the 254 million in the U.S.S.R. or 214 million in the U.S.A. A Common External Tariff of about six per cent on average regulated imports from the rest of the world, but a number of special arrangements were made, the most important being the Lomé Convention signed in 1975, an agreement by which 54 countries in the Caribbean, the Pacific and Africa may send the bulk of their exports to the E.E.C. without paying tariffs.

The Nine also coordinated their method of indirect taxation by agreeing to use value-added taxes (V.A.T.). They agreed on the free movement of labour, on common codes of practice for safety, transport and health regulations, and on mutual recognition of social welfare benefits and health insurance. Problems arose on the planned Economic and Monetary Union due in 1980, caused partly by the variations in the exchange values of members' currencies, and further discussions were necessary on the subject of a common currency. E.M.U. therefore had to be postponed.

The two subjects that caused greatest tension in the E.E.C. were agriculture and the budget contributions.

Agriculture was specially provided for in the Treaty of Rome on French insistence. In 1950, 28 per cent of the French work-force was involved in agriculture of a relatively backward standard. In 1962 a Common Agricultural Policy was established, consisting of guaranteed prices for farm produce and loans and grants for modernizing farming procedures. The drawback was that some food prices went up considerably, some goods were overproduced (creating 'butter mountains', 'beef mountains' and even 'wine lakes'), and some countries objected to the amount of money which they had to pay to the Community budget to support what they considered to be inefficient farming. Of the 1978 Budget, 74 per cent of the total of c.£8,000,000,000 went on agriculture. Britain, the only E.E.C. country with less than three per cent of its workforce in farming, paid £1,000,000,000 more into the Community than it received back in aid, to the extreme displeasure of both major parties, who tried to renegotiate the proportions.

Four per cent of the 1978 Budget was used to stimulate industrial investment in the poorer regions of Europe, including southern Italy, Eire, central Scotland, and south and west France. The European Investment Bank, a subsidiary body of the E.E.C., formalized its Regional Policy in 1974, and makes its grants to areas suffering from low per capita income, chronic and high unemployment, or declining population.

It is impossible to measure the success of the Common Market. Growth figures are misleading because they are affected by many more pressures besides Common Market regulations. But as Professor Hallstein, first President of the Commission, said, the figures all prove that 'it has not failed.' With Spain, Portugal, Austria and Greece all exploring the advantages of admission to the Market at the end of the 1970s, the economic dimension of a United States of Europe was well on its way to completion. Political union, however, was still beyond reach.

17 Britain since 1939

Wartime Britain

September 1939 to April 1940 was the period of 'phoney war', when, after Hitler's Polish campaign had finished, nothing else seemed to upset routine life. The panic evacuation from London (one and a half million people resettled in three days as war was declared), the universal issue of gas masks, and the nervous testing of air-raid sirens had involved the civilian population in the tensions of war, but having been keyed up for action, they found inactivity demoralizing, and Chamberlain's leadership failed to capture their imagination. The hectic days of April, May and June 1940, which included Churchill's promotion to Downing Street, brought significant changes: from then until 1945, there was 'total war'. (See Chapter 12 for Chamberlain's fall and military events.)

Churchill's ministry was a coalition, headed by a War Cabinet

The Evacuation of London. Parents and children study the carefully written instructions. Schools were the main units on which organization of the evacuation was based.

in which he was both P.M. and Defence Minister, Halifax retained his post as Foreign Secretary, Chamberlain was Lord President (he died within six months), Attlee (leader of the Labour Party) was Lord Privy Seal, and Greenwood, also of the Labour Party, was Minister without Portfolio. Men joined or left the War Cabinet as their skills or jobs demanded: Beaverbrook came, as Minister for Aircraft Production; Bevin, as an inspirational Minister of Labour; Woolton, as a forward-looking Minister for Reconstruction. Churchill's maxim was 'Everything for the war, whether controversial or not; and nothing controversial that is not needed for the war' and to this end he set up a benevolent dictatorship, efficient, but ruthless at times. Parliament granted him extra powers occasionally, and questioned him closely at other times, but his charisma carried him through; he was the right man for the people at that time.

The civilians of Britain played a key role in the war. Their heroic contribution to the Dunkirk evacuation demonstrated one aspect of military dependence on civilian help. Another was the production of over 100,000 aircraft, 25,000 tanks, 2,000,000 tons of Royal Navy shipping, and 6,000,000 rifles and machine guns between September 1939 and June 1944. They provided a volunteer Home Guard of some two million men (more than could be armed and equipped) as well as Air Raid Precautions teams, auxiliary firemen, civil defence and first aid personnel of all sorts. They dug up their parks and lawns in a 'Dig for Victory' campaign which reduced the country's dependence on food shipped across the perilous Atlantic; they saw their iron railings and their old saucepans requisitioned to be melted down, scrap metal contributing strongly to the production of weapons. They endured bombing raids that left 60,000 dead and one house in every 15 totally destroyed, and a further three in 15 damaged. They also endured food rationing that in 1941, for example, allowed each person, for a week, half a pound of meat plus a further four ounces of bacon or ham, eight ounces of sugar, eight ounces of fats (of which not more than two ounces could be butter), two ounces of tea, two ounces of jam or marmalade, and one ounce of cheese. Other foods were available 'on points', which allowed a certain amount of free choice but never enabled the customer to get much quantity.

The Start of Reconstruction

One effect of the hardship, the sharing and the agony of war was the fostering of a new democratic spirit. Bombs and bullets made no distinction between social classes, nor did hunger, grief, pain and death; nor did government regulations. Conscription was for everyone in the required age-brackets: the Registration for Employment Order of 1941 eventually drafted 94 per cent of all able-bodied males between the ages of 14 and 64 into the services, industry, or some 'reserved' occupation, while most single women in the 19–24 age-group were directed into the auxiliary branches of the fighting services, the 'Land Army' (a farming work-force) or some form of nursing or hospital service. Princess Elizabeth, now Queen Elizabeth II, was much publicized in her training as an army driver capable of doing basic mechanical repairs on her lorry. Rationing was for everyone. Increased taxation (at 50 per cent) hit everyone. Evacuation jumbled up the classes, the regions and the generations. The needs of industry brought former domestic servants and their former middle-class employers side by side in the same factory. The war brought awareness of 'how the other half lived.'

By 1942, Churchill's government was beginning to look beyond bare survival to the shape of the future for which all were fighting. The Beveridge Report of December 1942 called for new war on the 'five giants' that threatened human dignity, 'want, disease, squalor, ignorance and idleness', and in 1943, Lord Woolton joined the War Cabinet as Minister for Reconstruction. Government planning and organization were winning the war, and attention was now to be turned to the peace. 'Laissez-faire' was to be abandoned, as Butler's Education Act and the Town and Country Planning Act of 1944 anticipated.

The 1945 Election

The Labour and Liberal Parties withdrew from Churchill's coalition as soon as the war in Europe was over in 1945, in order to prepare themselves for the first General Election fought purely on party lines since 1929. Voting took place on 5 July, but with votes coming from servicemen all over the world, the result was not available until 26 July. When it came, it gave the Labour Party its first overall majority in the House of Commons: Labour 393 seats, Conservatives and allies 213, Liberals 12, Communists two, 'Independents' 20.

Churchill's defeat, unexpected before the election, was understandable. It reflected first of all a rejection, not of Churchill, but of pre-war ideas and conditions. Whereas after the First War, the voters had wanted to return to the gentle days of Edwardian England and had voted for the continuing leadership of Lloyd George, after the Second War they wanted to forget the past, especially the depressed, aimless 30s, and enter a new age. There was no nostalgia. Furthermore, the Conservative Party was the party of Munich: the public forgot how they had welcomed the 1938 Agreements, and remembered only how they had had to fight against the consequences. As for Churchill, he had no reputation as a peace-time politician. He had not been entrusted with ministerial rank in the 1930s, and his spell as Chancellor of the Exchequer (1924–29) had partly precipitated the General Strike of 1926.

Churchill personified the British fighting spirit as no-one else could have done, but he was now 71, and a nation brimming with respect and gratitude could not see him as the leader of a new age of peace. At the time, blame for his election defeat was put on his campaign, when he rashly compared the Socialists with the Gestapo and relied too much on the wordy rhetoric that had inspired resistance to Hitler. But what was most lacking in his campaign was a programme, a set of policies and promises in tune with the urgent desires of the electorate. The Conservatives could offer Churchill to the electorate, but little else.

Nationalization, 1945–51

The Labour Party, on the other hand, had published a policy document in 1942 called *The Old World and the New Society*, and had been pledged to a policy of Nationalization since the writing of their Constitution in 1918. For the State to take over certain industries was perfectly acceptable to most people: the Bank of England in 1946, the electricity industry and airlines in 1947 and the gas industry in 1948 attracted little comment as they came under government control. The Coalmines Act of 1946 and the Transport Act of 1947 (which covered docks, railways, London Transport and road haulage) were welcomed because they brought into government care industries whose inability to run efficiently and at a profit had plagued private enterprise since the First World War. It was unfortunate for the government that within a few weeks of the National Coal Board's creation, the country suffered the coldest winter for years and the worst fuel shortage in its history. So many power-stations were closed for lack of coal that there was no electricity at all for industry in the South, Midlands and North-West, and domestic electric fires were forbidden between nine a.m. and noon, and again between two p.m. and four p.m.

It was the Nationalization of iron and steel that caused the greatest controversy. The Conservatives felt not only that this industry would respond most efficiently and profitably to private enterprise, but also that government control here would lead to control of all the industries using iron and steel – building, car manufacture, all forms of engineering – and thus to economic dictatorship. In the House of Lords, the Conservatives vetoed the Iron and Steel Bill, the first use of the veto on a major piece of legislation since the Irish Home Rule Bill of 1912 and 1913. The result was a new Parliament Act, reducing the delaying power of the Lords from two years to one, and delaying the nationalization of steel until 1951, when, ironically, the Conservatives were in power.

The Welfare State

Not quite so controversial was the legislation which updated and extended the Welfare State. The National Insurance Act of 1946 provided for unemployment, sickness and retirement benefits as well as for family allowances and widows' benefits, in exchange for a flat-rate contribution made by all employed or self-employed people. The unremitting energy of Aneurin Bevan, Minister of Health, produced a National Health Service, which 95 per cent of the population joined within 12 months of its creation. It was opposed more by doctors and dentists than by anyone else because they feared that it would be cumbersome, inefficient and impersonal. It gave free consultations, medicine and treatment, including hospital treatment, and a free dental and optical service when originally set up. In 1951 Bevan and the young Harold Wilson resigned from the government when economy measures included a charge for spectacles and false teeth. Housing also came under the Ministry of Health, and by 1949 over a million new houses had been built, mostly on council estates. These still did not meet the high demands for housing as the post-war birth-rate pushed up the number of families with young children.

Other laws passed by Attlee's Labour government included a Trade Unions and Trade Disputes Act (1946) repealing that of 1927 (see Chapter 6); an Agriculture Act which set up the system of annual price reviews and subsidies for farmers, which stimulated production while keeping food prices low; a New Towns Act (1946) and a Town and Country Planning Act (1947) which took a radical new initiative in urban development policies.

Attlee's ministry ranks with the Liberal Ministry of 1906–1915

Ernest Bevin (left), Foreign Secretary 1945–51, and Clement Attlee, Prime Minister 1945–51, pictured at the Potsdam Conference, where they replaced the Conservatives Eden and Churchill.

as one of the great reforming ministries in British history. His quiet coordinating style was in sharp contrast to Churchill's forcefulness, but he ran a strong team: Bevin, the sincere and respected Foreign Secretary; Bevan, the fiery Minister of Health; Dalton, the Chancellor of the Exchequer, succeeded in 1947 by Sir Stafford Cripps, whose name became synonymous with rationing, shortages and austerity; Shinwell, Minister of Fuel and Power; Wilson, President of the Board of Trade. These were talented men who stuck to Labour's social objectives but kept the party broadly-based. In 1950 they won the General Election, polling two and a half per cent more votes that the Conservatives, but their majority was reduced to nine seats in the Commons. The strain on ministers became intolerable as they worked by day in their Departments and faced Conservative pressure as the Commons sat late into the night. Cripps retired through ill-health in 1950, Bevin in 1951. Attlee himself was exhausted, and in September 1951 he asked the King for a fresh election. Although the Labour Party still won more votes than the Conservatives alone, the Conservatives and their allies won 321 seats, Labour 295 and the Liberals six. At the age of 77, Winston Churchill became Prime Minister for the second time.

Britain in the Modern World – the Economic Reality

Before considering the political development of Britain after 1951, we must refer back to the economic difficulties last discussed in Chapter 6. The Labour Party's reforms brought about a change of ownership and organization in the 'commanding heights' of the economy, but they could not disguise the fundamental problems which still dog every British government.

Britain lives by trade and by manufacture. The population of the islands has been larger than can be supported by home agriculture for nearly 400 years, and the imported food has been paid for by exports of finished goods (cloth, machines, cars, for example, depending on the century) and of raw materials (wool and coal being the most important). Even so, there were only two years in the nineteenth century when Britain actually exported more goods than she imported. For the rest of the time her apparent prosperity was based on her 'invisible earnings', the money which came into England not in exchange for goods exported, but in exchange for services like shipping, insurance, and banking. Some of the invisible earnings were the dividends paid on overseas investment in the colonies or in South America. These invisible earnings paid in the nineteenth century for up to 40 per cent of British imports, exports paying for the remaining 60 per cent, and in many years they provided a surplus for re-investment and expansion at home and abroad.

Yet Britain's economic progress in the early twentieth century was like that of a tight-rope walker working his way up an ever-steepening wire as foreign competition and the using-up of domestic resources made survival more difficult. The effect of the Second World War was to make the tight-rope walker lose his balancing pole; in other words, in order to survive the war, Britain sold over £1,000,000,000 worth of foreign investments and had to watch the destruction of the investment of decades in areas captured by the Japanese. After the war, as India and Pakistan were granted their independence, more sources of invisible earnings vanished. By 1950, it was estimated that invisibles could pay for only 10 per cent of Britain's imports. The rest had to come from exports, which therefore had to be increased by at least 75 per cent. The problem faced by all Chancellors of the Exchequer since the war has been to create the conditions for that level of production. But while on one side of the tight-rope has yawned the gulf of Depression and unemployment, on the other lurk the perils of inflation and worthless money, and prices too high to be competitive.

The Labour Party's period in office from 1945 to 1951 was long enough to expose the particular problems of the post-war period and the general problems of Britain's economic structure. Hugh Dalton, Chancellor from 1945 until 1947, based his programme on a $3,750,000,000 loan from the U.S.A., negotiated by John Maynard Keynes when the Lend-Lease programme stopped. Sir Stafford Cripps, his successor, wrestled with supply shortages. Rationing in 1947 was stricter than it had been in 1941, for bread was now restricted. Clothes rationing ended in 1949, when the meat ration was still at its lowest point. In 1950, milk, flour, eggs and soap emerged from restrictions, but it was left to the Conservatives to remove the last food rationing (of cheese, butter, bacon and sugar) in 1951 and 1952. The 'age of austerity' was over, but balance of payments crises hovered. In 1949, Cripps had devalued the pound from its pre-war value of $4.03 to $2.80, and exports had risen greatly in response. Marshall Aid had added a further $12,000,000,000 to Britain's resources, and significant recovery had been made. But the 'sterling balances', money owed by Britain to other countries, amounted to £3,500,000,000 and at any sign of weakness in Britain's economy, those countries were likely to demand their cash.

Economics and the Conservatives, 1951–64

Churchill's election victory in 1951 was based on a promise to restore free enterprise in the economy and end rationing and controls, but the Conservatives unravelled very little of the fabric that Labour had woven. Iron and steel, committed by existing law to inevitable nationalization, were de-nationalized again in 1953, as was part of the road haulage industry, but the Welfare State was accepted in its entirety. The most striking economic achievement came from the Ministry of Housing under Macmillan, when the 'impossible' target of 350,000 new houses in a year was exceeded in 1954. At that time unemployment was low; taxation came down and hire-purchase regulations were eased; low interest rates encouraged borrowing and spending; it seemed at last as if the 'Age of Affluence' had arrived.

But affluence brought its own problems. Higher demand for goods put up prices: higher prices and a shortage of labour in some parts of the economy put up the pressure for higher wages. Soon a dangerous wages-prices spiral and a threatening balance of payments situation called for a reversal of policy. In 1956 taxes were raised, and higher rates of interest were introduced to discourage borrowing and encourage saving. The tactic worked; in 1957–58, the Chancellor Thorneycroft reduced taxes again. Slowly, the tight-rope walker could edge his way upward until Macmillan could say, in the 1959 Election campaign, 'You've never had it so good.' He was right, but only temporarily. The stimulation of the economy was reversed in 1960, when high rates of interest brought a new 'credit squeeze', and the government tried to impose a 'pay freeze', a fixed period of time in which no groups of workers should get increased wages or salaries. The idea was unpopular and did not work well. Those whose pay-rise had been postponed by the freeze pressed for a bigger rise as compensation, and in the long run, little had been saved. In 1962 and 1963 Reginald Maudling, the sixth Chancellor of the Exchequer since the Conservatives took office in 1951, reversed policy once again and by cutting taxes and interest rates, encouraged people to spend their way out of stagnation. The result of the spending spree was a huge increase in imports, and a balance of payments deficit which Maudling had foreseen as a necessary evil before British output picked up, and which the Labour Party saw only as an outcome of 'Thirteen Years of Tory Misrule.' This was an effective slogan, and in 1964, Labour narrowly won the General Election, largely because they were able to persuade the people that Conservative economic policy had failed.

The judgement was harsh in view of the underlying problems of the British economy, but the public was weary of 'Stop-Go' policies which lurched erratically and slowly towards a better standard of living. In 1951, they had voted for release from Socialist planning and controls and rationing; by 1964, there was an acknowledgement that the government had to play a more consistent role than occasionally touching the 'brake' or the 'accelerator' of the economy, and it seemed that the Labour Party was more prepared to take it on. In its final years the Conservative government had moved towards a more regulated, less laissez-faire system. It had tried to negotiate Britain's entry into the European Economic Community, which would have meant accepting a certain measure of outside regulation, but de Gaulle had vetoed the application in early 1963. It had also introduced a National Incomes Commission and a National Economic Development Council in 1962, but they could produce no results to save the Conservatives from defeat in 1964.

Politics and the Conservatives, 1951–59

Churchill's ministry from 1951 to 1955 was an undoubted success, not so much because of his ability but because of the end of austerity. The death of George VI in 1952 gave the nation a reason to reflect on how he had quietly and courageously led them from the constitutional crisis and the Depression of 1936 through the trauma of the war to their present improved situation. The Coronation of Elizabeth II in 1953 gave them a reason to look ahead optimistically to a new Elizabethan Age of revived vigour and greatness. The news that Hilary and Tensing had made the first ascent of Mount Everest, received on Coronation Day, symbolized hopes of new achievements. Television, greatly popularized by the spectacle of the Coronation, was further boosted in 1954 when the Conservatives allowed the establishment of Independent (commercial) television in competition with the B.B.C.

In 1955, Churchill handed over power to his nephew by marriage, Eden, who had been 'heir-apparent' since 1940. This predicted and over-due step was approved by the electorate when Eden went to the polls: the Conservatives, with 344 seats to Labour's 277 and the Liberals' six, had increased their majority, a thing which no other twentieth-century government had done until then. But Eden's long wait for power was followed by short tenure of it. The Suez Crisis (see Chapter 22) of 1956 destroyed his health and his confidence, and in 1957 he retired, leaving little of significance on the domestic statute book except the Clean Air Act of 1956.

R.A. Butler, former Minister of Education, Chancellor of the Exchequer, and Leader of the House of Commons, was strongly expected to replace Eden, for whom he had deputized when he was taken ill. However the man invited by the Queen to form a ministry, after she had taken much advice from senior statesmen, was Harold Macmillan, a man with a distinguished record as Housing Minister 1951–55, and with an air of Edwardian calm and charm which was a cartoonist's dream. Quickly caricatured by the *Daily Mirror*'s political cartoonist as 'Supermac', Macmillan actually benefited from this cynical title. He inspired confidence, and his keen political mind combined with an old-fashioned dignity made him much respected, both nationally and internationally. At home he rallied the Conservatives after the humiliation of the Suez failure and Eden's sudden departure. He led them through the passing of the Rent Act in 1957, which, by removing restrictions on rents, made them unpopular with all tenants. He supervised the boosting of the economy so that by 1959, it could be seen that real wages had gone up by 40 per cent while the Conservatives had been in office, and the average family now owned a car, a refrigerator and a television, all of which would have been luxuries in 1951. When he called an Election in 1959, the Conservatives won 365 seats to Labour's 258 and the Liberals' six. It was a remarkable triumph for 'Supermac'.

The End of the Conservative Era, 1960–64

The next four years were less successful. The quickening rate of inflation and pressure for wage settlements raised the number of strikes, and the general goodwill of British society was further upset by ever-increasing immigration of West Indians, Indians and Pakistanis into London, various industrial towns in the Midlands, and parts of Lancashire and Yorkshire. To industrial tension was added the complication of irrational colour prejudice. Although the immigrants were indispensable to many of Britain's vital services and industries (the hospitals, public transport, textiles, bricks), their presence stirred up resentment about wage levels, housing shortages and conditions, educational standards and public law and order. In 1962, the Commonwealth Immigration Act restricted entry to those with jobs or with certain skills. Racialism and political antagonism became bitterly intertwined, at a time when social standards were also being challenged by the 'Permissive Society'. Some blamed Macmillan's introduction (when he was Chancellor in 1956) of Premium Bonds, which they saw as State-

Two immigrant boys at a comprehensive school in Peckham learn how to make an electronic organ.

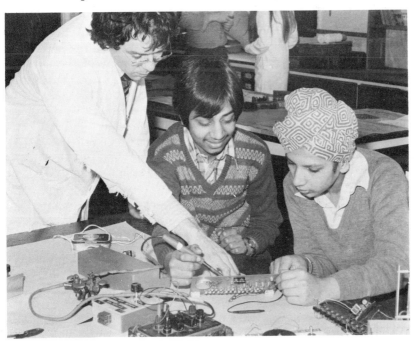

sponsored gambling; some blamed the Betting and Gaming Act of 1960 which authorized betting shops in every high street and turned cinemas into bingo halls; some blamed affluence and commercialism; some blamed the end of National Service. It did not help that Profumo, Secretary for War, became entangled in a much-publicized scandal in 1963, involving a call-girl and a Russian diplomat. His enforced resignation dented the Tory image.

The Conservatives also fell into disarray. In 1962, following a bad by-election defeat, Macmillan had sacked seven Cabinet Ministers and nine non-Cabinet Ministers in an effort to change both the image of the party and the direction of its economic policy. He was remarkably successful; 'Supermac' became 'Mac the Knife', but respect for him was undiminished. However, his sudden illness and resignation in the autumn of 1963 showed up the fact that the party was divided and uncertain. Butler, Hailsham, Maudling and Macleod were obvious candidates for the party leadership and the premiership, but there were strong 'Stop Butler' and 'Stop Hailsham' movements, and it was the Foreign Secretary, Lord Home, whom the Queen invited to form an administration. He was able to unite most of the party, though Macleod and Enoch Powell refused to serve under him. He disclaimed his peerage, and as Sir Alec Douglas-Home led the country with quiet care until the Conservatives narrowly lost the election of 1964. Labour won 317 seats, the Conservatives 304, the Liberals nine.

The Labour Party, 1964–70

As the Conservative Party became more bogged down and divided, the Labour Party had rediscovered its vigour. After Attlee retired from the leadership in 1955, Hugh Gaitskell had led the party with increasing authority and skill. His speech at the Labour Party Conference in 1962 was hailed as the sign of a man ready to be Prime Minister. His early death in 1963 led to the election of Harold Wilson as the new leader. In 1964, he became the youngest Prime Minister of England since Pitt in 1783.

Wilson, an admirer of President Kennedy of America, promised Britain 100 days of dynamic action to launch his ministry. He and his ministers also overstated the economic problems left to them by the Tories, in the hope of gaining full support for their measures. The result was that they talked Britain into an exaggerated balance of payments crisis. Overseas bankers looked at their measures (raising old age pensions and unemployment benefits, and removing prescription charges) with the same alarm as the bankers of 1931 had reviewed Ramsay MacDonald's Labour colleagues, and began to switch their holdings out of sterling. A loan of $3,000,000,000 from the International Monetary Fund (I.M.F.) stabilized the situation, and in 1965, with the introduction of a National Prices and Incomes Board, and a National Plan which

Harold Wilson (left), Labour Prime Minister 1964–70 and 1974–6, pictured on a visit to Moscow with the man who succeeded him as Prime Minister from 1976 to 1979, James Callaghan.

aimed for 25 per cent growth in the economy by 1970, Wilson seemed firmly in control, despite the fact that his Parliamentary majority had dropped to three, and by March 1966, to two. A General Election at the end of that month gave the Labour Party 363 seats, the Conservatives 253 and the Liberals 12.

Wilson's 1966–70 Ministry suffered between the hammer of left-wing expectations and the anvil of financial and economic realities. Although he could talk bravely of a new society, forged 'in the white heat of the technological revolution', the last word went to inflation fuelled by wage demands and strikes within the country and by rises in world prices (to which Britain, as an importing nation, was extremely vulnerable). In 1967, the Chancellor, James Callaghan, announced the devaluation of the pound from \$2.80 to \$2.40. The National Plan died amidst the financial chaos, as did a planned major reform of the Health Service. The re-nationalization of iron and steel had to wait until 1968. Industrial relations came under close scrutiny. The result of the Donovan Commission's Report of 1968 on Trade Unions and Employers Associations was a policy document called *In Place of Strife*, produced by Barbara Castle, Secretary of State for Employment and Productivity in 1969. It aimed to increase the government's ability to intervene in industrial disputes as well as to strengthen trade unions themselves in their efforts to cope with unofficial strikes. (In 1964–66, these made up 95 per cent of all strikes and cost 75 per cent of all working days lost through strikes.)

In Place of Strife, like an ill-fated plan to reform the House of Lords that had been proposed in 1968, produced a public rift in the party, and Wilson's majority of nearly 100 seats began to disintegrate as by-election after by-election returned anti-government candidates. In June 1970, encouraged by improved trade figures, Wilson called a General Election which superficially reunited his party. Contrary to the predictions of the opinion polls, Heath and the Conservatives won 330 seats to Labour's 287 and the Liberals' six. Later analysis seemed to indicate that the housewives' votes had swung strongly towards the Tories. The many social changes of Wilson's ministry – including the abolition of the death penalty (1965), the pressure on local authorities to turn to comprehensive schooling (1965), the Race Relations Act (1968), and the raising of the school leaving age (1970) – all failed to compensate for the feeling that prices, incomes and productivity were out of balance.

Politics in the 1970s

In 1964, Edward Heath had won great respect as the man who had led Britain's negotiations for entry into the Common Market. In 1965 he became the first leader of the Conservative Party to be elected to that post by his party, and now in 1970 he faced the same economic tight-rope that had tested all his predecessors since the war. His strong bid to find a new approach to it included successful negotiations for entry into the Common Market with effect from 1 January 1973, but part of the entry 'fee' was an inevitable rise in food prices. An Industrial Relations Act in 1971 was bitterly resented and resisted by the Labour Party and the unions, and as unemployment and prices rose, Heath had to fall back on a statutory Prices and Incomes policy, (Phase 1, 1972; Phase 2, 1973). By late 1973, industrial unrest had reached a new peak. In response to stoppages and overtime bans by electricity supply workers, train-drivers and miners, Heath announced a State of Emergency and eventually a three-day working week in all offices, shops and factories. This was to conserve fuel, which was in unusually short supply because of the Arab-Israeli War of 1973 (see Chapter 22) and the OPEC decision to double the price of crude oil. In February 1974, he appealed to the country in a General Election, but the belief that the Labour Party was better suited to sort out industrial grievances produced a slight swing in votes, and an indecisive result: Conservatives 296, Labour 301, Liberals 14, Ulster Unionists 11, Scottish Nationalists seven, Welsh Nationalists two, others three. After the Liberals had refused to enter into a coalition with Heath, he resigned.

In March 1974, Wilson formed a minority government, and in October, in a further General Election, the total of Labour seats was boosted to 319 (Conservatives 276, Liberals 13, Unionists 10, Scottish Nationalists 11, Welsh Nationalists three, others three), giving him an overall majority of three. Juggling this variety of parties enabled Wilson (1974–76) and Callaghan (1976–79) to

Britain's first woman Prime Minister, Margaret Thatcher, dominating a Press Conference.

hang onto power for a full Parliamentary span, but in 1979 Margaret Thatcher became the first woman Prime Minister of any Western country when the Conservatives won 339 seats to Labour's 268 and the Liberals' 11. The Ulster Unionists still held 10 seats, but the Scottish Nationalists and Welsh Nationalists had dropped to two seats each, and had lost any chance of pressurizing the government, as they had done in the preceding years, into granting them their own 'devolved' governments, with elected assemblies meeting in Edinburgh and Cardiff.

North Sea Oil

The pressure for devolution had been increased by Britain's entry into the Common Market. In his election campaigns in 1974, Wilson had promised to renegotiate Britain's terms of entry, and submit the result to a national referendum. This unprecedented action, in June 1975, with its two to one majority in favour of British membership, revealed that Scotland and Wales were less content than England. A further reason for Scotland's belief in devolution was the realization that North Sea oil, coming ashore in Scotland, could provide the source of revenue to give financial independence from England.

But North Sea oil was regarded by the politicians at Westminster as the new economic salvation, the 'balancing pole' that they had lacked since the war. With the first oil arriving by tanker in

June 1975, and by pipeline in November, the economic strategy could be revised, though in 1976 a major sterling crisis required an immediate loan of £2,300,000,000 from the I.M.F. Thereafter the balance of payments improved steadily, and from August 1977 Britain was producing a substantial trade surplus. Inflation and unemployment remained the twin targets of government policies. As Chancellor, Dennis Healey chose to introduce a series of small budgets to regulate the economy and avoid the excesses of 'Stop-Go'. Wage restraint was encouraged by a voluntary 'Social Contract' and a series of government-set percentage limits in annual pay bargaining. Left-wing socialists found little to please them in the period 1974–79, though comprehensive education was made compulsory for all local authorities, pensions and social security benefits were increased, and pay-beds in hospitals were restricted.

The Irish Question

For 40 years after the Government of Ireland Act of 1920 (see Chapter 6), the 'Irish Question' seemed to be buried if not dead, but in the late 1950s the reappearance of the Irish Republican Army (I.R.A.) in Northern Ireland indicated that the old problems still persisted there.

There were three obvious reasons for tension. Protestant-Catholic rivalry still existed with the fervour of the seventeenth century: one third of Northern Ireland's population was Catholic, and they had been discriminated against in employment and housing for decades. Secondly, there was still a racial and political split between the Unionists and Loyalists on one side, who favoured links with England, and on the other side those who saw more sense in uniting the whole of Ireland. Thirdly, there was economic tension: a country with a relatively poor economy and sadly lacking in investment and therefore immediate growth potential, Northern Ireland was clearly divided into rich and poor, 'haves' and 'have-nots'. One group of people felt aggrieved on all three scores: the Catholic working class, concentrated together in council estates in the poorer areas of Belfast and Londonderry. Here in the late 1960s, the Northern Ireland Civil Rights Association started to press for reforms, many of which were granted by the province's Prime Minister, Terence O'Neill.

The passing of some reforms of the laws affecting local government elections, housing policies and employment further divided all groups inside and outside Stormont (the province's Parliament in Belfast). The majority of the I.R.A. condemned the use of violence, and chose to put socialism before religion. Their attitude was that the working classes, Protestant perhaps as well as Catholic, would use political means to get rid of the exploiters. This Marxist approach was scorned by the extremists in the movement.

Calling themselves the Provisional I.R.A., they split away in 1969 and opted for violence. In that year there were 13 political murders in the province, in 1970 there were 20; in 1971, 173.

Protestant forces also used different approaches. The Ulster Volunteer Force and, later, the Ulster Defence Association were examples of 'para-military' organizations that chose to meet violence with violence. Ian Paisley voiced the extremist sectarian views of those who hated and distrusted anything that smacked of 'Popery'; William Craig led the hard-line 'Vanguard' party, while the Royal Ulster Constabulary and the 'B Specials' had distinctive Protestant leanings which cut across the impartiality expected of the forces of law and order.

The British Response

In contrast to the divisions in Northern Ireland, the major parties in Britain steadfastly supported each other's policies as they alternated in power in the 1970s. In 1969, Wilson sent British troops to Northern Ireland to enforce law and order. The R.U.C. was disarmed, the B Specials were disbanded, and the Catholics welcomed what they initially viewed as impartial protection. By 1971, distrust and violence had escalated again, and in August the

British troops in Northern Ireland. Their efforts to preserve peace could not prevent the new generation from being influenced by an atmosphere of violence.

new Prime Minister of the province, Brian Faulkner, introduced internment, i.e., imprisonment without previous trial. The use of this denial of basic civil rights represented a triumph for the violence of the I.R.A., for by forcing a democratic government to use dictatorial methods, they had won a 'moral' victory of a sort, especially when the government interned hundreds of Catholics but very few of the Protestant extremists. In January 1972, British soldiers shot 13 people in a Catholic demonstration in Londonderry. The breakdown of law and order became so pronounced that Heath accepted the resignation of Faulkner's government, and instituted direct rule from Westminster.

In 1973, a new Northern Ireland Assembly was elected by proportional representation, a novelty in British constitutional development. A 'power-sharing' executive of moderate Catholics and Protestants was formed, and in the Sunningdale Agreement of December 1973 it seemed that a liberal solution had been found, acceptable to Westminster, Dublin and Belfast. It was not so. The General Election of 1974 saw the success of 11 out of 12 anti-Sunningdale candidates, and an all-out strike in May called by the Protestant Ulster Workers' Union had the desired effect of destroying the Assembly and the Executive. Direct rule was reintroduced, with the moderates of each religion bitterly disappointed, and the extremists of each wing grimly prepared to win by violence.

In 1975–76 a new Constitutional Convention failed to hammer out an acceptable political formula. The constant violence took such a heavy toll (296 deaths in 1976, and many more deliberately mutilated, terrorized or made homeless) that a spontaneous 'Peace Movement' grew out of the efforts of two Belfast women, Betty Williams (a Protestant) and Mairead Corrigan (a Catholic) to restore political sanity and trust between members of the different religious sects. In 1977, their efforts were rewarded with the Nobel Peace Prize, but their sense of human dignity failed to touch the Catholic extremists. In 1978 and 1979, Provisional I.R.A. prisoners seeking special political (as opposed to criminal) status in gaol devised the 'dirty' protest, where they refused to use any of the clothing, washing and lavatory facilities of the prison but remained in stinking squalor for months. Whatever sympathy this action may have won for them was more than destroyed by the cold-blooded murder of Lord Mountbatten and two of his family in August 1979, and, in a separate incident on the same day, the murder by remote-controlled explosions of 18 British soldiers at Warren Point. Early in 1980, a new all-party conference met to try to find a political compromise once again. The death toll in this new 'time of troubles' exceeded 2,000 (in a little over 10 years).

China and Japan since 1941

CHINA

World War and Civil War

The war between China and Japan, that broke out in 1937 and merged into the Second World War in 1941, when the Japanese attacked Pearl Harbor (see Chapter 8), briefly halted the civil war that was already raging between the Kuomintang and the Communists. Chiang Kai-shek retreated from Peking, Nanking and Hankow to Chungking, far to the west up the Yangtse river, where, despite the loss of all ports and major towns and most of his army equipment and all his airforce, he was able to set up his government again, ruling over millions of people in the backward areas of 'Free China'. To the north, Mao Tse-tung and the Communists still held the territory that they had gained after the Long March, and they offered the Japanese not only conventional opposition but also guerrilla warfare. The Sino-Japanese War was harsh but fairly static in the years 1939–43. Until December 1941 Free China could be supplied from Burma and from Hong Kong, but when the Japanese advanced after Pearl Harbor, a new supply route had to be created by air, from Assam to Kunming in southwest China. This was the 'Hump' route, running along the southern edge of the Himalayas. In 1944 the Japanese attacked Assam to stop the 'Hump' – unsuccessfully – and stepped up their campaign in China itself, in order to cut the railways still in Nationalist hands. In this they were more effective, but it was their last success. From December 1944, they withdrew their most experienced troops to defend the other parts of their Empire, and the Chinese began to press them back.

At the same time, the competition between Kuomintang and Communists was growing again. In January 1941, heavy fighting broke out between the Communist New Fourth Army and Chiang's troops, causing hundreds of casualties, but thereafter the struggle was confined to political organization until after the Japanese surrender.

Chiang and the Kuomintang fared badly in the political rivalry against the Communists. Chiang's main source of allegiance was the army, and he made the mistake of using army personnel and army methods in his civilian administration. He set up a secret police force, the 'Blue Shirts', which came to number 300,000 men, spread all over China and the overseas Chinese communities, and which by its methods reminded people of the German S.S. Eventually it took over control of food supplies, emergency distribution, and industrial planning. His brother-in-law, T.V. Soong, became Finance Minister before the war broke out, and used the same authoritarian methods. In 1943, Chiang published his thoughts in *China's Destiny*, a book which became compulsory in all schools and which called for complete obedience and the revival of all ancient Chinese virtues. China's troubles, said Chiang, were really due to the intrusion of Western imperialism, which must be rejected. He called for a return to a land-based system not unlike that of the Manchu dynasty with its mandarins and its bureaucracy. Where industrialization was growing, it was to be under strict government control.

Mao Tse-tung, in contrast, had written *On New Democracy* in 1940, and was calling for the joint management of the state by the peasantry, the workers, the intellectuals and the petty bourgeoisie. He offered universal suffrage and 'a new democratic republic of genuinely new Three People's Principles with their Three Great Policies' (this was a subtle reference to the aims of Sun Yat-sen, the founder of the Chinese Republic). His organization was based on cadres of Communist party workers running village communities, labour unions, youth organizations and women's groups. It was a cooperative organization with a political, economic and military purpose, which fought against old-fashioned attitudes as well as the Japanese. By May 1945, the Communists claimed to have an army of nearly a million men and women, and an area under control which contained 90 million people.

The Communist Victory

When the Japanese formally surrendered in September 1945, Chiang Kai-shek was the official President of China, firmly backed by America. In November, General Marshall arrived to negotiate peace and cooperation between Nationalists and Communists, but by March 1946 his task appeared increasingly difficult, and in January 1947 he was recalled to Washington.

The area which precipitated the final spasm of fighting between the Kuomintang and the Communists was Manchuria, occupied in 1945 by the Russians, looted of much of its industrial equipment and then returned to the Nationalists. But although the Nationalists re-occupied most of Manchuria as well as the major cities of Peking, Nanking, Shanghai and Tientsin, the Communists organized the North East Democratic Allied Army under Lin Piao, which soon controlled a broad band of country from the north-west to the coast, effectively cutting many vital communication routes. From this, they attacked north into Manchuria, and south into Honan and Hupeh provinces, while all over China their political agents excited a campaign ('Speak bitterness') to overthrow the old landlord class and redistribute the land.

Sometime in 1947, the initiative passed to the Communists, even though they had less than half the number of troops of the Nationalists. Their morale was higher, their philosophy was more positive and forward-looking, their organization was considerably better run and more in touch with the feelings of the peasantry. While the Nationalists struggled to combat post-war inflation and tried to operate a new Constitution hurriedly offered to the people in 1947, the Communist stranglehold tightened. In October 1948, the battle of Huai-Hai brought 550,000 Nationalists into conflict with 300,000 Communists in the vital area between Peking and Nanking. After 65 days, the Communists claimed the victory, having wiped out a third of their enemy and captured the rest. In January 1949, Tientsin and Peking fell to them; in May, Nanking and Shanghai; in October, Canton and in November, the Nationalists' wartime centre, Chungking. By this time, Chiang Kai-shek had left the mainland to set up his Nationalist government on Taiwan, and the People's Republic of China had been proclaimed in Peking, under Chairman Mao Tse-tung.

Chairman Mao addresses the Second National Committee in 1949, flanked by Li Chi-shen on the left and Chou En-lai. Behind him, posters give equal prominence to Mao and Sun Yat-sen. The map on the wall includes the islands of Formosa and Hainan as part of Communist China.

Political Reforms

In 1949, Mao called again for the unification of the 'working class, the peasantry, the urban petty bourgeoisie and the national bourgeoisie', to 'establish people's democratic dictatorship'. A Chinese People's Consultative Conference was set up to be the main constitutional and law-making body, but when it was not in session, power was given to the National People's Congress. This in turn could be supplanted by the Central Executive Committee. In the early days, these bodies included a number of people who were not Communists: Madame Sun Yat-sen even became a member of the Central Executive Committee, and in the Congress some former Warlords and even Kuomintang generals found places. In 1954, a new Constitution was announced, based on local communities and congresses like the Russian Soviets, focussed on the State Council and the Executive Committee at the top, and completely interwoven with the Communist Party. Opposition was systematically eliminated.

In 1951, the 'Three Antis' campaign was launched against corruption, waste and bureaucratic inefficiency in all government institutions. In 1952 it was followed by the 'Five Antis', against bribery, tax evasion, fraud, leakage of information and theft of state property. These purges removed former Kuomintang officials and most 'middle class' businessmen, and put the Party into firm control of politics and the economy. 'Thought-reform' became an accepted practice; criticism of one's friends, neighbours, family and even of oneself was encouraged, so that in the ensuing discussions the 'Thoughts of Chairman Mao' could be introduced as proper guidelines. (In the mid-1960s these 'Thoughts' were set down in a little red book, carried constantly by everyone in China who valued freedom.) The old patterns of thought were obliterated: men and women were now social and political equals, a fact which alone upset the traditions of every aspect of Chinese life.

Economic Reforms

The Agrarian Reform Law of 1950 brought about the confiscation of the property of rural landlords and 'bureaucrat capitalists' (the more successful businessmen). During the redistribution of this land, Mutual Aid teams were set up, whereby peasants owned their plots of ground and their tools, but cultivated the land in teams. Ten million such teams, covering 70 million households, were set up by 1954, and further development came in the form of cooperatives which were introduced on an ever-growing scale. By the end of 1956, 88 per cent of peasant households were organized into cooperatives modelled on the Soviet collective farms, with strict government control of wage rates, work quotas and grain production targets. The cooperatives were also the centres of political education.

At the same time, towns were growing rapidly. The First Five Year Plan (1953–57), based heavily on credit and technical aid offered by the Soviet Union, aimed to add two hundred major new industrial undertakings to the economy, but the Plan was highly experimental and it did not predict accurately the problems of the transition from an agricultural to a more urban society. The urban population of 77 million in 1953 jumped to 99.5 million in 1957, while the 1953 census indicated that the total Chinese population was nearly 600 million, a third more than had been expected. As in Russia after the 1917 Revolutions, the level of food production in the countryside was the most vital measure of the success or failure of the regime, and of its likelihood of survival.

'The Hundred Flowers' and 'The Great Leap Forward'

In 1956, Mao relaxed his grip on what could be said and thought in China. 'The Hundred Flowers' movement ('Let a hundred flowers blossom, a hundred schools of thought contend') was a deliberate encouragement to the intellectuals of the country to discuss and even criticize Marxism and Communism. It was based on the assumption that the intellectuals would rapidly be persuaded of the rightness of the philosophy, so that they too would urge its general acceptance by the people. The plan misfired, partly because it overlapped with the bitter anti-Communist upsurge in Hungary, which provided much material for discussion. It became clear that many intellectuals doubted whether Communism was suited to China, and by February 1957 Mao began to restrict discussions to 'non-antagonistic contradictions'. By June 1957, it was clear that criticism of Communism was 'antagonistic', and would lead to liquidation or a spell of hard labour in Sinkiang Province. 'The Hundred Flowers' withered rapidly.

In 1958, the Eighth Party Congress called for bold leadership that would coincide with the Second Five Year Plan (1958–62) and achieve a 'Great Leap Forward' not only in economic output but in the attainment of true Socialism. The Second Plan aimed at doubling industrial output and increasing agricultural production by 35 per cent. 'The Great Leap Forward' set the patterns by which this was to be made possible. Emphasis was placed on the role to be played by the local Party official, the peasant from the cooperative and the urban dweller in his back yard. From local savings, irrigation schemes were started, power stations were built, factories were extended, and, most dramatically of all, steel furnaces were built by local party groups in small towns and villages. These enterprises were administered by new units, the Communes, which started in the towns but which were soon extended to the countryside, so that by the end of 1958 it was claimed that 99 per cent of the peasantry were living and working in them.

The Second Plan, the Great Leap Forward, and the Communes were all failures. First indications seemed to reveal tremendous success, but in 1959 Chou En-lai admitted that the figures which claimed a doubling of output were exaggerated and over-optimistic. Few production targets had been met. Levels had risen in most instances, but this had been achieved uneconomically, by the exceptional hard work of people stirred up by local pride and propaganda. It could not be maintained. The regimentation of the Communes also attracted great opposition. While the more prosperous villages resented being linked with poorer ones, the enforced break-up of the family, the traditional Chinese social unit, was hated even more. Men and women were expected to live in separate dormitories, eating in communal halls, working on communal projects, and being constantly deprived of a feeling of 'home' and 'family'.

The Great Leap Forward was followed by three years of disastrous harvests (1959–61) which completed its destruction. In 1961 China was forced to buy grain from Canada and Australia, by which time the leaders had reverted to encouraging Mutual Aid teams and cooperative farms of 20 to 30 households. Private ownership of land and of small businesses was allowed again. By 1962, the economy had recovered sufficiently for new plans to be made. Significantly, agriculture was given highest priority.

Changes in Leadership

In late 1958, when the failure of the Great Leap Forward was apparent, Mao voluntarily gave up the Presidency of the government, though he retained the chairmanship of the Party. In 1959 P'eng Teh-huai, Minister of Defence sharply criticized Mao, The Great Leap, the Communes and the attempt to rely on mass participation in economic realignment. He was soon removed from his position for being a right-winger, and was replaced by Lin Piao, hero of the Long March, the war against the Japanese and the Korean War. Nevertheless, 'moderates' soon filled the major positions of state. Liu Shao-Chi, the new President, headed a ministry that concentrated on practical problems of economic recovery and the planning of modest progress. These men were no longer Communist idealists, but pragmatic rulers of a Socialist state. By 1962, they were well pleased with their achievements.

It is now clear – though it was not so at the time – that by 1962 Mao Tse-tung had come to the conclusion that the policies of Liu and his followers represented a radical and unacceptable revision of true Marxism-Leninism. He felt that this 'revisionism', the same error of which the Soviet Union had been guilty under Stalin and his successors, betrayed the real Revolution that Marx had forecast. Capitalism and traditionalism would creep back unless the purity of ideal was maintained. It was necessary to intensify the violence of the class struggle and remove all those who might soften the harsh realities of the development of true Communism. To this end, Mao selected Lin Piao as his weapon of attack. While Mao remained in semi-obscurity, Lin Piao began to revitalize the People's Liberation Army on Maoist lines; it was he who issued the 'Little Red Book' to the rank and file of the P.L.A., and intensified the propaganda praising the 'Revolutionary Soldier'. The 1962 War against India (see Chapter 20) was portrayed as 'revolutionary' rather than nationalist, and in the same year a new Social Education Movement was launched. In 1963, this led to the purging of a number of intellectuals and artists. In 1964, the 'Four Clean-Ups' campaign was announced, against slackness in economics, politics, ideological thinking and organization.

'The Cultural Revolution'

In 1965, the pressure for a 'Cultural Revolution' built up within the Party. In January, Mao proclaimed in his 'Twenty Three Articles' that the real enemy of the Revolution was within the Party. In April, Lin Piao announced the end of rank in the P.L.A. In September, the Central Committee of the Party turned its back on massive continued support for Vietnamese Communists, and began to purge its own membership, starting with the Chief of Staff, Lo Jui-ch'ing.

In the summer of 1966, the full force of 'Great Proletarian Cultural Revolution' was unleashed. To the hard core of Lin Piao's Army, Mao added the restless energy and enthusiasm of the huge student population. Teenagers had already been used in the Social Education Movement, and this generation, which had been born at much the same time as the People's Republic itself was now encouraged to protect and purify the Red Revolution. In June 1966, schools and universities were closed for six months, and students were invited to criticize the education system, and to hunt down the 'handful of extremely reactionary bourgeois rightists and counter-revolutionary revisionists'. Eight massive demonstrations in Peking in the autumn of 1966 brought a million students on each occasion to the capital. On their journeys to and from the meetings, these 'Red Guards' dispensed their own forms of justice. Nothing and no one was safe from their prying and accusation. Denunciations, trials, resignations and executions became commonplace. Liu Shao-Chi, the President of the Republic, and Teng Hsaio-p'ing, General Secretary of the Party, offered self-criticisms and confessions which were rejected as inadequate shortly before both men were dismissed from their posts. In their wake, thousands of other leaders at all levels were humiliated and removed by the Red Guards.

Although Mao used the Red Guard movement to purge city administrations outside Peking and to try to build up a new framework of revolutionary town-country relationships, the process that he had started got out of hand. Red Guard groups, each with their own loyalties, accused others of being Liuist. Indiscriminate looting and disruption began to have an economic effect, and civil war threatened to follow the break-down of society, notably in Wuhan in July 1967. Late in 1967, the schools and universities were reopened, and the Red Guard groups began to dissolve. The more adult and disciplined P.L.A. reasserted its control, and Chou Enlai, who had been Premier since 1949 yet strangely unobtrusive since 1966, began to emerge as a mediator and conciliator. Chu Teh, Mao's lieutenant on the Long March but since disgraced as a Liuist, was now reinstated in favour. Chiang Ching, Mao's third wife and a central figure in the Cultural Revolution, disappeared from the limelight and appeared to have no more influence. In 1968 Mao spoke to the Party Central Committee of a new system within the Party, and early in 1969, Lin Piao confirmed that the era of violence was over, and that 'forgiveness' and 'unity' were the new themes.

Reconstruction

40 per cent of the Central Committee of the Ninth Party Congress elected in 1969 were serving members of the People's Liberation Army. The Politburo elected by the Central Committee had an overall majority of Army personnel. Reconstruction of the Party was therefore a subtle struggle between the Army and the politicians, for although Mao's personality and charisma dominated the Congress, and statues, banners, wall posters and millions of copies of the 'Little Red Book' proclaimed his name throughout China, the local cells of the Party had to be recreated, and at local level loyalties were still divided. In 1971, Lin Piao, Mao's officially named successor, suddenly disappeared, along with several senior military officers. It was rumoured that he had been killed in a plane crash in Mongolia. Two years later it was announced that he had been fleeing to Russia, after the discovery of his plot to assassinate Mao, when his plane crashed accidentally.

His disappearance elevated Chou En-lai to the position of Second-in-Command, but since he and Mao had been born in 1898 and 1893 respectively, he was an unattractive choice as successor. The Tenth Party Congress of 1973 appointed five vice-chairmen under Mao, including Teng Hsaio-p'ing, now rehabilitated after his disgrace as a Liuist in the Cultural Revolution. In the senior party committees, the mid-1970s was a time of regrouping and of apparently preparing a form of collective leadership to take over from Mao.

Chou En-lai died first, in January 1976. In the last few weeks of his life, advancing cancer had caused him to hand over administration to Teng, who thus became responsible for the coming Fifth

Five Year Plan (1976–80) as well as Chou's policy of 'The Four Modernizations' (science, agriculture, industry and defence). But Chou's death reopened the divisions within the Party.

'The Gang of Four'

Teng came under attack from the radicals in the Politburo who had sufficient confidence to claim Mao's support. Teng was referred to as an 'unrepentant capitalist-roader', under whose control 'both production and modernization will go astray if we abandon the key link of class struggle'. After huge popular demonstrations in all the major cities of China in memory of Chou En-lai, which were interpreted as being support also for Teng, Teng was suddenly dismissed from all posts 'on the proposal of our great leader Chairman Mao'. In his place, Hua Kuo-feng was elected First Vice-Chairman of the Central Committee of the Party, and Premier of China. Hua was clearly a compromise candidate between the moderates and the radicals, a man who had been relatively untouched by the Cultural Revolution, and who had only come to national prominence in the Politburo in 1973.

In September 1976, the death of Chairman Mao triggered the final clash between the moderates and the radicals. The 'Gang of Four', the four most radical members of the Politburo, led by Mao's widow Chiang Ching, were arrested for plotting to seize power by forging Chairman Mao's 'Last Advice' to the people of China. On the same day, 7 October 1976, Hua was elected Chairman of the Communist Party and Chairman of the Military

Confusion in China in 1976. Impassive students, wearing paper flowers in memory of Chou En-lai, listen to a denunciation of his successor, Teng Hsaio-p'ing, the 'unrepentant capitalist-roader'.

Chairman Hua. In 1980 a wave of opposition to Hua built up rapidly. Before he could consolidate himself in his apparent supremacy, Hua was speedily reduced to lowly rank and relative insignificance.

Affairs Commission, while retaining the Premiership. With the Party, the Army and the administration thus under his command, he held more power than Mao had ever been granted. He was then 56 years old, and it was clearly assumed that he would stay in power long enough to restore China's stability as well as complete 'The Four Modernizations'. Over the next 18 months, Teng was gradually rehabilitated while the Gang of Four received most of the blame for all the political disruption of the 1970s.

In February 1978, the Fifth National People's Congress adopted a new Constitution to replace that which had been suggested in 1975, and a Ten Year Plan to augment the Fifth Five Year Plan of 1976–80. Chairman Hua also promised a new emphasis on education, which, since the Cultural Revolution, had been falling in standard because of the lack of teachers with any authority.

Life in Modern China

Confucius, the greatest of all Chinese philosophers and teachers, who lived five hundred years before Christ, taught that 'To govern is to set things right.' That spirit has been the basis of all the authoritarian regimes of Chinese history, including those of the Dragon Empress, Chiang Kai-shek, Chairman Mao and, most recently, Chairman Hua. China is a one-party state, in spite of the Hundred Flowers, the Cultural Revolution and the recent liberalization. Communism has been built on the foundation of traditional obedience to the rulers, discipline and sacrifice.

Life is therefore still governed by unselfish uniformity. Clothes are drab, unisex and unaffected by 'fashion'; social behaviour is restrained; there is little distinction between the sexes in the work that they do or the pay that they receive. Young couples make few outward signs of affection that they may feel for each other. There is little freedom of expression. The 'Wall of Democracy' in Peking, where posters can be put up to voice opinions, is a mere 200 yards long. Education is dominated by the State, and everyone, however intellectual, is forced to do manual labour for two years during their 'teens so that they will always respect the 'working masses'. Reading matter is carefully controlled, as is news from the outside world. Most housing is still very basic, without running water for instance, since the resources of the economy are used for bigger capital projects. In 1979, a Western reporter recorded that in Shanghai, with 11 million inhabitants, 'one does not count in a day more than 30 cars on the streets, and no motor bikes either. The average salary is about £10 a month; a T.V. set costs two years' pay.' It is a life which the Western citizen would not tolerate and probably cannot understand.

China and Russia – the Vital Split in the Communist World

Until about 1956, the relationship between Russia and China was that of an older and a younger brother. Mao revered Stalin; the Chinese Revolution had many similarities to the Russian Rev-

Communist China's Involvement in East Asia

olution; the Chinese army and economy needed and received aid from Russia, especially in the context of the Korean War.

Yet after the death of Stalin, the relationship collapsed. Khrushchev's 'de-Stalinization' programme not only undetermined the personal standing of Mao, but also included a number of changes of doctrinal emphasis on which Mao had not been consulted. Furthermore, the visit of Bulganin and Khrushchev to India and Burma in 1955 seemed to indicate support for non-Communists, while the revolts in Poland and Hungary in 1956 'proved' that Khrushchev was mishandling Russian Communism. When, in 1958, the Russians offered no support for the Great Leap Forward, nor help in the Taiwan crisis of that year, and when in 1959 Khrushchev visited the U.S.A., the strain between the two great Communist powers became undeniable. In 1960, a series of International Communist Conferences in Rome, Warsaw, Bucharest and Moscow all confirmed the bitter division between China and Russia, which spilled over into the satellite countries. In Europe, Albania sided with the Chinese interpretation of Marxism. In Asia, North Korea and North Vietnam did the same in the 1960s, though in the late 1970s the Vietnamese turned more towards Russia, while the Kampuchean regime of Pol Pot followed a more Chinese line. In 1969, and again in the late 1970s, Chinese and Russian troops fought each other along the banks of the Ussuri River in Mongolia.

The difference between the two sides was not simply one of personalities, though undoubtedly Khrushchev was personally distrusted by the Chinese leaders, nor one of disagreement about

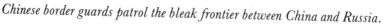

Chinese border guards patrol the bleak frontier between China and Russia.

specific world issues, though this too made matters worse. Underlying the whole argument is the Chinese belief that the Russians have become revisionists since the death of Stalin, giving up the sacred mission of world revolution and violent class struggle in favour of 'peaceful coexistence' and a consumer society. While the Chinese thus blame the Russians for losing the purity of Marxism, the Russians have taken the view that the Chinese approach is doctrinaire and therefore potentially harmful to the survival and spread of Communism.

Since 1971, Chinese foreign policy has been more like that of Russia after 1959. Since the disappearance of the 'Gang of Four'. Chinese domestic policy has been more like that of Russia since 1956. Whether reconciliation between the two Communist powers can be achieved will be one of the fundamental questions of the 1980s, for there is no escaping the fact that China, with a quarter of the world's population, huge mineral resources, vast lands and control of rocket and nuclear power, represents the biggest unknown factor in the balance of world politics. China and Russia combined could be overwhelming; China and Russia divided could be disastrous.

JAPAN

The Post-War Period

Historically, Japan developed in isolation from the West, shrouded in mystery and incurious about the origins of the few missionaries and traders who reached the islands. The arrival of American ships in 1853 is referred to in Japanese history as the 'opening of the doors', for it brought East and West into collision and stimulated the new thinking of the Meiji period (see Chapter 8). The defeat of Japan in 1945 was in some respects 'the second opening of the doors', bringing new ideas (some enforced by the outsiders) and new opportunities.

The Emperor Hirohito announced Japan's unconditional surrender on 15 August 1945, despite the attempts of some extremists to block the broadcast. The victorious nations had already promised, in the Potsdam Declaration of 26 July, that they would guarantee to the Japanese people freedom of speech, religion and thought; fundamental human rights; the removal of all obstacles to the revival and strengthening of democratic tendencies; and finally that Japan would not be 'enslaved as a race nor destroyed as a nation'. The formal surrender was signed on 2 September 1945, and on the same day General MacArthur assumed the Supreme Command for the Allied Powers (SCAP).

MacArthur's role was all-important. Although technically he represented a Far Eastern Commission of all the Allies, subject to an Allied Council of diplomats from Russia, China, Britain and

America, in practice he paid little attention to these controls and
devised his own method of working. He faced considerable Allied
pressure to abolish the Imperial constitution and introduce Ameri-
can-style republicanism, but he realized immediately that the
democratic decision of the Japanese people would be strongly in
favour of the preservation of the Emperor. Thus he set about the
destruction of the military aspects of Japanese society, while
maintaining a strong central administration. The armed forces
were demobilized and those who had held high military or political
rank were removed from office, and in some cases tried as war
criminals. General Tojo and ex-Premier Hirota were hanged
along with five others. 16 more prominent war leaders were
sentenced to life imprisonment, and thousands of others were
purged from their jobs, opening up the way for a general revision of
attitudes and organizations. The dictatorial Home Ministry and
Education Ministry were totally remodelled. The state religion,
Shinto, was disestablished and the Emperor renounced all claim to
divinity.

In 1946 SCAP produced a hastily-drafted new Constitution
which went into effect in 1947 after receiving the approval of an
elected Diet. It set up a bicameral legislature, elected by universal
suffrage (women had never voted in Japanese elections before
1946). The Prime Minister and Cabinet were to be chosen by the
Diet from among its members. There was to be an independent
judiciary, and the Emperor was to be a constitutional monarch,
'the symbol of the state, ... deriving his position from the will of the
people with whom resides sovereign power.' The old peerage was
abolished, but the most controversial clause came in Article Nine,
which laid down that 'the Japanese people forever renounce war as
a sovereign right of the nation... Land, sea and air forces will never
be maintained... The right of belligerency of the state will never be
recognized.' This unprecedented constitutional statement was in
practice compromised by SCAP itself when, in the Korean War, a
police reserve force of 75,000 men was authorized, which by 1972
had grown to the 250,000 strong 'Self-Defence Forces'.

Economic and Social Changes

Before 1945, Japanese society had been authoritarian and impersonal; individual human lives counted for little in a strictly
stratified society often threatened by earthquakes and typhoons of
vast destructive power. This deeply ingrained lack of regard for
individuals goes a long way towards 'explaining' the casual
indifference to the sufferings of prisoners-of-war, which in Western
eyes amounted to barbarity, and also the fanatical courage of the
Kamikaze pilots. The democratization of Japanese politics and
economics by SCAP and other Western influences ran contrary to
the whole Japanese tradition of utter devotion to the state and the

Emperor, so that despite the imposed changes, several aspects of Japan's development in the post-war world show signs of that same intense dedication and self-sacrifice in order to achieve the improvement of the whole of society.

Even before SCAP produced a plan for agrarian reform in 1946, Japanese politicians had started to dismantle the old feudal order. By the end of 1946, the law demanded that farmland and paddy fields should be taken from absentee landlords and from farmers with large holdings, and divided among the peasants. Thus a total of 4.8 million acres was compulsorily transferred from the original owners to over four million ex-tenants, giving a new political stability where before there had been unrest and discontent.

The huge business corporations, the zaibatsu, were also broken up so that they could no longer exercise monopoly power over the economy. Free and fair competition was thus stimulated, which speeded up the modernization of individual firms and led to intensive efforts to cut costs. Originally SCAP intended to investigate and possibly dissolve 1,200 companies; in fact only nine were totally broken up. Many others were shorn of subsidiary holdings, though most banks were left intact, another important factor in the post-war rate of investment and growth.

In 1946 and 1947, an attempt was made to further diminish the power of the industrialists by encouraging 'modern' trade unions. The Trade Union Act, the Labour Relations Adjustment Act and the Labour Standards Act were all intended to bolster the bargaining rights of workers, but companies each developed their own union and claimed to have the duty and right to look after the welfare of their workers. In 1947, there were 33,940 unions in Japan, with no concept of 'working class solidarity', except among the Communist Party.

A new education system was introduced (six years in primary school, three years in lower secondary school, followed by a voluntary further three years in upper secondary school and four years in college), but the quality of this scheme was severely tested by the numbers of students using it. (In 1975, 50 per cent of Japan's population was under the age of 30.) Classes in schools and colleges became huge, impersonal and bitterly competitive. The education system did however acknowledge equality between the sexes.

Economic Achievements

Like West Germany, Japan has achieved an 'economic miracle' since the Second War, but her economic base is more like that of Britain than that of Germany. She is an island nation, with a population larger than she can feed, and inadequate raw materials: 25 per cent of her food, 99.5 per cent of her oil, and 90 per cent of the needs of her heavy industries are imported. Of all her imports, 58 per cent are classified as raw materials, that must be processed

A Japanese production line. High investment in modern techniques made Japanese goods competitive all over the world.

and re-exported. But her share of world export trade is the third largest, after America and West Germany.

The means by which this record has been achieved, along with a rate of growth which averaged nine per cent from 1951 to 1955, 10 per cent from 1956 to 1961 and nine per cent from 1961 to 1973, are varied and interrelated. Much depended on the high rate of investment after the war, and the absolute determination of the Japanese workers and managers to restore national prestige. The fact that Japan was demilitarized, and therefore spared the heavy expense of a defence budget, freed much capital for more profitable use. The modernization of the land system greatly increased the productivity of the farmers, and released many agricultural workers to go to work in the industrial cities, where their productivity was immediately more valuable. This migration of workers from the countryside, together with the lack of effective trade unions, kept wages low and living conditions simple. The failure of SCAP to break up the zaibatsu completely meant that some big industrial corporations continued to exist and to compete in international markets. On the other hand, SCAP's suggested Constitution provided Japan with a strong and responsible executive power, which has been able to channel and direct all the economic energy of the country.

The Japanese recovery from its defeat in the Second War presents a truly remarkable story of persistence, determined hard work by an entire population, and considerable financial and diplomatic skill. But the economic miracle has not been achieved without human cost, and beneath the material satisfaction of the Japanese people lies deeper dissatisfaction. Issues like Tokyo's new international airport, pollution of sea and air from industrial effluents, examination systems, inadequate social services and, inevitably, foreign policy all provoke violence and bitterness. Terrorists of the right wing as well as of the 'Japanese Red Army' and other left wing groups use assassination, hijacking and bombs to draw attention to their demands. The patient acceptance of individual inequalities, which marked earlier periods of Japanese history, seemed to be wearing thin, just at the moment when Japan had regained her full international independence and importance.

19 International Affairs since 1950

The Korean War 1950–53

Korea had been administered by Japan since 1910 although in 1919 a provisional national government was briefly proclaimed under Syngman Rhee. In 1943, the country was promised independence, and at Yalta it was agreed that it should be divided along the 38th parallel of latitude between Russian and American troops until democratic elections could be held. In the South, Syngman Rhee set himself up as President, a nationalistic 70 year old right-winger with support from America. In the North, Kim Il-sung, a captain in the Red Army, was proclaimed leader of the 'Korean Peoples' Democratic Republic'. Neither side accepted the authority of the other to run elections throughout the country, and the Soviet Union blocked the attempts of the United Nations to mediate. President Truman declared that Korea had become 'a testing ground in the ideological conflict between Communism and Democracy', but in June 1949 he acknowledged that he could not keep American troops there indefinitely, and withdrew them. In June 1950, North Korean forces flooded across the 38th parallel.

Within 24 hours, the United Nations Security Council condemned the invasion and called on member-nations to assist in the restoration of peace. There was no Russian veto, because at that time the Russian delegation was boycotting the Council as a protest against the non-membership of the People's Republic of China. Within a further 24 hours, Truman had ordered American air and naval forces to Korea, followed shortly by ground forces. Fifteen other members of the U.N. also sent troops, but on a much smaller scale.

The early fighting favoured the North Koreans, who swept south until they controlled all but the south-east tip of the peninsula, but in September, General MacArthur, called from SCAP in Japan to command the U.N. forces, counter-attacked with landings at Inchon, deep behind the lines, cutting the Communist supply routes from the north. Within a fortnight, South Korea had been cleared of invaders, and by the end of October, North Korea itself was occupied, with U.N. troops reaching the Yalu river on the Manchurian border.

China had massed troops on the Yalu River as soon as U.N. forces entered North Korea. In November 1950 they advanced into Korea with a total disregard for appalling casualty figures. The tide of war flowed south again. In early 1951, Communist troops were in possession of Seoul, the South's capital, for a second time. A new offensive carried the U.N. troops back to the north in March 1951, and MacArthur now advocated carrying the war beyond the Yalu River and against China, a policy which was too aggressive not only for U.N. principles but also for the American administration. In April 1951 Truman abruptly dismissed MacArthur (see Chapter 15), and as the fighting got bogged down in the approximate area of the 38th parallel, the search for cease-fire terms began. Talks broke down when the Communists demanded the return of

The Korean War

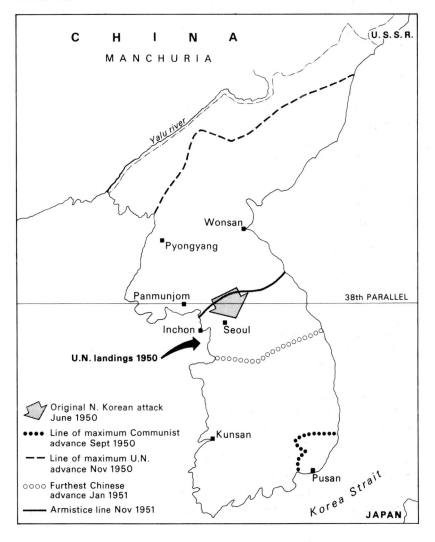

117,000 troops captured by the U.N. forces. The U.N. would not grant this because they knew that at least 50,000 of the prisoners did not want to return to the north; nor did they agree that the cease-fire line should be the 38th parallel, rather than the current front line. Ultimately an armistice was signed at Panmunjom, which effectively restored the situation that had existed before the original Communist invasion. Casualty figures indicated the human cost: 33,000 Americans killed, 47,000 South Koreans, and 3,000 from the other U.N. contingents. The Chinese had sacrificed 900,000 men, the North Koreans 520,000.

The Korean War was a major landmark. It showed that the U.N. could take strong action and would oppose aggression. It showed that 'Cold War' could boil up into military action, but that neither the American nor the Communist leaders wanted a 'duel to the death' with nuclear weapons. It badly disrupted the American and European economies which had just returned to a 'peace' footing, but at the same time it stimulated the Japanese economy, on which the U.N. forces relied for supplies of many types. It established India as a nation which tried to be a mediator, a foretaste of the future role of the 'non-aligned' countries. Finally it coincided with new leadership in America (as Truman handed over to Eisenhower) and in Russia (when Stalin died) just a few months before the armistice. Thus it marked the end of a distinct phase in international relations.

Vietnam and the 'Domino Theory'

Since 1953, there has been only one other major conflict of arms between Communist and Western forces, in Vietnam (see Chapter 20). The reasoning behind this war was, as far as the West was concerned, similar to that which took its troops into Korea, namely that of the 'domino theory'.

If a set of dominoes are placed on edge close to each other, and one is knocked over so that it falls against the next, the whole set will collapse even though only one was originally 'attacked'. In the same way, the Americans in particular felt that if one country in South East Asia were allowed to succumb to Communism, it would lead to the downfall of the next, and the next, and so on until the entire area was 'lost'.

Thus, after the French had evacuated Indo-China, leaving Ho Chi Minh and the Communists in charge of North Vietnam, the Americans propped up South Korea, the 'first domino', with promises, money, 'advisers', soldiers and weapons just as they had supported South Korea. They were conspicuously less successful. After the Americans eventually backed out in 1973, Cambodia (Kampuchea) and Laos followed South Vietnam into Communist control. The 'domino theory' seemed to be accurate after all.

Reasons for 'Thaw and Détente'

The Cold War 'thawed' after 1953. The reasons for the thaw go deeper than mere changes in the Heads of State, although Khrushchev's eventual emergence as sole leader of Russia in 1958 definitely produced a reassessment of Communism's relationship with Capitalism. Lenin had always preached the inevitability of war between the two creeds. Khrushchev produced the view that, because of Communism's evident success in the world at large, 'a real possibility will have arisen of excluding world war ... even before Socialism achieves complete victory on earth, with capitalism still existing...'. The 1960s and 1970s saw an increase in this 'détente' (meaning 'relaxation of tension') and in direct contact between Heads of State. From 1959, when Khrushchev met Eisenhower at Camp David in the United States, summit meetings have been regular features of international diplomacy, and in 1963 a 'hot line' was installed between Moscow and Washington for immediate and direct communication between the leaders.

The emergence of the sovereign, uncommitted nations of 'the Third World' (see below) was a further stimulus to the thaw. In 1960 Harold Macmillan spoke of the 'wind of change' blowing over Africa. It made the major powers aware that aggressive, semi-colonial policies were outdated. More subtle persuasion was required if they wished to win the support of the emerging nations. Britain and the Commonwealth had already launched the Colombo Plan for development aid in 1950. In 1950, the Americans also showed their interest in the underdeveloped areas of Asia, Africa and Latin America by sending technical assistance and economic aid under their 'Point Four' programme, so called because it arose out of the fourth point of Truman's inaugural address in 1949.

In 1961, the South American aspect of this aid was emphasized by the 'Alliance for Progress' project which pledged United States' help to 22 countries in the southern continent, aimed explicitly at the maintenance of democracy and the achievement of economic and social reform. In the same year, the American 'Peace Corps' was set up, under whose auspices American volunteers, backed by government money, were sent to underdeveloped countries to give specialist practical help, often at village and community level. Although by 1966, 10,000 volunteers were serving in 52 different countries, this programme was often regarded with suspicion by 'host' countries which feared that the volunteers represented a new form of political infiltration. The numbers in the Corps were sometimes reduced at their request. The Russians too sent technical aid to Africa, paying particular attention to Egypt, Somalia and the Congo. Although the Russians had some advantage in being revolutionaries with a reputation for dramatic economic growth in a short period of time, they were also as white as the European imperialists, and therefore politically unwelcome.

Postwar European blocs

The Chinese tended to get a better reception than either of the
superpowers.

After about 1956, the deteriorating relationship between China
and Russia was a further powerful reason for East-West thaw. With
Communist solidarity thus endangered, the thaw had to benefit.
Similarly, with the West divided over the Suez crisis and the
Eastern bloc preoccupied with Hungary, 'peaceful coexistence'
seemed a sensible policy on the global scale.

The 1950s

As the 'thaw' gathered speed (though not without setbacks), the
major powers made concessions and devised new 'rules' to reduce
international tensions.

In 1958, Dag Hammarskjöld clarified the principles by which
U.N. peace-keeping forces should be guided, because their use in
Korea and in Suez had been experimental and unstructured. It was
now agreed that U.N. contingents should never be drawn from

permanent members of the Security Council or from interested parties to a dispute, that they should never be stationed in a country without that country's consent, that they should never be used to affect the political outcome of a dispute, and that they should use arms only in self-defence. Exceptions have since been made: British troops were used in Cyprus from 1964 onwards because they were already there as mediators between the warring Greek and Turkish communities; and in the Congo in 1960–61, U.N. soldiers were used in a more than defensive role, to try to lessen the likelihood of civil war. Russia and France have reserved the right not to contribute financially to peace-keeping operations, especially any that might be based on a 'Uniting for Peace' resolution. America has always carried the main financial burden, though her troops have not been used since Korea. Britain's main contribution to peace-keeping is a standing offer of supply facilities and transport to any part of the world where the U.N. may be involved. Hitherto, U.N. peace-keeping forces have been used in six places: Korea (1950–53), the Israel-Egypt border (1956–67), the Congo (1960–64), Cyprus (1964 onwards), the Israel-Syria border (1973 onwards) and Lebanon (1978 onwards).

In 1959, Khrushchev announced to the 21st Congress of the Communist Party an economic programme which diverted money 'from guns to butter'. In the same year, his visit to America and his summit meeting with Eisenhower at Camp David raised the

The U.N. at work

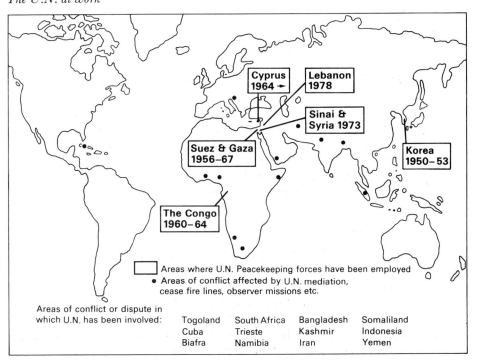

Cyprus 1964 →

Lebanon 1978

Sinai & Syria 1973

Suez & Gaza 1956–67

Korea 1950–53

The Congo 1960–64

☐ Areas where U.N. Peacekeeping forces have been employed
● Areas of conflict affected by U.N. mediation, cease fire lines, observer missions etc.

Areas of conflict or dispute in which U.N. has been involved:

Togoland	South Africa	Bangladesh	Somaliland
Cuba	Trieste	Kashmir	Indonesia
Biafra	Namibia	Iran	Yemen

brightest prospects of true peace since 1945.

The 1960s

Such hopes were dashed in 1960: an American U2 spy-plane was shot down while flying over Russia, taking photographs for intelligence purposes. The pilot was paraded in front of the world's press, and a new summit meeting, which had previously been organized to meet in Paris, collapsed in chaos. Before the year was out, Khrushchev was back in America, thumping his shoe on the desk in front of the General Assembly of the U.N., to emphasize Russian indignation.

Two more crises followed. In 1961 the construction of the Berlin Wall (see Chapter 16), and in 1962 the Cuban Missile crisis produced real fears of the world's first – and potentially final – nuclear confrontation. Cuba had already attracted attention in April 1961, when Kennedy had been persuaded to support a disastrous invasion of southern Cuba by Cuban exiles living in the U.S.A. All who took part were killed or captured in the Bay of Pigs. This humiliation for the President was soon obliterated in 1962. In October American spy-planes discovered Russian missile sites on Cuba, south of all the protective radar and anti-missile missile rings. Kennedy and his advisers toyed with the idea of 'a surgical strike' (bombing the missiles immediately) but settled for putting a naval blockade around Cuba, and stopping all ships approaching the island. Amid world-wide consternation, Kennedy and Khrushchev began to send a stream of messages to each other. An American U2 was shot down over Cuba; a Russian merchantman was stopped and inspected by U.S. naval patrols. Khrushchev claimed that Russian missiles in Cuba were no more or less threatening than American missiles in Turkey, and asked the United Nations to intervene. Eventually both sides backed down, the Russians removing all missiles from Cuba and the Americans promising not to invade Cuba nor support militant exiles.

The other outcome of the crisis was a better understanding between Khrushchev and Kennedy. They had met without success in Vienna in 1961, but now they agreed to a 'hot line' between Moscow and Washington (1963) and to a Nuclear Test-Ban Treaty (1963) forbidding above-ground tests. In 1967 tests in space were similarly ruled out, though both blocs continued underground testing. In 1968, the original nuclear 'club' (America, Britain and Russia) agreed to a Non-Proliferation Treaty which guarded against the spread of nuclear weapons among other states, by refusing to supply them to anyone, and by guaranteeing the security of other countries so that they might not be tempted to manufacture their own bombs. The positive aims of this Treaty were undermined by the refusal of France and China, nuclear powers from 1960 and 1964 respectively, to enter the agreement.

Since then, other countries have undoubtedly developed the know-ledge and the wealth to manufacture nuclear weapons; in 1979 the United States detected evidence of a nuclear explosion in the southern hemisphere for which no country claimed responsibility.

The 1970s – 'Ostpolitik', Helsinki and SALT

In 1970, Chancellor Brandt's policy of 'Ostpolitik' led to successful summits in Warsaw and Moscow in 1972, the mutual recognition of the two Germanies and their admission to the U.N. as full members. It also stimulated a 35-nation conference at Helsinki on Security and Cooperation in Europe. The subsequent 1975 Helsinki Agreement was not so much a peace treaty as an agreement for the sake of peace: its value was compared by some sceptics to that of Locarno in 1925, for it promised that frontiers would not be moved by force, and that there should be peaceful co-existence between *all* states. Much depended on interpretation: frontiers could still be moved by negotiation, and no provisions were made for countries divided internally between the ideologies. A further clause guaranteed basic human rights in all the signatory countries, a cause which President Carter of America chose to champion, challenging Russia to give better treatment to its Jewish population and those who wished to emigrate freely to the West.

In 1969, Strategic Arms Limitation Talks began in Vienna, leading to the 'SALT 1' Agreement in 1972, and later to the unratified 'SALT 2' Agreement of 1979. 'SALT 1' limited anti-ballistic missile systems; each country was allowed two systems, one around its capital and one around its offensive intercontinental missiles. The radius of each system was to be no more than 94 miles; there were to be no more than 100 static launchers, each with

Carter and Brezhnev with their advisers face the world's press at the SALT 2 meeting in Vienna, 1979. A Private Eye *cartoonist makes his own comment.*

a single warhead. Such rules about defensive weapons were
pointless without some control on offensive weapons, particularly
when each side was already capable of 'overkill', the power to
destroy the enemy many times over. For this reason, 'SALT 2' in
June 1979 produced a complicated formula concerning offensive
weapon launchers on both sides.

'The Third World'

During the 1950s, the phrase 'the Third World' came into popular
use, referring to the undeveloped or developing countries that were
not already committed to either Capitalism or Communism. The
adjective 'non-aligned' is often used to describe the same group,
but it is sometimes misleading because individual countries can
and do show a distinct leaning towards one side or the other at
various times. The essence of the Third World is that it is not
permanently attached to either super power. Each country retains
its independence of opinion and action, and in the 1960s and 1970s,
such independence proved to be powerful persuasion, especially in
the forum of the United Nations General Assembly.

It would be wrong to suggest that the Third World reacts as a

*The first major gathering of the 'non-aligned' nations in Belgrade, 1961. The
four leaders jointly inspecting the Guard of Honour are, from the left, Tito of
Yugoslavia, Nasser of Egypt, Ben Kedda of Algeria and Modibo Keita of
Mali.*

clear and identifiable bloc in all matters of world politics. In June 1979, 89 countries were accredited members of the 'non-aligned' bloc, and five others (Iran, Pakistan, Bolivia, Grenada and Surinam) applied to join at the Colombo Foreign Ministers' Conference in that month. But in the sixth summit meeting of the non-aligned countries, in Havana in September 1979, bitter divisions were revealed when Fidel Castro argued for closer links with Moscow, while President Tito of Yugoslavia, a founder of the movement, retaliated that 'We have never consented to be anyone's rubber stamp.'

The 'non-aligned' ideal can be traced further back than the first 'non-aligned' summit in Belgrade in 1961. Prime Minister Nehru of India did much to raise the diplomatic status of Third World countries by offering to mediate in Korea (1951) and in Vietnam (1954), and he won warm support from Dag Hammarskjöld. Indian troops were offered to U.N. peace-keeping forces in Palestine, the Congo and Cyprus. India's special position as the first non-white Dominion in the British Commonwealth made it acceptable to the West, whereas its strong anti-imperialism made it acceptable to the Russians.

Third World consciousness was further raised by the Bandung Conference of 1955. This had a particularly Afro-Asian flavour, being called by President Sukarno of Indonesia with support from Nehru. Of the 29 participants, six came from Africa. Chou En-lai came from China to address the meeting, but the growing tensions between China and India helped the Afro-Asian movement to lose its impact and become submerged eventually in the broader Third World.

The strongest binding force in the Third World has always been anti-colonialism. Most of the countries are former colonies of European powers, and an anti-Western feeling, often tinged with bitterness over the issues of race and colour, has been apparent, though not dominant, at all the summit meetings. But there has also been a second binding force: the need for economic cooperation within the Third World and between the Third World and the more advanced economies. The developing countries must sell their primary products (minerals, fibres, foodstuffs) and they must obtain aid in order to build up their hospitals, schools, roads and communications systems as well as their industries. In 1962 the United Nations Conference on Trade and Development (UNCTAD) was created, in order to ease economic relationships between countries in different stages of development. A permanent secretariat has negotiated numerous financing arrangements around the world, and the Lomé Convention (1975) is a prime example of a trading agreement between an advanced economic structure, the E.E.C., and a Third World group, in this case 54 countries in the Caribbean, the Pacific and Africa. 'Trade rather than Aid' sums up the philosophy of UNCTAD.

The Third World is the unpredictable feature of international relations. In purely political terms, it could be viewed as a *fifth* world, because East and West each have two centres: Russia and China, America and Europe. But in 1980 the Brandt Commission, reporting to the U.N., also made clear that it was a *second* world in economic terms. Forgetting political differences, Brandt placed all the developed countries into one category, which he called 'the North'. The undeveloped regions, 'the South' (the 'Third World'), deserved far more attention, understanding and help than 'the North' was currently affording, and he called for a reduction of political tensions in order to allow international concentration on true economic cooperation.

New States in East Asia   20

INDIA

The End of British Rule

As early as the 1930s, Britain was clearly contemplating the ending of her Empire over the Indians. What was not clear was when and how this would happen (see Chapter 6). The refusal of Gandhi's Congress Party to cooperate in the war effort brought Stafford Cripps to India in 1942 with the message that immediate help for Britain against Japan would result in the granting of a constitutional assembly to discuss the details of independence as soon as the war was over. Gandhi would not yield: 'Quit India' was the slogan of Congress, and despite Japanese successes in Burma, the British could not rouse Gandhi to the joint defence of India.

Meanwhile, the Muslims in India, whose hastily-organized Muslim League under Muhammed Jinnah had won 109 seats in the 1936 Parliamentary elections, began in 1940 to claim independence for the regions of north-west and eastern India where Muslims were in a majority. They believed that Britain was biassed in favour of Congress, and in 1945 they refused to cooperate when the viceroy Lord Wavell called a conference at Simla. In the 1946 elections, all the minor parties were swamped as Congress and the League drew apart to prepare for a major test of strength. In August 1946 Jinnah's call for a 'Direct Action Day' led to riots and 4,000 deaths in Calcutta alone. A rising tide of violence and non-cooperation left Wavell powerless, until in February 1947 the British Prime Minister, Attlee, announced the appointment of Lord Louis Mountbatten as the new viceroy. His task was to transfer the government into 'responsible Indian hands' by June 1948 at the latest.

Mountbatten immediately acknowledged that no half-measures could work now. India and Pakistan must be set up as Hindu and Muslim states respectively (the word PAKistan, 'Land of the Pure', also stands for 'the land of the Punjab, Assam and Kashmir'), and the 562 princely states of India, which would be technically independent when the Empire ended, could opt to join either or neither. The partition must be clearcut, and in some places, like the

Lord Mountbatten takes the oath as the last Viceroy of India, 1947.

Punjab and Bengal, it would lead to the division of ancient provinces because of unbridgeable religious divisions. The tensions of the coming change were bound to unleash more violent storms. Mountbatten brought forward Independence Day to 15 August 1947, leaving less than 10 weeks to arrange the partition of land, assets, public services, and population. While he urged individual princes and politicians into coherent new nations, more than seven million Muslims left their homes all over India, and migrated into the new areas which made up Pakistan, one in the north-west and one in the east. About the same number of Hindus moved in the opposite direction. Bitterness and bewilderment brought bloodshed which no authorities could check or even measure. The estimates of those killed range from 200,000 upwards; millions more were injured, made homeless or became prey to disease and starvation.

Of the princes, most joined India. In the far north, in Kashmir, where a Muslim majority lived under the rule of a Hindu Maharajah, an attempt at maintaining independence was wrecked by a popular movement against the Maharajah himself, and by interference from both India and Pakistan. By 1948 undeclared war was being waged by the regular troops of the two countries. A U.N. ceasefire was arranged in January 1949.

Gandhi

One indirect victim of the violence was Mohandas Gandhi, who in his own lifetime was given the title Mahatma, Great Soul. In January 1948 he was assassinated by a Hindu fanatic who believed

Mahatma Gandhi, who never abandoned his austere way of life and his simple Indian dress.

that Gandhi's appeals for peace and cooperation with the Muslims were threats to the Hindu domination of India.

Gandhi's influence on the modern world spread far beyond India because his work and belief had three vital elements: he opposed racialism, he opposed colonialism, and he opposed violence. Sometimes mocked for his simplicity, sometimes attacked for his stubbornness, he clung steadfastly to his ideals, enduring prison, fasts, rejection and disappointment throughout his public life. Yet from his example, many African leaders took heart as they worked for independence, and men such as Martin Luther King consciously copied his non-violent response to racial prejudice and discrimination.

Gandhi had not wanted the partition of India, but once it was set up, he was determined to make it work. His calm and courage undoubtedly saved many lives in the turmoil of late 1947.

India since 1947

From 1947 until his death in 1964, Jawaharlal Nehru was Prime Minister of India. A member of the Congress Party from its early years, he was imprisoned nine times by the British for his support of Gandhi, and from the mid-1930s he was acknowledged to be the Mahatma's deputy, even though his ideas on economic and political issues differed from Gandhi's. Nehru was a socialist, believing in government planning and the modernization of industry (rather than Gandhi's 'spinningwheel' approach, of individual self-sufficiency). He also believed in the creation of political and social equality, and for this reason he extended Gandhi's opposition to the old Indian 'caste' system. Gandhi's efforts made possible the creation of independent India: Nehru's efforts gave it its shape.

The Constitution adopted in 1950, when India became a Republic within the British Commonwealth, provided for a President, Prime Minister and Cabinet, and two houses of Parliament: the Lok Sabha representing the people of India directly, and the Rajya Sabha representing the States which make up the federal union of India. Because of its prominent role in the struggle for independence, the Congress Party dominated the first parliamentary elections, in 1952, winning 362 seats out of 489. The next largest party were the Communists, with 23 seats. Thus Nehru could make bold plans for the development of his new nation.

A series of Five Year Plans (1950, 1956, 1962, 1969) aimed to modernize India's village communities and agricultural systems and release men to work in industry (in 1961, only one per cent of the population worked in industry); an education programme was set up to stamp out illiteracy and to give basic, free, compulsory education to all children under the age of 14. Nehru turned to East and West to seek technical help and capital resources, thereby setting a pattern for the 'Third World' countries. By the early 1960s India's production had doubled, but her standard of living had scarcely improved because the population was rising alarmingly: 1951, 361 million; 1961, 439 million; 1971, 547 million. In 1956, the government began a major birth control programme, but as average life-expectancy had gone up from just over 30 years in the 1950s to just under 50 years in the 1970s, there was no chance of the population figures levelling off for many years.

Shastri and Mrs Gandhi

Nehru was succeeded as Prime Minister by Shastri, a mild disciple of Gandhi who commanded much respect among the moderates of the Congress Party, but who was criticized by the right wing. This split grew wider when Shastri died early in 1966. The inner councils of the Congress Party suggested Morarji Desai as his successor, but the Party at large chose Mrs Indira Gandhi, daughter of Nehru (and no relation of Mahatma Gandhi). From 1966 until the elections of 1977, a woman therefore ruled a country in which women had traditionally been subservient and without political status.

Mrs Gandhi chose Desai as her Deputy, but could not avert an open struggle for power inside and outside the Indian National Congress. Having won the election of 1967, she moved in a more

The young Indira Gandhi standing next to her father, Jawaharlal Nehru.

socialist direction, introducing land reforms and nationalizing the banks in a way that divided the party. Her 'Ruling' section was deserted by Desai and the 'Opposition' Congress, and although she won the 1971 election with a handsome majority (350 seats out of 520), her opponents picked away at her authority throughout the 1970s. In 1975 a court ruled that Mrs Gandhi could no longer be a member of the Lok Sabha because of 'corrupt practices' in the 1971 election (including the use of state funds to build platforms from which she spoke). The Opposition howled for her resignation from office, and in state elections she lost ground. A 'Twenty Point Programme' of economic reforms restored much of her popularity, but a complex series of legalistic arguments led to bitter political division, the declaration of a State of Emergency which allowed the arrest of Mrs Gandhi's opponents, and the postponement of the parliamentary elections due in 1976. When in 1977 the Emergency was ended, the politicians released and the elections held, the Congress Party retained only 153 seats, while the Janata Party, a combination of several opposition groups, won 295. Mrs Gandhi was defeated in her own constituency, and Janata chose the 81 year old Desai as the new Prime Minister. The political task facing him was formidable, for even at the moment of its first loss of office since 1947, the Congress Party had more unity and political tradition than any other party, and Mrs Gandhi had no intention of giving up the fight. Early in 1980, she returned to power with an impressive parliamentary majority.

PAKISTAN

Pakistan's development was always more problematic. It was a new country, and was divided into two regions a thousand miles apart. It had no common language, no vigorous industry, no political tradition. It had Jinnah, but he died in September 1948, just a few months after his old rival Gandhi. But whereas Gandhi's successor, Nehru, lasted for another 16 years, Jinnah's deputy Liaquat Ali was assassinated in 1951. No permanent constitution appeared. Under pressure from the Army, the civil service, the Muslim mullahs (religious leaders) and self-seeking parliamentarians, nine prime ministers wrestled with affairs of state until in 1958 President Mirza placed the country under martial law, administered by General Ayub Khan. Within three weeks, Khan had forced Mirza's resignation and exile.

The Drift into Civil War

Ayub Khan ruled from 1958 to 1969. After three and a half years of military rule, he established 'a blending of democracy with discipline' in a republican constitution published in 1962 and based on 80,000 local administrative units known as 'Basic Democrats'. Through these, irrigation schemes were fostered, small industrial plants were started, new houses were built, a totally new capital was built at Islamabad, and a new communication network was set up. But the growth rate was much higher in West Pakistan than in the East, where it scarcely covered the growth of population. Ayub Khan's government could not cope with the pressures of the economy combined with those of the war over Kashmir (see below), and the State of Emergency declared in 1965 triggered increasing political friction until 1969 when the Army under Yahya Khan reimposed military rule. Fresh elections, held in 1970 on the basis of universal suffrage, indicated that there were no realistic links between East and West Pakistan. In the East (where 54 per cent of the population lived) the Awami League under Sheikh Mujibur Rahman won a handsome victory with its policy of regional self-government. In the West (where the political capital stood and financial capital was more plentiful) the Pakistan People's Party under the former Foreign Secretary, Bhutto, captured 60 per cent of the seats with a policy of Islamic socialism. The results were incompatible. No true national government could be formed on this basis. Fruitless talks were followed by the imprisonment of Sheikh Mujibur, and then, in late 1971, by an attempt by West to invade East Pakistan. The resultant flood of Hindu refugees brought India into the civil war on the side of East Pakistan (now calling itself Bengal State or Bangladesh), and within two weeks, the forces of West Pakistan were compelled to surrender. Bangladesh was recognized as an independent state.

Pakistan and Bangladesh

Sheikh Mujibur was released from gaol to become Prime Minister of a devastated area. Racked by civil war, cyclones and floods, Bangladesh had roughly one doctor to every 9,000 people, one hospital bed to every 7,000, one teacher to every 50 students. The average daily food intake of the population was 20 per cent below the recommended minimum requirement for healthy living. By 1972, most major powers had recognized Bangladesh and many were sending aid, but further floods in 1974 had made government ineffective. In 1975, Mujibur was murdered in a power struggle and his flimsy parliamentary system was subjected to military rule again. In 1979, new elections marked the end of Zia Rahman's military rule, but he remained in power because his party, the Bangladesh Nationalist Party, won 207 of the 300 Parliamentary seats contested.

Meanwhile, Bhutto's government was also wrestling with the realities of power. Defeated in war, diminished in size and deeply demoralized, Pakistan needed a fresh start as much as did Bangladesh. In 1973 Bhutto produced a firm Federal Constitution, the first complete constitution since gaining independence from Britain in 1947, and set about reviving the economy with measures redistributing land and nationalizing a number of processes associated with agriculture (e.g. flour milling, cotton ginning). He introduced minimum wage levels, health insurance, and old age pensions.

When, in 1977, Bhutto called a new General Election, opposition to his party was unexpectedly vigorous and well-organized. The Pakistan National Alliance, a group of nine opposition parties, put up many candidates against the P.P.P., but Bhutto's party won all but 45 seats in the Assembly. Accusations of ballot-rigging and corruption were followed by street violence until the Army took power under General Zia-ul-Haq. In 1979, Bhutto was executed by the Army for conspiring to murder a political opponent, despite world-wide pleas for clemency. General Zia's government, though technically a civilian government after 1978, announced a return to the strict Islamic code of laws. Theft would be punished by the amputation of the right hand, rape by hanging, drinking alcohol by 80 lashes. The firmness of the government encouraged foreign observers to believe that it had the will and the ability to tackle Pakistan's main problems of poor resources and bad administration.

The Problems of Kashmir

Kashmir is like a cross-roads: to the south-west is Pakistan, to the south-east, India. China lies to the north-east, and Russia to the north-west, across a thin panhandle of Afghanistan. Thus its

geographical position gives it political and strategic importance, as
does the fact that the Indus River and its tributaries flow down
from Kashmir to give Pakistan its main supply of water. At the
time of partition in 1947, three-quarters of the four million
inhabitants of Kashmir were Muslim; 800,000 were Hindu, as was
the Maharajah, who wanted to remain independent of both India
and Pakistan. When Pathan tribesmen from the north-west attacked him in 1947, the Maharajah appealed for Indian help and
offered to accede to India. Pakistan offered immediate military aid
to the Kashmiri Muslims. In January 1949, the U.N. Security
Council called for a ceasefire, and a plebiscite to decide the future
of the area. The plebiscite was never held. Attempts at a negotiated
settlement failed in 1949, 1950, 1951, 1953, 1955 and 1957, by
which time India had virtually absorbed all but the north-west of
Kashmir.

In 1962, a border agreement between China and Pakistan
caused incidents between Chinese and Indian troops but
war between Pakistan and India was averted until 1965, when
a dispute about the desolate Rann of Kutch raised Pakistani
ambitions to gain Kashmir. Three weeks of full-scale war was
brought to an end by the U.N. In 1966 the Indian leader Shastri

India, Pakistan and Kashmir

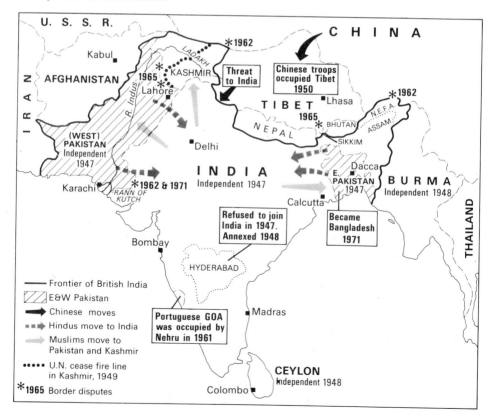

met Ayub Khan at Tashkent, where the Russian premier Kosygin persuaded them to sign a peace agreement on the basis of the existing situation. The uncertainty therefore continued, until in 1971, Indian troops took advantage of the civil war in Pakistan to occupy the Rann of Kutch and part of Azad Kashmir. Talks between Mrs Gandhi and Bhutto in 1972 drew new demarcation lines, leaving Kashmir divided. In 1978, Pakistan and China completed a road across the Karakoram Mountains, linking the two countries, despite loud Indian protests.

INDO-CHINA

Indo-China was the most prized area of the French Empire from 1884 until 1940. Divided into the five territories of Cochin-China, Tonkin, Annam (these three making up modern Vietnam), Cambodia and Laos, under a French Governor-General, the colony was ruled almost entirely for the benefit of the French economy and to the advantage of French settlers and a small class of native collaborators. The quantity of rice-producing land quadrupled between 1880 and 1930, but the peasants were less well-off by the end than they had originally been. In 1940, 80 per cent of the Vietnamese population was illiterate; there was one university for a population of 20,000,000 and two doctors for every 100,000 people. Significantly, there were few Vietnamese involved in trade and industry, apart from the sale of their own meagre produce, and therefore capitalism became associated with foreigners and exploitation.

Resistance to the French started in the 1880s, but ruthless repression smothered all attempts to set up a successful opposition movement until 1930, when Ho Chi Minh formed the Indo-China Communist Party and provoked widespread uprisings. In 1940 the French Governor-General Decoux, representing the Vichy government, agreed to allow the stationing of 30,000 Japanese troops in Vietnam. Ho Chi Minh withdrew to China, and with help from the Americans, he organized the 'Viet Minh' to harass the Japanese and the Vichy French administrators. Before the war ended, the Japanese formally ousted the French and allowed the puppet Emperor of Annam, Bao Dai, to declare the independence of Vietnam, but the Potsdam Conference in 1945 confirmed France's right to reoccupy the area, thus creating a three-way tension between the French, the Communists under Ho Chi Minh and the anti-Communist nationalists led by Bao Dai. In 1946 the French returned in force and seemed prepared to acknowledge a Viet Minh government based on Hanoi. But before the year was out, war had been declared and the Viet Minh had retreated into the mountains, where they easily survived with the aid of the majority of the peasantry.

The war of liberation lasted until 1954. In 1950, the French

*Ho Chi Minh (1890–1969),
Vietnamese nationalist leader, and
one of the most influential
Communists of the century.*

announced that they were prepared to concede the self-government of Laos, Cambodia and Vietnam within the French Union, with Bao Dai as ruler of Vietnam, but this was rejected as inadequate by the Communists and other nationalists. Despite the presence of 250,000 French troops in Vietnam, the Viet Minh became increasingly influential in Tonkin, Laos and the Mekong Delta, and when, under General Giap, they surrounded the major French garrison at Dien Bien Phu and forced its submission (March-May 1954), the French agreed to fresh negotiations.

Vietnam Divided

The Geneva Conference of 1954, attended by China, Russia, Britain and America as well as by the countries directly involved, agreed to a temporary division of the country along the 17th parallel of latitude; all French and 'State of Vietnam' troops were to withdraw to the south, while all Viet Minh ('Democratic Republic of Vietnam') forces were to retire to the north. Refugees were to be allowed to move to either side of the 17th parallel; France was to withdraw entirely; Laos and Cambodia were to become independent outside the French Union.

The North Vietnamese expected the temporary division of the country to be ended by elections, which they were confident of winning in July 1956. The South Vietnamese, under Bao Dai and then (1955–63) Ngo Dinh Diem, refused to administer such elections. They were conscious of the million refugees who had fled from the North, and of the strict Communism of the Ho Chi Minh government which penalized anyone who had cooperated with the French colonists. It was in the self-interest of the Diem regime not to hold the promised elections.

It was also in the interests of American foreign policy, which was based on the 'domino theory' (see Chapter 19). From 1955 onwards, the Diem government received American support in the form of money, arms and 700 military advisers (which were permitted by the Geneva Agreement). But Diem's regime was corrupt; a paltry land-reform scheme did nothing for the peasantry, and tyrannical persecution of Buddhists roused great opposition. By 1960, a National Liberation Front (N.L.F.) had appeared in South Vietnam, consisting of Communists and non-Communists who opposed Diem and who wanted to see the withdrawal of all foreign troops and the gradual reunification of Vietnam. As the N.L.F. came increasingly under the Viet Cong ('Vietnamese Communists'), so the Americans increased their support for Diem. In 1962 the number of 'advisers' had grown to 10,000; in 1963 (when Diem was murdered and political chaos ensued), the total was 17,000. At the same time, the Viet Cong had a fighting strength of 30,000.

War in Vietnam

In 1965, the Russian premier, Kosygin, visited Hanoi, the North

American artillery in Vietnam.

Vietnamese capital, and in so doing stimulated a new surge of Communist attacks on the South. As if in response, President Johnson of the United States authorized the systematic bombing of Northern supply routes and depots, and committed American ground troops to the fighting in South Vietnam. This was now an open battle between two ideologies: the Americans, representing the Western capitalist version of democracy, with huge resources and highly sophisticated technology (including napalm, 'gunships' in the form of heavily-armed helicopters, and defoliants for stripping the forests of all living plants) were tackling the Communism of village cells, guerrilla bands and unforgiving anti-colonialism. It was a battle of Goliath against David, and although the massive fire-power and economic backing of the Americans enabled them to seize the initiative in 1966–68, the 'Tet offensive' of February 1968 saw the Viet Cong capture 75 per cent of the towns in South Vietnam and hold them for some months, despite very heavy losses. It was enough to persuade the Americans that they must ultimately go to the conference table and not look for outright military victory.

In May 1968, after Johnson had ordered the end of the bombing of North Vietnam above the 20th parallel, the Communists agreed to come to peace talks in Paris, but no progress was made. In November, shortly before the Presidential Elections in which he was not a candidate, Johnson made one last attempt to break the deadlock by ending *all* bombing of the North. By this time there were more than half a million American combat troops in South Vietnam, fighting alongside three-quarters of a million South Vietnamese and 50,000 Allied forces from South Korea, Australia, New Zealand, Thailand and the Philippines. Estimates put the Viet Cong numbers at about 230,000.

'Vietnamization'

The election of President Nixon in 1968 (he took power in January 1969) gave America an opportunity for a new initiative, which home opinion was strongly demanding in massive political demonstrations. Nixon began to withdraw American troops (115,000 by April 1970) but at the same time introduced a policy of 'Vietnamization', namely the defence and administration of South Vietnam by South Vietnamese. In order to protect the transition, Nixon resumed the bombing of Communist supply routes, and in April 1970 actually extended the war into Cambodia to seek out guerrilla bases. In 1971, the bombing was extended to the supply routes that ran through Laos, but the intensive bombardment that would have obliterated Western roads and railways could not wipe out the 'Ho Chi Minh Trail', routes through the forests and mountains of Vietnam, Laos and Cambodia maintained by women with shovels and rush baskets for earth-moving, and traversed by carriers on

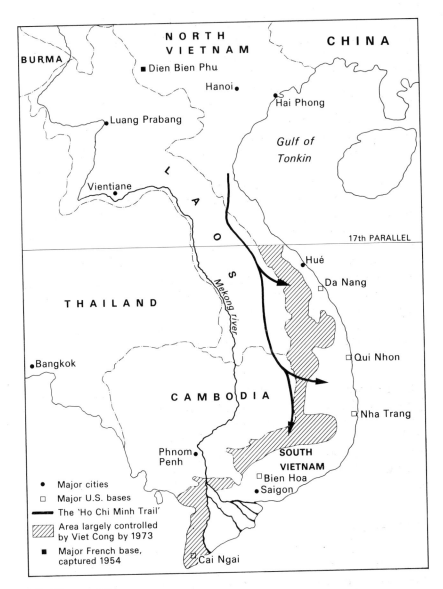

The Vietnam War

foot or on bicycles. By 1972 the bombing was heavier than ever, and Nixon gave orders to mine the approaches to North Vietnamese ports, to indicate his firm intention to complete the Vietnamization process.

In 1972, Nixon visited Moscow, and a flurry of diplomatic activity by his Secretary of State, Henry Kissinger, led to renewed talks in Paris between the Americans, the North Vietnamese, the South Vietnamese and the N.L.F. A ceasefire was arranged for the end of January 1973, and the Americans began the withdrawal of their remaining 25,000 ground forces and their Air Force. Within

60 days they had gone, leaving President Thieu in charge of the government in Saigon. The war had cost nearly 50,000 American lives on top of the million Communist soldiers and the 600,000 South Vietnamese soldiers and civilians killed.

Vietnam Since 1973

The government of President Thieu lasted until 1975. It had come to power with American support in 1967, and 'Vietnamization' meant that it had an army of a million men in 1974. Desertions however ran at the rate of 20,000 a month, and morale was correspondingly low. Civilians were no happier with an inflation rate of nearly 75 per cent per annum and unemployment at 20 per cent, and when the U.S. Congress refused further financial aid for 1975, Thieu's regime collapsed with very little extra leverage from the North. In April 1975 Viet Cong and North Vietnamese moved into Saigon, soon renamed Ho Chi Minh City, and in 1976 North and South Vietnam were formally reunited. In 1977, Vietnam joined the U.N., and in 1978, Comecon. Though there were no massive reprisals against the South, as some observers had expected, the Communist regime made no effort to stop the boatloads of refugees who put to sea in increasing numbers after 1976. In July 1979 it was estimated that 400,000 refugees, including 250,000 Vietnamese 'boat-people', had fled from Vietnam and Laos and were seeking resettlement. Tens of thousands more had died unseen as they attempted their escape.

Cambodia and Laos

As Vietnam recovered from the effects of the war, its neighbours fell into increasing disarray. Cambodia was governed by Prince Sihanouk after the French withdrawal; his policy of neutrality kept the country safe and stable until 1965, when, fearing American interference in his country, he began to align himself with the National Liberation Front and the North Vietnamese. Communist use of Cambodian territory in the war in Vietnam antagonized the right wing, and in 1970 Sihanouk was overthrown (while he was out of the country) by General Lon Nol. Sihanouk went to Peking, where he remained the nominal head of a government in exile. Lon Nol spent the next five years trying to govern Cambodia with American backing, but the Americans also caused great antagonism by their policy of attacking guerrilla bases (1970 onwards) and bombing the Ho Chi Minh Trail. In 1975 the capital, Phnom Penh, fell to the Communist 'Khmer Rouge' forces, and although Sihanouk returned from Peking to claim the leadership, he was brushed aside by more fanatical Communists who in 1976 set up the State of Democratic Kampuchea, under their leader Pol Pot. The Pol Pot regime attempted the most radical Communism ever seen. The towns of Kampuchea were deserted as all civilians were sent to work in the fields. The money economy was destroyed; barter returned. Secondary schools and universities were closed so that everyone should go into productive work. Pay, if it existed, was in surplus rice. The result was disastrous. In 1970, the Cambodian population numbered 7 million; in 1978, it was estimated to be 4 million, with every likelihood of dropping to just over 2 million in the next 12 months as famine and disease took an increasing toll, and war and reprisals rumbled on. In January 1979, the Khmer Rouge, though diplomatically supported by China, were over-thrown by Vietnamese forces with moral support from Russia. Whoever might win this struggle between Russian and Chinese Communism, Cambodia would certainly lose.

Conclusion

The leaders of the post-colonial states in Eastern Asia have had to perform a delicate operation. When the structure of the old colonialism was destroyed, new influences rushed into the vacuum. Racial and religious differences, always there but long suppressed by the imperialists, now became apparent, as in India and Pakistan. Class conflict, as in Indo-China, became more bitter. Political idealism was quickly seen to be hamstrung by political inexperience. Only by a combination of coercion and cajolery has it been possible to create relatively stable political and economic units, whether Communist or Capitalist. As in India, Pakistan and Vietnam, it has been the qualities of individual leaders which have forged the new nations. The same has been true in Indonesia, Malaysia and Singapore.

In Indonesia, formerly the Dutch East Indies, President Sukarno (1945–67) and President Suharto (1967–) welded together an area which includes 14,000 islands into an influential single unit; in Malaysia the Prime Minister Tunku Abdul Rahman (1957–70) brought together Malaya, Sabah and Sarawak, and for a brief period Singapore, until Lee Kuan Yew decided in 1964 to secede from the Federation. These three nations came together in 1967 with the Philippines and Thailand to form ASEAN, the Association of South East Asian Nations, which was designed to increase economic and political stability in the area, without trying to unite too closely races and nations which were enjoying their separate development. Their success has been considerable.

21 Nationalism in Africa

Africa was the last continent to be explored and exploited by the Europeans, yet by 1914, only Liberia and Abyssinia were not under some form of European control. In 1919, only Liberia and the Union of South Africa were considered eligible to join the League of Nations. After World War Two, Egypt and Abyssinia/Ethiopia joined these two as the four African founders of the United Nations Organization; the rest of the continent was still buried deep under

Africa in 1914

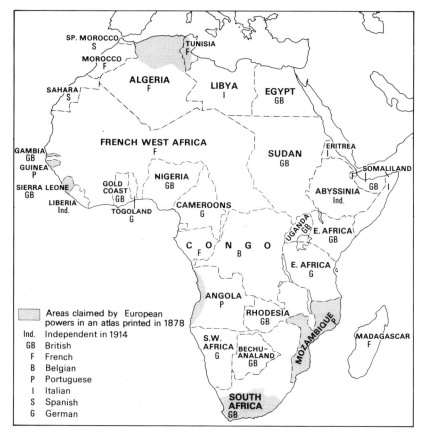

colonial rule. Nonetheless, between 1955 and 1968, thirty seven sovereign African nations joined the U.N. The European control of Africa collapsed more quickly than the 'grab for Africa' had occurred in the late nineteenth century (see Chapter 1).

One reason for the change was the mauling received by the colonial powers in the Second World War. Another was the fact that some colonies, especially those of occupied France, had virtually established independence during the war, and a third was that the original concept of colonialism, as understood by Britain and France, aimed at eventual independence, as made clear by the Statute of Westminster (1931) and as implied by the setting up of the 'French Union' in 1946. But the major cause of the collapse of European control in Africa was African nationalism.

African Nationalism

In Europe and in the European-populated countries of South America, 'nationalism' was a nineteenth-century ideal (see Chapter 1). In Asia, it found expression in the early twentieth century

Africa in 1980

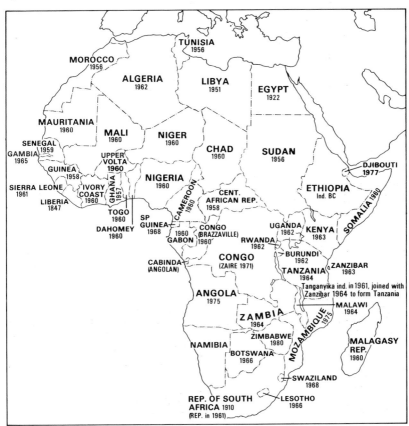

(Atatürk in Turkey, Sun Yat-sen in China, Gandhi in India) while in Africa it exploded in the 30 years after the Second World War.

Its causes were similar wherever it was found. Firstly, the presence of an alien power inevitably made the subject-peoples more aware of their own loyalties and common characteristics. Colonial powers automatically sowed the seeds of opposition to their own rule, by creating 'cultural consciousness'.

At the same time, the colonists introduced the ideas of the modern state: education, centralized law and order, a cash-based economy, more advanced communications. These features obliterated the restrictive, primitive social system that existed before the white men came, and opened up visions of a more advanced, wealthier, easier life in the future, especially if the white men at the top of the system could be done away with.

Increased awareness of political and economic opportunities was a third feature of the nationalist movement. Not only were the colonial powers becoming increasingly dependent on the undeveloped countries for raw materials like chrome, copper, natural gas, oil, gold, platinum and radium; they were also vulnerable because they were part of a world divided between two ideologies, and each ideology (Capitalist and Communist) wanted the support of the Third World.

Most nationalist movements started amongst small groups in exile or often in the prisons of the colonial powers, but in order to pressurize the colonial powers to grant independence, these 'élite' nationalists had to mobilize the forces of 'the people'. Propaganda and violence often resulted, later increasing the problems faced by the newly independent state. Once the common enemy had been expelled, the major emotional force that bound the people together evaporated, and tribalism reasserted itself. The old boundaries that had been artificially created by the colonists to suit their purposes were often unrealistic after they had gone, and warring tribes marked their departure as in Nigeria and the Belgian Congo, until new black dictatorships restored some form of order.

GHANA

Kwame Nkrumah

Originally known as the 'Gold Coast', Ghana became a British Crown Colony in 1874. Its unusually advanced economy, based on gold and cocoa, and its political stability encouraged hopes of early independence after the Second World War. In 1949, the British government approved the Coussey Constitution, which blended British experience with African optimism.

Opposition followed at once from Kwame Nkrumah and his

Nkrumah greets Queen Elizabeth II in Ghana in 1961.

Convention People's Party. Believing fiercely in African national-ism and anti-imperialism, he began a policy of non-cooperation and non-violence based on Gandhi's techniques. For this he was sent to prison, but when the first elections held under the Coussey Constitution gave his C.P.P. 34 out of the 38 Parliamentary seats, he was released to become Prime Minister in 1952. In 1957, the Gold Coast was granted independence under the ancient name of Ghana, becoming Britain's first black African partner in the Commonwealth.

Nkrumah was always authoritarian: his popularity was based on his achievements rather than his methods. Ghana's economy expanded rapidly, but part of the cost was the imprisonment without trial of 1,000 political opponents in 1959, and the creation of a Republic in 1960 in which Nkrumah, as President, could rule by decree. He diversified the economy by means of the Volta River Project (1961) which provided irrigation for agriculture and electricity for industry, thereby breaking Ghana's dependence on the annual cocoa crop.

Nkrumah was a founder of the Organization of African Unity

(O.A.U.), a believer in Pan-Africanism, and a leading international spokesman for the Third World. He was on a visit to Vietnam
and China when in 1966 the Army seized power in Ghana. For six
years he waited in neighbouring Guinea for a chance to reclaim his
power. It never came; he died in 1972.

Ghana since 1966

Since 1966, no government has held Ghana stable for long. Though
the Army under Ankrah was in power until 1969, they could do
little when government reserves of £4,000,000 were expected to
cover debts of £279,000,000. Dr Kofi Busia led a civilian ministry
from 1969 until 1972, but his policies of devaluation (1971),
restricting trade, increasing pleas for overseas aid, and even
banning trade unions still did little for a country where the system
of bribery was deeply rooted, and where well-placed individuals
made vast fortunes.

From 1972 until he in turn fell to a new coup in 1978, Colonel
Acheampong and his National Redemption Council tried to steer
the country, but the basic economic structure remained unbalanced, and the politicians insecure.

NIGERIA

Nigeria's problems were more complex than those of Ghana
because of its size and its constant tribal rivalry. Created by the
British in 1914, it was three times bigger than all Britain's other
West African colonies put together, and included a population
bigger than Britain's, divided into three major regions, at least 150
different tribes and more than 100 different languages.

The Northern section of Nigeria contained the majority of the
population, but they were the least united. Muslim chiefs of the
Fulani tribes had established a conservative, slow-moving rule over
most other tribes, but the area lacked capital, access to modern
trade routes, and desire to change. The southern section split into
two. In the West the Yoruba dominated; in the East the Ibo tribe
was centred, but the Ibo tribal structure was more fluid than most,
and many Ibos had left their agricultural origins to become
businessmen, administrators, technicians and teachers in other
parts of Nigeria.

In 1960 Britain granted independence to Nigeria, with a
Federal Constitution based on the three regions. Abubakr Tafewa
Balewa of the North became Prime Minister. From 1963, Nigerian
politics became a stormy scene of tribal jealousy, regional distrust,
religious squabbles and political immaturity, until in 1966, a group
of 160 officers rebelled against the government, murdering Balewa
and many leading politicians. Only the rapid assumption of power

by Major-General Ironsi, an Ibo but not a conspirator, prevented the complete break-up of the established order.

Ironsi lasted for six months. His proposal of a unitary constitution for Nigeria instead of a federal one was treated as an Ibo, southern trick to gain dominion over the north. He was murdered, and throughout Nigeria Ibos were faced with hostility and, in many places, massacre. They began to abandon their property and positions elsewhere in Nigeria, and fled back to the East. In May 1967, Colonel Ojukwu, military governor of the East since the original coup, declared it to be the independent state of Biafra.

The Biafran War, 1967–70

Colonel Gowon, who succeeded Ironsi in Nigeria, was a convinced federalist. The loss of Biafra was disastrous, for not only were there oilfields in the Eastern region which the Nigerian economy needed, but also the Ibos themselves were vital to Nigerian development. Their secession would almost certainly lead to the complete break-up of the Nigerian Federation, which would become a backward wasteland.

Gowon therefore called for a 'short surgical police action' to bring Biafra back. He miscalculated. Though the Organization of African Unity tried three times to mediate in the dispute, Biafra received support from France, the Ivory Coast, Gabon, and numerous charity organizations which were defending the principle of self-determination, and so was able to fight on, giving ground slowly. Nigeria received help from Britain, Russia, Egypt and most African states. The U.N. was powerless; it treated the problem as an internal one, therefore beyond its jurisdiction. U Thant visited Lagos when the war was over.

The war ended, suddenly, in January 1970 when Ojukwu's provisional capital Owerri fell to the federal troops. Ojukwu fled and his successor Effiong capitulated. The massacre that the Ibos feared would follow their defeat did not materialize. Gowon insisted on reconciliation, and by dividing the country into 12 states (later 19) in one federation, he reduced the tribal tensions which had contributed to the war. Nevertheless, an estimated two million Biafrans had died in the war, more from starvation than direct enemy action.

Nigeria since 1970

Thanks to oil (90 per cent of its exports), coal, tin and its own agricultural self-sufficiency, Nigeria's economy soared in the 1970s, though prices rose rapidly. For most of the 1970s half the annual budget supported the largest Army in Black Africa, just under 250,000 men.

Gowon's statesmanship after the Biafran War brought him support until 1975, but the distribution of wealth in Nigeria remained very uneven, and there was much corruption among the rich. Although Gowon promised that civilian rule would not be restored before 1976, he was deposed by Army officers who had lost confidence in him. Their leader, General Mohammed, was murdered in 1976, but General Obasanjo carried on his policies, restoring constitutional government in 1978. In August 1979, Alhaji Shagari was elected President of the new government.

Obasanjo's period in power saw not only the restoration of civilian government at federal and local level, but also a reduction in the rate of inflation, a lessening of tribalism in politics, and the development of a confident foreign policy based on Pan-Africanism and support for black rule in Southern Africa.

THE CONGO

The Congo faced the same problems as Nigeria. A huge area (nearly a million square miles) with 150 tribes, it had been allocated in 1876 to the 'International African Association' (in effect King Leopold II of the Belgians). In 1908, the Congo became an official Belgian colony rather than a private estate of the King, but the new officials had no new ideals. In 1955, a Belgian professor, van Bilsen, estimated that any transition to independence would take at least 30 years.

The independence of Ghana (1957), de Gaulle's offer to free the French Congo (1958) and the Pan-African Conference at Accra (1958) destroyed such a timetable. Congolese politics suddenly developed on tribal lines, and the Belgians hastily announced that independence would be granted by 1963. As turmoil grew, the date was changed to 1960. In that year Patrice Lumumba, leader of the Mouvement National Congolais, became Prime Minister and Joseph Kasavubu was elected President, while the Belgians withdrew rapidly.

Civil War in the Congo

Within weeks, the Force Publique (part police force, part Army) had mutinied and in the south, Moise Tshombe, leader of copper-rich Katanga, had declared independence and asked for Belgian military aid to protect his interests and their nationals. Lumumba and Kasavubu appealed for help from the U.N. A peace-keeping force was sent almost immediately because both Russia and America feared an explosion of nationalism all over Africa, but U.N. Secretary-General Hammarskjöld refused to allow his troops to be used to invade Katanga. In August 1960, when South Kasai also threatened to secede, Lumumba prepared his own invasion of Katanga, for which Kasavubu dismissed him in September. Amidst the chaos, the Congolese Army under Joseph Mobutu

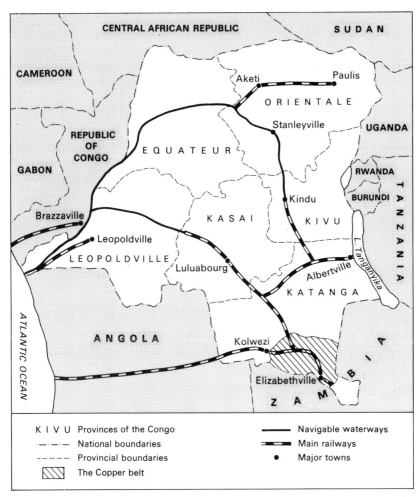

The Congo–Zaire

seized the capital, Leopoldville. In January 1961, Lumumba was murdered by his opponents.

In early 1961 there were therefore three competing Congolese centres: Leopoldville (under Kasavubu and Mobutu); Stanleyville (under Lumumba's deputy Gizenga); and Elizabethville in Katanga (under Tshombe). In August, the first two reunited. Tshombe now had to be coaxed or coerced into reconciliation. In September Hammarskjöld was killed in an air crash while travelling to negotiate with Tshombe, but his successor, U Thant, was able to achieve reunification of the Congo by diplomacy, in December 1962. Tshombe went into voluntary exile in Europe; U.N. troops finally evacuated the Congo in June 1964.

But the problems of the Congo were not solved. The Belgians, particularly the mining group, 'Union Minière', were still influential in Katanga, attracting hostility from black nationalists inside and outside the Congo. The economy was in tatters, as unemployment and prices rose simultaneously, and the reputation of the government fell accordingly. Guerilla bands appeared, whose most common target was the group of officers, civil servants and politicians who managed to thrive on other people's distress. Fragmentation was imminent, and the moderate policies of Prime Minister Adoula could not prevent it. As the U.N. forces finally pulled out, President Kasavubu invited Tshombe back from Europe to form a new administration over the whole Congo. This bold move met with military success when white mercenaries working for Tshombe dropped by parachute to recapture Stanley-ville from guerillas in November 1964, but the political rivalry between Kasavubu and Tshombe re-emerged and caused failure. In April 1965 Tshombe was sacked again, but in November the Army under General Mobutu, tired of the politicians' wranglings, ended all the uncertainty by taking total power themselves.

Mobutu and Zaire

Mobutu's government was tough, pragmatic and aggressively, proudly black. He cleared the country of white mercenaries (beating off an attempt to restore Tshombe in 1967), and he nationalized the Union Minière in 1967 and all other foreign-owned mining and agricultural holdings in 1973. In 1975 he nationalized the building trade and the distribution services. In 1971 he had ordered the Africanization of all place-names (the Congo becoming 'Zaire') and in 1972 he forbade the use of European Christian names, changing his own name from Joseph Désiré Mobutu to Mobutu Sese Seko. Having shown his power, he showed his statesmanship by negotiating technical and financial agreements with the Belgians and other Western countries, yet kept a neat diplomatic balance by establishing full diplomatic relations with China in 1972.

EAST AFRICA

East African development differed from that of West Africa, because a more temperate climate and a smaller number of black Africans in the region encouraged the belief that it could be 'White Man's Country' rather than an African tribal area with a few white missionaries and traders. It was a vain hope, further complicated by the presence of numerous Asians, who in the middle of the twentieth century became indispensable to the trade of the area. In each of the countries, the whites who settled were gradually forced to give way to 'Africanization' and political control by the blacks. The principle of African self-government was accepted in the 1950s, and independence was granted to Tanganyika in 1961, Uganda in 1962 and Kenya and Zanzibar in 1963. In 1964, Tanganyika and Zanzibar united to form Tanzania. Each of these countries found the traditions of government on the Westminster model impossible to maintain, and moved towards one-party rule.

Tanganyika and Tanzania

Tanganyika, then Tanzania, came under the leadership of Julius Nyerere, a strong, dedicated socialist leader who was elected President in 1962 by 97 per cent of the voters. Untroubled by tribalism, the area became stable and truly independent. Its economy was based on 'ujamaa' villages, where production was based on cooperative principles; its foreign policy was fearlessly 'non-aligned', and Nyerere became a highly respected statesman.

Uganda

Uganda, by contrast, was much affected by tribalism. Milton Obote established a one-party state but was forced to rely on the constant support of the Army, which in 1971 deserted him while he was at a Commonwealth Conference in Singapore. Into his place came Idi Amin, former sergeant of the King's African Rifles, but soon self-appointed general and holder of the self-awarded Victoria Cross. This unbalanced and irresponsible man ruled Uganda until he was overthrown by Tanzanian-backed rebels in 1979. His cruelty and unpredictability destroyed the unity and the economy of Uganda. In 1972 he expelled all Asians who did not hold Ugandan citizenship, despite the harmful impact on the economy. 20,000 refugees entered Britain in the next three months; 30,000 fled elsewhere. Thereafter he ruled by terror: 200,000 Ugandans were killed by his troops in the next seven years, many of them at the 'State Research Bureau' in Kampala. Evidence exists that he, and/or his bodyguard, ate the flesh of some of the victims. No-one was safe. The Bishop of Uganda was shot through the head, and his body planted in a faked car-crash. In 1976 his regime was responsible for the death of Mrs Dora Bloch, an elderly woman who became a hostage when a French aircraft was hijacked to Entebbe by members of the Popular Front for the Liberation of Palestine, supported by Amin. Despite universal condemnation, no European power had dared to move against Amin for fear of seeming racialist, and no black leader had dared to invade until there seemed a strong chance of victory.

Kenya

The situation in Kenya was different again, for in the late 1940s there grew up the most violent opposition to white rule in the form of the Mau Mau. This anti-white, anti-Christian, barbarous secret society was based among the Kikuyu tribe, and turned its savagery against other Kikuyus (over 8,000 killed) as well as against

A Mau Mau general gives himself up to Prime Minister Kenyatta who is wearing the hat, following the independence of Kenya in 1963.

Europeans (68 killed). The governor of Kenya, Sir Evelyn Baring, had to ask for British troops in 1952 to help to keep the peace, and the black leader, Jomo Kenyatta, was imprisoned for organizing the Mau Mau in 1954.

Nevertheless, when Kenya was granted independence in 1963, Kenyatta came rapidly to the forefront of the government, first as Prime Minister and then as President, until his death in 1978. His slogan of 'Harambee' ('Self-help') indicated that he was less socialist than Nyerere of Tanzania, but he was equally firm and fair in dealing with whites, blacks and Asians. Civil war threatened in the late 1960s when he sacked Oginga Odinga of the Luo tribe and when Tom Mboya, another Luo tipped to be Kenyatta's successor, was assassinated. But peace was maintained, and when Kenyatta died he was succeeded by Arap Moi of the Tugen tribe, with a largely Kikuyu Cabinet.

Zambia and Malawi

Zambia (formerly Northern Rhodesia) and Malawi (formerly Nyasaland) were joined in 1953 with Southern Rhodesia to form the 'Central African Federation': Sir Roy Welensky became Prime Minister in 1956, but neither he nor Garfield Todd of Southern Rhodesia could make the Federation politically stable. In 1964 Malawi became independent, under Dr Hastings Banda, who established a strict one-party state. Zambia also gained independence in 1964 under Kenneth Kaunda, who immediately had to wrestle with the problems posed by the existence of 73 different tribes within his country. He too turned to the solution of the one-party state, but this was no help in coping with Zambia's geographical problems. Rich in copper, Zambia was nevertheless the victim of its landlocked position, especially when economic sanctions were imposed on (Southern) Rhodesia in 1966, thus blocking Zambia's trade outlets.

Zimbabwe-Rhodesia

When Malawi and Zambia were granted independence in 1964, Southern Rhodesia remained a British colony, because political control there had passed from Garfield Todd and his successor Sir Edgar Whitehead into the hands of the more right-wing Rhodesian Front, representing the continuation of white domination. In 1964, Ian Smith was elected Prime Minister of Rhodesia (the adjective 'Southern' had been dropped when 'Northern Rhodesia' became Zambia), but Britain would not grant independence to a country where less than 250,000 whites intended to retain full power over the remaining 96 per cent of the population.

In 1965, Smith made a unilateral declaration of independence (U.D.I.), and Britain faced four choices: the use of force, the use of economic pressures, diplomatic negotiation, or the acceptance of an unpalatable fact. The first was unrealistic and might have sparked off a forest fire of racial war; the last was inconsistent with the whole principle of a multi-racial Commonwealth. Diplomacy was the only possible solution, against a background of increasing economic sanctions. Prime Minister Wilson met Smith aboard H.M.S. *Tiger* in 1966 and again on H.M.S. *Fearless* in 1969, without success. In 1971 the Conservative Foreign Secretary Douglas-

Bishop Muzorewa, Rhodesia's first black Prime Minister (1978–79), with Ian Smith, who declared the country's unilateral independence in 1965.

Home was equally unsuccessful when he visited Rhodesia, because each British party insisted on 'no independence before majority African rule' (NIBMAR). In 1965, Britain imposed immediate oil sanctions on the rebellious colony, and in 1966 and 1968 the United Nations Security Council endorsed the British action, widening the list of goods which were not to be sold to the Rhodesians and authorizing the presence of armed vessels off the coast of Mozambique to prevent 'sanction-busting'.

White Rhodesian inflexibility crumbled during the 1970s. In 1974 Smith released the black leaders Joshua Nkomo and Ndabaningi Sithole from prison, in order to prepare the way for constitutional talks held at the Victoria Falls in 1975 and in Geneva in 1976. Late in 1977, Smith announced that he accepted the principle of universal suffrage, and in 1978 Rhodesia's first elected racially-mixed government was sworn in under the moderate Bishop Muzorewa. But the elections were not accepted as being valid by most of the British Commonwealth or by the leaders of the 'Patriotic Front', Nkomo and Mugabe, who continued to lead a bitter guerilla campaign against the whites and those blacks who accepted Muzorewa's government. In September 1979, a new constitutional conference met in London to arrange a plan for fresh elections, preceded by a carefully controlled ceasefire. Agreement was reached early in 1980, and the plan was put into immediate effect under the supervision of Lord Soames as Governor of the colony. As soon as his authority was recognized by the white

Robert Mugabe (left) and Joshua Nkomo, leaders of the Rhodesia Patriotic Front forces, pictured at the Lancaster House Conference, 1979.

Rhodesians, the colony was accepted back into the Common-wealth, and all sanctions were lifted.

Robert Mugabe's wing of the Patriotic Front won 57 of the 100 seats in the Rhodesian parliament (the whites retained 20 by agreement, Nkomo won 20, and Bishop Muzorewa won three), but despite his Marxist guerilla background, Mugabe promised a government of reconciliation.

SOUTH AFRICA

From Colony to Dominion

The Dutch were the first white settlers in Southern Africa, establishing a colony on the Cape of Good Hope which was a vital staging post on the route from Holland to the Dutch East Indies. The English links with India similarly encouraged British coloniza-tion in the nineteenth century, but differences in religion, economic attitudes and colonial policies divided the British from the Dutch (Boers). In 1835, the Boers left the Cape Colony and trekked north-east to found the Transvaal and later the Orange Free State, leaving Britain in control of Natal and Cape Colony. The discovery of diamonds near Kimberley and gold near Johannesburg inten-sified the rivalry between the two nations. The first Boer War (1880–81) resolved nothing, but the second Boer War (1899–1902) ended in British victory and the annexation of the two Boer colonies. The Treaty of Vereeniging, 1902, aimed immediately at creating one 'South African' nation. In 1910, the Union of South Africa was formed out of the four original colonies, with one central government and parliament, in which Boers and British mingled in a ratio of about two to one, the Boers therefore having the greater influence and providing (to this day) all the Prime Ministers and most of the policies. The whites made up less than 20 per cent of the population. Black Africans comprised about 70 per cent, and the remainder were Asians (Chinese and Indians) and other 'coloured' people, a phrase denoting racially mixed backgrounds.

The first Prime Ministers, Botha (1910–19) and Smuts (1919–24) were moderate men; from 1924 to 1939, Hertzog was in power with the Nationalist Party, but he shared many of Smuts' policies, and a splinter group, the Afrikaaner (Boer) Nationalists under Dr Malan, broke away. They won power in 1948. Their racial policies have isolated them from harmonious contact with any other nation.

Apartheid

Apartheid is the Afrikaans word for 'apartness'. In 1948, it became the official word to describe the racial policies of the South African government, which are based on the separate development of the black and white races, and, on the domination of the black majority by the white minority. The British settlers of the nineteenth century believed in a measure of white supremacy; the Boer prejudice was stronger, more rigid and more obstinate. It was backed up by the preachings of the Dutch Reformed Church, and by vague biological beliefs that blacks were naturally inferior and that people of mixed race were possibly worse. Malan campaigned in 1948 against the 'Black Menace', and his words touched the deep fears of those whites who felt that the black majority might challenge them for economic and political power. The more this attitude was criticized around the world, the more the Afrikaaners fell back into the 'laager mentality', the stubborn determination of the original Boer settlers to tackle every enemy and obstacle, and never to concede an inch (a 'laager' was a defensive ring of ox-wagons).

In 1913, blacks' rights to own land were limited, and in 1936 an Act of Parliament allocated 12½ per cent of the area of South Africa to the four million blacks, 87½ per cent to the one and a quarter million whites. Acts in 1911 and 1926 introduced an official colour bar into employment, since when average black wages have been under 10 per cent of average white wages. Since 1927, sexual relations between blacks and whites have been forbidden; so have mixed marriages since 1949. Since 1953, black trade unions have been forbidden, and in 1956 non-whites lost the right to vote. 'Pass laws' required that blacks should remain in their own areas and not travel out of them without specific permission. Special townships were created on the outskirts of white urban areas for the necessary black workers. In 1959, eight 'Bantustans' were created, reserves where blacks could live and develop in political and economic independence, a theory which was challenged by the hard facts of the Transkei, where 16,000 square miles of poor soil was expected to support two million Africans. The Transkei was given 'sovereign status' in 1976: in 1977 Bophuthatswana became the second independent 'homeland'.

Three other areas that were once British protectorates, Bechuanaland, Basutoland and Swaziland, became independent as Botswana (1966), Lesotho (1966) and Ngwane (1968), but their geographical and economic dependence on South Africa makes them similar to Bantustans in all but legal definition. South West Africa, a former German colony, became a South African mandate after the First World War. Apartheid spread there despite a ruling by the International Court of Justice in 1950 that it must not become a province of the Republic. Throughout the 1960s and 1970s, guerrilla warfare and legal wrangling threatened the future of the area, but in 1978 South Africa accepted a U.N. Resolution that it should become independent, under the name of Namibia.

Southern Africa, 1980

Successive Prime Ministers reinforced apartheid: Malan (1948–54); Strijdom (1954–58); Verwoerd (1958–66, when he was assassinated); and Vorster (1966–78), but not without opposition, internal and external.

Internal Resistance

The earliest resistance to racialist policies in South Africa was led by Mohandas Gandhi, with a programme of non-violent protests against laws discriminating against Indians, in the years 1913–15. From then until 1948, no champion of black rights appeared, but as apartheid tightened, some whites began to oppose it through the Liberal and Progressive Parties, and the blacks began to use the boycott of buses as an economic weapon, and silent vigils by black-sashed women as a dignified and subtle psychological pressure. The Communist Party attracted support among whites and blacks, and was banned by the Suppression of Communism Act of 1950, which gave massive powers to the Minister of Justice. The Public Safety Act of 1953, the Criminal Law Amendment Act of the same year, the Riotous Assemblies Act of 1956, the Unlawful Organizations Act of 1960 and the Terrorism Act of 1967 all increased the power of the Bureau of State Security (BOSS) and made resistance to the policies dangerous. In 1960, a demonstration against the pass laws provoked a panicky reaction from the local police at

Sharpeville and at Langa. A total of 83 Africans were shot dead and 350 injured, almost all in the back. Thousands more were imprisoned as the protests continued. In 1961, Chief Luthuli organized a three-day strike; he was deprived of his chieftaincy. In 1976, the frustration of the Africans reached a new peak of violence, when rioting in the township of Soweto, near Johannesburg, left dozens dead, hundreds injured, and unrest rippling through all black areas. Then in 1977, Steven Biko, founder of the Black Consciousness movement and supporter of reconciliation rather than confrontation, died of head wounds received while in police custody: 20,000 blacks attended his funeral, as well as many representatives of European countries.

External Opposition

The outside world became increasingly critical of South African policies as they contrasted more and more with the trend towards majority rule and racial equality in the rest of the world. The early 1960s were the turning point. In January 1960, Verwoerd announced that South Africa would become a republic; in March came the Sharpeville massacre. When Verwoerd came to a Commonwealth Conference in London in 1961, the hostility of demonstrators and the bitterness of the Afro-Asian politicians at

The British Daily Mirror's *view of apartheid in 1961, after Dr Verwoerd had called it 'a policy of good neighbourliness'.*

the Conference astounded him. After a week of negotiation, he withdrew his request for South Africa to remain in the Commonwealth, despite her republican status. His country was now without a diplomatic ally, apart from the right-wing Portuguese regime of Salazar.

The racial discrimination of apartheid was condemned by the United Nations in 1961, 1962 and 1963, at a time when many new African nations were joining the organization and rejoicing in their freedom from white domination. In Britain and America, pressure rose to organize a boycott of all South African produce, an idea which was scarcely practicable because of the Western world's reliance on the gold and diamond reserves of South Africa. Wilson's Labour government refused to sell arms to South Africa, a ban which the Conservative government reversed in 1970 because of its worries about the strategic importance of the Southern Ocean in the struggle against Communism. South Africa was banned from the Olympic movement, and when New Zealand maintained its rugby-playing links with South Africa, most black African nations boycotted the 1976 Olympic Games to indicate their disgust.

Vorster's successor as Prime Minister, P.W. Botha, gave an immediate impression of being more liberal than his predecessors. In 1979, he visited Soweto; at the same time, the organization of multiracial sport seemed to be opening a crack in the rigid barriers of apartheid, with rugby tours to and from the British Isles. Most far-reaching of all, Botha announced a relaxation of the 'Immorality Laws', making marriage between blacks and whites more likely.

22 The Middle East

ISRAEL AND THE ARAB STATES

In the year 70 A.D., the Romans sacked Jerusalem. From then until 1948, the 'Land of Israel' always formed part of some bigger empire – Roman, Byzantine, Arab, Crusader, Mameluk or Ottoman. In 1918, when the Ottoman Empire collapsed, the League of Nations allocated Iraq, Jordan and Palestine to Britain as mandates (and Lebanon and Syria to France). It thus became Britain's responsibility to cope with 'Zionism', the movement which aimed at recreating a Jewish state in Palestine. Centuries of oppression had made the Jews conscious of the need to stick together. It was a Jewish writer, Herzl, who called together the First Zionist Congress in Switzerland in 1897, and his ambitions were furthered by a Jewish research scientist, Chaim Weizmann, born in Russia and educated in Switzerland before settling in England.

The Balfour Declaration and the British Mandate

The British government was broadly sympathetic to the Jews. In 1903, when Russian Jews suffered a new wave of persecution, the Colonial Secretary, Joseph Chamberlain, suggested that part of Uganda might be made available as a temporary homeland for Jewish refugees. Nothing came of the idea, but Weizmann, drawn into scientific work on behalf of the British munitions industry in the First World War, was able to turn British sympathy into British support. In November 1917, the Foreign Secretary Balfour wrote to the Jewish banker Lord Rothschild, 'His Majesty's Government view with favour the establishment in Palestine of a national home for the Jewish people, and will use their best endeavours to facilitate the achievement of this object, it being clearly understood that nothing shall be done that may prejudice the civil and religious rights of existing non-Jewish communities in Palestine...'.

In 1915–16, the British High Commissioner in Egypt had carried on a correspondence with Sharif Hussein ibn Ali of Mecca, in which he promised the Arabs post-war independence if they would give Britain active support against the Ottoman Empire.

This 'MacMahon Correspondence' was popularly believed to have invalidated the later Balfour Declaration, though MacMahon always claimed that he had made it clear that 'Palestine west of the Jordan' was not within the terms of the agreement, and the Arab leaders understood this. Certainly in 1918 and 1919, there was a large measure of public agreement and goodwill between Jew and Arab; Weizmann and Hussein's son, Feisal, met in Aqaba, London and Paris, with T.E. Lawrence 'of Arabia' acting as an intermediary, and a written agreement between them was published in January 1919.

Britain was awarded the Mandate of Palestine at the San Remo Conference of 1920. The Council of the League of Nations ratified it in 1922, stating that the main purpose of the Mandate was to put the Balfour Declaration into effect. Almost immediately one part of Palestine, Transjordan, was separated from the rest because of anti-Jewish riots: Hussein's second son, Abdullah, was made Emir, still under the mandate, while Feisal became King of Iraq.

Jewish Immigration

In 1922, there were approximately 84,000 Jews in Palestine, about 11 per cent of the total population, but in the early 1920s immigrants arrived from Russia and Poland in increasing numbers, and in the 1930s, persecution in Germany added to the total. Between 1933 and 1936, 164,000 Jews came to Palestine legally while thousands more slipped in anonymously. By 1936, 30 per cent of the population was Jewish, and Arab resentment of the increase led to riots and the appointment of a Royal Commission to consider the problem. In 1937, the Peel Commission recommended the partition of Palestine into a Jewish and an Arab state (the latter to merge with Transjordan) and a small British enclave. The Jews reluctantly accepted the idea; the Mufti of Jerusalem rejected it from the Arab side and demanded that all Jewish immigration should stop, and that Western Palestine should become an independent Arab state.

In 1939, the British Colonial Secretary, Malcolm MacDonald, proposed in a White Paper that immigration should be limited to 10,000 a year for five years, and thereafter that it should be subject to Arab approval. This scheme was bitterly resented by the Jewish leaders who were deeply aware of the Nazi persecution; it caused an anti-British feeling which increased the determination of the Jews to establish their own independent homeland. When the war was over, Britain seemed intent upon sticking to the White Paper policy. Sympathy for the quarter-million Jewish survivors of Hitler's atrocities did not stretch as far as allowing them access to Palestine, and when boatloads of illegal immigrants headed for the eastern Mediterranean, they were intercepted by the Royal Navy and interned in Cyprus.

Three days before the final British evacuation from Palestine in 1948, yet another ship packed with Jewish immigrants arrives in Haifa, to set up the new state of Israel.

The Establishment of Israel

The British mandate was due to expire in 1948, and Britain had no desire for its extension. In 1947, Ernest Bevin, Foreign Secretary, referred the whole problem to the U.N. A Special Committee on Palestine made up of 11 member-states recommended partition into separate Jewish and Arab states, with Jerusalem as an international enclave. Two-thirds of the land would be Jewish. The Jews accepted the plan and the Arabs opposed it, but as more than the required two-thirds of the U.N. General Assembly approved it, it was put into effect. In May 1948, the State of Israel was declared, within the boundaries set by the U.N. The Jewish homeland had been created.

Within 24 hours, it had been invaded by Egypt, Transjordan, Syria, Iraq, Lebanon and Saudi Arabia, but the Israeli people were not prepared to be deprived. Their fanatical retaliation, backed up by official American recognition, won an unlikely victory. In 1949 separate armistice agreements were made with each of the invaders, and Israel was left in possession of more territory than had been allocated in 1947 (see map on p.343). During the period of fighting, nearly a million Arabs living within the boundaries of the new Israeli state fled, encouraged on their way by the massacre of the inhabitants of one Arab village and by acts of terrorism committed by the 'Stern gang', a vehemently anti-British organization which was prepared to fight anyone by any means to achieve an independent Israel. In 1948, the Stern gang murdered Count Bernadotte, the U.N. mediator. As a result of the emigration, the

Jews became the majority group in Israel.

The 1949 armistice (which was not considered by the Arab countries to be a final peace settlement, nor a recognition of the right of Israel to exist) removed 'Palestine' from the map. Lebanon, Jordan and Egypt gave up their claim to those parts of Palestine which they had been allocated by the U.N. in 1947; Transjordan incorporated its part, which included most of Jerusalem, and henceforth became known as the Hashemite Kingdom of Jordan.

The Government of Israel

In 1949 the Israelis elected their first Knesset (parliament); a series of Basic Laws established the form of government, and Chaim Weizmann was elected to the (largely ceremonial) post of President, while David Ben Gurion became Prime Minister, at the head of a coalition dominated by the Mapai (Labour Party). Ben Gurion remained Prime Minister until 1963 (except for the period 1953–55). He was succeeded by Eshkol until 1969 and Mrs Golda Meir until 1974. In 1977, the Likud 'Union' Party, led by Menahem Begin, once the commander of an extremist organization, became the largest party in the Knesset.

Every citizen over the age of 18 can vote for the Knesset, which has 120 members elected for four year periods. There is a system of proportional representation which has meant that there has always been a range of parties. Until 1977, the left wing predominated with the Labour-Mapai Alignment, but in 1977 the Likud group, a coalition of five liberal parties, took 45 seats to Labour's 32. The National Religious Party has always held about a dozen seats in the Knesset and has been essential to the formation of ministries, thereby being able to insist upon the passing of laws preserving the orthodoxy of Judaism (which about one third of the population scrupulously observe). The small size of the Knesset and the system of representation enables Israel to enjoy a very democratic government. The Jewish people suffered so much at the hands of tyrannical governments elsewhere in the world that they have created a state which places great importance on individual rights. Men and women are equal in duties and in rights (though women only do two years National Service to the men's three), and the idea of equality and sharing is constantly fostered. The use of the Hebrew language, the education programme for children and adults, the development of kibbutzim (collective farm-villages) and moshavim (co-operatives): all these, as well as the absolute right of any Jew to immigrate into Israel, emphasize the new nationhood and the philosophy of the Jewish people.

Israel and her Neighbours

For 30 years after its establishment, Israel remained unrecognized by any Arab state because of the problem of the Palestinians – the Arabs who had fled from, or remained in, the old mandated territory of Palestine. Unwilling to recognize the sovereign existence of a Jewish state, they became what the Jews had been before 1948, a minority group campaigning by any means to claim what they believed to be their historically justified right to a sovereign state. Their plight, and the right of Israel to exist, have been the central issues in three wars and a period of attrition in the Middle East.

In 1950, a Tripartite Declaration between Britain, France and the U.S.A. tried to avert future trouble by guaranteeing the existing frontiers in the Middle East and by limiting arms sales to both sides, so that neither had the power to overcome the other. This failed when Czechoslovakia and the U.S.S.R. supplied arms to Egypt in 1955.

The Egyptian Connection

In the nineteenth century, British interest in Egypt was primarily economic, though economic interests were usually backed by military potential. In 1851–56, the British built a railway from Alexandria to Cairo, and in 1858 continued it to Suez on the Red Sea, thereby considerably improving their communication with India. Simultaneously the French engineer, de Lesseps, was winning the concession to cut a canal from Port Said to Suez, which was opened in 1869. This double injection of Western capital into Egypt did not save its Khedive from bankruptcy. In 1875, he sold his shares in the Suez Canal to a delighted Disraeli, but three years later was forced to accept supervision ('Dual Control') of his finances by a French and British commission. In 1882, this limited interference in Egyptian affairs was extended when British troops entered Egypt to crush an army revolt (the Battle of Tel-el-Kebir), and for the next 70 years, Britain exercised an unintended controlling hand, supporting and guiding the Khedives and then the Kings of Egypt. When war broke out in 1914, the declaration of a Protectorate was merely a formality. In 1922, the Protectorate was replaced by a constitutional monarchy under King Fuad, until 1936, and then his son Farouk, until 1952.

After the war, Egyptian nationalist demands increased for Britain to leave the Canal zone and to hand over control of the Sudan. In 1947, Egypt asked the U.N. to arbitrate; in 1948–49, Britain attracted more resentment because of the setting up of Israel and because of Egypt's humiliating defeat in the resulting war. By 1951, the British troops in the Canal zone were the victims of constant harassment. In June 1952, Farouk was overthrown and forced into exile by the Revolution Command Council under General Neguib and his deputy, Colonel Nasser.

The political turmoil of the Egyptian revolution took four years. A Republic was declared in 1953, Nasser became Prime Minister in 1954, but not until 1956 was the internal power struggle resolved by his appointment as President. In the meantime the British agreed to leave the Sudan (1953) and the Canal zone (1954, with the final evacuation in 1955). But to achieve his socialist, nationalist revolution, Nasser needed financial support and diplomatic recognition from abroad.

Suez and the War of 1956

In September 1955, Egypt announced an arms deal with Czechoslovakia, seeming therefore to align itself with the Communist bloc, but in December 1955, it was announced that the World Bank would provide a loan of $20 million towards the building of the Aswan High Dam, to add to an American loan of $56 million and a British contribution of $14 million. However the Western money was to be loaned on condition that Nasser loosened his ties with the Communists, a condition that he was not prepared to meet, if he could get help from both super-powers. In July 1956, American Secretary of State Dulles withdrew the proffered aid; Britain followed suit, but the pressure rebounded. On 26 July 1956, Nasser declared that he had nationalized the Suez Canal, in order that the revenues would finance the Dam.

In one stroke, he was furthering Egyptian socialism, Arab nationalism and the independence of his foreign policy. At the same time, his action was seen by Britain as an illegal and irresponsible threat to a vital international waterway and a move of great strategic danger. A crisis conference of Canal users met in London in August, but Britain and France became aware that America, now in an election year and largely unaffected by what happened to the Canal, was unlikely to take positive action to restore the Canal to its rightful owners. Nasser, emboldened by his success and by tacit Russian support, now increased his attacks on Israel and in October formed a joint military command with Syria and Jordan; he also blocked the Straits of Tiran, thus completing an Egyptian stranglehold on the northern end of the Red Sea. At this point the French, further angered by Egyptian support for rebels in Algeria, proposed a plan, whereby Israel should counterattack in the Sinai peninsula, thus giving the British and French a reason to reoccupy the Canal zone on the pretext of protecting international waters. This plan, denied until years later, was put into effect. Israeli troops moved into Sinai on 29 October; a day later an Anglo-French ultimatum called for the withdrawal of the Egyptian and Israeli forces to lines ten miles back from the Canal, a position

Egyptian block ships in the Suez Canal in 1956, the legacy of the Anglo-French invasion.

which favoured the Israeli advance. On 5 November, British and French paratroopers were dropped on Port Said, which had already been subjected to heavy air attack since 30 October.

Intense diplomatic activity followed. Russia threatened the use of force against the 'imperialist aggressors'; America condemned Britain and France; the Labour Party in England was violently critical of the Conservatives' policy. On 6 November, seeing all opinion united against them, the French and British accepted the U.N. call for a cease-fire, and began to withdraw. They had lost 32 men killed; the Israelis about 200; the Egyptians nearly 3,000. The result was humiliation for Britain and France. For Egypt it was a diplomatic victory if not a military one.

The Conflict Continues

The bitterness between Israel and her neighbours remained. In 1964 the Palestine Liberation Organization (P.L.O.) was founded, as well as a secret organization 'al-Fatah', ('the Conquest'), and guerilla bands made increasing numbers of attacks on Jewish settlements. In late 1966 the Syrian border became the scene of bombardments and reprisal raids, and Nasser pledged his support for Syria in the event of an Israeli invasion. In May 1967, Cairo Radio announced 'All Egypt is now prepared to plunge into total war which will put an end to Israel,' and Arab nationalism was stirred into a state of high excitement. Nasser called for the withdrawal of the U.N. Emergency Force, received promises of support from Saudi-Arabia, Algeria and Iraq, and made a treaty with King Hussein of Jordan; he also closed the Straits of Tiran.

The Arab world followed Nasser's lead, expecting to arrive at the end of the Israel-Palestine problem by means of the eradication of the Jewish homeland. Arab troops massed on the frontiers.

In Israel, Eshkol appointed General Moshe Dayan, hero of the 1956 Sinai campaign, as Minister of Defence. Preferring attack to defence, he ordered a surprise attack on the Egyptian Air Force

Palestine and Israel, 1920–78

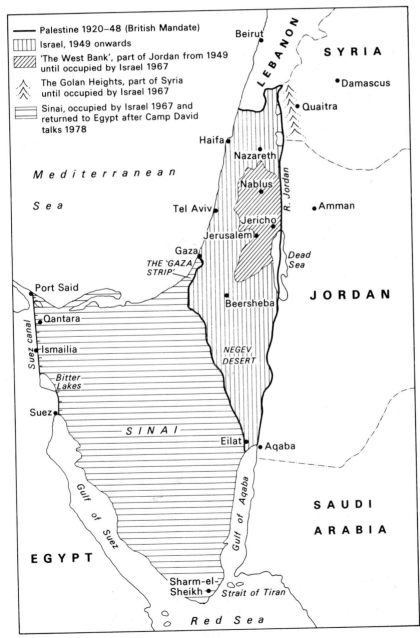

while it was on the ground, followed by an immediate assault on all fronts. Deprived of air cover, the Arab forces were rolled back on all fronts. In six days, the Israelis occupied the Sinai Peninsula up to the east bank of the Suez Canal, Jordan on the west bank of the river (including the whole of Jerusalem) and the Golan Heights in Syria as well as the approach to Damascus. By the time that the U.N. Security Council could arrange a cease-fire, the Arabs had suffered a major psychological and military defeat, and the Israelis were in a position from which they would not retreat without a guarantee of permanent recognition and security.

The Six Day War of 1967 came close to involving the 'super-powers'; Russian sympathies lay clearly with the Arabs and American sympathies with the Israelis. In November 1967, the U.N. Security Council tried to find a peace formula through Resolution 242, which made five basic points: Israel must with-draw its troops from occupied areas; belligerency must stop and sovereignty must be respected throughout the Middle East; there must be freedom of navigation in all the international waterways of the area (the Suez Canal was now blocked by ships sunk deliberately); the refugee problem must be justly settled; and the rights and territories of each state must be guaranteed by measures which included demilitarized zones. This Resolution was accepted by most Arab states, but the Israelis rejected it, because it seemed to them to give away their gains and return them to the unsatisfactory position that they had been in before the war.

There followed a war of attrition, of air raids, outrages and terrorism in which the super-powers restocked the two sides' armouries with highly sophisticated weapons while the Palestinians became so assertive of their rights that in 1970 they caused civil war in Jordan before being expelled by Hussein's troops. The P.L.O. and al-Fatah extended their campaign to the hi-jacking of airliners (four were seized and destroyed in September 1970), gunning down innocent passengers at Tel Aviv airport (1972) and seizing a party of Israeli athletes as hostages at the Munich Olympics (1972). Talks arranged by the U.N. Special Envoy Gunnar Jarring failed to find solutions.

In 1973, Egypt and Syria launched a new attack on Israel on 6 October, Yom Kippur, the holiest day in the Jewish calendar. On the defensive for two days, the Israelis showed the resilience and enterprise which had saved them in 1948. A counter-attack across the Suez Canal into Egypt, and across the Golan Heights towards Damascus showed that they would not be beaten. The super powers drew back from all-out support of the separate sides, and arranged a new cease-fire. Syria lost a further 300 square miles of territory.

The wars had solved nothing. They had added to the number of refugees, and found no new home for the Palestinians. They had cost the luckless Hussein of Jordan much of his kingdom, and after his expulsion of the guerillas in 1970, they had aggravated civil war in Lebanon where the Palestinians settled as a last refuge. They had blocked the Suez Canal, leaving the Western world to obtain its Middle Eastern oil by super-tanker around the Cape of Good Hope. They had cost millions of dollars and thousands of lives.

Sadat and the Acceptance of Israel

In 1974, Anwar as-Sadat, who had succeeded Nasser on his death in 1970, ordered the clearing of the block-ships from the Suez Canal and the rebuilding of the ruined cities on the Canal's edge. These actions, and a request for a Geneva Peace Conference, were an indication of a new peace initiative, which the U.S.A. was quick to recognize and foster. Secretary of State Kissinger 'shuttled' around the capitals of the Middle East, and by the end of 1975 the Canal was open, and Israeli, Egyptian and Syrian troops had all withdrawn from the confrontation positions that they had occupied since 1973. While Lebanon became the new centre for Palestinian raids against Israel and fell into civil war, Egypt established a new relationship with the U.S.A. and buried its former friendship with Russia. Nixon visited the Middle East, Sadat visited Washington.

In 1977, Sadat's position in Egypt was threatened by riots and internal unrest which stemmed from complaints about high food prices and low standards of living, the legacy of high military expenditure in the past. It was a further stimulus to peace. While most of the Arab world stuck to its anti-Israel policies, Sadat

A picture which marked a major change in Middle Eastern politics: Prime Minister Begin of Israel and President Sadat of Egypt meet for peace talks.

announced to the Egyptian Parliament in November 1977, 'There is no time to lose. I am ready to go to the ends of the earth if that will save one of my soldiers... I am ready to go to the Knesset to discuss peace with the Israeli leaders.' This brave gamble, condemned immediately by Algeria, Libya, Syria, Iraq, the Yemen and the P.L.O., was welcomed by Prime Minister Begin of Israel, and within three weeks, Sadat had addressed the Knesset.

Throughout 1978, the impetus for peace was maintained despite occasional flashes of the old hostility from both sides. In September 1978, President Carter invited Sadat and Begin to Camp David, near Washington, from where after two weeks of tough bargaining, a draft peace treaty was produced. Though it did not cover the future of Jerusalem or the fate of Israeli settlements in the areas that they had occupied after the 1967 War, it laid down a programme, phased over five years, which spoke of 'self-governing authorities' in the Gaza Strip and on the west bank of the Jordan, the areas most occupied by Palestinian Arabs, and of Israel's gradual withdrawal from Sinai. Most important of all, it contained the first recognition by an Arab state of Israel's right to exist. It was this that led to its utter rejection by the 21 countries of the Arab League, meeting in Baghdad in November 1978.

OIL AND OPEC

Oil is the ultimate weapon of the Middle East. In 1977, the total oil reserves of the world were calculated to stand at 652,000,000,000 barrels. Of these, the Middle East claimed 56.3 per cent, compared with Russia's 12 per cent, Africa's 9.3 per cent, America's 5.7 per cent and Western Europe's 3.8 per cent. The table of consumers showed a completely different picture: the U.S.A. accounted for 28.6 per cent of the world's consumption, Russia 13.2 per cent, Germany, France and Britain a total of 12.1 per cent and Japan 8.8 per cent. The dependence of the rest of the world on the Middle East has been obvious throughout the twentieth century, and it has become especially marked since the United States has started to use more oil than it can produce. In 1960, the major oil producers of the world formed the Organization of Petroleum Exporting Countries (OPEC), to unify their policies and to protect their interests. Of the 13 member states, Saudi Arabia, Iran, Iraq, Kuwait, the United Arab Emirates, Libya, Algeria and Qatar represent broadly the Middle Eastern block, and control more than three-quarters of the total OPEC production.

When the Suez Canal was closed after the 1956 Sinai War, and blocked again for eight years after the 1967 War, the cost of transporting oil from the Persian Gulf to the Western world rose rapidly, but the fact that consumption scarcely dropped indicated that the West was prepared to pay the price. This knowledge, together with the more sobering thought that their strong bargain-

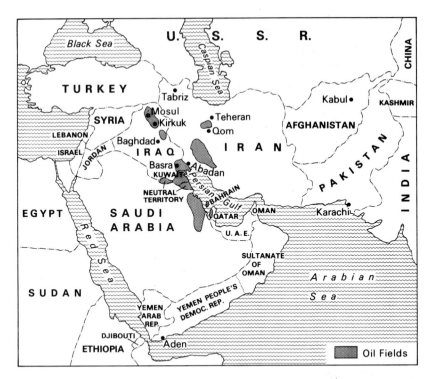

Iran and the Oil-Producing Nations

ing position would last only as long as their oil reserves, persuaded OPEC to raise prices further. In the aftermath of the 1973 war, OPEC quadrupled the price of oil. The effect on the world economy was dramatic; most Western countries sank into a recession in 1974–75, from which they found it hard to recover, as world prices soared and unemployment increased. At the same time, under-developed countries were hit even more severely, as they had fewer means of earning the money needed to pay for imported oil.

But while oil-consuming countries were falling into debt, the oil-rich countries were accumulating wealth rapidly. Those with larger populations were able to import goods from the West and thus use some of their profits: their remaining surplus cash was invested in the West wherever interest rates were high, thus further fuelling inflation. As inflation reduced the real value of their earnings, some of the OPEC countries urged even more price rises, arguing that they should get the highest price possible for their oil, with a view to maximizing immediate profits, as well as prolonging the life of their oil stocks, by forcing the West to reduce its demand.

Two results emerged from the price rises. One was a flurry of exploration and development by oil companies seeking reserves in Alaska, Africa, the North Sea and elsewhere. The other was the unbalancing of the economies of the OPEC countries, particularly illustrated by events in Iran.

IRAN

Foreign Influences

Nineteenth-century Iran (called Persia) was a feudal desert empire, untroubled by foreigners except for trade missions and occasional entrepreneurs seeking a chance to make quick profits. In 1865, the British built a telegraphic link between Europe and India which crossed Iran. In 1901, a private individual was granted an oil concession for 60 years, which was quickly turned into the Anglo-Iranian Oil Company. In 1914, the British government invested two million pounds in the company, and bought 51 per cent of the shares. Meanwhile the five northern provinces of Iran came under Russian influence, a fact recognized by British diplomats, who negotiated an agreement with the Russians in 1907.

The First World War was a chaotic period in Iranian politics: the Parliament that had been created in 1906 became corrupt and ineffective, and traditional land-owning families re-established their power. In 1921, an Army officer seized power, and by 1925 was able to declare himself Reza Shah, undisputed occupant of the Peacock Throne. Reza Shah's achievements rank with those of Kemal Atatürk of Turkey: he created the modern nation, officially changing its name from Persia to Iran in 1935. He reduced the power of-the mullahs (Muslim priests), and freed women from many of the restrictions under which they had suffered for centuries. He modernized the communication system, opening Iran's first railway in 1938. He renegotiated the oil concession with the Anglo-Iranian Oil Company, reducing the area over which the A.I.O.C. had rights by three-quarters, in exchange for extending the remaining rights until 1993. Fear of Communism drove him in 1939 towards the German side; British concern about oil supplies brought an Allied invasion in 1941, and after three days' resistance, Iran capitulated and Reza Shah abdicated in favour of his son, Muhammed Reza Pahlavi.

After the war, the British troops left Iran according to a previously agreed timetable. The Russians, who had occupied the province of Azerbaijan, were slower to honour their promise to move out at the end of the war. They hoped to turn Iran into a satellite, and to this end encouraged not only the Tudeh (Communist) Party, but also Kurd nationalism. They were outmanoeuvred by the Iranians, who had become fully aware of the value of their oil reserves. In 1949, they negotiated a new concession from the A.I.O.C., whereby royalties went up immediately by 50 per cent and a lump sum of £5.1 million was handed over to Iran. This whetted the appetites of various political groups in Iran; in late 1951 power fell into the hands of Dr. Musaddeq, an emotional and powerful nationalistic leader, impulsive and often irrational, who won wide support for his sudden nationalization of the A.I.O.C.

Mussadeq lasted until 1953, but his gamble on oil failed. Without foreign assistance, the nationalized company became inefficient and unprofitable. The 'majlis' (Iranian Parliament) voted full powers to Mussadeq, but his dictatorial methods were opposed by the army and by the young Shah. After near civil war, Mussadeq was tried for treason and imprisoned for three years. Thereafter he had no political following; he died in 1967.

In 1954, normal relations were restored with Britain. The Iranian oil fields remained nationalized, but an agreement was worked out with a new consortium of oil companies from Britain, France and America, in which British Petroleum had a 40 per cent share. This consortium was granted control over the principal oilfields for the next 25 years, a move which satisfied both Iranian nationalists, who felt it was still *their* oil, and foreign businessmen who were confident that they could organize supplies and markets properly.

Internal Revolutions

By 1961, the Shah had patiently established his political independence, and in order to push through a package of reform, he dissolved the majlis, knowing that it was too conservative and self-interested to accept his measures. In 1962, his Land Reform Law forced the redistribution of the estates of the 'thousand families', the traditional feudal overlords of Iran. State funds were used to set up irrigation schemes; collectives were organized; profit-sharing was introduced in industry; a huge education programme was undertaken. In 1963, the Shah was strong enough to hold a national referendum seeking approval for his 'White Revolution'. He won it overwhelmingly. The average per capita income went up by 70 per cent in six years as the people began to share in the wealth generated by the oil reserves. Iran became a consumer society, and as the oil profits were reinvested, massive plans were made for hydro-electric power, new communications systems, offices, universities and all the trappings of 'modern' civilization. Even before the quadrupling of prices in 1973, Iran's oil revenue exceeded $2,000,000,000 a year. By 1975, it had reached $18,200,000,000.

Despite all the Shah's planning, the 'White Revolution' went too fast. From the start, the ayatollahs (leading Muslim priests) had condemned the importation of Western attitudes and customs, which contradicted much of their Islamic teaching and discipline. The importation of Western money also upset the economic and social structure of Iran: inflation became rampant in the mid-1970s, and the opportunities for quick profits encouraged the growth of corruption. The Shah's dictatorial methods depended increasingly on the Army and on 'Savak', the State security organization, and he became cut off from the realities of daily life

The Ayatollah Khomeini, focal point of the Iranian Revolution of 1979.

for many of his subjects. In 1978, the stresses appeared all over Iran, in riots and demonstrations. From Paris, the exiled Ayatollah Khomeini kept up a constant stream of condemnation, and just as the Shah had taken all the credit for the best aspects of the 'Shah-People Revolution' of the 1960s, so now he received all the blame for its failings. An attempt to find a compromise ministry under Bakhtiar failed. In January 1979, the Shah and his family left Iran 'for a period of rest' (which was clearly likely to be permanent exile). In February 1979, Khomeini re-entered the country, and began the process of restoring order through strict use of 'Islamic Courts', lavish use of executions, and constant reference to the teachings of the Koran. He attracted a wide measure of support, but the fundamental economic problems which had beaten the Shah were no closer to solution.

Relations with the West became strained by the capture of the U.S. Embassy and its staff in Teheran by Iranian students, while the Russian occupation of Afghanistan posed a threat not only to Iran's government, but also to its oil, and therefore, to the delicate balance of world diplomacy.

Into the Twenty-First Century

When, in the twenty-first century, historians sit down to write their own *Histories of the Modern World*, they may well be tempted to start by looking at the broad trends of the late twentieth century. If so, they will probably pass quickly over the 'isms' which launched the first chapter of this book – capitalism, socialism, imperialism, nationalism and democracy – in order to concentrate on new areas of concern. Those 'isms' will still exist, but against a background that few could have foreseen in 1901, and a background which will be more challenging, and perhaps threatening, than anything previously imagined.

One aspect of challenge will be the size of the world population. In 1976 the most informed estimates put world population at about 4,000,000,000, with an annual growth rate of 1.6–2.2 per cent per annum. This would lead to a doubling of the world population in 43 years at the most, and 33 years at the least. Much of this growth will take place not in the richer and more sophisticated countries, where education programmes, birth control and material selfishness already limit the rate of expansion, but in the poorer, more primitive countries of the Third World, where hunger and poverty are already widespread.

The ability to feed the world's population will be the second challenge. In the short run, this is less a question of production than of distribution and international finance. The development of new strains of rice and wheat, of synthetic protein-laden 'meat' and of sea-bed farming, as well as highly efficient use of land and chemicals, has pushed back the spectre of world starvation for a while, but left unsolved the problem that the poor cannot buy the food produced expensively, and possibly far away, by the rich. The butter mountains and beef mountains of the E.E.C. are of no use to the Kampuchean refugee.

Thirdly, the world is already challenged by the rapid disappearance of its fossil fuels (especially oil but also coal) and its other vital natural resources like timber and numerous minerals. The first 'point of no return' has already been reached, where known reserves of oil are diminishing in total while demand for oil continues to increase. The emphasis increases on instant availability of every form of material improvement. The production of goods around us, the provision of transport, entertainment, comfort, hygiene, food, clothing, defence, communication: all these drain a limited supply of resources.

At the same time, the processing of these resources and the provision of goods and services is leaving its scar over, in and under the earth. From the threatened pollution of the upper atmosphere by high-flying planes, to the pollution of the air we breathe by lead fumes from cars and sulphur dioxide from industrial processes, to the pollution of land and sea by waste products, man's environment is increasingly contaminated by his own actions.

Two final challenges are evident in the very 'solutions' which are being devised to meet the demands of the first four. The development of nuclear power, while providing a massive source of energy, brings with it the threat of accidental or deliberate radiation or explosion, and in either case, destruction. In 1979, the world was fully alerted to such danger when a nuclear reactor at Harrisburg, Pennsylvania nearly ran out of control, despite all the safety measures built into its design.

Finally, the whole development of modern technology has accelerated the speed of change and the tensions that go with it. Although the stimulus has usually been the desire for human improvement, the result has often been greater stress and greater complication. The official elimination from the world of smallpox, announced in 1979, is a brilliant human achievement. But it has been produced by a society in which heart disease and mental stress are on the increase. The phenomenal triumph of putting men on the moon brought a 'spin-off' not only of medical, astronomical, physical and electronic knowledge (including the beginning of the 'micro-chip' revolution); it also increased the capacity of men to kill each other with increased accuracy and efficiency.

These matters will be reviewed by the historian of the twenty-first century. That he will be able to do so depends on the success of some of the processes and institutions referred to in the previous chapters of this book. World government is unlikely, but there has been a hopeful increase in world cooperation, illustrated by the many agencies of the U.N., by the cohesion of the Third World and by the development of groups of nations like the E.E.C., the Arab League, the Organization of American States, the British Commonwealth, the Organization of African Unity and Comecon. No less important is the increase in understanding and knowledge of the evolving world of the twentieth century. It is on the awareness of you, the reader, that the bridge to the year 2001 will be built.

Index